The Cultures of Knowledge Organizations

WORKING METHODS FOR KNOWLEDGE MANAGEMENT

Knowledge Economies and Knowledge Work
Bill Lafayette, Wayne Curtis, Denise Bedford, and Seema Iyer

Knowledge Assets and Knowledge Audits
Pawan Handa, Jean Pagani, and Denise Bedford

Critical Capabilities and Competencies for Knowledge Organizations
Juan Cegarra-Navarro, Alexeis Garcia-Perez, Susan Wakabayashi, Denise Bedford, and Margo Thomas

Designing and Tracking Knowledge Management Metrics
Alexeis Garcia-Perez and Farah Gheriss

Translating Knowledge Management Visions into Strategies
Angel Williams, Monique Ceruti, and Denise Bedford

Assessment Strategies for Knowledge Organizations
Dean Testa, Johel Brown-Grant, and Denise Bedford

Learning Organizations
Malva Daniel Reid, Jyldyz Bekbalaeva, Denise Bedford, Alexeis Garcia-Perez, and Dwane Jones

Knowledge Networks
Denise Bedford and Thomas W. Sanchez

Communicating Knowledge
Denise Bedford, Ira Chalphin, Karen Dietz, and Karla Phlypo

Organizational Intelligence and Knowledge Analytics
Brian McBreen, John Silson, and Denise Bedford

Forthcoming

Knowledge Preservation and Curation
Margie Foster, Hossein Arvand, Hugh Graham, and Denise Bedford

Knowledge Translation
Constantin Bratianu, Alexeis Garcia-Perez, Francesca Dal Mas, and Denise Bedford

The MASK Methodology – Knowledge Books
Jean-Louis Ermine, Alexeis Garcia-Perez, and Denise Bedford

Knowledge Places and Spaces
Jayne Sappington, Alexeis Garcia-Perez, and Denise Bedford

Strategic Intelligence for the Knowledge Economy
Brian McBreen, Cory Cannon, Pawan Handa, Liz Herman, Michael Molina, Alexeis Garcia-Perez, and Denise Bedford

Knowledge Ethics
Norman Mooradian, Jelina Haines, Malgorzata Zieba, Benjamin Anyacho, Cynthia Hilsinger, and Denise Bedford

Knowledge and Communities
Nancy J. Meyer, Leni Oman, John Edwards, Pat Kerrigan, Alexeis Garcia-Perez, and Denise Bedford

The Cultures of Knowledge Organizations: Knowledge, Learning, Collaboration (KLC)

BY

WIOLETA KUCHARSKA

Gdansk University of Technology, Poland

AND

DENISE BEDFORD

Georgetown University, USA

United Kingdom – North America – Japan – India – Malaysia – China

Emerald Publishing Limited
Emerald Publishing, Floor 5, Northspring, 21-23 Wellington Street, Leeds LS1 4DL.

First edition 2023

British Library Cataloguing in Publication Data
A catalogue record for this book is available from the British Library

ISBN: 978-1-83909-337-1 (Print)
ISBN: 978-1-83909-336-4 (Online)
ISBN: 978-1-83909-338-8 (Epub)

Printed and bound by CPI Group (UK) Ltd, Croydon, CR0 4YY

INVESTOR IN PEOPLE

Contents

Introduction

Knowledge sciences as a discipline have a rich and diverse history dating back to the 1950s. In the past 70 years, the discipline has drawn theory and practice from economics, engineering, communications, learning sciences, technology, information sciences, psychology, social sciences, and business and organization management. To craft this discipline, we have developed our own language and terminologies, established our own peer-reviewed journals, built a rich research foundation, created gray literature, and established a series of networks and conferences. Over the decades, there have been many knowledge management education programs, but there is no consistent curriculum and few have been sustained. It has been challenging for new practitioners to gain an understanding of the field. While the practice of knowledge management is growing around the world, it has not yet achieved the expected organizational stature. For knowledge management to rise to the stature of other business functions and operations, it must be able to speak the language of business, align with and support the way the organization works.

This series is designed for business and knowledge management practitioners. Working Methods in Knowledge Management is a multi-year and multi-volume series designed to address each and all of the methods required to establish and sustain an organization-wide knowledge management function. The goal of the series is to provide a business perspective of each topic. Each book begins by grounding the method in the business context – then translates established business models and methods to a knowledge management context. It is often the case that this translation expands and extends the business model and method.

The knowledge management literature is rich with introductory handbooks, guidebooks, cookbooks, toolkits, and practical introductions. This literature is an important starting point for anyone new to the discipline. We recommend any and all of these books as a way to build a fundamental understanding of the scope and coverage of the field. These texts will provide a good 10–20 page introduction to all of the key issues you need to be aware of as you embark on a new career in the field or have been assigned a new knowledge management role or responsibility. Once you have that grounding, though, we recommend that you look to the Working Methods in Knowledge Management texts as an intermediate source for understanding "What comes next? What now?"

Just as this series is not intended as a starting point for the field, neither is it an ending point. Each text is designed to support practical application, and to foster a broader discussion of practice. It is through practical application and extended discussion that we will advance theory and research. The editors anticipate that as practice expands, there will be a need to update the texts – based on what we are learning. Furthermore, the editors hope the texts are written in a way that allows business managers to extend their work to include knowledge management functions and assets. We will learn most from expanding the discussion beyond our core community.

Joint Enterprise, Mutual Engagement, and a Shared Repertoire

From the outset, the publisher and the editors have established a new and different approach to designing and writing the books. Each text is supported by a team of authors who represent multiple and diverse views of the topic. Each team includes academics, practitioners, and thought leaders. Every author has grappled with the topic in a real-world context. Every author sees the topic differently today than they did when the project began. Over the course of several months, through weekly virtual discussions, the scope and coverage were defined. Through mutual engagement and open sharing, each team developed a joint enterprise and commitment to the topic that is enduring. Every author learned through the discussion and writing process. Each project has resulted in a new shared repertoire. We practiced knowledge management to write about knowledge management. We "ate our own dog food."

Acknowledgements of Early Support

The series is a massive effort. If there is value in the series much of the credit must go to two individuals – Dr Elias Carayannis, George Washington University, and Dr Manlio Del Giudice, University of Rome. It was Dr Carayannis who first encouraged us to develop a proposal for Emerald Publishers. Of course, this encouragement was just the most recent form of support from Dr Carayannis. He has been a mentor and coach for close to 20 years. It was Dr Carayannis who first taught me the importance of aligning knowledge management with business administration and organizational management. Dr Del Giudice has been generous with his guidance – particularly in setting a high standard for any and all knowledge management research and practice. We are grateful to him for his careful review and critique of our initial proposal. His patience and thoughtful coaching of colleagues is rare in any field. The field will reach its full potential as long as we have teachers and editors like Dr Del Giudice.

Preface

Overview of the Subject Matter

This book focuses on seeing, understanding, and learning to shape an organization's essential cultures. The book is grounded on a fundamental assumption that every organization has a de facto culture. These "de facto cultures" appear at first glance to be serendipitous, vague, invisible, and unmanaged. An invisible and unrecognized de facto culture can undermine business goals and strategies and lead to business failures. The authors believe that humans can learn to "see" culture around them and understand their influence on individuals, teams, organizations, and societies. At its core, the book lays out the levels of culture to help the reader "see" and learn how to shape a knowledge organization's cultures.

Learning to see and understand the culture, mainly organizational culture, is critical in today's hyperdynamic knowledge economy. Culture will always dominate strategy in any economy. However, it can play an even more significant role in the knowledge economy, where knowledge is the primary form of capital and the most critical production factor. To thrive and survive in the knowledge economy, managers must "see" their company culture's power to shape the company's course and learn to gain and sustain knowledge, learning, and collaboration (KLC) cultures synergy. Hyperdynamic business reality requires smart actions. When managers "see" their cultures as an asset, they have an opportunity to shape those cultures and use them for the company's best.

This book reviews the current models and theories around organizational culture and presents a new perspective that treats organizational culture not as a static conceptual model but as a dynamic, complex adaptive system. The authors consider how organizational cultures must and will shift in a knowledge economy. Specifically, they consider how de facto organizational (e.g., what the authors refer to throughout the book as a company culture) cultures might function in a hyperdynamic knowledge economy. The authors describe a new approach to three internal cultures –KLC – knowledge, learning and collaboration cultures. The synergy between the business culture and the KLC cultures synergy is essential to business success and survival in the hyperdynamic knowledge economy. These three focal cultures – knowledge, learning, and collaboration – must be designed and nourished to leverage the knowledge and intellectual capital needed for innovativeness and sustainability. Knowledge and intellectual capital are the critical value-creation factors in the knowledge economy. The authors also go beyond the traditional treatment of organizational cultures to identify and address cultural tensions, complexities, conflicts, and paradoxes. These challenges are often demonstrated in the cultures of public-sector organizations.

As background for writing this book, the authors conducted an extensive literature review of culture and organizational culture. They assessed the existing cultural tools and methods. They covered the peer-reviewed and gray literature on the organizational cultures of both commercial and public-sector organizations. In addition to this background research, the authors conducted several conversations with two leading cultural researchers – Drs Richard Lewis and Iouri Bairatchnyi – to gain insights into their experiences. Both experts have written extensively about culture, but not all of their knowledge has been formally encoded. In synthesizing knowledge and information, the authors considered the conceptual treatment of culture in the economics concept, anchoring on the core concept of value. This background work informed the new perspective on the role of culture in a knowledge-driven economy. The authors formulated a new KLC-approach and supported it with current and relevant case studies. In addition, the authors drew upon their research and experience to speak to practical implications and applications. The profound connection between theory and practice given in this book has opened the door to discovering critical paradoxes and conflicts that may be at play in any complex cultural context.

In this text, the authors further synthesize the fragmented discourse around factors that shape culture in varying contexts and at varying levels. The authors also highlight the need for more robust and informative cultural assessment methods and tools and some potential approaches. In addition, the book highlights the need for a more holistic approach to seeing and shaping organizational cultures. Finally, the book speaks to the need to reconsider the effectiveness of traditional industrial-era business cultures. Considering how these traditional business cultures will function in a hyperdynamic knowledge economy is essential.

Furthermore, this book makes a case for new approaches to describing an organizational culture. The authors also highlight the importance of expanding the knowledge base of organizational culture practice and relating it to existing research. It is what the thought leader, John Edwards, commonly refers to as "research on practice." Aligning practice and research will surface new knowledge gaps in the field and identify new theoretical and applied research topics. Culture is no longer just an academic topic. It is a purposeful company asset that has significant effects on real-world business performance and strategies. Today's managers need practical guidance on how to apply the driving force of company culture to the company's development culture, on how to assess it, design it that aligns with and supports business goals and help the workforce understand their role in shaping culture.

Where the Topic Fits in The World Today?

Like the other books in the series, this text draws from and integrates research and practice from several disciplines. The primary goal of the series is to create stronger ties between the business management and knowledge management fields. In the current peer-reviewed literature, the most critical theoretical research focuses on culture at the national level. There is some theoretical research at the regional level. Case studies comprise the bulk of the literature at the organizational level. There is not yet a focused body of knowledge that addresses organizational cultures across a broad spectrum of organizational types, sizes, or sectors. There is substantial theoretical literature on the elements of culture by international thought leaders.

While rigorous and widely accepted conceptual models exist, the field lacks a comprehensive and integrated framework. Therefore, to complete the research for this book and other research, the authors reviewed the literature on culture and anthropology, communications, learning and education, knowledge sciences, organizational design, business management, economics, and psychology. The extensive list of factors influencing culture highlights the importance of reaching beyond the primary domain to find relevant work. Today's managers need a practical, working framework they can use as a tool to assess and manage their organization's cultural competencies and capabilities. The framework should also identify areas where conflicts and paradoxes might surface.

The most significant challenge of this topic is that culture is often treated as a static concept – when it is a dynamic and complex system. Culture is a continuous interplay of factors – across levels, domains, sectors, and over time. Culture changes continuously – one individual at a time – but in aggregate, it changes slowly. In the context of the shifting economic landscape, culture takes on the form of a complex adaptive system. The literature on complex adaptive systems is extensive but does not address culture or portray it as a complex adaptive system.

Important new research on internal organizational cultures has originated in applied research and is now translated into rigorous theory. It is in the early stages but holds promise for expanding our understanding of the role of culture as a knowledge and intellectual capital asset. This new research is the work of this book's primary author.

Where the Book Fits in the Literature Today?

The book augments and expands the seminal work of cultural thought leaders such as Schein, Hofstede, Lewis, and Denison. In addition, the book adds to the body of knowledge about organizational culture by integrating the cutting-edge research conducted by Professor Kucharska. It also incorporates the lessons from Dr Bedford's graduate students in the organizational culture at Georgetown University. Also, it aggregates and critically evaluates the research on public sector cultures. Finally, the book sets the stage for new assessment methods and tools and identifies new topics for a future research agenda.

There are gaps in the literature that the academy should fill before we can move forward to incorporate practice. First, there should be a synthesis and integration of what is known or has been learned about cultures by types, sizes, and sectors of organizations. Second, what is known should be mapped to and tested against the theory. Where there is not a good match, we must ask whether our theoretical knowledge is complete or what gaps exist. Where there is a conflict, we must ask why and how the conflict might be reconciled. Third, there is a need to encourage more rigorous "on-the-scene" practical research that can reinforce, revise or reject the existing theory. Finally, what is known in theory must be translated into management methods that characterize and categorize existing company cultures and help managers understand what cultural foundations are critical to their business goals and strategies. This book answers these needs.

The book considers practice for the business management literature and ties it to established theory. It elevates and aligns the existing case study literature to research factors. The authors strive to identify the critical practical needs of business managers. The book speaks not only to current needs in the industrial economy but looks forward to the needs of the knowledge economy.

This book also expands the coverage of the Working Methods for Knowledge Management series. It is the 11th book in the Working Methods in Knowledge Management series. The text focuses on understanding, assessing, and effectively managing organizational cultures. The book fills a significant gap in knowledge management and knowledge sciences literature. While culture is acknowledged as one of the primary forms of structural capital, there is little peer-reviewed literature explaining how it develops. This book empirically examines company cultures. Company cultures play a vital role in shaping human capital. Through the development of individual human capital, they contribute to the company's structural capital – which affects business capabilities and performance. The existing peer-reviewed literature offers case studies and anecdotes, which may provide selective insights into the company culture. In general, these insights have neither been validated nor generalized. Neither have the results been compared to the foundational theory of culture studies. The authors hope to lay the foundation for a new round of research in the field of knowledge sciences. To incentivize new research, the authors have shared their thoughts on future topics during their book research.

The Intended Audience for the Book

This text is written for executives and business managers interested in exposing, understanding, shaping, and managing their organization's culture, and for executives and managers who understand the importance of preparing their organizations for the knowledge economy. It means developing new organization-wide ways of knowing, learning, collaborating, communicating, and networking. Moreover, it means understanding how company culture aligns with business structure and strategy. Finally, the book is intended to guide managers who want to ensure their culture is well aligned with business strategies and leverage the value of the organization's knowledge capital.

The book is written primarily for knowledge management practitioners and other professionals charged with ensuring that cultural capital is transformed within an organization by human-related components of intellectual capital and finally recognized as structural capital. And those investments are made in

KLC synergy to grow and leverage the entire company's intellectual capital and innovativeness. The book is designed to bridge the gap in perspectives between knowledge managers and business managers who must work together to adapt the organization's culture to thrive in the hyperdynamic knowledge economy.

The book is also written for academics searching for a textbook that bridges theory and practice. A cursory review of organizational culture courses suggests there is a need for further development and for academics searching for research topics with significant real-world practical value.

This book can also be valuable for knowledge management or strategic management teachers seeking exciting company culture case studies to discuss with students.

Finally, the book is also written for students and anyone who wishes to self-study the field and for anyone who wishes to engage in a renewed dialog around organizational culture.

Structure of the Book

The book is organized into three sections and 12 chapters. Section 1 sets a context for understanding the elements of culture defined by the thought leaders in the field and reviews the five levels at which culture operates. To this foundation, the authors expand the foundation to increase our understanding of culture as a dynamic system. The section further expands our understanding of the culture at a practical level by examining culture as a dynamic and complex adaptive system in any organization. Finally, the section translates theory into meaningful practice for managers.

Section 2 presents the theoretical assumptions of the new KLC approach to the cultures of knowledge organizations, resulting from the powerful synergy of KLC cultures to shape all intellectual capital components and expose their meaning for innovativeness performance. This section provides the persuasive rooted in the relevant literature and a set of interesting case studies that support the KLC-approach relevance under formulated lessons learned.

Finally, Section 3 applies the lessons learned and guidance provided in Section 2 to one of the most understudied but complex organizational culture environments, public sector organizations. These organizations are commonly seen as one-dimensional in the peer-reviewed literature. Yet, they provide meaningful contexts for understanding the complex interactions and dependencies highlighted in Section 2. This section provides a broad overview of public service cultures and reifies the lessons of Section 2 in four domains – defense, agriculture, space exploration, and diplomacy.

SECTION 1. THE FUNDAMENTAL OF CULTURE

- Chapter 1. Culture as a System
- Chapter 2. Organizational Culture as a Complex Systems
- Chapter 3. How Organizational Culture Dominates Strategy
- Chapter 4. KLC Approach to Knowledge Organization Culture Building

SECTION 2. THE SYNERGISTIC POWER OF KNOWLEDGE, LEARNING, AND COLLABORATION CULTURES

- Chapter 5. Knowledge Culture Opens Minds
- Chapter 6. Learning Cultures Grow Minds
- Chapter 7. Collaborative Culture Enhances the Network of Minds

SECTION 3. KLC AND THE COMPLEX CULTURES OF THE PUBLIC SECTOR

- Chapter 8. Public Sector Cultures
- Chapter 9. The KLC Approach and Public Sector Diplomacy
- Chapter 10. The KLC Approach and Public Sector Military
- Chapter 11. The KLC Approach and Public Sector Space Exploration
- Chapter 12. The KLC Approach and Public Sector Agriculture

Appendix A. Pulling It All Together
Appendix B. The Empirical Evidence of KLC Approach
Appendix C. Surveying Knowledge, Learning and Collaboration Cultures
Appendix D. Questions for Future Research

Chapter Summaries

Each chapter provides background information on the topic and references to additional resources – both theory and practice. In addition, each chapter highlights the thought leaders and practitioners in that topic. Appendix A provides a high-level project plan that the reader can use as a template for designing their approach. Each Task and Subtask in the project plan traces back to a chapter in the book. Finally, Appendix B presents the empirical evidence in Section 2 KLC-approach theory.

Chapter 1 defines culture and explains the different conceptual models developed by critical researchers in the field. First, the authors explain why it is essential for us to learn how to see our cultures. Next, the chapter breaks the conceptual models into five essential elements: assumptions, beliefs, values, behaviors, and artifacts. Next, the authors explain why and how each organization's culture is unique – and walk through the factors that influence our organizational cultures. Finally, the chapter reminds us that it is hard to deliberately change an organization's culture because it is inherently dynamic. Instead, each organization should strive to understand how these factors affect our organizations.

In Chapter 2, the authors focus the discussion of culture on the middle level of organizations. The critical role culture plays in any organization is discussed. The authors further explain how the other levels of culture influence organizational cultures. Those factors that influence each level of culture are identified and discussed. The potential effects of these cultural factors may have on organizational capabilities. Finally, the interplay and interactions of organizational cultures are highlighted.

Chapter 3 focuses on corporate cultures as critical focus points for the knowledge economy. The authors explain how culture is a crucial intangible asset in the hyperdynamic knowledge economy. Those de facto business cultures in every organization – visible or invisible – are also discussed. The authors describe the four common types of company cultures – bureaucracy, market, clan, and fief (Boisot, 2010). Finally, the importance of aligning culture and strategy is explained. In the event of culture, this chapter explains why culture will always prevail in any conflict.

In Chapter 4, the authors explain the KLC-approach value to cultural capacity building in knowledge-driven organizations. Moreover, this chapter also expresses the importance of the company's multilevel interactions to coherently expose and enable experiencing a company culture. The authors reinforce that culture is experienced and defined by all our shared and individual experiences. The role of leadership, hierarchy, and maturity in company culture capacity at the individual, team, and organizational levels is also discussed. Finally, the chapter details a step-by-step introduces a methodology and a set of sample questions for taking stock of an organization's cultural capacity.

Chapter 5 addresses the meaning of knowledge culture. This chapter provides a deeper dive into the workings of knowledge cultures. The authors explain how a knowledge culture can shape an organization's knowledge processes and work. The chapter covers how knowledge cultures create intellectual capital. The authors also provide insights into the tension created by these knowledge paradoxes. Additionally, the interplay of knowledge paradoxes and cultural collisions is considered. Practical use cases are provided to illustrate the ideas defined in the chapter.

Chapter 6 defines a learning culture and discusses the relationship between knowledge and learning. The authors explain why learning is essential to bringing knowledge to life to incentivize knowledge flows and use. The chapter addresses the interplay between knowledge cultures and learning cultures. A key point in the chapter is the value of mistakes as learning opportunities. The authors explain how mistakes are viewed in the industrial economy and how this perspective impedes critical organizational learning. Specifically, we define mistakes, explain the double cognitive bias of mistakes, explain the tendency and impact of hiding mistakes, the side effects of double mistake bias, learn to learn from mistakes, and take on the challenge of reconciling mistake acceptance and avoidance. Finally, the chapter addresses the importance of cultivating a learning climate to realize you're learning culture. So, the awareness of how employees know culture is a key to implementing and managing company culture. The chapter is supported by practical use cases that illustrate the points in the chapter.

Chapter 7 exposes the value of a culture of collaboration and explains how collaborative cultures are essential to developing networked intelligence in any organization. The authors explain how collaborative cultures relate to three critical business processes: trust, risk, and critical thinking. The chapter addresses how important collaborative cultures are to developing these capabilities in knowledge organizations and the knowledge economy. How collaborative cultures help organizations to become more resilient and adaptable to the hyperdynamic change at the core of the knowledge economy is also explained. Moreover, this chapter also addresses how collaborative cultures help organizations maintain and sustain their business performance in chaotic environments. This chapter is supported by practical use cases that illustrate the points in the chapter.

Chapter 8 addresses the potential for KLC cultures in public sector organizations. Public sector organizations are among the most complex for introducing or nourishing a KLC approach because there are multiple levels of cultures with varying levels of influence. We describe these complex cultures as tiers. First, we define the business goals, purpose, and strategies of the public sector organizations. Then, the authors translate and interpret all five levels of culture for public sector organizations. The chapter also details the nature of cultural complexity, namely the four tiers of public sector cultures: (1) company culture (Tier 1); (2) the public service culture (Tier 2); (3) the culture of the external environment (Tier 3); and (4) the internal KLC cultures (Tier 4). This chapter establishes a framework for describing an organization's complex culture and determining the best KLC-approach for the context.

Chapter 9 describes the business goals, purpose, and strategy of public diplomatic services. It reinforces diplomatic organizations' fundamental bureaucratic company culture (Tier 1). The bureaucratic culture of diplomacy is deconstructed, and each of the five layers is described in detail. The authors also explain why focusing on the artifacts and behavior layers are the dominant and essential starting points for analysis in diplomatic cultures. The public service culture (Tier 2) overlays and mediates the bureaucratic culture. Additionally, the authors describe the influence that political appointees as leaders may play in shaping public service cultures. The authors explain how diplomatic cultures reflect the core values of a state's culture. Next, the chapter outlines the landscape of external influencing cultures (Tier 3) in diplomacy. Finally, the KLC culture of diplomacy is considered, with opportunities for future growth (Tier 4).

Chapter 10 describes the business goals, purpose, and strategy of public defense and military services. It reinforces defense and military organizations' fundamental bureaucratic company culture (Tier 1). The authors describe the influence that political appointees as leaders may play in shaping public sector cultures. The bureaucratic culture of diplomacy is deconstructed, and each of the five layers is described in detail. Additionally, the authors explain why focusing on the beliefs layer is the dominant layer and the most critical starting point for analysis in military cultures. The public service culture (Tier 2) is a mediating and grounding culture for the military. It is firmly grounded in the foundational values of the state. The chapter outlines the landscape of external influencing cultures (Tier 3) in the defense and military landscape. Finally, the potential value and challenges of developing internal KLC cultures (Tier 4) are explored.

Chapter 11 describes public space exploration services' business goals, purpose, and strategy. It reinforces space exploration organizations' fundamental bureaucratic company culture (Tier 1). The authors describe the influence that political appointees as leaders may play in shaping public sector cultures. Next, the public service culture (Tier 2) is deconstructed, and each of the five layers is described in detail. Additionally, the authors explain why focusing on the beliefs layer is the dominant layer and the most critical starting point for analysis in space exploration cultures. Next, the chapter outlines the landscape of external influencing cultures (Tier 3) in the space exploration landscape. Finally, the potential value and challenges of developing internal KLC cultures (Tier 4) are explored.

Chapter 12 describes public agriculture services' business goals, purpose, and strategy. It reinforces agriculture organizations' fundamental bureaucratic company culture (Tier 1). The authors describe the influence that political appointees as leaders may play in shaping public sector cultures. The bureaucratic culture of agriculture is deconstructed, and each of the five layers is described in detail. Additionally, the authors explain why behavior is the dominant layer and the most critical starting point for understanding military cultures. The public service culture (Tier 2) brings an essential element of leveling, access, and equity to the larger context. It brings the focus back to service to the people and community rather than performance. It also gives greater emphasis to the role of safety and well-being. The chapter lays out the landscape of external influencing cultures (Tier 3) in agriculture. Finally, the potential value and challenges of developing internal KLC cultures (Tier 4) are explored.

Appendix A provides a template for a project plan. It is a summary of the issues addressed in each of the chapters. It is a starting point, which we expect you will adapt to your situation and goals. Appendix B explains the research and supporting evidence behind the KLC approach. Detailed hypotheses, data, and results are presented. Appendix C provides a simple tool to use to assess your current and potential KLC cultures. Finally, the grounding work for this book was done over two and a half years. During that time, the authors encountered many other questions and ideas that were related to the topic, but not core to the text. We chose to list those questions for the reader in Appendix D, in the event that you might have an interest in refining, refocusing, or carrying them forward.

How the Book Impacts the Field?

The authors hope the book will contribute to business management literature by expanding the discourse about organizational cultures beyond the traditional literature to include new insight from real-world practice. The book anchors the discussion of organizational culture in a business context and interprets culture in a way that aligns it with knowledge economies, knowledge work, and intellectual capital. The book also aligns the research on intellectual and knowledge capital.

Ideally, the book adds rigor to the discussion of organizational culture and creates an extended body of knowledge grounded in practice. The authors hope the book will increase knowledge sciences' visibility across management and culture by portraying culture as an essential knowledge capital asset and a critical business capability. The text also attempts to refocus culture discussion from theory to practice.

How to Read This Book?

The authors faced a challenge in putting this book together. We recognize that substantial work will not be read in an afternoon or two-hour airport layover.

So, how do we recommend you read this book? The book's core message is the importance of the KLC approach described in Section 2. Culture is a complex and dynamic topic that has remained mainly in the theoretical world. We needed to make it practical. To understand the KLC approach in context, it was necessary to provide a brief overview of culture in Section 1. Sections 1 and 2 are written for managers and practitioners who must translate theory into practice. Armed with a practical understanding of culture and the KLC approach, managers and practitioners can develop relevant and suitable strategies for their organizations. Because of the KLC approach and the synergies they create in an emerging topic, it was essential to provide both the supporting research evidence and a "desk-check" of the theory in companies and organizations familiar to the reader. Appendix B provides the research evidence. The business stories in Chapters 3–7. and the extended public service "desk checks" of Chapters 8–12 provide real-world examples of the importance of culture and the KLC culture approach.

For practicing managers, we recommend you to read Sections 1 and 2 and select a chapter of interest from Section 3. We recommend scanning Appendix A as a template for your organizational culture. For academics and students of culture who already have a grounding in culture, we recommend you begin with Section 2, review the research evidence in Appendix B, and then select relevant chapters from Section 3. For knowledge management practitioners, we recommend you begin with Section 2 to understand the critical synergies among KLC cultures, and review Chapter 2 to understand the layers of organizational culture. Finally, for researchers, we suggest you also review Appendix C for future research topics.

Notes from the Authors

The authors have collaborated on this text during a period of significant change and challenges. We wish to acknowledge the critical contributions to our thinking from Dr Richard Lewis and Dr Iouri Bairatchnyi, two thought leaders in the field. Their early advice and guidance were invaluable.

Reference

Boisot, H. (2010). *Knowledge assets.* Oxford University Press.

Section 1

The Fundamentals of Culture

Chapter 1

Culture as a System

Chapter Summary

This chapter defines culture and explains the different conceptual models developed by critical researchers in the field. First, the authors explain why it is essential for us to learn to see our cultures. Next, the chapter breaks the conceptual model of culture into its essential elements, including assumptions, beliefs, values, behaviors, and artifacts. The authors explain why and how each organization's culture is unique – and walk through the factors that influence our organizational cultures. Finally, the chapter reminds us that it is hard to deliberately change an organization's culture, because it is inherently dynamic. Instead, each organization should strive to understand how these factors affect our organizations.

Why We Care About Culture?

Culture governs our behaviors and assumptions and is core to our beliefs, but it does so unconsciously. While largely invisible, culture is a force that influences a community or an organization's behavior. Culture can support or impede strategy and performance. Culture is a dynamic force in every organization, but it is not a simple force that is easy to manage (Alvesson, 2012; Deshpandé & Farley, 1999; Lewis, 2010; Neuijen et al., 1990; Pettigrew, 1990). Instead, it resembles a complex adaptive system.

Every organization has an inherent culture defined and designed to support its business goals and aligned with its business strategies. There are well-researched and tested characteristics of the business cultures of industrial organizations (Rashid et al., 1997; Schall, 1983; Scholz, 1987; Schwartz & Davis, 1981; Van Maanen & Barley, 1984). These business cultures are complex. However, knowledge organizations' cultures are exponentially more complex than those of industrial organizations. It is more complex because an organization cannot be said to be a knowledge organization unless it has a vibrant and dynamic knowledge culture, a learning culture, and a collaborative culture.

The Cultures of Knowledge Organizations: Knowledge, Learning, Collaboration (KLC), 3–24
Copyright © 2023 by Wioleta Kucharska and Denise Bedford
Published under exclusive licence by Emerald Publishing Limited
doi:10.1108/978-1-83909-336-420231001

Managers and decision-makers need a framework for understanding the cultures in place in the workplace and for designing cultures for a knowledge economy (Alexander et al., 1990; Corbett et al., 1987; Corbett & Rossman, 1989). It is challenging, though, because it means modeling the dimensions of those cultures. What we have to work with today comes from peer-reviewed literature (Choe, 2003; Gordon & DiTomaso, 1992; McGuire et al., 2003; Sadri & Lees, 2001). The literature reflects an anthropological perspective and tends to focus on national or regional cultures rather than more complex and dynamic organizational cultures. As a result, what we know is mainly theoretical and static. While there are case studies, these practical examples have not been tied to the theory. The research of Kucharska (2017, 2021), Kucharska and Bedford (2020), or Kucharska and Rebelo (2022), and primarily the empirical evidence provided in this book (Appendix B) are essential to building out the theoretical and foundational organizational cultures of the knowledge economy (KLC approach). This essential new research helps us understand how culture works, what factors shape it, and how the structural levels of organizational culture influence the entire company's shared mindset. In essence, it provides practically what managers need to know to introduce and manage a company culture.

Culture – Definitions and Characterizations

Culture has many definitions in scholarly and popular literature. However, the most common characterization of culture is a pattern of shared underlying assumptions that a group learned as it solved problems of external adaptation and internal integration, which has worked well enough to be considered valid and, therefore, to be taught to new members as the correct way to perceive, think, and feel about those problems (Schein, 1992).

On a practical level, culture can be defined as the set of assumptions, beliefs, values, and behaviors a group has developed over time, enabling it to survive in any environment (Cooke & Rousseau, 1988). Assumptions, beliefs, values, and behavioral patterns form its identity. Culture is taught to the new members of a society as the correct way to think and feel about problems and challenges. It is the total of all the shared assumptions and beliefs a group has learned throughout its history. Culture is the structure and control system that generates behavioral standards.

Culture is viewed as a shared mental model that influences how individuals interpret behaviors, and they often behave without being aware of the underlying assumptions. Culture is learned, reinforced, and handed on as learning to the next generation and new members of groups. Cultures are reinforcing – they can hold us hostage to traditional beliefs, prejudices, and perspectives. And cultures can be liberating – they can create new assumptions and help us to develop and instill new values and behaviors. Perceive success will reinforce the culture and make it stronger. An organization or group will develop its distinct patterns of behaviors and beliefs to support the culture and the internal socialization process.

Culture is inherently the outcome of human active and passive experiences. These experiences shape perception. They determine how culture is shaped and how it shapes attitudes and behaviors is complex. There is not one culture – there are many cultures at play in any situation – the individual's culture, the group's culture, the organization's culture, and the national culture. Culture is inside people's heads and somewhere between the heads of a group of people, interactions, and material objects – it describes our behaviors, social events, institutions, and processes. Culture is like air – we breathe it every day without even knowing it is there.

Culture – The Static Perspective

There are two prominent perspectives on culture in the literature. The first is the perspective of a static conceptual model in the research and analytical literature. Static models take two forms – theoretical models developed by researchers and analytical frameworks developed by organizational analysts and consultants. The second is a dynamic system at work in every organization, at every level. Unfortunately, there are fewer examples of dynamic systems in the literature.

Research Models

The first type of static model is the theoretical model of group cultures developed by researchers. In the research community, there is a general agreement that culture can be referred to as a set of values, beliefs, and behavior patterns that form its core identity and shape everyday behaviors (Deal & Kennedy, 1982; Deshpandé & Farley, 1999; Heskett & Kotter, 1992; Jones, 1983; Pheysey, 2002; Schein, 1992; Van der Post & De Coning, 1998). Four researchers have developed the dominant models – Hofstede, Frost, Dennison, and Schein.

Hofstede (1998) defines culture as a process to which each of us has been subjected since birth. When parents returning from the hospital carry you over the threshold, they have often already made their first culturally-based decision. Frost defines culture as rituals, myths, stories, legends, and interpretations of events, ideas, and experiences that are influenced and shaped by the groups within which they live. Culture includes values and assumptions about social reality. Culture provides the shared rules governing cognitive and affective aspects of membership in an organization and the means by whereby they are shaped and expressed. Culture is central and describes our behaviors, social events, institutions, and processes. Culture provides group members with a shared understanding, feelings of clarity, direction, meaning, and purpose.

Dennison characterizes culture as an iceberg. Dennison (1990) tells us that only about 10% of an iceberg is visible above the water – 90% is below the surface. Consider how this aligns with Schein's model – assumptions, beliefs, and values are likely the 90%. Behaviors and artifacts are the 10% we can observe – and they are motivated by and determined by the 90%. What is beneath the surface is what will sink your organizational strategies and decisions. Dennison reminds us that culture is learned. It is filled up from the accumulated principles we learn as we survive together. The lessons from the past shape our survival strategies for the future. Our mindset and worldview shape the way we use the lessons of the past to forge strategies for the future.

Schein, though, provides the most detailed and structured conceptual model. Schein (1992) defined organizational culture as a pattern of underlying assumptions invented, discovered, or developed by a group as it learns to cope with its problem of external adaptation and internal integration problems. These values are then taught to new members of the organization as the correct way to think and feel about those problems. For Schein (1992), culture is the total of all the shared, taken-for-granted assumptions a group has learned throughout its history. Also, culture is determined to be the residue of success. Culture is also the structure and control system to generate behavioral standards. Corporate culture has to be kept strictly from similar concepts like corporate identity, organizational climate, or national culture. Corporate culture is the implicit, invisible, intrinsic, and informal consciousness of the organization that guides the individuals' behavior and shapes itself out of the behavior.

Schein (1984, 1988, 1990, 1992) defines culture in a particularly useful way for organizational management. Shine defines organizational culture as a pattern of shared underlying assumptions that a group learned as it solved its problems of external adaptation and internal integration, which has worked well enough to be considered valid and, therefore, to be taught to new members as the correct way to perceive, think, and feel about those problems. *Shein*'s classical approach divides culture into three levels. First, he argues that basic underlying assumptions lie at the root of culture and our unconscious, taken-for-granted beliefs, perceptions, thoughts, and feelings. Espoused values are derived from the basic underlying assumptions and the espoused justification of strategies, goals, and philosophies. Finally, at the top level are artifacts, defined as the visible yet hard-to-decipher organizational structures and processes.

Analytical Models

The cultural assessment frameworks and tools developed in recent decades represent the analytical perspective. They are the second type of static model. The frameworks are designed to generate a cultural profile of an organization, group, or community. There are few published accounts of organizational culture assessments because most examples are business proprietary. While the profiles are generally not publicly available, the frameworks are well documented in the literature. Traditionally, there have been two approaches to culture assessment – culture-centered and personality-centered. Researchers have added a third in the past 10 years – cultural competence assessment or cultural intelligence (Earley, 2002; Kumar et al., 2008).

Culture-centered approaches are qualitative methods of culture assessment and are derived primarily from cultural anthropology. The personality-centered approaches consist in obtaining quantitative measures for identifying and describing cultures. Cultural competence or intelligence assessments are applied to individuals.

Culture-centered approaches are grounded in ethnological research intended for cultural comparisons. This type of research is often qualitative, drawing from sociological, psychological, or anthropological methods. Ethnographic description begins with observations of social structures, artifacts and collective behavior, then used to develop conclusions about groups. This approach reflects anthropologists' view that cultures are so complex that they cannot be measured, only observed and described. This approach is essential for understanding national, regional, and local community cultures. Moreover, these studies are essential to understanding the context in which our communities and organizations operate because each individual has a national and community culture.

Additionally, every organization is located "somewhere," and we know that "somewhere" influences how the organization behaves. In today's global economy, where a company is located may be a complicated consideration – consider Goodyear Corporation, which is headquartered in Akron, Ohio, but has manufacturing plants in Brazil, China, and Poland and research facilities in Germany and Brussels. A company's subsidiary cultures are simultaneously shaped by the culture of the country in which they are located and the company culture at headquarters. The national and company cultures of subsidiaries are interwoven by the individuals working in the subsidiary.

The personality-centered approach label is somewhat misleading because the final assessment is not necessarily a personality profile. Instead, this approach focuses on how personalities affect group and community behaviors and consider how companies treat people and do things. This approach uses information about behaviors, psychology, and personalities to develop a profile of the culture of teams and organizations. This approach aims to illuminate potential problems with an organization's current culture. The most widely used personality-centered assessment is based on the Competing Values Framework developed by Quinn et al. (2015), which has two dimensions – the internal and the external. Internal orientation focuses on the development, collaboration, integration of activities, and coordination. External orientation focuses on the market, the latest technology, competitors, customers, and diversification. Like the culture-centered approach, the competing values approach is descriptive and analytical but does not guide how to respond to any challenges.

The third framework focuses on an individual's cultural competence. Traditionally, cultural competence was defined as understanding, communicating, and effectively interacting with people across cultures. Cultural intelligence is also seen as a non-academic intelligence (Kumar et al., 2008) that represents a personal competence in functioning in cultural variety environments (Earley & Ang, 2003). Cultural competence encompasses being aware of one's worldview. And it means developing positive attitudes toward cultural differences. This traditional definition is essential to building an organization's cultural capacity, but it is only one small part of that culture. In the context of a twenty-first-century knowledge economy and a knowledge organization, cultural competence also includes being aware of the value and liabilities culture can pose to business and information strategies. It also includes an individual's ability to adapt and shape cultural norms and behaviors to support the organization.

Culture – The Dynamic Perspective

Culture is complex. It is an aggregation of the cultures of today's individuals, business units, and the entire membership of the group or organization. Culture is refined and expanded by each individual in the organization – as individuals arrive and depart. The culture shifts to small degrees. Culture is multi-directional. Culture is how we do things around here, what we do when we think no one is looking, and what if everybody is looking. Culture is the code, the core logic, the mind's core software, It defines our attitudes, beliefs, values and behaviors. It develops from the lessons that we have learned that are important enough to pass on to the next generation (Denison, 1990; Denison et al., 2012).

The static models of culture can only go so far in describing the culture in play in any context. Culture is complex in its fundamental elements – assumptions, beliefs, values, behaviors, and artifacts. It is multi-layered because individuals contribute to group culture, and groups contribute to organizational cultures. Everyone brings a culture, whether an employee or a Chief Executive Office. The challenge is to discover these cultures and understand how they do or do not fit and how they influence the organization's "whole" culture.

Conceptual models help understand the anatomy of culture – but they are not productive for understanding culture at work in everyday environments. We need more than a conceptual model – we need a system model that allows us to "see" how the culture plays out in the real world. As shown in Fig. 1, there are three dimensions to a model of a cultural system. The first dimension is structural – the degree of impact and influence of the culture. Culture exists at the individual level, the group level, the organization level, the national level, and today even at the global level. The second dimension addresses the essential elements of culture we find at each level and the factors that characterize those elements. By elements, we include assumptions, beliefs, values, behaviors, and artifacts.

Finally, we have the context – the activity or point in time – where we see the culture at work. Culture constantly changes in small ways – it adapts, expands, and shrinks as people enter and leave. It is impossible to document and track every factor at every level because, ultimately, culture is made up of and practiced by people. If we know what to look for, where and when, we can learn to align it with our goals and strategies and leverage it to support how we work.

Culture is like a dynamic prism. The first facet is the essential elements of culture – assumptions, beliefs, values, behaviors, and artifacts. The second facet is the scale or level – ranging from individual to global cultures. And a third facet is the context in which culture is most apparent – the events, activities, and decisions affected by culture. For explanation purposes, the authors select three organizational behaviors that can be significantly affected by culture. Of the three facets, the most dynamic and complex is the level of culture. Each level has its own set of influence factors. As a result, the cultural prism is challenging to hold sufficiently

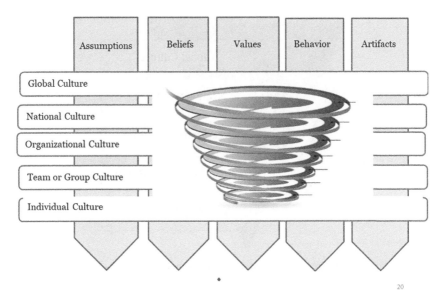

Fig. 1.   Spiral Model of Culture – Interplay Across Levels and Components.

constant to understand which factors are at play in any given context. In the following sections, the authors explain each facet of the prism.

Levels of Culture

Levels of culture pertain to the scale at which a culture may be defined. For example, the lowest level is an individual's culture (Fig. 2). The culture scale then increases to include the cultures of teams and business units, the organization's culture, and the cultures of the countries or locations where they live and work. Finally, the highest level of culture is a global culture.

Culture as a shared meaning system can be formed at any level. The organizational culture is formed by factors at play at three general levels: (1) the global and national level, (2) the organization and team level, and (3) the individual level. While the authors describe the role of all three levels, the primary focus of this text is on the meso- and micro-level cultures. These levels are the most relevant to business and information management strategies.

Global Culture – Dynamic Factors

Our organizations and business environments are increasingly global. Global culture is not just a sum of national cultures but a blending and shaping of a new international perspective at the organizational level. Our workplaces and work teams are increasingly representations of many national cultures – rather than one dominant culture. Global teams shape new blended cultures (Berson et al., 2004). The global environment creates a new cultural identity that blends national and

Fig. 2.   Seeing Culture from the Structural Perspective.

organizational cultures. An international identity means that people develop a sense of belongingness to a universal organizational culture by adopting the values and behaviors of the organization while still retaining their assumptions, beliefs, behaviors, and values. Oddly, international culture has the most significant impact on the individual because it is at the individual level that these two different cultures must align (Naisbitt, 1994; Tajfel & Turner, 1979). Global culture is individuals drawing upon and blending their national and organizational cultures.

National Culture – Dynamic Factors

National cultures include factors that shape how our organizations work, how we manage and our expectations for work. When we think of national cultures, most people will think of cultural artifacts – those visible representations that distinguish one culture from another. The most easily recognized artifacts of national culture might include how we dress, our art and crafts, how we build our homes, or the food we eat. These are ways that cultures distinguish themselves from one another. However, national cultures run much more profoundly than artifacts and are much more pervasive. National cultures also include essential beliefs and assumptions, behaviors, and values. Our national cultures are what we learn from our families, our communities, and our upbringing. They are the first cultures that each of us develops, and they are the cultures that remain throughout our lives. According to Hofstede, these primary cultures determine the mental models, assumptions, and beliefs we acquire during the first 10 years of our lives. Of all the structural levels of culture, the national culture aligns most clearly with the lowest level of culture – assumptions and beliefs. We note that these are not only the most pervasive and long-lasting but are the hardest to change. A wise organizational manager will understand that it is essential to shape but not attempt to change a national culture.

Organizational Level – Dynamic Factors

Nested within the national culture is the level of organizational culture, often defined as a set of beliefs and values shared by members of the same organization which influence their behaviors (Miron et al., 2003; O'Reilly, Chatman, & Caldwell, 1991; Rousseau, 1990; Schein, 1961, 1992; Schneider et al., 2002). The organization-level culture is officially sanctioned, presented to the external business environment, and promoted internally. The organizational culture is a result of all the decisions made and all the actions taken in an organization over time. Culture is slowly formed by people interacting and repeating behaviors that lead to success as defined by the organization.

There is a common assumption that organizations have a single, uniform culture (Gregory, 1983). However, organizations rarely have a shared, overarching set of beliefs and systems of meanings. What we find instead is a culture that is espoused by the organization and one that is lived by its workforce. Culture at this level shapes how we learn, how we work together, how we share knowledge, and how we problem-solve. It is the lived culture that is demonstrated in everyday organizational behaviors. In understanding those lived cultures – at the functional and individual levels – we are better positioned to continually align and adjust the organization's espoused culture. It is the most critical level to see our culture. At this level, we can also see the complex interplay of factors across levels. The point of aligning espoused and lived cultures is that the members share a set of problems commonly defined to be the problems of all and routinely take actions based on collective understandings of the group (Van Maanen & Barley, 1984). Whose problem interpretations and actions will prevail is the key question in organizations where there are multiple and possible cross-cutting cultures in play.

Unit and Team Culture – Dynamic Factors

From a 50,000-foot view or the outside, an organization's espoused culture may appear consistent and synchronized. Upon closer inspection, though, every organizational culture has multiple subcultures. An organization's culture is a composition of its subcultures (Martin, 1992, 2002; Schein, 1996). Martin and Schein suggest that organizational cultures may be (1) cohesive and unitary, (2) integrated and collections of subcultures, or (3) differentiated. A fragmented culture is ambiguous and open to members' multiple interpretations (Meyerson & Martin, 1987). Furthermore, each subculture interacts uniquely with others (Bloor & Dawson, 1994; Martin, 2001; Martin & Siehl, 1983). Therefore, we must understand subcultures at an individual level and understand whether and, if so, how they contribute to creating a productive, supportive, and "whole organization" culture (Rose, 1988; Sackmann, 1992; Trice & Beyer, 1993). By considering cultural cohesion and strength, we acknowledge that subcultures exist and can develop within strong cultures without weakening the overarching culture.

Two sets of factors influence this level of culture, specifically (1) factors that are a reflection of and are inherited from the organizational culture; and (2) factors that derive from the composition of the unit or team – what the individuals bring to the unit. These two sets of factors might be viewed as top-down and bottom-up factors.

The unit and team culture level is critical from a cultural understanding perspective because it is where the collective and the individual cultures meet, it is the optimal level in organizations for blending and shaping culture. As a result, it is a bit more challenging to develop a cultural profile of the unit. It also means that unit cultures are a starting point for understanding the interaction of cultures across units and the organization. These factors are discussed in greater detail in Chapter 2.

At this level, culture is influenced by both the organization's culture and the culture of the composition of the team or unit. The culture they create may be consistent with or different from the organizational culture. Therefore, managers must consider how these factors may change when they reach the unit level. Is there a different cultural effect of each factor, i.e., do the factors interact differently? How does the unique composition of the individual cultures or registers affect the inherited factors? How do they affect the cultural composition of the unit?

At the unit and team level culture, equal weight is given to the cultural factors inherited from the organizational culture and the cultures of the individuals who make up the unit. It is a level of synthesis where the lived organizational culture is formed. Inherited organizational factors may be commonly defined across organizations – but the cultural registers of individuals that make up a unit give it its unique cultural character. As noted earlier, a unit is defined by the individuals who comprise it at any given time and their cultural registers. The set of compositional factors is a bottom-up description of a unit's culture. They are more dynamic than inherited factors because they change with the arrival or departure of each individual. The composition of a unit is defined by the people assigned to it at any time.

Individual Level – Dynamic Factors

Every individual comes to work with a mindset shaped by multiple cultures experienced, meaning they operate within multiple cultures daily–family, national, social, and political. We can observe how the organization works and behaves at this level. However, shaping culture at this level is the individual's responsibility. Shaping culture means empowering individuals to shape their cultural register to support the strategy. In comparison, achieving the most effective level of alignment is also challenging.

The Interplay of Levels of Culture

While we have described five distinct levels of culture, the levels continuously influence each other. The individual level is the most dynamic of all levels and the level that is the most authentic representation of a lived or actual culture. The cultures that represent a larger or higher scale tend to represent the espoused culture of the organization. The espoused culture is the preferred culture that represents the organization's goals and aspirations.

An added complexity in the prism is the continuous interplay of cultures (Fig. 3). The team's culture continuously challenges or reifies an individual's culture. The organization's culture is continuously challenged or reified by the nation's culture, though the rate of change and influence may be slower than at the team level. Understanding organizational cultures are challenging because all four other cultures continuously influence them.

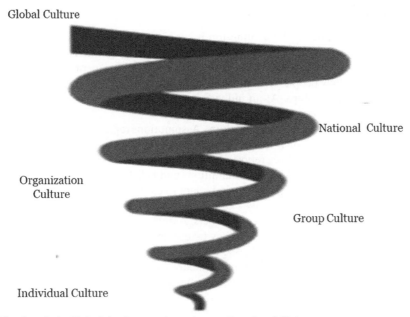

Global Culture

National Culture

Organization Culture

Group Culture

Individual Culture

Fig. 3.   Spiral Model – Interactions Across Levels of Culture.

The Element Dimension

While specific models and characterizations may differ, the essential elements of organizational culture are consistent across researchers. Organizational culture includes assumptions, beliefs, fundamental values, behaviors, and artifacts (Schein, 1984, 1990). Culture is manifested in rituals and routines, stories and myths, symbols, power structures, organizational structures, and control systems. There are several characterizations and models of organizational culture. Given the author's research and experience, we suggest five levels each affect the overall culture (Fig. 4).

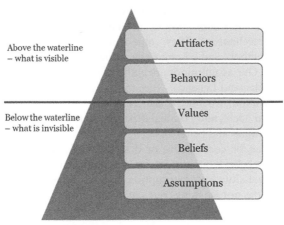

Above the waterline – what is visible

Below the waterline – what is invisible

Artifacts

Behaviors

Values

Beliefs

Assumptions

Fig. 4.   Five Elements of Culture.

Assumptions

What are assumptions? An assumption is something we accept as true without question or proof. Assumptions are thoughts we take for granted and believe to be true. They aren't based on facts; they are based on past experiences. Assumptions describe how people perceive situations and make sense of events, activities, and human relationships. At an individual level, assumptions are a part of our human capital – reflected in our attitudes.

Assumptions are at the core of culture. Assumptions represent how individuals build their beliefs into their thought patterns and how they perceive and interpret the world around them. They represent individuals' beliefs about human behavior, relationships, reality, and truth. Assumptions and beliefs are formed over time as people learn to cope with problems and adapt to change. Assumptions are tacit – they live below the waterline. We can only see them as individuals express them through their behaviors, values, and beliefs. Assumptions evolve with encountering new situations and challenges. They take shape and become embedded when they work to help an individual cope with their environment. When an assumption is repeatedly made, and when it repeatedly serves the purpose, it becomes an essential part of an individual's beliefs. Assumptions represent our mental stability and our defense mechanisms. Different cultures make different assumptions about others based on their beliefs and values. If people are treated consistently with certain underlying assumptions, they eventually behave according to them to make their world stable and predictable. Our assumptions affect what we pay attention to, how we interpret things, react emotionally, and what actions we are likely to take and when. Like other elements of culture, assumptions influence and are influenced by beliefs, values, behaviors, and artifacts.

Assumptions are the deepest level of culture we can find in an individual. They are the most challenging to "see" and to change. Not all assumptions are mutually compatible or consistent. We build our assumptions early in life and are reinforced, questioned, contradicted, or challenged over time. If we are never exposed to anyone with different assumptions, we will never have a reason to test our assumptions – we will never have a chance to validate them, invalidate them, or even call them into question. If you have little virtual access to people with different assumptions, the chances of any tests of your assumptions are small.

Where do our assumptions come from? They represent our mental stability and our defense mechanisms. They come from family and heritage, faith and belief systems, neighbors and communities, education systems, work experience, and other sources. Our assumptions are embedded in family stories and histories, in fairy Tales, Myths, and Legends – the stories we read or hear, in our religious training and education, what we learn from our neighbors, our teachers and peers, and from our social and political experiences. In other words, assumptions are influenced by values and behaviors.

Assumptions can be constructive or destructive. Assumptions start causing problems when we believe our way of interpreting a given situation is the only way to interpret that situation. Assumptions can be destructive when we assume that anyone who does not see things our way is somehow "less than us." Everyone has a different set of assumptions – no two people can have the same set of life experiences. We make assumptions and believe we are right about the assumptions; then, we defend our assumptions and try to make someone else wrong.

Not all assumptions are mutually compatible or consistent. If a group holds the assumption that all good ideas and products ultimately come from individual effort, it will not readily assume that groups can be held responsible for the results. Or those individuals will put a high priority on group loyalty. If a group assumes that the way to survive is to conquer nature and manipulate the environment aggressively, it cannot have the same time as soon. The notion that business should be profitable, that schools should educate, or that medicine should prolong life is an assumption. They do not rise to the level of cultural values.

Beliefs

Beliefs are underlying assumptions about the world and how it works. Because many facets of physical and social reality are difficult or impossible to experience personally or to verify, people rely on others they identify with and trust to help them decide what to believe and what not to believe. Beliefs held for a long time without being violated or challenged may be taken so much for granted that we are no longer aware of them. It is why organizational members frequently fail to realize the profound influence culture has on them. It is why it can be difficult to "see" our cultures. Beliefs are our brain's way of making sense of and navigating our complex world. They are mental representations of how our brains expect things in our environment to behave and how things should be related – the patterns our brain expects the world to conform to. A belief is an attitude that something is the case or that some proposition about the world is true. Philosophers use the term "belief" to refer to attitudes about the world, which can be either true or false. A belief is an opinion or something a person holds to be true. Faith in God is an example of a belief.

Where do our beliefs come from? Beliefs originate from what we hear – and we keep hearing from others since we were children. The sources of beliefs include environment, events, knowledge, past experiences, visualization, what we know to be true in our worlds, and what helps us survive. Beliefs are inherent to the society in which we live. Limiting beliefs are false beliefs that prevent us from pursuing our goals and desires. Limiting beliefs can keep you from doing important things, like applying for your dream job or finding the relationship you want (or leaving the one you don't want). Limiting beliefs comes from the different things that happen in your life. Many limiting beliefs develop in childhood when you aren't always able to process what happens to you. When something traumatic happens, that moment's feelings can remain in your psyche. Beliefs can manifest themselves as prejudice or persuade someone to blow up themselves and others in the name of a political cause.

How do we learn what we believe? Belief takes the concept of memory a step further. It is a mental architecture of how we interpret the world – we learn our beliefs as we navigate and survive. Some neuroscientists suggest beliefs are similar to memories – memories are formed in the brain as networks of neurons that fire when stimulated by an event – the more our neural network is employed, the more it fires and the stronger the memory becomes. We have lots of fluid things moving by but how we make sense of the world is crystallized knowledge – if we did not have those beliefs, every time we woke up, we would not know who we are or how to navigate the world.

What reinforces our beliefs? The human being is best at interpreting all new information so that their prior conclusions remain intact. When it has once adopted an opinion, human understanding draws everything else to support and agree with it. Even though there are a more significant number and weight of instances to be found on the other side, it will ignore and reject those other instances. Confirmation bias is linked to our memories – we prefer to recall and reference evidence that backs up our beliefs – we are susceptible to selective recall.

What causes us to question our beliefs? First, beliefs provide stability – when a new piece of sensory information comes in, it is assessed against these knowledge units before the brain determines whether it should be incorporated. Second, we need cognitive consistency – everyday information comes from other people, the media, our experience, and various other sources. People call their beliefs into play when they test a politician's credibility or hear about a paranormal event. Third, we develop cognitive shortcuts and models that enable us to encode, store, and retrieve the ideas we are exposed to. Finally, we ignore contradictory evidence because it is so unpalatable for our brains – we think differently only when we are held to account by others around us.

How do we live our beliefs? Living our beliefs means translating them into value systems and behaviors. Lived or actual beliefs are found in our everyday choices, actions, and decisions. We may say we espouse a set of beliefs (e.g., a belief system, a well-articulated philosophy, and so on), but they may be at variance with our true beliefs. For example, consider how we might characterize a celebrity or politician or a leader as "false" or when we say that someone has "betrayed" their beliefs – it means we think their espoused beliefs are not their lived or actual beliefs.

Values

Beliefs and values are closely related, though different. Beliefs and values are different, though closely related. Values tell us what is important. They guide our choices and actions. Essentially, values define what actions to take, and how to live to survive. Values reflect a person's sense of right and wrong or what "ought" to be – a society, a community, or an organization often establish values. Values guide our behaviors and actions. They describe the significance of something to an individual. Values tell us what is good, desirable, or worthwhile – the motive behind purposeful action. Values tell us why people behave the way they do. Values are underlying assumptions that convey an implicit *ought* (Schein, 1988).

Where do our values come from? Like our beliefs, our values come from family and friends, colleagues, the work environment, our industries and professions, our communities, and our religious and spiritual community. What reinforces our values? In a nutshell, lived experiences and successful, positive experiences reinforce our values. Values are reified when they are lived, when we succeed as a result of following them, when we see others living those values when those values are reinforced in conversations, recognized and rewarded by others around us, when they are integrated into how we work, and when people who violate these values are corrected.

Values are closely related to norms, morals, and ethics. Norms are behaviors and attitudes considered normal, while values are things people consider important to them. Values are the social norms that define the rules that govern how people behave. Individuals demonstrate their compliance or opposition to norms in how they behave in the community, workplace, family settings, and every other aspect of their lives. Morals are society's standards of right and wrong, similar to ethics. Finally, ethics are a structured system of principles that govern appropriate conduct for a group, including professional ethics, compassion, commitment, and cooperation.

Values are complex. The research offers several characterizations and refinements of values to explain this complexity. Specifically, the research speaks to:

- core and universal values
- espoused and actual-lived values
- pivotal and peripheral values
- aspirational and fashionable values
- corrective values.

At the heart of most cultures, we will generally find a *core* or *universal* set of values. These values are central to most spiritual and belief systems. They speak to those characteristics of individuals most valued in society, including trustworthiness, respect, fairness, fidelity, charity, responsibility, caring, and good citizenship. These values reflect the values of the broader society and its beliefs.

Espoused values those promoted by or attributed to the organization. Espoused values are at the foundation of what the firm believe. They are the practical results of the values that the members of an organization espouse. Espoused values may be distinct from practiced values. We distinguish between openly stated explicit values (e.g., espoused values) and unstated implicit values (e.g., actual or lived values). In a healthy, open, and creative organizational culture, there will be minimal discrepancies between explicit and implicit values. In a weak organizational culture, the espoused and actual-lived values may conflict. For instance, management espouses creativity and initiative but punishes any risk-taking or variation from established work practices. *Actual values* refer to the values that individuals across the organization or community hold. These values reflect what an individual understands to be the values held and enforced in practice and the values they must adhere to survive in the environment. These are observable in an individual's everyday behaviors, language, decisions, and choices. An organization's credo might say one thing, but the operating culture might have a slightly different character and set of values. In supportive cultures, subunits can act on the values necessary but peripheral to the organization's functioning, leaving the organization's core values intact (O'Reilly & Tushman, 2008).

Pivotal values are central to an organization's functioning. Pivotal values are exclusive – members are required to adopt and adhere to them. Those who do not are excluded from the culture (Chatman, 1989; O'Reilly & Chatman, 1996). Pivotal values include (1) actual and (2) corrective values. *Peripheral values* are desirable but are not believed by members to be essential to an organization's functioning. Members are encouraged to accept peripheral values but can reject them and still function fully as members. Peripheral values include (1) aspirational and (2) fashionable values. Pivotal values included high professional standards and a commitment to client satisfaction. Workers within the organization simultaneously embrace core values and focus on ethical behavior and client advocacy. Because there is the agreement that the pivotal values are essential and peripheral, do not interfere with the organization's pivotal values and do not detract from the strength of the dominant organizational culture. Strong pivotal and varying peripheral cultural values can coexist.

Aspirational values are lofty but achievable goals. However, depending on the degree of aspiration and its alignment with a current state and culture, they may not be achievable. *Fashionable values* are a kind of aspiration value that reflects the values in society, which may be more transitory. In some cases, fashionable values can transition to aspirational values, e.g., being green to becoming an environmentally sustainable organization, denouncing discrimination to embracing corporate social responsibility policies.

Corrective values represent those values that cannot be broken or disregarded. We find corrective values in organizations with the most cohesive cultures. Corrective values are often found in cults and prisons. Corrective values can become pivotal in some environments where they are so widely adopted or enforced that they preclude the emergence of peripheral values (Bloor & Dawson, 1994; O'Reilly & Chatman, 1996; Schein, 1961; Van Maanen & Barley, 1984).

In reality, most organizations do not operate with well-defined values (Trice & Beyer, 1993). And it is realistic to assume that some of those values may be more dynamic than others. We might expect actual-lived values to be more persistent than espoused values. Espoused values may change with the leadership team. Pivotal values are likely to be more persistent across the organization, but peripheral values may vary with the leadership style of a department or division. It is these variations in values that allow subcultures to emerge. Subculture values can nourish an organization's culture where they are not in conflict. They can, though, be destructive to organizations where they emerge in opposition to espoused or pivotal values.

Behaviors

Just as there are dependencies between beliefs and values, so are their dependencies between values and behaviors. It is impossible to understand our values outside our beliefs and separate them from assumptions. Behaviors and habits are what an external observer can see. Individuals, communities, and societies communicate them through their everyday actions. Behaviors include work behaviors, learning styles, knowledge-sharing practices, and willingness to work with others.

Behaviors are also represented in the language we use, how we communicate, how we dress or present ourselves, how we make decisions, how we reward others, our relationships, and even how we respond to change or crises.

Individuals tailor their behaviors to suit the context. For example, consider how you dress, conduct yourself, interact with and communicate with others when you are in an office environment, a faith or spiritual context, the gym or exercise context, a maker space, a formal, a college classroom, or an open public space or on public transport. Each of these behavioral adaptations is grounded in our value systems – and each of these different environments causes us to adapt and translate to meet the expectations of others around us.

Work practices are core organizational behaviors. They are central to organizational and operational routines and habits that have been established to run the organization. The espoused values and corresponding justification heavily influence decision-making processes. Work practices include the organizational structure and hierarchy, both formal and informal, decision-making processes, organizational skills and capabilities, workflow processes, and Performance Management reward and compensation systems. National cultures profoundly impact organizational work behaviors (Hammerisch & Lewis, 2012; O'Reilly & Tushman, 2008).

What can we learn by observing how someone thinks, learns, approaches problem-solving, and works with others? Relationships are an essential indicator of behavior – how do people develop relationships, how are groups organized, and are there designations, ranks, or protocols honored? Behaviors are learned through interaction with our environment, and all behaviors are learned through experience. For example, we might encounter something new based on a natural occurrence in our world, and over time, we continue to respond in the same way – it becomes how we behave. Or, we can learn as a consequence of action – how or how not to behave because of the consequences of our previous behaviors. Both of these processes occur over time and are learned through experience. Every individual's behavior is a result of their personal learned experiences.

Artifacts

Artifacts are tangible and visible objects that reflect and reinforce culture. Artifacts are things we can see, hear, and feel. They are visible products and things – architectures of places and spaces, our language, the technology we use, the products we adopt, our choice and style of clothing, our manners of address, the stories we tell, and the organizational myths we believe, the art we prefer, the heroes we regard, the rituals and ceremonies we observe (Deal & Kennedy, 1982; Hofstede, 1991; Trice & Beyer, 1984; Wuthnow & Witten, 1988). For example, we can observe a building's physical workspaces, the logos and symbols representing an organization, its promotional and branding, and its organizational charts. They are easy to observe but may be difficult to decipher by outsiders.

Artifacts are symbols of our current and past cultures. Artifacts are the physical things that are found to have particular symbolism for a culture. Artifacts can also be everyday objects, such as flowers in reception. The main thing is that they have special meaning, at the very least, for the people in the culture. Artifacts remind people who are part of a culture of its rules, beliefs, and meaning (in good and bad ways).

Artifacts are part of culture above the waterline – what we can see. Seeing our culture – becoming aware of it – is challenging, because culture is complex. Sometimes the best place to start is to look at our artifacts and learn what we can from them. Artifacts are Cultural Reinforcements. Artifacts help to establish recognition (branding) to shareholders, customers, and the general public – consider some common institutional symbols such as the Toyota emblem or Google logo. They also create culturally accepted, inspirational symbols for internal stakeholders, e.g., the skull and bones of the pirate ship flag. Tangible artifacts are significant to the success of a society or an organization because they give individuals something tangible to relate – to associate with and feel that they are part of that larger culture. Artifacts can help to build spirit and camaraderie among a unit or team. Artifacts can create inspiration in broader environments.

Artifacts are visible, but they may be open to interpretation. They may be ambiguous. How can we "see" our artifacts? And how do we interpret them? How do others interpret them? How do artifacts affect or define culture? Do the artifacts support a productive culture? What may need to change? An organization May reveal significant information about its embedded values from visible artifacts. Is the boss in a prominent corner off? Can an individual's status in the hierarchy be determined based on the size and position of their desk or office? By the type of car, they drive? Is an organization's headquarters located in a modest building in an industrial area, or is it an iconic building on a prominent plot in the center of town? This type of information about the company and its people can tell us much about deeply rooted beliefs (Hammerich & Lewis, 2013).

The Interplay of Cultural Elements

While we can understand and "learn to see" each of the five elements of organizational culture, it is also critical to understand how they build upon and relate to each other (Fig. 5). For example, we may discover our assumptions and beliefs by reviewing our organizational visions or codes of ethics, but are these consistent across all levels and areas of the organization? Do our cultural artifacts reinforce our assumptions and beliefs, or do they tell us something more deep-seated about what we truly believe? Do our values come through in our behaviors? Moreover, do they embody our espoused beliefs?

Where these five elements are not aligned, the culture will be fractured. While every organization has at least one culture, most organizations will have many subcultures, groups, and individual cultures. In this text, we are less concerned with whether a culture is productive or unproductive and more interested in whether and how to fit it into the business strategy. Culture in and of itself is neither positive nor negative. Our interest in culture is in how it aligns with and reinforces strategy. We must ensure that each of the five elements of our culture aligns with and "fits" the elements of our strategies.

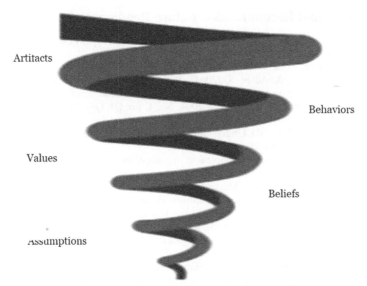

Fig. 5. Spiral Model of Interactions Across Components of Culture.

Chapter Observations

We can see the effects of culture in the everyday behaviors of individuals, groups, and the organization and the most impactful actions of leaders and managers. Events, activities, and decisions are behaviors – they are what we can see. These behaviors are above the waterline in Denison's model. As a result, we can better understand what factors influence these behaviors and choices and how we see and understand the cultures in our organizations and societies. In this text, we take three common behaviors to all organizations for illustration and explanation purposes – knowledge sharing and transfer, learning, and collaboration.

Chapter Review

After reading this chapter, you should be able to:

- describe the static and dynamic models of culture.
- define culture and explain the different conceptual models.
- explain why it is essential for us to learn how to see our cultures.
- describe the five essential elements: assumptions, beliefs, values, behaviors, and artifacts.
- describe how culture is a system.
- explain why and how each organization's culture is unique.
- identify the factors that make your organization's culture unique.
- explain why it is hard to change an organization's culture.

References and Recommended Future Readings

Alexander, J. C., Seidman, S., & Seidman, S. J. (Eds.). (1990). *Culture and society: Contemporary debates.* Cambridge University Press.

Alvesson, M. (2012). *Understanding organizational culture.* Sage.

Berson, Y., Erez, M., & Adler, S. (2004). Reflections of organizational identity and national culture on managerial roles in a multinational corporation. In *Academy of Management Proceedings* (Vol. 2004, No. 1, pp. Q1–Q6). Briarcliff Manor, NY: Academy of Management.

Bloor, G., & Dawson, P. (1994). Understanding professional culture in organizational context. *Organization Studies, 15*(2), 275–295.

Chatman, J. A. (1989). Matching people and organizations: Selection and socialization in public accounting firms. In *Academy of management proceedings* (Vol. 1989, No. 1, pp. 199–203). Academy of Management.

Choe, J. M. (2003). The effect of environmental uncertainty and strategic applications of IS on a firm's performance. *Information and Management, 40*(4), 257–268.

Cooke, R. A., & Rousseau, D. M. (1988). Behavioral norms and expectations: A quantitative approach to the assessment of organizational culture. *Group and Organization Studies, 13*(3), 245–273.

Corbett, H. D., Firestone, W. A., & Rossman, G. B. (1987). Resistance to planned change and the sacred in school cultures. *Educational Administration Quarterly, 23*(4), 36–59.

Corbett, H. D., & Rossman, G. B. (1989). Three paths to implementing change: A research note. *Curriculum Inquiry, 19*(2), 163–190.

Deal, T. E., & Kennedy, A. A. (1982). *Corporate cultures* (pp. 110–134). Addison Wesley.

Denison, D. R. (1990). *Corporate culture and organizational effectiveness.* John Wiley and Sons.

Denison, D., Hooijberg, R., Lane, N., & Lief, C. (2012). *Leading culture change in global organizations: Aligning culture and strategy* (Vol. 394). John Wiley and Sons.

Dennison, D. R., & Neale, F. (1996). *Dennison organizational culture survey: Facilitators' guide.* Ann Arbor, MI: Aviat.

Deshpandé, R., & Farley, J. U. (1999). Executive insights: Corporate culture and market orientation: Comparing Indian and Japanese firms. *Journal of International Marketing, 7*(4), 111–127.

Earley, P. C. (2002). Redefining interactions across cultures and organizations: Moving forward with cultural intelligence. *Research in Organizational Behavior, 24,* 271–299.

Earley, P. C., & Ang, S. (2003). *Cultural intelligence: Individual interactions across cultures.* Stanford University Press.

Gordon, G. G., & DiTomaso, N. (1992). Predicting corporate performance from organizational culture. *Journal of Management Studies, 29*(6), 783–798.

Gregory, K. L. (1983). Native-view paradigms: Multiple cultures and culture conflicts in organizations. *Administrative Science Quarterly,* 359–376.

Hammerich, K., & Lewis, R. D. (2013). *Fish can't see water* (pp. 121–131). John Wiley and Sons, Ltd.

Heskett, J. L., & Kotter, J. P. (1992). Corporate culture and performance. *Business Review, 2*(5), 83–93.

Hofstede, G. (1991). Empirical models of cultural differences. In N. Bleichrodt & P. J. D. Drenth (Eds.), *Contemporary issues in cross-cultural psychology* (pp. 4–20). Swets & Zeitlinger Publishers.

Hofstede, G. (1998). Attitudes, values and organizational culture: Disentangling the concepts. *Organization Studies, 19*(3), 477–493.

Jones, G. R. (1983). Transaction costs, property rights, and organizational culture: An exchange perspective. *Administrative Science Quarterly,* 454–467.

Kucharska, W. (2017). Relationships between trust and collaborative culture in the context of tacit knowledge sharing. *Journal of Entrepreneurship, Management and Innovation,* *13*(4), 61–78. https://doi.org/10.7341/20171344

Kucharska, W. (2021). Leadership, culture, intellectual capital and knowledge processes for organizational innovativeness across industries: The case of Poland. *Journal of Intellectual Capital, 22*(7), 121–141.

Kucharska, W., & Bedford, D. A. D. (2020). Love your mistakes! – They help you adapt to change. How do knowledge, collaboration, and learning cultures foster organizational intelligence?*Journal of Organizational Change Management, 33*(7), 1329–1354. https://doi.org/10.1108/JOCM-02-2020-0052

Kucharska, W., & Rebelo, T. (2022). Knowledge sharing and knowledge hiding in light of the mistakes acceptance component of learning culture- knowledge culture and human capital implications. *The Learning Organization*, ahead-of-print. https://doi.org/10.1108/TLO-03-2022-0032

Kumar, N., Rose, R. C., & Subramaniam, N. K. (2008). The effects of personality and cultural intelligence on international assignment effectiveness: A review. *Journal of Social Sciences, 4*(4), 320–328. https://doi.org/10.3844/jssp.2008.320.328

Lewis, R. (2010). *When cultures collide*. Nicholas Brealey Publishing.

Martin, J. (1992). *Cultures in organizations: Three perspectives*. Oxford University Press.

Martin, J. (2001). *Organizational culture: Mapping the terrain*. Sage publications.

Martin, D. G. (2002). Constructing the 'Neighborhood Sphere': gender and community organizing [1]. *Gender, Place & Culture, 9*(4), 333–350.

Martin, J., & Siehl, C. (1983). Organizational culture and counterculture: An uneasy symbiosis. *Organizational Dynamics, 12*(2), 52–64.

McGuire, J., Dow, S., & Argheyd, K. (2003). CEO incentives and corporate social performance. *Journal of Business Ethics, 45*(4), 341–359.

Miron, E., Erez, M., & Naveh, E. (2004). Do personal characteristics and cultural values that promote innovation, quality, and efficiency compete or complement each other?. *Journal of Organizational Behavior, 25*(2), 175–199.

Meyerson, D., & Martin, J. (1987). Cultural change: An integration of three different views [1]. *Journal of Management Studies, 24*(6), 623–647.

Naisbitt, J. (1994). *Global paradox*. William Morrow & Co., Inc.. 304.

Neuijen, B., Ohayv, D. D., & Sanders, G. (1990). Measuring organizational cultures: A qualitative and quantitative study across twenty cases. *Administrative Science Quarterly, 35*(2), 286–316.

O'Reilly, C. A., & Chatman, J. A. (1996). Culture as social control: Corporations, cults, and commitment.

O'Reilly III, C. A., Chatman, J., & Caldwell, D. F. (1991). People and organizational culture: A profile comparison approach to assessing person-organization fit. *Academy of Management Journal, 34*(3), 487–516.

O'Reilly, C. A., & Tushman, M. L. (2008). Ambidexterity as a dynamic capability: Resolving the innovator's dilemma. *Research in Organizational Behavior, 28*, 185–206.

Pettigrew, A. (1990). Organizational climate and culture: Two constructs in search of a role.

Pheysey, D. C. (2002). *Organizational cultures: Types and transformations*. Routledge.

Quinn, R. E., Bright, D., Faerman, S. R., Thompson, M. P., & McGrath, M. R. (2015). *Becoming a master manager: A competing values approach*. John Wiley and Sons.

Rashid, M. Z. A., Anantharaman, R. N., & Raveendran, J. (1997). Corporate cultures and work values in dominant ethnic organizations in Malaysia. *Journal of Transnational Management Development, 2*(4), 60–72.

Rose, G. (1988). Locality, Politics, and Culture; Poplar in the 1920s. *Environment and Planning D: Society and Space, 6*(2), 151–168.

Rousseau, D. M. (1990). Assessing organizational culture: The case for multiple methods. *Organizational Climate and Culture, 153*, 192.

Sadri, G., & Lees, B. (2001). Developing corporate culture as a competitive advantage. *Journal of Management Development, 20*(10), 853–859.

Schall, M. S. (1983). A communication-rules approach to organizational culture. *Administrative Science Quarterly*, 557–581.

Schein, E. H. (1961). Management development as a process of influence. *Industrial Management Review (pre-1986)*, *2*(2), 59.

Schein, E. H. (1984). Coming to a new awareness of organizational culture. *Sloan Management Review, 25*(2), 3–16.

Schein, E. H. (1988). Organizational socialization and the profession of management. *MIT Sloan Management Review, 30*(1), 53.

Schein, E. H. (1990). *Organizational culture* (Vol. 45, No. 2, p. 109). American Psychological Association.

Schein, E. H. (1992). *Organizational culture and leadership*. Jossey-Bass.

Schein, E. H. (1996). Culture: The missing concept in organization studies. *Administrative Science Quarterly, 41*(2), 229–240.

Scholz, C. (1987). Corporate culture and strategy – The problem of strategic fit. *Long Range Planning, 20*(4), 78–87.

Schneider, J. A. (2002). Social Capital and Community Supports for Low Income Families: Examples from Pennsylvania and Wisconsin. *The Social Policy Journal, 1*(1), 35–55.

Schwartz, H., & Davis, S. M. (1981). Matching corporate culture and business strategy. *Organizational Dynamics, 10*(1), 30–48.

Tajfel, H., & Turner, J. C. (1979). An integrative theory of inter-group conflict. In W. G. Austin & S. Worchel (Eds.), *The social psychology of inter-group relations* (pp. 33–47). Monterey, CA: Brooks/Cole.

Trice, H. M., & Beyer, J. M. (1984). Studying organizational cultures through rites and ceremonials. *Academy of Management Review, 9*(4), 653–669.

Trice, H. M., & Beyer, J. M. (1993). *The cultures of work organizations*. Prentice-Hall, Inc.

Van der Post, W. Z., & De Coning, T. J. (1998). The relationship between organisational culture and financial performance: Some South African evidence. *South African Journal of Business Management, 29*(1), 30–40.

Van Maanen, J., & Barley, R. S. (1984). Occupational communities: Culture and control in organizations. *Research in Organizational Behaviour*.

Wuthnow, R., & Witten, M. (1988). New directions in the study of culture. *Annual Review of Sociology, 14*(1), 49–67.

Chapter 2

Organizational Culture as a Complex Systems

Chapter Summary

This chapter focuses on the middle level of organizations. It is a critical synthesis level for culture. The authors explain how this level is influenced by the higher and lower levels of the organizational culture. The authors discuss how factors from the higher and lower levels may affect this level. It is at this level that culture has the greatest effect on an organization's business capabilities, and therefore its operations and performance.

Why We Care About Company Culture?

The cultural competence, intelligence, and assessment literature refer to the middle layer in the "culture stack" as organizational culture (Kristof, 1996; O'Reilly et al., 1991). The research literature refers to this level generically to emphasize that culture applies to for-profit, not-for-profit, non-profit, and public-sector organizations. This text may refer to this middle layer as business culture, company culture, or corporate culture. The label we use is more a reflection of the context or environment. In all cases, the reader should assume we are referring to the middle level.

We care about company culture – the middle level – because this level of culture has the most significant effect on business performance and success in the business environment (Martin, 1992, 2001; Martin & Siehl, 1983; O'Reilly, 1989; Schein, 1996; Stevenson & Bartunek, 1996; Maanen & Barley, 1982). An organization's culture is a part of its knowledge capital and ability to compete and survive in any market. However, culture is too complex and dynamic to *manage* daily (Chao & Moon, 2005; Marchington et al., 2005). Instead, organizations can learn to see and understand the culture to ensure it supports rather than impedes essential business capabilities and goals. As we noted in Chapter 1, culture is both faceted and dynamic. It is challenging to learn to see it and even more challenging to influence the people who practice that culture.

The Cultures of Knowledge Organizations: Knowledge, Learning, Collaboration (KLC), 25–38
Copyright © 2023 by Wioleta Kucharska and Denise Bedford
Published under exclusive licence by Emerald Publishing Limited
doi:10.1108/978-1-83909-336-420231002

The most effective organizational cultures result from continuous awareness, adaptation, adjustment, and alignment of the organization's mental model to make it relevant to the business context and shared. The most effective organizational cultures develop from the individuals' shared mental models, beliefs and values collectively representing the organization's perception of the internal and external business and environment. It means that every individual in the organization has a stake in being aware of the organizational identity reflected in culture. An individual's commitment to the organization's activities and goals depends on how closely the organization's culture aligns with and supports its identity and culture.

Organizational Culture – Definitions and Characterizations

As noted in Chapter 1, the level of culture pertains to the scale at which a culture may be defined. The lowest level is an individual's culture (Fig. 1). The culture scale then increases to include the cultures of teams and business units, the organization's culture, and the cultures of the countries or locations where they live and work. Finally, the highest level of culture is a global culture.

Culture as a shared meaning system can be formed at any level. Therefore, factors at all five levels form the company culture. While the authors describe the role of all five levels in forming a particular business culture, the most important is the organization level which we define as the meso level. In the following sections, we explain how the factors at each level can contribute to the formation of these cultures. At this level, we also see the most significant alignment of culture and strategy.

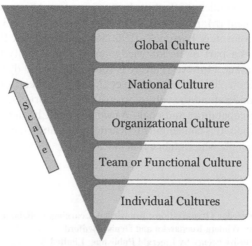

Fig. 1.   Seeing Culture from the Structural Perspective.

Organizational Culture – Definitions and Characterizations

Organizational cultures reflect the values, behaviors, and artifacts of the organization. First, it is the customs, beliefs, and assumptions developed by the people within an organization. These have developed over time and reflect both what the organization has learned about surviving in the market and what individuals have learned about surviving in the organization. An organization's culture also reflects the cultures of its geographical locations and the global or national markets in which it must perform. Finally, an organization's assumptions, beliefs, and values reflect the espoused or preferred values (e.g., those formally written and promoted by leadership) and those that are unwritten (e.g., the actual or lived cultures of the individuals in the organization). We can see examples of an organization's culture by observing how it treats its stakeholders, workforce, and environment and how it shapes other relations when conducting its business.

Organizational culture helps individuals to make sense of things and to understand what is and is not acceptable behavior. It can influence an individual's satisfaction with the work environment and define their commitment to the organization's business goals and processes. Culture is an invisible force in the organization's business performance. Effective organizational culture is grounded in shared values and reinforced through rituals and artifacts. A harmful or destructive culture will put the organization at risk.

Organizational culture is complex because it is shaped externally by the national and global environment and internally by the cultures of all of its individuals (individual and functional) (Fig. 2).

The factors influencing an organization's culture have been discussed in the literature. That literature, though, is fragmented and scattered. As a result, we can draw upon no single authoritative model of cultural factors. Instead, the authors have researched these factors to explain their effect on an organization's

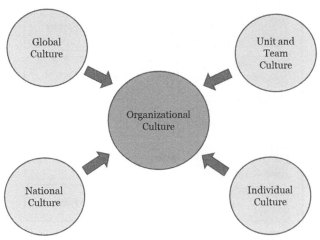

Fig. 2.   How Macro and Micro Cultures Shape the Organizational Culture.

culture. This chapter aims to guide business managers to see and leverage the factors influencing culture, and understand how they may support or impede critical business capabilities and processes.

Factors That Influence Organizational Culture

Managers who learn to see the factors that shape the organizational culture will be more effective and productive. It includes understanding how global and national cultures influence the organization and those in play at the team and individual levels. The authors have these factors do not behave in a straightforward additive way – some may have a more significant effect than others. Managers need to see how individual and team cultures play out daily. Organizations need to "see" the full scope of our organizational culture and to understand it sufficiently well to "shape" or "fit" it to support strategy. The following sections of this chapter walk the reader through discovering and describing your organization's business culture.

The authors have discovered 50 factors that may influence an organization's culture (Fig. 3). We organize these factors as a framework that managers may use to guide them to see and better understand how these cultures may affect capabilities and strategies. The following sections briefly explain how these factors may influence an organization's culture.

Global Culture – Dynamic Factors

Our organizations and business environments are increasingly global. Global culture is not just a sum of national cultures but a blending and shaping of a new international perspective at the organizational level (Leung et al., 2005;

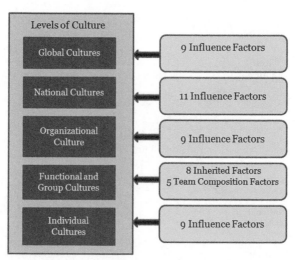

Fig. 3. Levels of Culture and the Factors that Shape Them.

Lewis, 2003; Soares et al., 2007; Trompenaars, 1996). Our workplaces and work teams are increasingly representations of many national cultures – rather than one dominant culture; global teams shape new blended cultures (Berson et al., 2004). The global environment creates a new cultural identity that blends national and organizational cultures. An international identity means that people develop a sense of belongingness to a universal organizational culture by adopting the values and behaviors of the organization while still retaining the assumptions, beliefs, behaviors, and values of their national cultures (Arnett, 2002). Individuals who work in international organizations or global environments adopt multiple identities. How well these identities and cultures align depends on the global and local cultures' similarities. Our research suggests that the factors that influence our national cultures also influence our global cultures. The difference, though, is in a more remarkable synthesis of cultures at the organizational and global levels. Global cultures may supersede national cultures. They may also tend to strengthen or reinforce global institutional cultures.

National Culture – Dynamic Factors

When we think of national cultures, most people will think of cultural artifacts – those visible representations that distinguish one culture from another. For example, the most easily recognized artifacts of national culture might include how we dress, our art and crafts, how we build our homes or the food we eat. These are ways that cultures distinguish themselves from one another. However, national cultures are much more profound than artifacts, and they are much more pervasive (Punnett & Shenkar, 2004; Fey & Denison, 2003; Gregory, 1983; Lewis, 1999, 2010; Morris & Peng, 1994; Murakami & Singelis, 2002; Newman & Nollen, 1996; Rose, 1988; Schwartz, 1992; Smith et al., 1995, 1996).

National cultures include essential beliefs and assumptions, behaviors, and values. Our national cultures are what we learn from our families, our communities, and our upbringing. They are the first cultures that each of us develops, and they are the cultures that remain throughout our lives. According to Hofstede (1980, 1983, 1984, 1998), national cultures determine the mental models, assumptions, and beliefs we acquire during the first 10 years of our lives. Of all the levels of culture, the national culture aligns most clearly with the most invisible aspects of culture – assumptions and beliefs – because these are the first forms of culture individuals learn. We note that these are the most pervasive and long-lasting of all levels and the hardest to change (Ingersoll et al., 2000; Meyerson & Martin, 1987; Rashid et al., 2004). A wise organizational manager will understand that it is essential to shape but not attempt to change a national culture.

- Our general approach to *work* – some countries prefer to work in teams while others have a more individualistic approach to getting the job done (factor 1).
- Whether we are *process-oriented* or *people-oriented* (factor 2).
- Whether we are highly individualistically oriented and focus on individual *competition* and individual rewards or place a higher value on cohesiveness and *collaboration* (factor 3).

- Whether we are *risk-takers* or *risk-avoiders* (factor 4).
- Whether we value *financial rewards* and compensation or *social rewards* (factor 5).
- How we *manage meetings* and events (factor 6).
- What we consider to be effective *leadership characteristics* (factor 7) (Baumgartner, 2009; Cullen et al., 2012; Den Hartog et al., 1999; House & Mansor, 1999; Schein, 1992).
- Our underlying assumptions and beliefs about the *role of managers and workers* (factor 8).
- Our underlying assumptions and beliefs *of engagement and social behavior* (factor 9).
- How we approach *decision-making* and whether we are comfortable with *open discussions and debates* (factor 10).
- How we *learn*, where we learn and whom we learn from – a reflection of national education philosophies (factor 11).

Organizational Culture – Dynamic Factors

The published research on this level of culture tends to focus on those factors that affect the espoused or preferred (e.g., written and supported) culture (Dansereau & Alutto, 1990; Dellheim, 1987). These factors most significantly define an individual's behavior in the organization. And they are factors most closely tied to an organization's business goals and performance (Rousseau, 1990). Primarily, factors at this level are intended to reinforce behaviors that contribute to the organization's preferred or espoused ways of working. They serve as a guide to success for individuals and teams across the organization. The intent is that when in the work environment, an individual will adopt their values and behaviors (e.g., lived or actual cultures) to align with the organization's espoused or preferred values and behaviors. In this text, the authors consider how the organizational cultures of private sector organizations may differ from those of public and non-profit sector organizations. And why it is often challenging for individuals to adapt to organizational cultures when they change working sectors.

Through an extensive review of the literature, the authors identified nine factors that play a role in defining the organization's culture, including:

1. the *leadership style*
2. the *life cycle stage* of the organization
3. its *geographic location*
4. its institutional *ethics and rewards*
5. the *business sector and industry* in which it operates
6. the organization's *position and role* in the market
7. the *business goals* of the organization
8. the *internal structure* of the organization
9. its *management control* systems.

These factors play an essential role at the unit level – but they may be interpreted differently. The culture they create may be consistent with or different from the organizational culture (Alderfer & Smith, 1982; Ardichvili et al., 2006). Managers must consider how these factors may change when they reach the unit level. Is there a different cultural effect of each factor, i.e., do the factors interact differently?

Unit and Team Culture – Dynamic Factors

Two sets of factors influence this level of culture, specifically (1) factors that are a reflection of and are inherited from the organizational culture; and (2) factors that derive from the composition of the unit or team – what the individuals bring to the unit. These two sets of factors might be viewed as top-down and bottom-up factors. It is a critical cultural integration level simply because it is where the most generalized and individualized cultures meet and blend. As a result, it is a bit more challenging to develop a cultural profile of the unit. However, it also means that unit cultures are a starting point for understanding the interaction of cultures across units and the organization.

Team Composition Factors. A unit is defined by the individuals who comprise it at any given time and their cultures. As individuals share their cultural behaviors and values with others – they influence everyone they come in contact with. The collective culture of a business unit is defined at a given time and by the nature of their work (Aasi et al., 2016; Bloor & Dawson, 1994; Bunderson & Sutcliffe, 2003; Edmondson, 2002; Gordon, 1991; Grimshaw, 1995; Kunda, 1992; Phillips, 1994; Lyons et al., 2006; Meterko et al., 2004; Riley, 1983; Shermont & Krepcio, 2006; Tajfel & Turner, 1979; Trice & Beyer, 1993; Maanen & Barley, 1982; VanderVen, 1999). It makes it more challenging to define and describe. A change in membership or leadership can significantly change the compositional culture. While culture is manifested in the collective, it is lived by each individual. Individuals absorb elements of every culture they are exposed to – it becomes part of their fundamental attitudes and behaviors.

The authors have identified six elements of individuals' cultures whose aggregate composition impacts the unit's culture. These six factors include:

1. the unit's *gender makeup*
2. the unit's *national cultural* makeup
3. the *generational composition* of the unit
4. the *size* of the group
5. the nature of *relationships and networks* within and beyond the group
6. the *language* composition of the unit.

The set of compositional factors is a bottom-up description of a unit's culture. They are more dynamic than inherited factors because they change with the arrival or departure of each individual. Research treats these factors as "demographic differences" (Pelled, 1996). In this text, the authors attempt to break them down and consider how they might play out and how we might shape them to support an organization's capabilities and processes.

Individual Culture – Dynamic Factors

Every individual comes to work with their own complex set of cultures. In addition, they operate within multiple cultures daily – family, national, social, and political cultures. At this level, we can best observe individual behaviors – the visible level of culture. The shaping of an individual's culture is generally external to the organization. These individual cultures are primarily lived and actual rather than espoused or preferred (Jermier et al., 1991). While the most effective level of alignment, it is also the most difficult to see and understand because it is intangible. Nine factors may influence an individual's culture, including:

1. *role and responsibilities* in the unit
2. *experience* and *management preferences*
3. *experiences within* the current and former organization
4. individual's *nationality*
5. individual's *skills and competencies*
6. individual's *levels of expertise* (Miron-Spektor et al., 2006; Moore, 2014; Hein & Brinley, 2004; Medin et al., 2002; Novinger et al., 2005; Sackmann, 1992)
7. individual's *gender* (Andreoni & Vesterlund, 2001; Ayman & Korabik, 2010; Croson & Buchan, 1999; Fischer & Manstead, 2000; Kashima et al., 1995; Korabik & Ayman, 2007; Mills, 1988; Shinnar et al., 2012)
8. individual's *age* (Weerstra, 1994)
9. individual's *networks*.

Effect of Cultural Factors on Organizational Capabilities

Every organization has a unique culture. The culture is unique because it is shaped by many factors (e.g., global, national, functional, and individual). Nowhere else will we find a replica of these factors and their interactions. Each culture is particularly unique when we consider that they are all dynamic and interacting in a particular business context. It is unique because the business environment and goals evolve. Each culture is unique at a given point in time. There is no typical organization with a typical culture. We can develop cultural frameworks or prototypes that may be used for comparison or learning purposes. In the end, every organization must define what culture best suits its business goals and how it works. To this end, we offer general advice and guidance. The advice and guidance are intended to be adapted and interpreted with special attention paid to a particular business context. In its current form, it represents a universal or generalized approach. The advice and guidance are derived from observing and experiencing organizations of many sizes, structures, types, and geographies. As a context for this advice, we consider the effect organizational culture may have on business strategies, knowledge exchange capabilities, learning capabilities, and collaboration capabilities. Section 2 considers how culture can affect these capabilities in private-sector organizations. Section 3 considers how culture can affect these capabilities in the public sector and non-profit organizations.

Interplay of Organizational Cultures

Its goals, objectives, purpose, and vision reflect a rigorously defined and managed organizational culture. Ideally, it also aligns with and is "visible" in the company strategy. The strategy-culture alignment is the foundation of the company's development. Long-term, dynamic company cultures should evolve to fit and support the company's business challenges. Strategies cannot be successfully implemented without the company culture's support. It is the foundational assumption of the power of company culture. It is the background against which all various types of company cultures exist. All these various types of functional cultures are embedded in the organizational culture core and are influenced by it.

In this book, we present three functional cultures whose synergy is essential to successful strategy implementation in knowledge-driven organizations, including (1) a knowledge culture; (2) a learning culture; and (3) a collaboration culture. The knowledge culture is a fundamental culture of the knowledge economy. It reflects an appreciation for today's critical resource for value generation – knowledge. Organizations must have a knowledge culture to survive and thrive in the knowledge economy. Learning cultures fuel a knowledge economy. Organizations with strong knowledge cultures that are not supported by a learning culture are static and do not develop because they are stuck in the safe stage and rely on the verified (old) knowledge only that one day occurs to be not relevant anymore. These knowledge culture-dominated organizations focus on explicit and static information rather than dynamic knowledge. As a result, these cultures generate neither new knowledge nor innovative ideas. A culture of collaboration provides the context and incentive for a learning culture. Knowledge only grows and is leveraged in a collaborative culture that facilitates networked minds' smooth functioning.

Often knowledge-driven organizations see the KLC cultures in separate and distinct ways. For companies to smoothly and continually adapt to the hyperdynamic economy, knowledge-driven organizations must align their functional, knowledge, learning, and collaboration (KLC) cultures in a way that supports those functions that are critical to the company's sustainable development (Fig. 4). It is the synergy of these that shapes the organization's whole culture. Today's knowledge-driven organizations should see the synergy of KLC cultures as vital to sustainable development. These cultures are less influential when they function independently and exponentially influential when they work together.

A knowledge culture may be espoused but not lived. Or it may be constrained by the nature of the organization's administrative structure and company culture. Many organizations assume that if they espouse and even live a knowledge culture, by definition, they have a learning culture and a collaboration culture. All four of these cultures are interdependent. And each needs to be designed and curated based on understanding how they affect other cultures. And each of

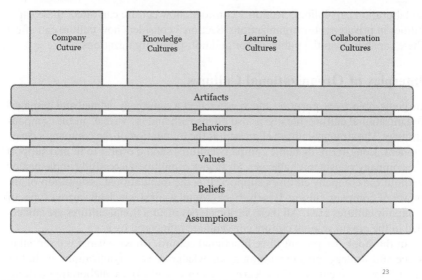

Fig. 4.   The Interplay of Organizational Cultures.

these cultures needs to exist and be visible at the organizational level, the team, department or functional level, and the individual level. For example, collaboration culture must be visible at all three levels, or the cultures are sub-optimized and will affect business performance. Likewise, learning culture must be visible at all three levels, or the cultures must be sub-optimized. Chapters 4–6 explore the interdependencies across these cultures in greater detail.

Chapter Review

After reading this chapter, you should be able to:

- define the culture at an organizational level.
- explain the critical role culture plays in any organization.
- identify the factors that influence each level of a culture.
- explain how the global, national, team, and individual cultures each influence organizational culture.
- describe the effects these factors have on organizational capabilities.
- explain the interplay and interactions of organizational cultures.

References and Recommended Future Readings

Aasi, P., Rusu, L., & Han, S. (2016). The influence of organizational culture on IT governance performance: Case of the IT department in a large Swedish company. In *2016 49th Hawaii International Conference on System Sciences (HICSS)* (pp. 5157–5166). IEEE.

Alderfer, C. P., & Smith, K. K. (1982). Studying intergroup relations embedded in organizations. *Administrative Science Quarterly, 27*, 35–65.

Andreoni, J., & Vesterlund, L. (2001). Which is fair sex? Gender differences in altruism. *The Quarterly Journal of Economics, 116*(1), 293–312.

Ardichvili, A., Maurer, M., Li, W., Wentling, T., & Stuedemann, R. (2006). Cultural influences on knowledge sharing through online communities of practice. *Journal of Knowledge Management, 10*(1), 94–107.

Arnett, J. J. (2002). The psychology of globalization. *American Psychologist, 57*(10), 774.

Ayman, R., & Korabik, K. (2010). Leadership: Why gender and culture matter. *American Psychologist, 65*(3), 157.

Baumgartner, R. J. (2009). Organizational culture and leadership: Preconditions for the development of a sustainable corporation. *Sustainable Development, 17*(2), 102–113.

Berson, Y., Erez, M., & Adler, S. (2004). Reflections of organizational identity and national culture on managerial roles in a multinational corporation. In *Academy of management proceedings* (Vol. 2004, No. 1, pp. Q1–Q6). Academy of Management.

Bloor, G., & Dawson, P. (1994). Understanding professional culture in organizational context. *Organization Studies, 15*(2), 275–295.

Bunderson, J. S., & Sutcliffe, K. M. (2003). Management team learning orientation and business unit performance. *Journal of Applied Psychology, 88*(3), 552.

Chao, G. T., & Moon, H. (2005). The cultural mosaic: A metatheory for understanding the complexity of culture. *Journal of Applied Psychology, 90*(6), 1128.

Croson, R., & Buchan, N. (1999). Gender and culture: International experimental evidence from trust games. *American Economic Review, 89*(2), 386–391.

Cullen, K. L., Palus, C. J., Chrobot-Mason, D., & Appaneal, C. (2012). Getting to "we": Collective leadership development. *Industrial and Organizational Psychology, 5*(4), 428–432.

Dansereau, F., & Alutto, J. A. (1990). Level-of-analysis issues in climate and culture research. *Organizational Climate and Culture, 193*(236), 333–349.

Dellheim, C. (1987). The creation of a company culture: Cadburys, 1861–1931. *The American Historical Review, 92*(1), 13–44.

Den Hartog, D. N., House, R. J., Hanges, P. J., Ruiz-Quintanilla, S. A., Dorfman, P. W., Abdalla, I. A., & Akande, B. E. (1999). Culture specific and cross-culturally generalizable implicit leadership theories: Are attributes of charismatic/transformational leadership universally endorsed? *The Leadership Quarterly, 10*(2), 219–256.

Edmondson, A. C. (2002). The local and variegated nature of learning in organizations: A group-level perspective. *Organization Science, 13*(2), 128–146.

Fey, C. F., & Denison, D. R. (2003). Organizational culture and effectiveness: Can American theory be applied in Russia? *Organization Science, 14*(6), 686–706.

Fischer, A. H., & Manstead, A. S. (2000). The relation between gender and emotions in different cultures. *Gender and Emotion: Social Psychological Perspectives, 1*, 71–94.

Gordon, G. G. (1991). Industry determinants of organizational culture. *Academy of Management Review, 16*(2), 396–415.

Gregory, K. L. (1983). Native-view paradigms: Multiple cultures and culture conflicts in organizations. *Administrative Science Quarterly, 28*(3), 359–376.

Grimshaw, A. (Ed.). (1995). *Information culture and business performance*. University of Hertfordshire Press.

Hein, L., & Brinley, J. (2004). *Reasonable men, powerful words: Political culture and expertise in twentieth century Japan* (Vol. 16). Univ of California Press.

Hofstede, G. (1980). Culture and organizations. *International Studies of Management and Organization, 10*(4), 15–41.

Hofstede, G. (1983). National cultures in four dimensions: A research-based theory of cultural differences among nations. *International Studies of Management and Organization, 13*(1–2), 46–74.

Hofstede, G. (1984). Cultural dimensions in management and planning. *Asia Pacific Journal of Management, 1*(2), 81–99.

Hofstede, G. (1998). Attitudes, values and organizational culture: Disentangling the concepts. *Organization Studies, 19*(3), 477–493.

House, R. J., & Mansor, N. (1999). *Cultural influences on leadership and organizations: Project globe* (Vol. 1). Advances in Global Leadership.

Ingersoll, G. L., Kirsch, J. C., Merk, S. E., & Lightfoot, J. (2000). Relationship of organizational culture and readiness for change to employee commitment to the organization. *JONA: The Journal of Nursing Administration, 30*(1), 11–20.

Jermier, J. M., Slocum Jr, J. W., Fry, L. W., & Gaines, J. (1991). Organizational subcultures in a soft bureaucracy: Resistance behind the myth and facade of an official culture. *Organization Science, 2*(2), 170–194.

Kashima, Y., Yamaguchi, S., Kim, U., Choi, S. C., Gelfand, M. J., & Yuki, M. (1995). Culture, gender, and self: A perspective from individualism-collectivism research. *Journal of Personality and Social Psychology, 69*(5), 925.

Korabik, K., & Ayman, R. (2007). Gender and leadership in the corporate world: A multiperspective model. In J. C. Lau, B. Lott, J. Rice & J. Sanchez-Hudes (Eds). *Transforming leadership: Diverse visions and women's voices.* (pp. 106–124) Malden, MA: Blackwell.

Kristof, A. L. (1996). Person-organization fit: An integrative review of its conceptualizations, measurement, and implications. *Personnel Psychology, 49*(1), 1–49.

Kunda, G. (1992). *Labor and social change. Engineering culture: Control and commitment in a high-tech corporation.* Temple University Press.

Leung, K., Bhagat, R. S., Buchan, N. R., Erez, M., & Gibson, C. B. (2005). Culture and international business: Recent advances and their implications for future research. *Journal of International Business Studies, 36*(4), 357–378.

Lewis, R. D. (1999). *Cross cultural communication: A visual approach.* Transcreen Publications.

Lewis, R. D. (2003). *The cultural imperative: Global trends in the 21st century.* Intercultural Press.

Lewis, R. (2010). *When cultures collide.* Nicholas Brealey Publishing.

Lyons, S. T., Duxbury, L. E., & Higgins, C. A. (2006). A comparison of the values and commitment of private sector, public sector, and parapublic sector employees. *Public Administration Review, 66*(4), 605–618.

Maanen, J. V., & Barley, S. R. (1982). Occupational Communities: Culture and Control in Organizations. *Research in Organizational Behavior.* Interin Technical Report. Defense Technical Information Center, Arlington VA. Accessed online on March 31, 2023 at: ADA122826.pdf (dtic.mil)

Marchington, M., Grimshaw, D., Rubery, J., & Willmott, H. (Eds.). (2005). *Fragmenting work: Blurring organizational boundaries and disordering hierarchies.* Oxford University Press on Demand.

Martin, J. (1992). *Cultures in organizations: Three perspectives.* Oxford University Press.

Martin, J. (2001). *Organizational culture: Mapping the terrain.* Sage Publications.

Martin, J., & Siehl, C. (1983). Organizational culture and counterculture: An uneasy symbiosis. *Organizational Dynamics, 12*(2), 52–64.

Medin, D. L., Ross, N., Atran, S., Burnett, R. C., & Blok, S. V. (2002). Categorization and reasoning in relation to culture and expertise. In *Psychology of learning and motivation* (Vol. 41, pp. 1–41). Academic Press.

Meterko, M., Mohr, D. C., & Young, G. J. (2004). Teamwork culture and patient satisfaction in hospitals. *Medical Care, 42*, 492–498.

Meyerson, D., & Martin, J. (1987). Cultural change: An integration of three different views. *Journal of Management Studies, 24*(6), 623–647.

Mills, A. J. (1988). Organization, gender and culture. *Organization Studies, 9*(3), 351–369.

Miron-Spektor, E., Erez, M., & Naveh, E. (2006). The personal attributes that enhance individual versus team innovation. In *Annual Meeting of the Academy of Management, Atlanta, GA*.

Moore, I. (2014). Cultural and Creative Industries concept: A historical perspective. *Procedia-Social and Behavioral Sciences, 110*, 738–746.

Morris, M. W., & Peng, K. (1994). Culture and cause: American and Chinese attributions for social and physical events. *Journal of Personality and Social Psychology, 67*(6), 949.

Murakami, F., & Singelis, T. M. (2002). Social axioms: The search for universal dimensions of general beliefs about how the world functions. *Journal of Cross-Cultural Psychology, 33*(3), 286–302.

Naisbitt, J. (1994). *Global paradox. The bigger the world economy, the more powerful its smallest players*. William Morrow and Company. Inc.

Newman, K. L., & Nollen, S. D. (1996). Culture and congruence: The fit between management practices and national culture. *Journal of International Business Studies, 27*(4), 753–779.

Novinger, S., O'Brien, L., & Sweigman, L. (2005). Challenging the culture of expertise: Moving beyond training the always, already failing early childhood educator. In *Practical transformations and transformational practices: Globalization, postmodernism, and early childhood education* (pp. 217–241). Emerald Group Publishing Limited.

O'Reilly, C. (1989). Corporations, culture, and commitment: Motivation and social control in organizations. *California Management Review, 31*(4), 9–25.

O'Reilly, C. A., Chatman, J., & Caldwell, D. F. (1991). People and organizational culture: A profile comparison approach to assessing person-organization fit. *Academy of Management Journal, 34*(3), 487–516.

Pelled, L. H. (1996). Demographic diversity, conflict, and work group outcomes: An intervening process theory. *Organization Science, 7*(6), 615–631.

Phillips, M. E. (1994). Industry mindsets: Exploring the cultures of two macro-organizational settings. *Organization Science, 5*(3), 384–402.

Punnett, B. J., & Shenkar, O. (Eds.). (2004). *Handbook for international management research*. Ann Arbor, MI: University of Michigan Press.

Rashid, Z. A., Sambasivan, M., & Rahman, A. A. (2004). The influence of organizational culture on attitudes toward organizational change. *Leadership and Organization Development Journal 25*, 161–179.

Riley, P. (1983). A structurationist account of political culture. *Administrative Science Quarterly, 28*(3), 414–437.

Rose, R. A. (1988). Organizations as multiple cultures: A rules theory analysis. *Human Relations, 41*(2), 139–170.

Rousseau, D. M. (1990). Normative beliefs in fund-raising organizations: Linking culture to organizational performance and individual responses. *Group and Organization Studies, 15*(4), 448–460.

Sackmann, S. A. (1992). Culture and subcultures: An analysis of organizational knowledge. *Administrative Science Quarterly, 37*(1), 140–161.

Schein, E. H. (1992). *Organizational culture and leadership*. Jossey-Bass.

Schein, E. H. (1996). Culture: The missing concept in organization studies. *Administrative Science Quarterly, 41*(2), 229–240.

Schwartz, S. H. (1992). Cultural dimensions of values: Towards an understanding of national differences. *International Journal of Psychology, 27*(3), 540–540.

Shermont, H., & Krepcio, D. (2006). The impact of culture change on nurse retention. *JONA: The Journal of Nursing Administration, 36*(9), 407–415.

Shinnar, R. S., Giacomin, O., & Janssen, F. (2012). Entrepreneurial perceptions and intentions: The role of gender and culture. *Entrepreneurship Theory and Practice, 36*(3), 465–493.

Smith, P. B., Dugan, S., & Trompenaars, F. (1996). National culture and the values of organizational employees: A dimensional analysis across 43 nations. *Journal of Cross-Cultural Psychology, 27*(2), 231–264.

Smith, P. B., Trompenaars, F., & Dugan, S. (1995). The Rotter locus of control scale in 43 countries: A test of cultural relativity. *International Journal of Psychology, 30*(3), 377–400.

Soares, A. M., Farhangmehr, M., & Shoham, A. (2007). Hofstede's dimensions of culture in international marketing studies. *Journal of Business Research, 60*(3), 277–284.

Stevenson, W. B., & Bartunek, J. M. (1996). Power, interaction, position, and the generation of cultural agreement in organizations. *Human Relations, 49*(1), 75–104.

Tajfel, H., & Turner, J. (1979). An integrative theory of intergroup conflict. In W. Austin & S. Worchel (Eds.), *Social psychology of intergroup relations* (pp. 33–47). Monterey, Brooks/Cole.

Trice, H. M., & Beyer, J. M. (1993). *The cultures of work organizations.* Prentice-Hall, Inc.

Trompenaars, F. (1996). Resolving international conflict: Culture and business strategy. *Business Strategy Review, 7*(3), 51–68.

Van Maanen, J., & Barley, S. (1985). Organizational culture: Fragments of a theory. *Organizational Culture, Beverly Hills, Sage,* 31–53.

VanderVen, K. (1999). You are what you do and become what you've done: The role of activity in development of self. *Journal of Child and Youth Care, 13,* 133–147.

Weerstra, J. (1994). The boomer generation: For such a time as this. *International Journal of Frontier Missions, 11,* 129–132.

Chapter 3

How Organizational Culture Impacts on Organizational Strategy Implementation

Chapter Summary

This chapter focuses on corporate cultures as critical focus points for the knowledge economy. The authors explain how culture is a crucial intangible asset in the hyperdynamic knowledge economy. The de facto business cultures in every organization – visible or invisible – are also discussed. The authors describe the four common types of business cultures – bureaucracy, market, clan, and fief. Finally, the importance of aligning culture and strategy is explained. In the event of culture, this chapter explains why culture will always prevail in any strategy-culture conflict. The chapter is supported by practical use cases.

Why we Care about the Relationship Between Culture and Strategy?

Culture is a pattern of behaviors embedded in our mindset. Such a pattern is learned throughout our lifetime, unconsciously rather than consciously. Children mirror their parents' behaviors they observe and become more critical of them when they grow up, but some behaviors stay with them "forever." They are unconsciously learned and unconsciously applied and are very difficult to unlearn and re-learn. *Culture is a kind of software of the mind* (Hofstede et al., 2010). Culture, in other words, is an inner algorithm of behaviors that affects everything an individual does and thinks – how we learn to perceive happiness, misery, success, failure, beauty, and ugliness. Culture constitutes our perception of the things and actions we undertake. Culture is compelling. When we follow cultural norms, we believe we do what is right.

It is not surprising that organizations are increasingly aware of culture's role in supporting or impeding strategies. Peter's Drucker adage – *culture eats strategy for breakfast every day* – indicates that even the most brilliant strategy is doomed to failure if it isn't aligned with the company culture.

The Cultures of Knowledge Organizations: Knowledge, Learning, Collaboration (KLC), 39–54
Copyright © 2023 by Wioleta Kucharska and Denise Bedford
Published under exclusive licence by Emerald Publishing Limited
doi:10.1108/978-1-83909-336-420231003

Company culture is vital for business success and performance. It reflects the company's shared perception of the business, the employees' self-identity as a part of this business, and their shared vision of the future. A company's culture is reflected in its goals, aims, and dreams. Company culture is a shared mindset visible in beliefs, attitudes, and behaviors toward the company's current state and position. It is visible in its dreams and aspirations for a better future. A shared, positive vision of the future is an important driver and incentive that motivates an organization's workforce to work together to realize that better future.

Shared goals and expectations for the future are best achieved by developing a shared pattern of attitudes, behaviors, and beliefs in each person, team, and organization. It is the definition of an organization's culture. While complex and challenging to see and understand, organizational culture is worth all efforts required to develop and sustain it. An organizational culture espoused and lived at all levels is essential for organizational strategy fulfillment, knowledge, and intellectual capital development. The more widespread the adoption of a common culture, the greater the chance that a shared vision of a future will be achieved. And that it will be sustained through effective cooperation among all employees. Company culture strongly affects its ability to achieve its business goals. It is why company culture matters so much – it holds power to grow or deplete a company's knowledge and intellectual capital. And, as Drucker reminds us, it can support or impede a company's business value and goals. Therefore, a company must define, implement, cultivate, or re-frame its corporate culture.

Developing a consistent company culture, especially in multinational companies, is challenging. It requires diligent attention and effort from managers. While defined and designed by leadership, the global company culture is influenced by the functional and individual cultures of the company's workforce. The cultures of individuals formed at home, school, and neighborhood come into play in the company daily. Corporate culture also is strongly influenced by the national culture of its location. As noted in Chapter 2, there are many layers of factors that shape an individual's attitudes and behaviors. Managing and calibrating these layers to support company goals is challenging. Despite the complexity of company culture, its influence is worthy of the company's full attention and effort. It is critical to focus on company values and ensure they are lived and actual rather than just espoused. Company values should be adopted, translated into individual mindfulness, and observed in their behaviors.

Culture as a Key Intangible Asset in the Hyperdynamic Knowledge – Economy Context

Knowledge is a vital asset of the current economy because it is essential to company intelligence. Feuerstein et al. (1979) defined intelligence as the ability to adapt to change. Change is a characteristic of the current economy. In the knowledge economy, creating and adapting to change are what organizations and individuals do to exist and create value. Existing in a fast-changing environment requires making change a part of daily organizational routines. How organizations think about and respond to change is reflected in their formal and non-formal cultures.

Knowledge is a critical source of capital and competitive advantage in the knowledge economy. Those societies, organizations, and individuals that develop and adapt a knowledge culture will survive and thrive in the new economy. These knowledge cultures highlight the value of continuous knowledge creation and absorption. Modern markets require organizations to learn and adapt constantly. Teece refers to the ability to create, adapt, and absorb knowledge as The Dynamic Capability Theory (Teece, 2018; Teece et al., 1997). Dynamic capabilities are defined as higher-level change routines (Winter, 2003). Over time they become new core capabilities through environmental monitoring, learning, knowledge integration (collective shared knowledge creation), and resource coordination (Handa et al., 2019; Moreno et al., 2020).

Knowledge capital and dynamic capability building are the base for sustainable development. Moreover, well-being and resilience building are critical societal responses to shocks and the need for sustainable development (Chaigneau et al., 2022). In a hyperdynamic knowledge economy, a company culture that supports the organization's ability to learn dynamically is critical to organizational survival and development.

The hyperdynamic environment shifts the company culture at all levels, affecting formal norms, ethics, rules, values, behaviors, procedures, strategies, and policies. Creating new rules and procedures in an environment of rapid change is challenging. We may develop new espoused values, behaviors, and beliefs, but it takes time to become a lived and actual culture across the organization. As a set of shared assumptions, beliefs, and behaviors, company culture can act as a universal and stabilizing compass to guide and show the way in times of change. Hofstede (2001) explains culture as the collective programming of the mind affected by a particular group's perception of things that distinguishes one group from another. Accordingly, the company culture is a shared mindset or a group with the same perception. Culture conveys the company values and reflects employees' attitudes, beliefs, social norms, and behaviors. It is one of the essential determinants in the actions or non-actions a company may take in a dynamic business environment. Individual and collective intelligence and culture affect these actions or lack of action. Culture provides verified behavior patterns and teaches us how to act "wisely."

Case Study – "Shape of Future"

John, the owner of a small but successful construction developer of commercial space named "Shape of Future," launched his most promising project of the last decade during the COVID-19 pandemic. This project concerned the public space, a shopping and office center located in the middle of a big city. The design aimed to highlight the modern and sustainable character of the local society. The project idea was developed and promoted by John, who always approached his projects with an "open mind." John realized, though, that COVID-19 had changed many of his traditional assumptions and beliefs. He realized that such a public space in a city center with vast office spaces and a shopping center no longer aligned with the new society where people work remotely and shop online. John realized he needed to develop a different idea to make this space attractive and profitable in the new "normality."

John's team, which always shared his passion for the creative trans-formation of public space to suit the norms, conventions, and lifestyles, quickly organized the meeting to discuss the needs for "new reality public spaces." They decided there was a high probability that people would need a sustainable space where people of any age, color, gender, or religion could come together to have fun. Such a space would use environmen-tally friendly materials. And its design would create positive experiences, inspire, motivate, and develop the knowledge capital of the local society. It is an essential new cultural value in a knowledge-driven networked society that values each individual's knowledge capital. This new dynamic real-ity forced John's team to take note of adaptability to the social changes around them.

After trend analysis and brainstorming, the team decided to create a sports center dedicated not to professional performance arenas but to arenas for casual people who care about physical and mental health – a healthy body and mind. The team realized that physical needs and limitations are a shared value of those casual people. This value is held equally and firmly by everyone. Sport teaches us to recognize and address our weaknesses. The physical effort made in person (contrary to this watched on television) teaches us how to both excel and accept our limi-tations. This result is inevitable. However, sports also teach us to discover our strengths, rise after difficult experiences, or rise after failure. John and his team decided that such a sports center for ordinary people would be the most valuable contribution to sustainable society building in their city. Indeed, the "United Sports Center Social Club" became one of the favorite places in the city very quickly.

The hyperdynamic knowledge economy forces us to adapt quickly to changing conditions and environments. Part of this hyperdynamism is the constant growth and development of new knowledge. Open minds are essential to recognizing and absorbing this new knowledge. National, company, team, and individual cultures that expose an open-minded attitude enable the organization to adapt to a "new normal." People, teams, organizations, and societies are highly interdependent in this new economy and business environment. And it is the knowledge that nour-ishes these dependencies.

Knowledge capital is an intangible asset contributing to company value in a networked economy (Tapscott, 1999; Ujwary-Gil, 2020). These are crucial intangible capital (Boisot, 2010; Ray et al., 2022). Intangibles contribute to value in many ways, but in recent decades, the interest has focused on how they contribute to innovation and growth. A company's culture is at the foundation of everything it does, particularly its ability to create value. These essential company assets determine the success or failure of any organization's strategies. And ultimately, it determines a company's performance. Bedford and Kucharska (2020) explained that a culture-strategy alignment is critical for successful strategy execution. It is a critical facilitator of any company's actions because it is firmly embedded in the employees' minds and shapes their attitudes and behaviors. If the company culture is seen as an asset, it should be managed like any other asset. And, since it is a critical asset, it requires special attention and diligence.

The critical question is how can we manage a company culture? We offer the following guidance:

1. Design and define the culture (fundamental values, procedures, and rules of human interactions with others, duties, tasks, and the entire environment at work).
2. Train managers and develop their cultural competence (they are company culture mirrors).
3. Employing people for their professional skills and individual and functional cultures allows them to identify with the company culture (their national and personal cultures align or are close to the company's).
4. Nurture the culture you define; align espoused-aspirational values with lived-actual values. Variations in values, rules, and procedures can adversely affect projects, programs, and strategies. Coach or, if necessary, replace leaders who do not mirror the company culture – at any level. Professional skills or positions should not be an exception for tolerating company culture misalignment.

Since the company culture is a "shared software of the mind," it only works when installed and operational. It must be officially introduced in the organization and demonstrated to be learned and lived daily. The consequences of operationalizing a company culture can be seen in everyday behaviors, actions, and decisions.

De Facto Company Cultures

Whether we want it or not, we always have a company culture. Even if we do not design and define it, it will exist. People always come to the company with their own "software of the mind" programmed by all the cultural experiences they gained, and strong personalities can impose their "software" on others. So, the company culture always exists but does not always serve the company's "best good." A company is a people. A company develops if people develop. So as long as this organic company culture serves the entire organization's best interest, all is fine. But it is essential to know what that culture is and whether it serves the company and its people. Even if we recognize that a company culture exists, we must consider Step 1 in the guide. Step 1 allows us to identify the culture and its levels and consider whether it contributes to or detracts from the company and its people achieving their goals.

If your current culture serves only strong personalities or strong groups, it may impede instead of facilitating the company's performance and development. Following this line – the quality of the society resonates with the cultures of companies existing in this society. Naturally, the national culture and the industry or branch culture and owners or formal and informal leaders' culture and management style are other strongly influencing powers that "organically" shape the company culture. It is why "an organic company culture" may not always serve the company's best interests. The culture may focus on a particular individual and promote their interests at the company's and others' expense. What happens if we skip step 1 from the list above and do not consciously design company culture? There may be competing and contradictory interests. The prevalence of contradictory cultures in companies today is significant – not only at the local level but also at the international level. Contradictory or variant cultures are particularly prevalent in international companies where the mix of cultures is, by definition, extensive. Constructively controlled, variant cultures can create a vibrant and innovative company culture. However, if not managed, cultures may clash and create performance challenges for the company.

If they are not designed and managed, national cultures, management styles, and many other factors found at the organizational level will determine organizational results (Hofstede et al., 2010; Moonen, 2017; Soloviov, 2022). For example, in the hyperdynamic knowledge-driven economy – knowledge is seen as a critical source of value. Following this line, Boisot (2010) explored a company's culture type and noted that corporate cultures differ in their ability to acquire and process knowledge and classified the type of corporate culture: bureaucracy, market, fiefdom, and clan in terms of the disposition to acquire and process knowledge. In particular, he called out how traditional management styles and organizational structures – bureaucracy, market, fief, and clan (Boisot & Child, 1988; Ouchi, 1980) affect a company's culture.

Bureaucratic Cultures

Bureaucracies operate on the "need for knowledge" principle, controlling the diffusion of encoded (explicit) knowledge from and to selected roles in the administrative hierarchy and per their levels of authority. A hierarchical culture gives individuals in positions of authority a strategic information advantage that can be converted into power over subordinates. In this type of organization, relationships are transactional and impersonal. Since there is hierarchical coordination of processes, sharing values and beliefs is unnecessary. In this case, the culture can constrain the growth of the company's knowledge assets and create a strategic disadvantage in the market. Moonen (2017) noted that high power distance and high uncertainty avoidance are critical cultural dimensions in bureaucracies. Innovativeness and asset development are not strength of such organizations. Control dominates in bureaucratic cultures. Smaller and less mature organizations, such as start-ups, are often faster, more flexible, agile, and more innovative than larger, mature, hierarchical and bureaucratic cultures. As a result, they are often better-resourced organizations that gain a greater return on their knowledge assets

(Goncalves et al., 2020). More prominent, experienced, and mature organizations also find it more challenging to change well-established processes, behaviors and "ways of working" (Kucharska, 2021). As a result, they often focus more on controlling their "internal order" than on adaptability to change and development.

Market Cultures

Market cultures also leverage codified, explicit knowledge, but rather than being constrained to selected individuals, it is more widely diffused throughout the organization. In these cultures, access to knowledge is not a tool of power and control. These cultures are fascinating because access to knowledge and sources of information allows for self-regulating internal markets. When we focus on explicit or codified knowledge, relationships in these market cultures remain impersonal and competitive. The trend, though, suggests that as we focus more on the other types of knowledge – those intangibles such as human capital, structural capital, and relational capital – relationships may resemble more personal transactions between individuals. Shared values and beliefs are unnecessary when the system is coordinated through impersonal markets. Market cultures serve as a pure market transactional type of relations among organization members. Moonen (2017) explains how low power distance, low uncertainty avoidance, high individuality, and high masculinity can predominate in market cultures.

Fief Cultures

Fief cultures are grounded in the charismatic power of leaders, which is grounded in their intangible knowledge capital. Specifically, charisma is visible in a leader's human capital – their attitudes, behaviors, personalities, and communication skills. It is also grounded in their procedural capital – their ability to work with others – and their cultural capital. Most important, though, it is grounded in a leader's relational capital – their reputation and the network of relationships they have built. These assets are challenging to articulate and intentionally share with others. The challenge with charisma is that it is only shared or exchanged with others through face-to-face interactions. The more a charismatic leader interacts with individuals throughout the company, the greater opportunity to share or at least to make that intangible knowledge visible. In a charismatic culture, relationships and exchanges may depend on individual leaders, but they are also still hierarchical. There is a submission to superordinate goals and hierarchical coordination in these cultures. For fief cultures to work, values and beliefs must be shared and align with the company's business goals. The charismatic authority of these leaders is grounded in their tacit professional knowledge, social skills, and personal qualities. In these cultures, subordinate loyalty grows based on trust and shared values. Moonen (2017) suggests that these power relationships enable fief cultures to achieve their business goals. However, if the power distance is too significant, it can impede the freely communicating of new creative and potentially risky ideas. In any hierarchical culture, communication, idea generation, and influence may be afforded to some rather than all individuals. In these cultures, a charismatic leader will be the organization's center.

Clan Cultures

Clan cultures are grounded in shared experiences. Human capital, e.g., tacit knowledge, skills, and competencies, and relational capital, e.g., existing relationships, are at the foundation of clan cultures. As human and relational capital is, by nature, intangible, it is shared or diffused throughout an organization primarily through face-to-face interactions. Clan cultures are prevalent in smaller organizations with greater access to other individuals. Relationships in clan cultures are personal and equal rather than hierarchical. Horizontal coordination and knowledge exchange predominate. Negotiation and resolution among members afford opportunities to share values and beliefs. It leads to effective interactions, supporting the company's business goals. Moonen (2017) explains that clan cultures are highly collective and create an effective environment for generating new and out-of-the-box ideas that may lead to crucial cutting-edge and market-redefining inventions.

Working from Cameron and Quinn (2006) company cultures taxonomy, Tseng (2010) revealed an adhocracy culture that is very close to a fief culture as initially described by Boisot (2010). Tseng suggested that an adhocracy culture fosters company performance more efficiently than clan and hierarchy cultures because they enable knowledge creation and conversion. Boisot (2010) noted that company cultures vary in their abilities to absorb and process knowledge. They also vary in how they leverage knowledge to influence the company's performance. We have made the case that knowledge is a significant factor in an organization's ability to survive, compete, and grow in a hyperdynamic knowledge-driven economy. For this reason, we suggest that a company's culture is a critical intangible asset. For this reason, it is essential to manage and monitor company cultures.

Successful knowledge-driven organizations are highly dependent on the capability of their employees to produce, acquire, and apply knowledge to create value. Therefore, the free and easy flow of knowledge among employees and interactions that enable them to create this value is critical. The fundamental values, procedures, and rules of human interactions at work matter for organizational success – they are the essence of the company culture. As they are intangible, they are less visible, and their effects are difficult to see.

The cultures described above were analyzed from a multifaceted perspective to understand their organizational knowledge processes, support for collaboration, the power distances in their relationships, and uncertainty avoidance behaviors. All of these are critical cultural dimensions that support knowledge creation and sharing. Clan and fief cultures seem to be the most inclined toward dynamic knowledge creation and learning, specific intangible knowledge capital assets. Bureaucracy and market cultures seem more inclined toward static knowledge consumption, e.g., explicit and encoded knowledge capital assets. Dynamic knowledge creation leads to dynamic capabilities development in organizations. Dynamic capabilities are responsible for organizational change adaptability to hyperdynamic knowledge-economy reality. Dynamic capabilities are higher-level competencies that determine the organizational response to a changing environment (Teece, 2018). Learning is at the center of such capabilities (Uhl-Bien & Arena, 2018). Organizations exposing bureaucracy and market cultures tend to focus less on learning than do fief and clan cultures. The result may be that they are less able to optimize opportunities and continuously adapt to new challenges.

The same observations apply to the cultures at the local community and national levels. Cultures with a high disposition for social collaboration generally have shorter power distance in their relationships. They also tend to have a greater tolerance for uncertainty avoidance. These characteristics support knowledge creation and sharing, allowing these organizations to adapt to change more rapidly and effectively. National culture is the shared, national software of the mind. When national cultures are both espoused and shared in assumptions, beliefs, values, and behaviors, countries may be able to adapt to change more effectively. Where we find gaps in nationally espoused and actual assumptions, beliefs, values, and behaviors, it may be more challenging for a country to transition to the new economy. These cultures may face challenges in retaining values in a transition, particularly where there is little awareness or reconciliation of values. Culture is deeply embedded and long-lived. Cultural transformation is slow and complex. These cultures can significantly affect the cultures of multinational companies, particularly where cultural differences among employees are not recognized, valued, and aligned. Having an espoused or "official company culture" does not address the actual and lived "software of many minds" problem. Multinational companies must learn to see, value, and align these individual variant cultures to construct a lived organizational knowledge-rich culture.

Case Study – Wilma's Problem of Cultural Collision

Wilma was working for a knowledge-driven solid international pharmaceutical company whose headquarters was located in Europe. The company had a long-standing challenge in its relationships and collaboration with colleagues from Asian countries. The challenge focused on variations in assumptions and beliefs related to respect and behaviors toward superiors in the management hierarchy. The variations stem from essential differences in respective national cultures. Wilma was the manager of the R&D division. Whenever Wilma completed a presentation, her culture suggested she ask for questions and clarifications with the expectation that each individual would share openly. The response was always the same – "Yes, it is all clear. There are no questions." As a result, the individuals in her chain of command usually agreed with her on everything. On a practical level, tasks were often misunderstood and left uncompleted. Had Wilma understood the essential difference in assumptions and beliefs, though, she would have understood that asking questions and for clarifications in their culture suggests a lack of knowledge or understanding. In turn, it suggests they may not be sufficiently knowledgeable to do their work. From their perspective, it may also have suggested that they thought Wilma – their superior – could not express herself clearly. Giving this impression would have been considered disrespectful and rude. Offending a superior would have been a profoundly serious problem. A simple lack of understanding of national cultural variations may have created severe knowledge exchange and performance situations. The company frequently performed "cultural workshops" to implement a culture that supports knowledge creation, sharing, and collaboration, builds short power distances, and encourages low uncertainty avoidance. Where these workshops are designed around the cultural assumptions and beliefs of one culture rather than all the cultures represented in the R&D division, they will be suboptimal. Those employees whose mental models aligned with those of the workshop gained new knowledge. Those who were different may not have participated in the workshops. The knowledge value of the workshops would have been far greater had they been designed with all cultures in mind. Companies sometimes value the lower costs of an Asian workforce but fail to understand the potential knowledge value of those individuals. It is an effect of industrial economy cultures which needs to be reconsidered in the knowledge economy. Value is financial and direct cost grounded. The opportunity costs of not leveraging or sub-optimizing the knowledge of that workforce are a significant price to pay. It is a loss in value for any company. Wilma resigned from further cooperation with the Asian teams. Wilma recognized that it was not an intentional mistake or error. Instead, it was a simple cultural misalignment.

Cultures naturally collide if we do not take the time and make an effort to see beyond what is visible (Lewis, 2010). The following chapters focus on how we learn to see cultures and better align culture and strategy.

How do Culture and Strategy Align or Misalign?

Company culture results from a shared mindset visible in behaviors that reflect shared values, beliefs, and attitudes. To align culture with the strategy, we also need to understand strategy. Strategy is a company-specific plan for developing new or existing business models which create value for customers and society. Strategies enable organizations to monetize value effectively. A strategy is a higher-level plan composed of actions coordinated to achieve a company's business aims and goals. A strategy specifies what, when, and how a company intends to achieve these goals and assigns the resources required to support it. The corporate-level strategy speaks to the organization's goals, resources, and endeavors – all of its entities, bodies, and divisions. Top and middle managers develop functional and process-level strategies that support this broader strategy and allow the organization to achieve it efficiently and effectively. It is the only way to achieve performance aggregation and synergy across all entities. The first step is the decomposition of the strategy into the functional component. Next, the company aggregates the accomplishments of all entities into a whole strategy. Everything an organization manages, e.g., brand, market, and production, will be supported by a development plan or a dedicated strategy tailored to the unique business context.

When the organization and its management are complex (i.e., a complex market, a complex product or service line that involves multiple markets), when an asset is essential to the business goals (e.g., brand or knowledge) and function (e.g., logistics), decomposition of the broad strategy is essential. The individual managers of these assets, markets, or functions must understand their role in achieving the broader goals and aims. Therefore, it is essential to achieving the broader strategy. The ease or difficulty in achieving this depends on how the strategy is developed – a simple action plan or a more complex endeavor.

Strategies are like "trip plans" – there is often more than one way or method to reach a destination. There are benefits to all strategic approaches, but it is essential to remember that one size does not fit all organizations. Finding the option that best fits the particular organization in a given business context is essential. The company should shape the strategy to fit its business goals and aims and the available resources – physical, financial, and knowledge capital assets.

Strategies are translated into plans. A good strategy will define the tasks and the expected results of each task in the plan. The plan will also include methods to accomplish each task and metrics to measure achievement (key performance indicators – KPIs). Assuming that all these plans, resources, and actions are perfectly deconstructed for action, we often assume it will be successful. However, we overlook another critical consideration that the strategy and its plans may fail to consider the company culture. Success is unlikely where culture and strategy are not well aligned.

In the knowledge economy, driven every day by the fresh set of big data transformed into information and then into knowledge, company strategy must be knowledge-driven to adapt to the constantly changing business environment. Change is the only way to create value today. Hence, the company needs to be powered by up-to-date knowledge to survive. To do this, the company strategy needs to be supported by a knowledge strategy. What is knowledge strategy? It is a company-specific development of knowledge processes to support a new or existing business model to create value. Knowledge management processes required to do this are knowledge identification, next capturing, storage, security, distribution, usage (application), re-usage (verification), and new knowledge production.

Organizations must align their knowledge strategies with organizational cultures to succeed in the knowledge-driven economy. It is the first and most critical step in knowledge management. A knowledge strategy aims to leverage the knowledge capital essential to the organization's business goals. Aligning the knowledge strategy and the organizational cultures de facto addresses strategic gaps in any knowledge organization. The highest company strategies must be aligned with and supported by the knowledge strategy and must continue to align as they evolve. Maximum business success depends on this alignment. Aligning a knowledge strategy and the organizational culture requires the development of a whole organization's knowledge culture.

Why is a knowledge culture so important? Even a very clever and sophisticated business strategy cannot succeed in such a fast-changing business environment without strong knowledge grounding. The reason is simple. Well-formed and well-articulated strategies mean nothing if everyday routines, behaviors, actions, and decisions do not support them. All of these are guided by assumptions and beliefs – the core elements of culture. The knowledge culture and its core assumptions and beliefs about knowledge are essential today. The authors make a case for developing knowledge cultures that support knowledge strategies. The moral of this story is to pay attention to the actions, behaviors, and choices of every individual to ensure they are grounded in knowledge cultures and aligned with the organization's general and knowledge strategies. It means leveraging all forms of knowledge capital – from human capital to explicit knowledge (e.g., data and encoded information) – to enable the company to adapt to a fast-changing world. Ignoring the company culture is a risk you can't take.

Realizing change is challenging in organizations where individual employees believe in and trust traditions, feel a sense of belonging, and derive personal security from repetition and routine. It is also challenging in organizations with well-entrenched protocols – "the way we've always done things." Such assumptions and beliefs do not leave room for learning or entertaining new ideas. Instead, they are misaligned with learning, change, and development. Imagine that you want to introduce a strategy of higher market flexibility to such an organization. How will you accomplish this when people are attached to repeating learned activities without thinking beyond the immediate task or using their current skills? Remember that the people are the company. It is naive to believe that organizational behavior may change when an individual's behavior does not change. Therefore, it is vital to establish espoused behaviors grounded in values, beliefs, customs, and assumptions. And why these espoused behaviors must align with business goals and strategies. It is why a company strategy and culture alignment are essential.

The workday of individuals is comprised of established routines and tasks. While more attention and value may be associated with "big decisions" and official organizational-level actions, they may affect the performance less than individuals' actions and choices. The individual and team cultures, rooted in functional assumptions and beliefs, routines, and informal behaviors, best reflect the actual and lived company culture. It is why it is essential to understand and align the actual-lived cultures and align them with espoused cultures to achieve business performance. These lower-level cultures may be dominant and highly significant for the final performance. Their sheer volume and frequency may have more significant effect on business performance.

We achieve our best performance when we align high-level strategic decisions with the high volume of daily attitudes and choices of individual goals and actions. This alignment will create synergy. It is why aligning a company strategy and culture matters so much. The adage – *culture eats strategy for breakfast every day* – is an indication that even the most brilliant strategy is doomed to failure if it isn't aligned with the company culture. Aligning culture and strategy is essential. When culture and strategy are in harmony, an organization can maximize its knowledge capital to achieve all strategies. When culture and strategy are aligned, individuals, teams, and business units have a work environment that incentivizes them to contribute their knowledge, skills, competencies, attitudes, personal assumptions, beliefs, values, behaviors, networks, and reputation. A cultural environment that offers such incentives enables an organization to support its strategy and achieve its goals. A working environment that discourages the pooling of knowledge assets will see the strategy undermined and sub-optimized. Culture will always take precedence over strategy. Those managers and workers who understand the culture and its behavior can shape it to support or undermine it. Organizational culture is a complex phenomenon: understanding what or who shapes it and managing it to make it consistent with strategic aims. Therefore, business managers must first understand what affects their culture and ensure it is aligned with and supports their strategy if they are serious about business development.

Why Culture Always Wins?

Culture always wins, thanks to its undeniable impact on value creation. The strength of company culture to create value in the hyperdynamic knowledge economy depends upon its degree of influence on knowledge practices. A company's general raison d'etre in a knowledge economy is the ability to create value that consumers and society appreciates and are willing to pay for in the form of a price for its products or services. The better access to knowledge supporting all organizational processes, e.g., the knowledge about markets and customers or the knowledge about technology usage, the better chance for superb value delivery. How a company monetizes this value is defined in its business model and the ability of the business model to achieve an advantageous position in the market. Value is created and implemented by leveraging employees' knowledge capital and knowledge interactions. The company culture is a set of shared values, attitudes, beliefs, and behaviors that govern these interactions' nature. The quality of these interactions is the essence of an organization's capability to achieve any goal and deliver value. An organization is nothing more than a group of individuals organized to achieve complex business goals which may not be achieved through the actions of any individual. The complexity of the new business environment requires the cooperation and coordination of groups of individuals. Therefore, a company culture that generates value creation is essential to business performance.

The strength of company culture is optimal where:

- Company orientation and values can be visible in a *shared mission* that leads to *a shared vision;*
- *A shared vision* takes a tangible form in a strategy formulation;
- Cultural consistency across the company can be visible in a *shared mindset;*
- *A shared mindset* determines company culture;
- Culture-strategy alignment can be visible in the materialized organizational vision given in the particular strategy. Thanks to company culture-strategy alignment, strategy implementation is possible.

Company culture is vital for business success because it reflects a shared mindset evident in shared values, beliefs, attitudes, assumptions, behaviors, artifacts, and the company's self-identity and vision. Company culture is a visible pattern of employees' collective attitudes and behaviors reflected in personal, team, and organizational actions and behaviors. The more common this pattern is, the stronger the culture. In other words, the more common the shared vision of the company, the more effective the cooperation among members, and the greater the probability of achieving business goals.

Case Study – Jerome's Strategy and the Modern Eagles Culture Misalignment

Jerome was the new CEO of Modern Eagles. He was hired to take full advantage of the sustained post-pandemic demand for courier services and improve the company's performance. The demand had grown so fast that the company's full attention was focused on satisfying it. Now that the situation is under control, it is time to shift attention to operational improvement and optimization. Jerome loves optimization – constant improvement is his passion. He felt highly motivated, excited, and simply happy when he identified areas for improvement. Jerome has handled the preparation of the implementation plan like a puzzle game. He is an authentic transformational leader excited about having the opportunity to implement change. With genuine passion, he analyzed the entire business environment inside and out and developed a new strategy based on a continuous improvement culture. Implementing Jerome's critical strategic goals required all employees to focus on progress and constantly optimize their work. Jerome quickly realized that the collision of the culture needed to accomplish the strategy and the culture that existed in the company was more profound than he assumed. The truth was that the Modern Eagles employed people who were comfortable repeating the same tasks in the same way. They felt happy and safe performing the same work to the same standards every day. Modern Eagles was a market leader, which instilled pride in the employees' work. They saw no need to change. Unfortunately, Jerome's attitudes, values, goals, and vision were out of sync with his employees. Jerome's new strategy collided with the existing company culture. They were misaligned.

However brilliant, Jerome's strategy failed at the implementation stage. The entire idea was at variance from how The Modern Eagles employees were run so far, and how the current company culture performs. As a result, Jerome alone could not implement his strategy. He and Modern Eagles employees did not develop a shared mindset which enabled them to build a common company culture – to create a shared vision. Without a shared vision, they could not move on to formulate and implement a common strategy.

In summary, a company's culture is a compelling capital asset. Moreover, if developed to support the company's goals, mission, and vision, it is an essential facilitator of strategy formulation and implementation. Conversely, if the company culture and strategy are misaligned, there is little hope for the company's long-term success.

Chapter Review

After reading this chapter, you should be able to:

- describe how the knowledge economy will affect corporate cultures in the future.
- explain why culture is a key intangible asset critical to a hyperdynamic knowledge economy.
- describe how to make existing organizational cultures visible.
- describe the four common types of business cultures, bureaucracy, market, clan, and fief.
- explain why it is important to align culture and strategy.
- explain why culture will always prevail over strategy in any conflict.

References and Recommendations for Future Readings

Bedford, D., & Kucharska, W. (2020). *Relating information culture to information policies and management strategies*. IGI Global.

Bontis, N. (2001). Assessing knowledge assets: A review of the models used to measure intellectual capital.*International Journal of Management Reviews, 3*(1), 41–60.

Boisot, H. (2010). *Knowledge assets*. Oxford University Press.

Boisot, M., & Child, J. (1988). The Iron Law of Fiefs: Bureaucratic failure and the problem of governance in the Chinese Economic Reforms. *Administrative Science Quarterly, 33*, 507–527.

Cameron, K. S., & Quinn, R. E. (2006). *Diagnosing and changing organizational culture: Based on the competing values framework*. Jossey-Bass.

Chaigneau, T., Coulthard, S., Daw, T. M., Szaboova, L., Camfield, L., Chapin, F. S., Gasper, D., Gurney, G. G., Hicks, C. C., Ibrahim, M. James, T., Jones, L., Matthews, N., McQuistan, C., Reyers, B., & Brown, K. (2022). Reconciling well-being and resilience for sustainable development. *Nature Sustainability, 1*(7). https://doi.org/10.1038/s41893-021-00790-8

Feuerstein, R., Feuerstein, S., Falik, L., & Rand, Y. (1979). *Dynamic assessments of cognitive modifiability*. ICELP Press.

Handa, P., Pagani, J., & Bedford, D. (2019). *Knowledge assets and knowledge audits*. Emerald Group Publishing.

Hofstede, G. (2001). *Culture's consequences: Comparing values, behaviors, institutions, and organizations across nations* (2nd ed.). Sage Publications.

Hofstede, G., Hofstede, G. J., & Minkov, M. (2010). *Culture and organizations*. McGraw-Hill.

Goncalves, D., Bergquist, M., Bunk, R., & Alänge, S. (2020). Cultural aspects of organizational agility affecting digital innovation. *Journal of Entrepreneurship, Management, and Innovation, 16*(4), 13–46.

Kucharska, W. (2021). Wisdom from experience paradox: Organizational learning, mistakes, hierarchy and maturity issues. *Electronic Journal of Knowledge Management, 19*(2), 105–117. https://doi.org/10.34190/ejkm.19.2.2370

Lewis, R. D. (2010). *When cultures collide: Leading across cultures*. Nicholas Brealey International.

Moonen, P. (2017). The impact of culture on the innovative strength of nations: A comprehensive review of the theories of Hofstede, Schwartz, Boisot and Cameron and Quinn. *Journal of Organizational Change Management, 30*(7), 1149–1183. https://doi.org/10.1108/JOCM-08-2017-0311

Moreno, V., Cavazotte, F., & Carvalho de Souza, W. (2020). Business intelligence and analytics as a driver of dynamic and operational capabilities in times of intense macroeconomic turbulence, *Journal of High Technology Management Research, 31*, 100389.

Ouchi, W. (1980). Markets, bureaucracies and clans. *Administrative Science Quarterly, 25*, 129–141.

Ray, P., Ray, S., & Kumar, V. (2022). A knowledge-based view of emerging market firm internationalization: The case of the Indian I.T. industry. *Journal of Knowledge Management*, ahead-of-print. https://doi.org/10.1108/JKM-08-2021-0660

Soloviov, V. (2022). Linking regional autonomy – Embeddedness value orientation and innovation. *Journal of Innovation and Enterpreneurship, 11*, 18. https://doi.org/10.1186/s13731-022-00218-3

Tapscott, D. (1999). *Creating value in the network economy*. A Harvard Business Review Book, Boston.

Teece, D. J. (2018). Business models and dynamic capabilities. *Long Range Planning, 51*, 40–49.

Teece, D. J., Pisano, G., & Shuen, A. (1997). Dynamic capabilities and strategic management. *Strategic Management Journal, 18*(7), 509–533.

Tseng, S. (2010). The correlation between organizational culture and knowledge conversion on corporate performance. *Journal of Knowledge Management, 14*(2), 269–284. https://doi.org/10.1108/13673271011032409

Uhl-Bien, M., & Arena, M. (2018). Leadership for organizational adaptability: A theoretical synthesis and integrative framework. *The Leadership Quarterly, 29*, 89–104.

Ujwary-Gil, A. (2020). *Organizational network analysis: Auditing intangible resources*. Routledge.

Winter, S. G. (2003). Understanding dynamic capabilities. *Strategic Management Journal, 24*, 991–995.

Chapter 4

KLC Approach to Knowledge Organization Culture Building

Chapter Summary

In this chapter, the authors explain the value of the KLC approach to building cultural capacity in knowledge-driven organizations. This chapter also explains the importance of coherent multilevel interactions to expose and experience a company culture. The authors reinforce that culture is learned simultaneously, consciously and unconsciously, through all company's related experiences. The effects of leadership, hierarchy, and maturity on cultural capacity are discussed at the individual, team, and organizational levels. Finally, the chapter provides a step-by-step methodology and sample questions for taking stock of an organization's cultural capacity.

Why the KLC Approach is Critical to Building Culture in a Knowledge Organization

The essential value of the KLC approach to culture building in knowledge organizations is the synergy among functional cultures of knowledge, learning, and collaboration (KLC). This synergy produces dynamic capabilities, innovation, and sustainable development. Winter (2003) defines dynamic capabilities as higher-level change routines in response to the reality of the hyperdynamic times and environments we live in. A learning culture is critical to this process. Furthermore, a learning culture must go beyond the status quo and expand the existing body of knowledge. Organizations that rely only on exploiting static knowledge will not progress beyond the knowledge-orientation stage of development.

In many organizations, the traditional, proven ways of working and operations are preferred and valued over the search for new opportunities, solutions, and risk-taking. Consequently, the opportunity to learn from mistakes related to these new approaches is lost. Organizations that rely chiefly on proven knowledge often prefer to "keep things as they are." They prefer maintaining a "safe, control-oriented environment based on well-known routines." These organizational attitudes may hinder their organizational development. The antidote to this appears

The Cultures of Knowledge Organizations: Knowledge, Learning, Collaboration (KLC), 55–75
Copyright © 2023 by Wioleta Kucharska and Denise Bedford
Published under exclusive licence by Emerald Publishing Limited
doi:10.1108/978-1-83909-336-420231004

to be a continuous learning culture. To be efficient, the learning cultures of learning organizations must be multilevel. And, by definition, to be multilevel, they must be collective.

From the organizational perspective presented in this book, there is no culture of learning without the culture of knowledge. And there is no learning without collaboration. These three cultures are exponentially valuable when they are all in place and working together. No one of them is as powerful alone as they are together. Appendix B presents the empirical evidence of the synergistic effect they can have on internal innovation and performance.

Company Culture is Learned from Experience

Company culture is learned from experience. It is affected by a set of multilevel interactions taking multiple forms, including formal and informal. Many factors, including structure, size, maturity level, leadership, and the network of employee relationships, determine company's formal and informal interactions. A company's culture is experienced and learned through this communication structure. Formal and informal verbal and non-verbal communications and interactions make a company culture visible. The most effective way to learn about a culture is through experience and immersion. For example, how a company is organized and managed will influence how employees perceive one another, experience one another and treat each other and those around them, including the entire business environment.

Therefore, we define, implement, and manage company culture through a prism of experiences, enhancement, design, and delivery. The prism perspective is conducive to logical thinking, imagination, and empathy. When we design or re-design a company structure, we need to understand how the change will affect an employee and everyday communication and management. Company maturity level often affects the attachment to "old" rules and procedures that significantly affect the range of possible actions. Company maturity may also have a significant effect on experiences and affects the accepted leadership style. Leadership style can shape culture, but long-lasting traditions might also shape leadership methods. For the KLC approach to be efficient, it must be multilevel. Therefore, structure, maturity, and leadership issues are essential to an organization's capacity for KLC culture implementation.

Company Structure

An organization is a group established to fulfill complex goals and tasks that individuals working independently could not accomplish. Human interactions foster organizational learning and the dissemination of knowledge. Knowledge cultures affect the relationships and social interactions that affect the company's capacity for adaptation to change. Company structure determines social interactions, which in turn influence knowledge cultures. Company structure determines how groups are organized to achieve those goals. It is reflected in the hierarchy – the outline of the company's goals, roles, and responsibilities as they are designed and assigned across units, groups, entities, and individuals. Structure undoubtedly affects employees' formal interactions. The more complex a company's general business goals, the more people are engaged across the organization. The more general the business goals, the higher it resides in the company hierarchy.

Hierarchy is a complex dynamic incorporating vertical and horizontal organizational processes and practices. And these hierarchical dynamics depend on managers' social and epistemic distance from the operations and work processes. The organization's size can determine the scale and slope of the hierarchy. A steep hierarchy may be justified where the company's goals are aligned with the highest levels of the structure and decomposed with each level. Boisot (2010) observed that a steep hierarchy is not a good structure for the free flow of knowledge across the organization. Everyday human actions occur in network structures, which are significantly different and distinct from a formal hierarchical structure. Even if we organize ourselves into a formal hierarchy, external and internal human interactions will flow in a network structure. Where very steep hierarchical structures exist, they will collide with democratic structures. In steep hierarchies, knowledge is accepted only if it aligns with a company's complex business goals and comes from authoritative levels. In network structures, knowledge may align with task and process needs and address the gaps in employee competencies. The more a company's administrative structure and social interactions, both formal and informal, align with the company's goals and its national and social culture, the greater the probability that collaboration will support the company-culture strategy alignment.

Kucharska and Bedford (2020) and Kucharska (2021) indicate that low-hierarchy working environment is characterized by high adaptability to change. At the same time, though, they observed that the mistakes acceptance level does not influence the organizational competency of adaptability to change. They noted that employees working in less hierarchical organizations adapt to changes much more effectively than those who work in high-hierarchy conditions. Acceptance of mistakes does not significantly contribute to the adaptability to change of low-hierarchy organizations. In low-hierarchy organizations, adaptability to change is generally high and unrelated to the level of mistake acceptance. It suggests that low-hierarchy organizations learn and adapt to a dynamic business environment faster and more effectively. It is, though, not related to the organization's ability to learn from mistakes. Instead, they learn more rapidly by adapting to the business environment.

The opposite effect was observed by Kucharska (2021) in hierarchical organizations – learning via the acceptance of mistakes enables them to adapt to changes much better than they do not accept making them. But what is interesting, it works only if the mistake acceptance level is high. When low-hierarchical organizations' adaptability to change is also very low. Therefore, high-hierarchy organizations that truly accept mistakes achieve better results for adaptability to change than low- and medium-hierarchy organizations.

What other factors influence hierarchical organizations? In addition to the complexity of organizational goals, we also explore how operating rate, size, and maturity level may determine whether an organization has a low, medium, or high hierarchy.

Company Maturity Level

Organizations with a low maturity level often demonstrate a high level of adaptability to change because they adapt to and align with the market leaders' rules and standards. These organizations not only achieve but exceed these standards to succeed in the market. Mature organizations develop through continuous improvement. Terouhid and Ries (2016) observed that organizational maturity is grounded in organizational processes. They noted that the most successful organizations demonstrate maturity, sustainability, and leadership in every aspect of their operations. And mature organizations operate within a complex environment where continuous operational improvement is the most crucial growth strategy. Given what we know about the critical value of learning in the business environment, new errors may be seen as valuable indicators of change. These indicators may be critical in large, hierarchical organizations with complex monitoring and management methods. In well-established business environments and markets, every new error may be a warning signal of change or an opportunity for change. It is how mature organizations learn, adapt, and grow their intelligence. In sum, young organizations learn and develop by adaptation, and mature organizations learn from anomalies that are symptoms of change, e.g., mistakes.

Transformational Leaders

Change is the new normal in the hyperdynamic networked knowledge-driven economy. Authentic leaders, as change agents, are vital sources of cultural influence in the company. Transformational leaders are prominent because they generate bold new ideas and visions, create strong bonds with employees, motivate employees, and are supportive and inspirational (Busari et al., 2019). These leaders can effect change through the development of organizational culture (Brandt et al., 2019; Kucharska & Rebelo, 2022). Organizational culture is the quintessential representation of the organizational mindset. Leaders who are on changing organizational policies rather than changing the organizational mindset often fail to improve performance (Schwartz, 2018).

For tacit knowledge flows and exchange to generate value, we need the support of leadership. Mabey and Zhao (2017) suggest that intentional leadership grounded in a collaborative ethic is necessary for creating a "shared" space where informal knowledge exchange occurs. Leaders must facilitate group and collaborative learning to transform tacit knowledge into explicit knowledge. Organizations must also develop a culture where employees can learn, unlearn, and relearn in a safe climate (Nold, 2012). Indeed, leadership can positively impact the psychological safety climate of organizations (Shao et al., 2017). The climate and accepting mistakes constitute a learning culture (Kucharska & Bedford, 2020). The organizational climate is vital for learning. But, the ready to be the wrong attitude is crucial for all individuals who wish to learn (Senge, 2006).

Mature leaders can only reconcile the paradox of learning without making mistakes. Therefore, an authentic leadership style is critical to developing a knowledge culture. In turn, the knowledge culture drives collaboration, learning policies, and practices to manage errors. The critical challenges for learning organizations are:

- the creation of internal mechanisms to support safe learning from mistakes;
- the development of effective communication methods that bridge technological and non-technological mindsets, especially in the context of learning from mistakes;
- that existence of mature leaders in positions of influence and authority.

Only truly mature leaders can introduce a constant learning culture, including the element of mistakes acceptance. Only truly mature leaders can stop the illusion that an organization will continuously learn without making mistakes. A good manager in a hierarchical learning organization should be a learner by example, a learning leader, a coach, and a patient teacher, not a *mistakes hunter*. It is a challenge for managers working in "learning organizations" today – as it is contrary to the traditional image of management cultures that define what it means to be a manager. Managers in learning organizations should inspire, motivate, and help others to grow instead of hunting errors and assigning blame. It is how leaders mature. The paradox of continuous learning presents contradictions when not accepting mistakes destroys what is needed for human development.

Knowledge Workers

There can be no knowledge-driven organization without knowledgeable workers. Knowledge workers are knowledge producers who transform existing, explicit knowledge into new knowledge: first tacit, then explicit. It is the effective and efficient functioning of collaboration networks fueled by the minds of knowledge workers. This group is critical. Knowledge workers do not need or want to be directed or led – they want to be inspired. They want to lead themselves and follow their inspiration. The common, shared leadership model introduced by Bergmann et al. (1999) aligns well with the concept of a collaborative intelligence network. The concept of shared organizational leadership means leveraging every mind to achieve organization-wide capacity. It means building total employee engagement by distributing leadership and decision-making responsibilities. This level of engagement liberates, inspires, and motivates everyone to higher achievement and maximize their contributions to affect productivity and business results. It profoundly affects knowledge workers who do not want to be managed at work but rather to be inspired. Inspiring them increases their commitment to the organization, rather than micro-managing or directing them. To do this, we offer five suggestions:

1. There is no development without change. The idea of change inspires some and, at the same time, terrifies others. Employ those with long-term value and will invest in their knowledge capital. It is not a trivial effort to continuously grow knowledge, seek new solutions, and continuously re-configuration of knowledge assets effectively for the short-and long-term development.

Working with those who do will persevere and find adapting to change exciting rather than terrifying.

2. Personal employee motivation and adopting company values serve as an internal compass, reflecting preferences towards particular attitudes and behaviors at work. Employees seek organizations that values are close to theirs. In this context, knowledge workers should be natural KLC culture fanciers. Their attitudes and behaviors are often motivated by their natural curiosity and the need for knowledge possession and extension. Knowledge workers also care about their recognition as knowledgeable people. So, they often build their personal brand image based on their personal knowledge, exposition, and sharing (Kucharska, 2022). Knowledge workers build their personal brands on their personal and professional knowledge, motivation, ability to learn and collaborate. This is a perfect tool for implementing the KLC approach.

3. The company, division, or team leaders inspire their teams to continuous learning and cooperation, supporting adaptation to change through acceptance of mistakes. Making mistakes can be a costly lesson, but it can be a valuable opportunity to leverage new knowledge.

4. Inspiring knowledge workers is the challenge of finding a good balance between creating a supportive environment of a learning climate where people feel safe and stimulated to think freely to solve new, challenging tasks that satisfy their ambitions and between the corporate rigor of rules, policies, and procedures that serve for the need for uncertainty avoidance.

   Continuous critical thinking, questioning, and opposing collective stupidity are needed more than bureaucracy and control to secure organizational growth. Leaders must be ready to serve as coaches rather than pursue control and "corporate orderliness."

5. Make your company structure as flat as possible to encourage knowledge flows. Transform it into a network where possible. Knowledge workers are intelligent people who do not want to be managed. Instead, they prefer to be wisely led and gently inspired by someone they respect.

Case Study

As a highly experienced CEO (25 years of work), Anthony found that the best way to maintain his employees' adaptability skills was to allow them to adapt to changes. Opportunities might include changing jobs, departments, positions, and even desk locations. According to Anthony, employee mental flexibility loss is a serious concern. It can happen when employees lose a fresh perspective and become content to have achieved mastery in their work. Why does this occur? "They follow their primary instinct and devote energy to maintaining their 'territory.' It is human nature to ensure your security – and I understand that," – Anthony says. "But it blocks the company's development. I noticed that a feeling of work security is attributable to attributes such as position, office facilities, and tools. So, I standardized position attributes and visibly and verbally rewarded my team instead of individuals for their accomplishments. I reward teams instead of individuals to sustain cooperation, but the shared reward is grounded in the contributions of the team leader. It is a significant but periodic reward. Rewards are time-sensitive. They are not long-term. This reward philosophy helps to counter mental complacency. This reward philosophy is practical because the company employs 50 people, and 60% of the workforce has worked together for over 20 years. Yes, I am a transformational leader. Anthony admitted and continued his story with strong self-confidence and passion. Within my team, I am a fan of continuous improvement. Therefore, we constantly freely discuss our options for work improvements. Yes, we learn a lot every day. We must be up to date with new regulations and the situation in any given market and understand our clients' requirements. We continuously learn professionally and socially. We are a high-functioning network of professional statutory auditors. Anthony concluded proudly.

To make my organization flexible and adaptable to change, I decided to design the company structure as a network. In this network, some individuals are functional nodes serving as hubs for a team. Because the proficiency level is consistent across the team, individuals can step into the central node role as needed. We shift central nodes frequently. We change project roles, department positions, and even desk locations frequently. How do we do this? One day per year, we organize an obligatory desk-changing activity – to change our perspectives. It is both a symbol and a practice – everyone takes on a fresh perspective – to see things differently. It helps everyone come up with solutions beyond the norm – which we constantly want – Anthony closed.

In sum, fundamental company factors such as structure, size, maturity level, leadership, and employee profile determine the communication practices among individuals and their experiences and shape the company culture.

Providing and Absorbing Experiences at Work

The most effective way to learn about any culture is to experience it. It is why national and home cultures have such power to shape an individual's assumptions, beliefs, values, and behavior. Each person is immersed in these cultures from infancy without ever being conscious. From infancy, our mind is programmed with assumptions, beliefs, attitudes, and behaviors our society teaches us – to help us survive and thrive. We absorb this culture, and it becomes embedded in our minds. It determines our actions and behaviors. Therefore, experience is the most effective method of learning culture.

Organizations have officially espoused cultures –"manifestos" that describe good practice. Unfortunately, many espoused cultures describe platitudes and general principles that do not reflect the culture lived in the organization daily. As a result, organizations often underestimate the importance of aligning lived or actual cultures with espoused cultures. As a result, they fail to develop a more precisely defined set of values, norms, and behaviors. A vague culture encourages vague social patterns and, in the end, produces a weak culture that has little impact on individual behaviors. Defining a culture of more specific values, norms and behaviors is essential for an authentic knowledge culture to thrive. Why is it important? It is essential for two reasons. The first reason is technical. When we describe something precisely, we can shape it – the concept is no longer "intuitive" and open to interpretation and misunderstandings. The second reason is that when a concept is shared and codified, it is easier to understand, interpret, and discuss with workmates. Through discussion with workmates the concept will be improved and there will be greater engagement. And, the concept will be implemented in practice.

The business world is full of unrealistic ideas that reflect managers' aspirations about what they would like to achieve than what they can achieve in a particular organizational context. For example, today, many companies espouse being "knowledge-driven," "flexible," and "open-minded" while the employees live and work in an entirely different culture. Managers must dream and aspire to more meaningful goals, be ambitious and creative, generate bold new ideas, and be realistic. The culture will not be lived if the culture exists only as an artifact – a manifesto or poster on the wall. It will never become the actual culture. If no one lives the culture, no one will believe or adhere to it.

The best way to learn and instill culture is by making it visible, explicit, and lived. Therefore, the best option for teaching and promoting an organizational culture is to demonstrate its "organizational soul." When the culture is authentic and robust – we can think of it as an actual and lived "cultural soul." We offer a few key observations:

1. Company culture is learned through experience. Therefore, it must be visible and lived every day.
2. Employ people whose individual cultures – assumptions, beliefs, values, and goals – align with the organization.
3. An authentic knowledge culture is reflected in individuals' everyday behavior, demonstrated and reified in leaders' behaviors, actions, and decisions. Authentic cultures begin with each living it and reinforcing it in decisions and choices.
4. For a culture to be evident in the pattern of beliefs, attitudes, and behaviors, organizations should make that culture explicit and reified at each level.
5. Joint organizational leadership development will facilitate rapid cultural adoption and implementation.

Only authentic leaders can introduce an authentic knowledge culture and ensure its adoption. Cultures do not shift easily or quickly, mainly where the company is mature, and that culture is deeply ingrained. Embedding a new or adapted culture takes a robust, consistent, and long-term effort.

Organizational culture exists – whether we have intentionally created it or not, whether we care about it or not. Culture is what a group or community has learned over time that helps them survive in any environment, not just in a country or a natural environment but in an organization. Wherever there are people, we will always have a culture. Often culture is defined and promoted by influential or powerful groups and individuals. It is essential to consider the discrepancy between the culture we experience every day and the culture we aspire to and want to experience. It is where discrepancies exist that we find opportunities for growth and adjustment. Cultural change in an organization is challenging and rare (Burnes, 2011). But when the environment changes, the culture will also change if it is what people need to do to survive. As the environment changes, so do individuals' cultures and mindsets. Severe and transformational change is impossible without a shift in mental models. Scientific research suggests that transformational, radical changes affecting an entire organization require a shift in organizational culture (Kezar & Eckel, 2002). People's behavior is rooted in their mindsets – their assumptions, beliefs, values, norms, and behaviors.

The everyday working environment in most organizations is comprised of a set of small routines. While the "big decisions" and official actions receive more attention, they do not dominate many choices and actions taken by individuals performing those small routines and informal behaviors. These small actions and decisions define the company's actual culture. Therefore, they have great significance for the company's business performance – not by a one-time impact but by their sheer volume and frequency. Optimum performance is achieved when strategic decisions are aligned with the individual assumptions, beliefs, and values that determine those small choices and actions. We create synergy when the company strategy and culture align.

Reinventing a new strategy or refreshing a culture will always introduce a risk. It is a significant effort, and the result is not guaranteed. The risk is worth taking, though, when considering the greater risk and cost of conflicting strategies and cultures. Bedford and Kucharska (2020) give a detailed view of this issue, but the main observation we draw from their work is that if your company culture fails or is suboptimal, your strategy will also fail.

Case Study – Adam

Jenny is the new successor in a family-owned business – BikesMasters. The company has systematically lost market share and position for the last few years. Jenny noticed that the team had lost much of its earlier creative spirit and that employees relied on traditional methods unsuited to the new business reality. The younger employees, especially those with some external training, have suggested changes, but John, the CEO, has ignored them. Jenny has also proposed new ideas, but John was uncomfortable with them, preferring to fall back on his former market successes.

Finally, when Jenny felt she had exhausted her ability to communicate with John and to find a shared vision of BikesMasters's future, she let him go. It was a courageous decision, but Jenny knew it was a pivotal moment for her company. The company needed an immediate change of culture that would never have happened if the old attitudes and behaviors continued to be reinforced by John. She hired Adam, an experienced, dynamic enthusiast, for improvement. Soon it became apparent that there was a misalignment between Adam's leadership style and the actual company culture. The company team had survived in a robust hierarchical culture dominated by a well-established structure, control, and stability. It would be challenging to adjust to the new leader's style. Adam's first important decision was to explore the reasons for lower performance and a weaker market position. It involved conducting detailed analyses to identify weak points and shortcomings. The team was initially resistant because they had always performed their work diligently and according to standards. It was true – they did perform the same duties diligently every day but without critical thinking or self-reflection. There were no opportunities to learn something new because all their work was on John's historically best years. Adam realized that the company culture did not value or reward reflection and learning. He realized the company culture needed to change.

Adam saw himself as a transformational leader. Because the team saw him as a model and mirrored his behavior, Adam saw an opportunity to use his behavior to encourage teamwork, reflection, and knowledge sharing. The team began to model these behaviors. Over time, they unlearned their old habits and behaviors and internalized new ways of working. The new learning culture took hold and created a learning climate. This new learning climate included learning from mistakes and critical thinking.

Adam routinely gave an engaging presentation outlining the new strategy. Next, he began working closely with the management team. First, he led by example. He was patient, enthusiastic, motivating, and inspiring to build support. And indeed, the majority of company managers followed his lead. Those who did not follow his patterns of new culture lost their managerial positions. He needed managers who believed in and practiced the new culture to be strong examples in their divisions. Next, Adam engaged middle managers and team leaders in the same effort. He always made sure he reinforced positive changes and rewarded all early adopters.

Adam noticed that while company headquarters quickly adopted the changes, some subsidiaries, especially those located a long distance from headquarters, had and continued to follow different cultures. Specifically, the production subsidiary in a small town in the country's south had a strong hierarchical culture. Sales teams that were widely distributed worked in an adhocracy culture. And the design subsidiary located in the most creative city of the country – functioned in a clan culture. The most challenging task for John was the introduction of a learning culture, including mistakes acceptance and a learning climate, in those subsidiaries with hierarchical cultures. The critical thinking needed for learning from mistakes was more easily achieved in those subsidiaries operating in a clan culture. Salesforce teams functioning in an adhocracy culture developed a learning climate but faced challenges adopting the reflection component. Reflection requires time and emotional distance to take the entire lesson from the particular event. Sales teams work under constant time pressure. They must close sales targets in a specific period, and they focus on it. Therefore, their time for calm reflection is very limited. To address this constraint, Adam worked closely with the leaders of the subsidiaries to develop a strategy to introduce the new culture to all subsidiaries "step by step." This strategy was based not only on professional training but mostly on teams' professional and mental support by their leaders'.

The starting point for introducing a culture of KLC is to assess the current state of the company's mindset and determine areas where the espoused and actual cultures do not align. We suggest you begin by answering the following questions:

- Does knowledge strategy align with the business strategy of your company?
- Does knowledge culture align with your knowledge strategy?
- What is the current state of KLC cultures in your organization?
- How do you want it to be?
- What discrepancies can you identify? – each discrepancy is a space for work.
- How might we create a plan for how to transform the current state to the desired KLC culture level?

The current state of the culture is possible to assess the following three-step methodology:

- Step 1: Observation *(How do you experience company culture?)*
- Step 2: Survey *(How do others experience the company culture)*
- Step 3: More-In-Depth Interviews *(To better understand some problematic issues)*

Step 1: Observation

Where a knowledge culture exists, it will be visible. This step is vital. Through observation, researchers can determine whether knowledge culture layers exist or not and can assess the current state of the knowledge culture. It is a simple and essential step. The drawback is that observation is time-consuming. If a researcher wants to gain a deep understanding of the layers of the existing organizational culture, they must spend time in the organization. It requires a person who is outside of the organization – and can objectively describe the culture. Individuals inside the organization, and a part of the culture, may do their best to observe, but their observations will not be as objective as those of an outsider. The researcher must be objective and also "invisible" to gain insights. It is essential not to disturb or influence the natural behaviors and interactions among individuals. Nevertheless, observation is a significant step that produces meaningful insights that can lay the groundwork for a productive survey.

Step 2: Survey

Surveying the organization is the fastest and most efficient method for seeing and understanding the fascinating layers and levels of an organization's culture. The critical success factor, though, is the quality of the tool. In most cases, the tool will be a questionnaire. It is having a foundation from observation from STEP 1 that is so important and should not be omitted. It is vital to ensure that all the questions presented are relevant to the organization and are thoughtfully and objectively presented. It is challenging to collect information about a subjective topic like culture in an objective way.

Sample Questionnaire

A. Questions related to knowledge culture and organization
　1. In my organization, knowledge culture exists formally
　　　a) in "knowledge book" (formal policy)
　　　b) in symbols (posters, slogans, gadgets that expose the formalities in a friendly & inspirational way)
　　　c) in formal events focused on knowledge culture
　　　d) other, please specify
　2. Knowledge attitudes and values
　　　a) exist common focus on knowledge (knowledge is a value)
　　　b) exist common understanding of what knowledge culture is
　　　c) exist common understanding of how vital knowledge culture is
　　　d) other, please specify
　3. Knowledge culture behaviors
　　　a) we care about the knowledge quality
　　　b) we care about the knowledge relevance
　　　c) we share knowledge among employees
　　　d) we learn every day
　　　e) we constantly look for new and better ways of working – the best solutions
　　　f) we are not ashamed to make a mistake
　　　g) we are ready to change how we think to gain a better understanding and do better
　　　h) other, please specify
　4. Knowledge beliefs
　　　a) knowledge culture helps us achieve our goals
　　　b) knowledge culture is something that makes our organization unique
　　　c) we are market leaders because of our culture
　　　d) we are open-minded
　　　e) we constantly re-frame and adjust our mental models
　　　f) other, please specify
B. Questions related to the knowledge culture and you
　5. I respect my organizational knowledge culture
　　　a) I am familiar with the formal policy in the "knowledge book" – I read and understand it

    b) I respect our artifacts (symbols, insignia, posters, slogans, gadgets) and the friendly and inspirational way they represent our formal culture

    c) I attend formal events focused on knowledge culture

    d) other

6. Knowledge attitudes and values
    a) I am focused on knowledge (knowledge is a value)
    b) I understand what knowledge culture is
    c) I understand how vital knowledge culture is
    d) other

7. Knowledge culture behaviors
    a) I care about the quality of knowledge
    b) I care about the relevance of knowledge
    c) I share the knowledge with other employees
    d) I learn every day
    e) I am constantly looking for new and better ways of working, striving for the best solutions
    f) I am not ashamed to make a mistake
    g) I am ready to change the way I think to gain a better understanding and do better
    h) other

8. Knowledge beliefs
    a) Knowledge culture helps me achieve my goals
    b) Knowledge culture is part of my culture
    c) I am open-minded
    d) I can re-structure my mental model

Details about Respondent:

1. Position: Employee Manager Board
2. Gender: M F
3. Work experience general: >1; >5; >10; >15; >20
4. Work experience in this organization: >1; >5; >10; >15; >20
5. Age:
6. Division/unit (if the company is small, it is better to mark questionnaires to divisions or groups to identify them without jeopardizing anonymity)

Well-designed survey instruments can provide the information needed to describe the current state of an organization's knowledge culture. The information collected through the survey should reflect the employees' views on organizational culture. Before designing or administering, survey instruments should be reviewed by high-level managers and leaders. Surveys can be high-profile activities, and it is essential to ensure they will provide the information the leaders need to meet their aspirational goals and practically achieve them.

Step 3: More-In-Depth Interviews

This step provides a deeper understanding of the survey results (STEP 2). We first conduct an in-depth analysis of all the data gathered in the survey. The researcher must be trusted within the organization and in the broader field. Follow-up and in-depth interviews will only generate honest answers and provide deeper insights where the interviewer is trusted. Interviews allow for a more in-depth exploration of critical issues, i.e., motives, significant issues, new, unusual, or simply exciting insights into information identified in an earlier stage. As a result, we can better design practical actions with a deeper understanding of issues and contexts.

It is good to assess the state of the organizational culture from the perspective of employees, managers, and the board. Comparing these perspectives enables us to identify and assess any discrepancies. We know that position may strongly influence an individual's perception. For example, Kucharska and Kowalczyk (2019) proved that managers rate their performance much higher than their employees. Only through an evaluation of employees', managers', and board views, we can identify the areas of discrepancy and understand the roots of those discrepancies. This insight comes through more in-depth interviews. These insights are critical to developing a strategy for designing, implementing, and executing a plan. At this stage, it is vital to a*ssess the discrepancies and establish goals*. The "moment of the truth" is critical to the process.

The 3-Step method provides a complete picture of the organizational culture. It allows you to:

- assess the layers of culture in your organization.
- identify and compare the consistency and discrepancies in individual, group, and organizational cultures.
- assess the consistencies and discrepancies in employee-manager cultures.

The 3-step process enables you to understand your organization better and to take into account the organization's situational context. You can then tailor subsequent steps to suit the situation: establish your aims and prepare and execute a plan. Understanding the company's context is vital to determining effective methods and actions.

Introducing Cultural Change – Planning & Execution

Introducing a new culture is not as simple as deciding to change. As with most management issues, the essence of success is execution. To succeed, you need a plan. Unfortunately, there is no one-size plan to suit all organizations or all situations. While we cannot offer you a plan that will work for you, we can offer a framework from which you can design a plan that will fit.

1. *Understanding & Importance.* Knowledge workers need to understand the purpose and goal. Make your motives for changing the culture clear. Knowledge workers need to feel that they are essential, to see that what they do contributes to something that matters. Highlight how significant a change in their attitudes and behaviors is to accomplishing the goal.

2. *Benefit.* Knowledge workers need to see the value of the change to them and from their perspective. The need for growth often incentivizes a cultural shift. Growth is an excellent benefit for the organization. It is critical to prepare a communication plan for each employee to show that changing their habits will lead to personal growth. Do this in an inspirational way!

3. *Leaders First.* Make sure the change begins at the top. Ensure that behavior changes are persistent, consistent, and consequential. Make it, start the change from your behavior, and be persistent, consistent, and consequential. Leaders both build it and execute it – they lead by example.

4. *Gamify.* Gamification is the application of game-design elements and game principles to non-game contexts. Create a 21-day competitive or game scenario where teams rather than individuals win. It will build a team spirit and foster leadership. Reward the change leader of the day for sustaining motivation and maintaining the focus.

5. *Prove It.* Prepare a virtual or physical space where employees can share lessons learned from experiences. For example, it could be an intranet where employees may share their "new skills" and "lessons learned": best practices, methods for changing behaviors and attitudes, and the effects these experiences produced. Reward people who help others learn new skills and empower change.

6. *Real Empowerment.* Implementing any planned changes begins with leaders. It is critical to empower leaders to make and live the change. Their behaviors set standards that are mirrored by others.

Successful implementation of the 3-step plan depends on a well-timed implementation plan, including detailed communication plans, tactics and actions, timing and sequencing. The plan should define the who, what, when, where, and how. In addition, it is critical to identify and list the risks inherent in your plan and to have mitigation strategies, and emergency plans in place should those risks occur. The most significant risk you may face is high resistance from staff – where the change is too painful or drastic. The longer it takes to implement the plan, the more significant opportunity there is for solid resistance to form. Therefore, it is essential to be ready to reconfigure your human capital assets where necessary.

It is worth highlighting that a KLC culture successfully fosters a working culture when it is embedded in every aspect of the workday. We know that cultural transformation is a huge challenge. It is not easy to change the behavior we have learned and have become accustomed to since childhood. We also know that while change is inevitable, personal development and growth require deliberate, intentional, continuous learning. And by learning, we mean learning new skills, attitudes, and behaviors.

It is challenging to introduce and manage an authentic KLC-driven culture in any organization. Cultural change in an organization is challenging and rare, but sometimes it is necessary to change the "organization's mental model" to grow and progress. Any other intentional, transformational change will not be possible without a culture change. Introducing the KLC culture is not as simple as deciding what it is or deciding to create it. A lesson common to any management challenge – the essence of success is – the first plan and then execute. The organizational context is always the most critical consideration. A universal plan that fits all companies to transform their culture from existing to desired does not exist. This chapter has provided a helpful frame for developing a deep understanding of and a strategy for empowering an organization to change its culture. Appendix C offers additional KLC assessment and implementation tools.

Case Study – Nicola

Nicola was a company's CEO in the fast-moving consumer goods (FCMG) market. HcHcompany produced household chemicals that had consistently lost market share. It was evident to George, the company's owner, that the root of any company's problems was its culture. HcHcompany was a significant domestic market player, a prominent and mature company with a steep hierarchy and an overwhelming bureaucracy that was challenging for everyone. While everyone complained about it, they nonetheless tolerated it. While there was widespread agreement that the company needed to be reframed, everything continued to function "as usual." George realized that mental barriers were the root cause of the company's inability to change behavior. Under time pressures, everyone works their best, doing what is generally accepted – "the usual." Time pressures are the new normal, so if left unaddressed, the company will be stuck in an organizational structure and culture that block its development. There is no internal means or power to make the change. George decided the company needed a transformational leader, and it needed it quickly.

Nicola, the new CEO, was charismatic. He had successfully transformed a company-wide mindset in his previous position. For this reason, George and Nicola thought he could achieve equal success at HcHcompany. So Nicola set about preparing a new plan based on three months of analyses and observations.

Nicola began by analyzing and diagnosing the situation. He then verified that the company had a good market position – a number 2 producer with a 22% market share and 30% market value. However, the truth was that this was not a good market position because it represented a decline over two years. Two years ago, Hcompany was the number 1 producer with a 30% market share and 40% market value. He also noticed that the market trend was generally going up, which meant that the actual market loss was higher than it appeared at first glance.

Nicola traced margin levels and realized that margin had been systematically lost. He then traced the margin creation line with the company's process effectiveness in critical categories and products to determine where the margin was lost. Finally, Nikola compared HcH results with those of competitors. He realized that margin was being lost in those categories that had lost their competitiveness. To Nicola, this suggested the company had lost its internal and external ability to innovate.

Based on his analysis, Nicola established new business goals. Nicola understood that many internal processes had lost effectiveness, and some industry segments and products had lost market positions. His new business goals aimed to improve processes and products through increased innovation. Next, Nicola asked himself: what kind of company culture will support innovation? And what kind of culture does HcH currently exhibit? In answering these questions, Nicola identified a considerable discrepancy between the existing and espoused bureaucratic, hierarchical company where the climate was dominated by control and obedience to siloed product line monitors and pseudo leaders. He realized that workers follow these influencers blindly to keep their jobs and survive in the company. Instead, they needed a culture and environment that supported agile learning and collaboration across a network structure. The company needed a network of open-minded, creative people where knowledge could flow. The company needed chemical and market knowledge leaders who continuously challenged their assumptions and beliefs to create new ground-breaking products. These new products would bring new value to society and improve the company's market position. Nicola concluded that his new company strategy needed realignment to win back the market leader position and shift the company culture.

Nicola developed a new tactical plan to support his new strategic business goals. First, he planned to restore the company's *capacity for innovation*. He set up an internal innovation improvement program (IIIP) that rewards innovations focused on internal processes: logic, efficiency, and effectiveness. Employees offer ideas, and the best of these are accepted and rewarded. He also set up an external innovation improvement program (EIIP). The EIIP brought together the most innovative minds across the company into project teams to recommend market-focused innovations. These innovations focused on potential product *improvements or new product developments. Second, Nicola* developed an organizational climate that motivated everyone to think innovatively. This new climate focused on seeking opportunities rather than creating barriers to change. All employees are expected to propose work and process improvements every Friday. This obligatory exercise aims to accustom employees to shift their mental focus from seeing barriers to seeing opportunities. The exercise is required because it is essential to shifting the company's mindset from seeing problems to seeing opportunities. The Friday exercise identifies ideas that are essential for internal and external innovation. It also identifies people who are best suited to carry these ideas forward. Nicola also developed a plan to dismantle the old company culture, *in effect, a* total dismantling.

Since the old HcH culture was firmly embedded in employees' minds, this would be a challenge. Nicola decided to communicate the change throughout the organization. Nicola decided that after 20 years, the only chance of changing the company culture was to send a strong message that the way we do business has changed. Whenever Nicola asked an employee why they did something in a particular way, the answer was always, "I've always done it in this way, and it was good!." Nicola's primary challenge then was to communicate clearly and firmly to all that "there is no longer any business as usual." To achieve this, he decided to make a physical change that reinforced the message – he changed the location of the company's office. The office lease agreement had expired, and this presented an excellent opportunity. It was a much better choice than simply swapping division offices. Workers could not simply work as usual because the workplace was different. A new place helped everyone see work from a new perception. When "everything around is different," the mindset will adapt to the new environment.

Nicola also flattened the company structure by eliminating two levels of management. It provided an opportunity to promote some leaders with potential expertise to "board advisors." As a result, their knowledge would remain in the company. And space was created for those creative employees with experience in the company and the market to thrive. All of these actions reinforced the company's intention to shift culture. Nicola replaced leaders with their more culturally aware subordinates wherever possible without causing other adverse effects.

In some cases, he swapped managers across departments because he knew they would work together effectively. These actions accelerated my understanding of other perspectives. Conversely, those who could not change or adapt were incentivized to leave.

Nicola introduced all of these changes thoughtfully and cautiously, explaining the reason for each change and describing the value to the company and the benefit to every employee. Of course, the most significant benefit was personal development. Some employees realized that the change might be uncomfortable in the short run. However, new competencies would bring many personal and professional benefits in the long run.

Nikola was not naïve. He knew it would be stressful for the first two years. He understood that a period of adjustment was necessary after years of accumulated mental and cultural experiences. The adjustment period was necessary because the traditional culture had been in place for a long time without any change. He anticipated that the cumulative effect of the shift would cause psychological distress and threaten workers' sense of security and safety. Nicola worked with the human resources department to prepare a psychological assistance program that would apply to everyone. It was readily available to everyone. No one needed to ask for it. The program supported all changes by identifying potential reactions and addressing the concerns with guidelines. The guidelines focused on how to see and positively react, to see the value of the changes, and to become part of the change.

Nicola also developed a plan for implementing the new company culture. Nicola wanted to establish a new culture based on KLC. He put knowledge first as a base for all decisions the organization makes. *Priority One* was to use the best knowledge when doing anything or making decisions in an organization. If knowledge deficits are discovered, they will be quickly filled leveraging internal or external sources. The core knowledge needed to support the fundamental business and its sources is defined and secured. This knowledge is accessible to individuals based on their business needs. It is integrated into the company structure and aligned with roles, responsibilities, and levels of authority. Nikola organized regular "knowledge-sharing meetings." These meetings aim to share knowledge, new ideas, and lessons learned from recent events. These meetings were organized at each management level.

Employees are encouraged to break with conventions, experiment and innovate, and freely discuss new ideas. It is acceptable not to know everything, but it is not acceptable to not make progress and not develop oneself. Priority Two is personal progress. The new culture is tolerant of mistakes. Mistakes happen, and mistakes are managed. Mistakes should be reported and shared. Critically reflect on your actions and ideas, and discuss them with more experienced staff. Learn new lessons, formulate guidelines, share new knowledge, and implement change to avoid repeating mistakes. Nicola instituted a new *Reflect&Change* rule. If someone hides mistakes, the consequence will be a loss of bonuses during the billing period.

Nikola also ensured that Single, Double, and Triple loop organizational learning rules were formally implemented across the organization. Single loop learning means learning to do something well or better, i.e., differently, more effectively or efficiently than how you are accustomed to doing it. Double loop learning means continuing to do something well, but based on your unique skills and competencies, take on something new that might generate greater value. Keep your mind open to new opportunities and focus more on the business goal of what you do rather than adhere to rules and procedures. Double loop learning also includes changing the business model to achieve more significant value. Triple loop learning means learning to learn collectively. Nicola focused Priority Three on collaboration. Nicola highlighted the importance of a collaborative culture. An organization is a network of people. Collaboration is the foundation for organizational knowledge exchange for achieving efficiency and effectiveness in any activity, including knowledge identification, absorption, production, creation, application, or sharing.

Nicola implemented his plans and designed a method to evaluate the progress of each component in his strategy. He approached implementation and evaluation as his top priority and highlighted sustainability as an essential objective. He operated from a fundamental assumption – rules and procedures that are good for us today can be useless tomorrow. With sustainability in mind, each organization member could understand that continuous improvement is part of their daily responsibilities.

If an authentic culture of KLC contains a sustainability component, it will generate organizational learning. Double and triple loop learning leads to continuous improvements. Effective and wise continuous improvements will lead to sustainability and development. Internal and external collaboration naturally generates shared value. Knowledge brings truth. Truth brings trust. Trust brings collaboration (and vice versa). So, when the organization strives to generate value over the long run, a synergy of KLC cultures is a meaningful, effective, and sustainable approach to growth. Appendix B presents the empirical evidence that the synergy of functional cultures of the KLC approach to knowledge organizations' culture building – is vital to support their innovativeness. Innovation is a proxy for sustainability that always requires creativity and invention to adapt to inevitable business environment changes.

Chapter Review

After reading this chapter, you should be able to:

- explain KLC approach to cultural capacity building in knowledge organizations.
- explain the role of company communications in seeing and shaping the company culture.
- describe how company structures affect communications at all levels.
- describe the relationship of company maturity and age to its adaptability.
- define the role of transformational leaders in building cultural capacity.
- define the role of knowledge workers in building cultural capacity.
- explain that every individual experiences culture.
- conduct a step-by-step assessment of your organization's cultural capacity.

References and Recommended Future Readings

Bedford, D., & Kucharska, W. (2020). *Relating information culture to information policies and management strategies.* IGI Global.

Bergmann, H., Hurson, K., & Russ-Eft, D. (1999). *Everyone is a leader. A grassroots model for the new workplace.* Achieve Global.

Boisot, H. (2010). *Knowledge assets.* Oxford University Press.

Brandt, E., Andersson, A., & Kjellstrom, S. (2019). The future trip: A story of transformational change. *Journal of Organizational Change Management, 32*(7), 669–686. https://doi.org/10.1108/JOCM-09-2017-0358

Burnes, B. (2011). Introduction. Why does change fail, and what can we do about it? *Journal of Change Management, 11*(4), 445–450.

Busari, A. H., Khan, S. N., Abdullah, S. M., & Mughal, Y. H. (2019). Transformational leadership style, followership, and factors of employees' reactions towards organizational change. *Journal of Asia Business Studies, 14*(2), 181–209. https://doi.org/10.1108/JABS-03-2018-0083

Hofstede, G., Hofstede, G. J., & Minkov, M. (2010). *Cultures and organizations.* McGraw Hill.

Kezar, A., & Eckel, P. (2002). Examining the institutional transformation process: The importance of sensemaking, interrelated strategies, and balance. *Research in Higher Education, 43*(3), 295–328.

Kucharska, W. (2021). Wisdom from experience paradox: Organizational learning, mistakes, hierarchy and maturity issues. *Electronic Journal of Knowledge Management, 19*(2), 105–117. https://doi.org/10.34190/ejkm.19.2.2370

Kucharska, W. (2022). *Personal Branding in the Knowledge Economy: The Inter-relationship between Corporate and Employee Brands.* Routledge.

Kucharska, W., & Bedford, D. A. D. (2020). Love your mistakes! – They help you adapt to change. How do knowledge, collaboration and learning cultures foster organizational intelligence? *Journal of Organizational Change Management, 33*(7), 1329–1354. https://doi.org/10.1108/JOCM-02-2020-0052

Kucharska, W., & Kowalczyk, R. (2019). How to achieve sustainability? – Employee's point of view on company's culture and CSR practice. *Corporate Social Responsibility and Environmental Management, 26*(2), 453–467. https://doi.org/10.1002/csr.1696

Kucharska, W., & Rebelo, T. (2022). Transformational leadership for researcher's innovativeness in the context of tacit knowledge and change adaptability. *International Journal of Leadership in Education.* https://doi.org/10.1080/13603124.2022.2068189

Mabey, C., & Nicholds, A. (2015). Discourses of knowledge across global networks: What can be learned about knowledge leadership from the ATLAS collaboration? *International Business Review, 24*(1), 43–54. https://doi.org/10.1016/j.ibusrev.2014.05.007

Mabey, C., & Zhao, S. (2017). Managing five paradoxes of knowledge exchange in networked organizations: New priorities for HRM? *Human Resource Management Journal, 27*(1), 39–57. https://doi.org/10.1111/1748-8583.12106

Nold, H. A. (2012). Linking knowledge processes with firm performance: Organizational culture. *Journal of Intellectual Capital, 13*(1), 16–38. https://doi.org/10.1108/14691931211196196

Schwartz, T. (2018). Leaders focus too much on changing policies, and not enough on changing minds. *Harvard Business Review*, June 25, 1–6.

Senge, P. M. (2006). *The fifth discipline: The art & practice of the learning organization.* Crown Business.

Shao, Z., Feng, Y., & Wang, T. (2017). Charismatic leadership and tacit knowledge sharing in the context of enterprise systems learning: The mediating effect of psychological safety climate and intrinsic motivation. *Behaviour & Information Technology, 36*(2), 194–208. https://doi.org/10.1080/0144929X.2016.1221461

Terouhid, S. A., & Ries, R. (2016). People capability: A strategic capability for enhancing organizational excellence of construction firms. *Journal of Modelling in Management, 11*(3), 811–841. https://doi.org/10.1108/JM2-04-2014-0028

Winter, S. G. (2003). Understanding dynamic capabilities. *Strategic Management Journal, 24*, 991–995. https://doi.org/10.1002/smj.318

Section 2

The Synergistic Power of Knowledge, Learning, and Collaboration Cultures

Chapter 5

Knowledge Culture Opens Minds

Chapter Summary

Chapter 4 addresses the importance of internal knowledge cultures. It provides a deeper dive into how internal knowledge cultures can contribute to a company's performance. The authors explain how knowledge culture shapes practical knowledge processes and fosters intellectual capital. The authors also provide insights into a critical knowledge paradox and discuss the interplay of knowledge paradoxes and cultural collisions. The chapter is supported by practical use cases that illustrate the points in the chapter.

Why We Care about Knowledge Culture?

Company cultures with short power distances and low levels of uncertainty avoidance characterize value social collaboration. They encourage and nourish effective and efficient knowledge flows. These cultures develop higher levels of knowledge capital. They also adapt to change more quickly and achieve higher levels of business performance than hierarchical and bureaucratic cultures. Hierarchical and bureaucratic cultures tend to constrain knowledge creation and impede access to knowledge capital. They also tend not to encourage workplace collaboration. And we know that knowledge capital creation and access are limited where workplace collaboration is limited and procedural only. It further limits an organization's ability to develop those dynamic capabilities essential to surviving in the knowledge economy.

Knowledge-driven organizations that strive to develop dynamic capabilities value collaboration over hierarchies. They foster knowledge exchange which generates new knowledge and ensures that organizational knowledge is accessible to the workforce. These knowledge-oriented companies are grounded in knowledge cultures and mindsets, where knowledge is acknowledged as a critical capital asset. Knowledge cultures resemble a prism through which assumptions, beliefs, values, behaviors, and business goals may be seen. In a knowledge culture, there is an implicit assumption and belief in the value of knowledge. Knowledge cultures should be evident and in practice at all levels and across all departments of an organization. Knowledge is appreciated and leveraged every day in every decision and every action. It is valid

The Cultures of Knowledge Organizations: Knowledge, Learning, Collaboration (KLC), 79–93
Copyright © 2023 by Wioleta Kucharska and Denise Bedford
Published under exclusive licence by Emerald Publishing Limited
doi:10.1108/978-1-83909-336-420231005

if it is acknowledged as a source of capital value by senior leadership. The organization sees every action, choice, and decision as a facet of the knowledge culture prism. Knowledge is visible in the company's espoused culture, regardless of the type of business culture, i.e., bureaucracy, market, fief, or clan (Boisot, 2010; Cameron & Quinn, 2006).

Cultures with shared assumptions and beliefs – shared mindsets – tend to build strong relationships and mutual support. They also place a high value on collaboration and learning. These cultures are referred to as learning cultures – they value all forms of learning and knowledge. A shared value of learning is reflected in the organization's business priorities. A company's survival, resilience, and growth depend on learning in the knowledge economy. Cultures dedicated to learning will make learning visible in assumptions, beliefs, values, behaviors, and artifacts. The synergy created by cultures of knowledge, cultures of learning, and cultures of collaboration is vital to success in the knowledge economy. These cultures can exist in any company culture, including bureaucracy, market, fief, or clan (Boisot, 2010; Cameron & Quinn, 2006). Some business cultures, though, can leverage these cultures to better advantage. When effectively designed and implemented, these cultures create the conditions in which knowledge, learning, and collaboration thrive.

Knowledge Culture Shapes Knowledge Processes

Knowledge is the lifeblood of organizations (Mabey & Zhao, 2017). Knowledge culture facilitates the creation and distribution of knowledge across the organization (Aramburu et al., 2015). Knowledge cultures raise employees' awareness of the value of all forms of knowledge and encourage the smooth flow of knowledge throughout the organization. The principal focus of knowledge-driven organizations is to create and maintain the conditions and methods for leveraging knowledge to create a competitive advantage (Leone & Schiavone, 2019). Knowledge culture dominates in knowledge-oriented organizations, where professional knowledge is required to perform daily in every stage of any action. Knowledge economy characterizes the strong participation of knowledge in value creation. Therefore, organizations cannot succeed in the knowledge economy without a culture of knowledge that supports knowledge processes (e.g., knowledge gaining, creation, storage, protection, usage, re-usage, development, and sharing). Knowledge cultures also support the effective management of organizations of all types and levels.

Knowledge management is defined as a dynamic and systematic process (García-Fernández, 2015) consisting of a set of capabilities (Cheng & Leong, 2017; Cegarra-Navarez et al., 2021) designed to support the nature of knowledge and all aspects of its creation, discovery, growth, organization, preservation, access, and exchange (LaFayette et al., 2019; Raudeliuniene et al., 2018). Knowledge management capabilities resemble dynamic and systematic processes. These capabilities demonstrate that high-quality knowledge is a fundamental organizational value. It is more likely that knowledge assets will be managed and cultivated where knowledge assets are recognized for their business and organizational value and reified by a knowledge culture. It is also more likely that the organization's commitment to managing and leveraging knowledge will be sustained (Intezari et al., 2017).

Each of the eight types of knowledge assets – tacit and explicit – requires unique management and use strategies. Each approach calls upon a particular mindset. The tacit component of knowledge reflects novelty and uniqueness because it reflects an individual's absorption and interpretation of knowledge they have encountered. Tacit knowledge creation and acquisition require an open mind rather than only recognizing existing encoded knowledge and information. Crane and Bontis (2014) defined tacit knowledge as "acquired unconsciously and automatically, but capable of influencing action." Explicit forms of knowledge – encoded information and data – are packaged in ways that enable preservation and sharing (e.g., books, reports, documents, and databases).

In contrast, tacit knowledge is associated with human beings and cannot be shared without social interactions. Tacit knowledge is context-specific; it is created and stored in the human mind (Polanyi, 1966). In light of the theory of dynamic knowledge creation (Nonaka, 1994), Kucharska and Erickson (2023) revealed that tacit knowledge acquisition is a critical organizational process for innovation. Tacit knowledge acquisition is fostered by social interactions supported by trust and critical thinking. From there, it follows that tacit knowledge acquisition capacity at the organizational level is a direct, undeniable, and crucial competency determining competitive advantage creation in the knowledge economy context. It means that sharing is also an economic transaction where personal values (e.g., altruistic motives, trust, reputation, status, expertise, risk, and so on) are factors that govern the transaction. Most tacit knowledge processes are unconscious and occur inside the human mind. When they are shared – they are revealed. Learning from and with others and collaborative work offer opportunities to reveal tacit knowledge (Asher & Popper, 2019; Kucharska, 2017; Olaisen & Revang, 2018). Explicit knowledge is more amenable to being captured by the organization and then shared through formal processes and procedures. Furthermore, explicit knowledge can be an essential foundation for building tacit knowledge and a source of knowledge exchange.

An organization's explicit knowledge acquisition and management are fundamental parts of structural capital (Abualoush et al., 2018; Agostini et al., 2017; Agostini & Nosella, 2017). Structural capital is perceived then as an effect of explicit knowledge integrated into information systems and as the result of knowledge conversion (Asiaei et al., 2018). Therefore, simplifying the implemented knowledge culture is fundamental for organizations' structural components of intellectual capital development. Furthermore, without a shared understanding of the value of knowledge, there is no chance for efficient management within an organization.

Knowledge exchanges and transactions are only effective when knowledge from one source is absorbed into the knowledge store of another source. Nonaka (1994) provides one of the earliest explanations of essential transactions for knowledge expression and absorption in his concept of "ba." "Ba" describes the discovery moment when an individual encounters or expresses knowledge and realizes the need to absorb it into their conscious tacit knowledge. Nonaka describes four types of exchange that may lead to absorption – internalization, externalization, socialization, and combination. These four processes can be found in any organization and the learning activities of individuals. Therefore, a

Case Study – Angela's Post-Doctoral Experience

Angela was awarded a post-doctoral position at a reputable university. She approached her position with high expectations of extensive personal development based on the inspiration of other well-known colleagues. She anticipated sharing and extending ideas through open discussion with others. She also hoped to develop her research and international collaboration skills. These enhanced skills and capabilities often determine access to funding and other future career opportunities. Her dreams of collaboration were realized, but only within her direct work team. She also noticed that competition among faculty members for resources could be intense. Moreover, administrative requirements and conditions can affect a researcher's enthusiasm by requiring multiple levels of requirements, documentation, compliance, and signoffs.

Regardless of the resource access-related barriers, the dominant culture of knowledge paradoxically also created a barrier to development. The department with the wealthiest knowledge culture was the library. The library provided rich access to explicit knowledge sources in books, databases, archives, artifacts, and networks. Collections included historical and current sources and were easy to access and use. In addition to access to explicit sources, the library had a dominant culture of *knowing*. Individuals portrayed themselves as "knowers" or experts. Angela also had to present herself as a knower to survive and thrive in this culture. She learned to hide what she did not know at home and as quickly as possible so she might not be seen as *not knowing*. In some situations, Angela chose to remain quiet and pretend to be invisible than take a risk, ask a question, and be seen as someone who *did not know*. As a result, she accelerated her learning and grew her knowledge capital more quickly than ever. She was motivated to fill her knowledge gaps to be seen as a peer with others. While this was an efficient way to build her knowledge base, it was also very stressful. The obsession with perfection had a negative effect on her creativity, self-esteem, and confidence. It taught her to focus on rigid forms and requirements, unreflective ways of thinking and working, and structured tools. Angela recognized the conflict with her assumptions, beliefs, values, and behaviors. She did not learn from prominent scientists directly, somewhat only indirectly. She was motivated under pressure. While it was efficient, it was not sustainable. She was exhausted.

Angela realized she was experiencing a cultural conflict. The conflict was not just between her learning values and those of the university but more fundamental. When the cultures of individual researchers are competitive rather than additive, the values of organizations and divisions (i.e., administrative, scientific, and teaching) will conflict. In this case, the visible culture was a knowledge culture heavily focused on the values of excellence, perfection, and hierarchical position. Angela realized that in a hierarchical culture, investments in and distribution of human capital value accrue to a few rather than the whole. As a result, these organizations cannot fully leverage human capital value. It means that some individuals in the hierarchy have a more significant opportunity to develop and lower incentives to engage in sharing and grow the human capital of others. Angela realized that knowledge competition rather than knowledge-building culture is not sustainable. She understood that these cultures would discourage many individuals from investing in their human capital because there is no clear return.

Angela observed firsthand how the strategies of individuals, groups, scientific, educational departments, and administrative units could conflict. These fundamental conflicts lead to conflicting strategic goals at the whole organizational level. In this case, the university's shared values, mindset, and vision did not reflect those of individuals at the lower levels. After two years of working at the university, Angela realized the significance of cultural challenges and paradoxes. It caused Angela to consider how an organization with a misaligned culture and business goals could still exist.

knowledge culture that encourages the flow and exchange of all forms of knowledge is essential to survival in the knowledge economy.

A knowledge culture where employees' attitudes, values, beliefs, and behaviors are treated with deep respect and appreciation will create a knowledge-rich environment. In a knowledge-rich environment, knowledge is created at all levels, flows throughout the organization, and is leveraged at every level to achieve competitive advantage. These flows are required for the development of new and cumulative knowledge capital. Knowledge cultures support intellectual capital development (Kucharska, 2021). By supporting and realizing knowledge processes, knowledge cultures contribute to the knowledge capital sources critical to a networked, hyperdynamic knowledge-driven organization. Knowledge capital is a determining factor in organizational performance. An organization's business culture and its knowledge assets are heavily independent.

Knowledge Processes Support Intellectual Capital Creation

Knowledge management processes enable organizations to build and leverage intellectual capital. Knowledge cultures are critical to both (Seleim & Khalil, 2011). Intellectual capital influences organizational intelligence and the development of dynamic capabilities. In turn, organizational intelligence and dynamic capabilities directly affect an organization's business performance, fostering its adaptability and resilience.

Intellectual capital is conceptualized as a set of knowledge-based assets organizations need to achieve and maintain a competitive advantage (Handa et al., 2019;

LaFayette et al., 2019; Yang et al., 2015). Intellectual capital is also defined as the "stock of knowledge" possessed by an organization. It represents the organization's cumulative human and structural capital and its internal and external relational and reputational capital (Jardon, 2015). Relationships are critical to the business infrastructure in the new networked economy. Bontis (1998) presents this view of a holistic typology of knowledge capital, including human, structural, and relational capital. Relational capital is determined by an organization's internal and external social relations, quality, and quantity. In the networked economy, relationships are essential to the company's position in the business network. They are as critical assets as tacit knowledge, skills, attitudes and behaviors, explicit information, procedural knowledge, and cultural capital. Human capital is the employees' knowledge, capabilities, education and learning, soft and professional skills, and personal characteristics, which are critical sources of value. Structural capital reflects an organization's collective knowledge infrastructure, often enhanced by technology (Hussinki et al., 2017). It enhances the value of those explicit knowledge assets, such as databases, repositories, registers, and library collections. Kianto (2008) addressed an organization's ability to grow and renew these knowledge assets. Knowledge capital renewal is an organization's ability to re-invent all assets (Yang et al., 2015). Just as organizations reinvest in financial and physical capital, so must they reinvest and renew their knowledge assets. We believe that knowledge cultures, fueled by knowledge assets, will determine organizational innovativeness (Kucharska, 2021, 2022a, 2022b). Knowledge cultures' direct and indirect influence on organizational networks makes it a critical asset. All forms of knowledge capital (explicit and tacit) affect organizational forces.

Knowledge processes contribute to the building of all types of knowledge capital. The cultivation of different types of capital, though, requires different methods and tactics. Saint-Onge (1996) noted that forms of tacit knowledge, such as human capital, leverage different knowledge management processes. Wang et al. (2014) and Kucharska (2022a, 2021) demonstrated variations in the impacts of different types of specific knowledge capital, both tacit and explicit. Human capital, the best-known form of tacit knowledge, is reflected in mindsets, assumptions, beliefs, and biases. Another form of tacit knowledge – relational capital – is represented in the collective mindsets and perceptions. Another form of tacit knowledge – structural capital – is represented in the collective culture, norms, and behavior patterns. Building tacit knowledge to create an innovative mindset and strengthen business performance means leveraging various knowledge management methods and processes. Tacit knowledge sharing is a significant challenge for organizations today. It is produced and stored in employees' minds and can only be transferred to tangible form through individuals' voluntary actions and engagements. Organizations may influence or incentivize individuals to share tacit knowledge but cannot compel or force individuals to share. A company's culture significantly affects this level of knowledge exchange and sharing. The more an organizational culture promotes cooperation, invention, risk-taking, and rule stretching, the greater the probability that tacit knowledge will be recognized, valued, and shared. As this awareness and interaction build at the individual level, the greater the likelihood they will develop into organizational norms. As norms and values grow, so do the productivity and innovation of the workplace.

Critical knowledge processes contribute to the flows of both explicit and implicit knowledge – visibly and invisibly. The company's knowledge culture also takes both visible and invisible forms. As described in Chapter 2, artifacts and assumptions are visible and above the waterline. Assumptions, beliefs, values, and norms are invisible and below the line. And, those aspects of the waterline may be espoused or actual. It means there are two versions of assumptions, beliefs, and values – one visible. The other version reflects the actual or lived assumptions, beliefs, and values that individuals follow and demonstrate in their everyday behaviors, actions, and decisions. Promoted by the organization and is reflected in some behaviors and company artifacts. Any organization's goal is to align the visible and invisible, the espoused and the actual cultures, as closely as possible. A company culture cannot exist solely as an espoused or aspirational phenomenon created by leaders. While aspirational cultures may reflect desired values and behaviors, they will not reflect how individuals behave or the choices they make in reality. Aspirational cultures should be aligned with actual cultures, with the intent of moving the actual culture closer to aspiration. However, a false culture will serve no purpose in realizing the desired culture. Neither will it stimulate the development of intellectual capital assets. It is because false culture is a culture that exists barely as an official statement but is far away from the company's daily life; therefore, being totally illusory, it can't serve the company assets development at all. It is particularly true when we think about how Human Capital, Structural Capital and Relational Capital grow and what they contribute to the company's overall capital. If we do not see the actual or lived knowledge culture, we risk neglecting the critical knowledge capital that allows companies to develop company intelligence, dynamic capabilities, innovation, resilience, and systematic adaptability.

Traditionally, knowledge science has focused on formal knowledge management processes and tactics. These processes and tactics have derived mainly from the information and data science domains. Following the traditional focus of those domains, the focus has been on one type of knowledge capital – explicit or tangible knowledge. However, there are critical dependencies across all types of knowledge capital. It is mainly the case for explicit knowledge, as it can be seen as fuel for building other forms of knowledge. For example, explicit procedural or design manuals may reflect a team's structural knowledge. Also, work and functional teams routinely leverage data and information from databases, repositories, libraries, registers, and reports (Abualoush et al., 2018). While essential, these explicit assets represent knowledge at a given point in time – while tangible, they are also static. Often, we find that procedural and design manual lag behind the actual methods and ideas that a team is working on each day.

The challenge for companies today is managing both types of knowledge – tacit knowledge, a conceptual and dynamic source of innovation, and the explicit, a static but fundamental asset. Managing tacit knowledge is much more challenging than managing explicit knowledge because it means managing people and the environment in which they work and interact and can only be accessed, shared, or reused when the individual chooses to do so. Tacit knowledge sharing is not easy. First, the "ba" - the tacit knowledge awareness moment (knowledge revelation) must occur to make tacit knowledge sharing even possible (Kucharska & Erickson, 2023). It matters because tacit knowledge is relatively more unconscious than conscious. And when the individual is coming to the tacit knowledge awareness, then this new knowledge can be shared if only the knowledge owner intends to share and has the skills and competencies to articulate or demonstrate it. In such a case, tacit knowledge can be distributed among the workmates' in the company's knowledge workers' minds network. Precisely, internalization ("ba moment") is a starting point for tacit knowledge externalization, combination, experimentation, and again internalization according to the knowledge spiral idea of Nonaka and Takeuchi (1995). We know from the literature (Bedford et al., 2022) that individuals absorb knowledge differently, depending on a wide range of factors. These factors are built into an individual's assumptions, beliefs, and values. The renewal component of knowledge capital is primarily responsible for the organization's ability to create new solutions and procedural knowledge (Kucharska, 2021, 2022a). This tacit aspect of knowledge capital has the most significant effect on the organization's ability to create new ideas and innovate internally and externally. Internal innovations enable organizations to improve organizational efficiency, whereas external innovation increases the organization's competitiveness and performance in the larger market.

Case Study – GREENzone

Norman owned GREENzone – a fresh vegetable delivery company that delivered fruits and vegetables to large traditional retail networks and door-to-door bars and restaurants. Based on current market trends, they recently introduced a new product named "GREENbox." The new product was intended to replace the classic "office sandwich" lunch with a selection of fruits and vegetables. Norman developed this new product after he noticed a significant change in consumption habits. The changes he observed identified noted an increasing population living mainly in large cities with consumption habits with significantly lower levels of meat and carbohydrates. Instead, their consumption patterns demonstrated increased levels of nuts, vegetables, and fruits. GREENbox became increasingly popular and quickly expanded to include a GREENbox: breakfast, lunch, and dinner offering. And the rich selection of healthy options further enhanced the product line. And Norman introduced the GREENstyle of living, followed shortly by GREENplaces, a diverse offering of gym & bar. All went well with the newly expanded product lines.

Norman critically reviewed and analyzed his sales figures, general traffic data, frequency of attendance and visits, the performance of complementary products and services, customer loyalty, and basket value. He was a master at analysis and relied heavily on GREENzone's customer relationship management (CRM) system. The CRM allowed Norman to monitor each transaction and each customer. He developed his new product lines carefully and strategically, building from the CRM data. Leveraging the CRM data depended on Norman's critical analytical and software skills and competencies. He leveraged these skills and competencies to collect and transform the CRM data – a form of tangible and explicit knowledge. And he interpreted and translated these data to create other forms of human, structural, and relational capital. He built structural capital that generated additional human and relational capital to renew their knowledge capital continually.

Norman has always been a knowledge-oriented businessman. He believed that the more he knew about the market and his clients, the better he could position and manage his businesses. He always approached challenges with open eyes, ears, and minds. He tried to be as familiar with his target groups as possible, leveraging his relational and reputational capital. Furthermore, this is what he expected from his employees. Traditionally, Norman has employed people with strong professional knowledge, skills, and competencies, but also whether their cultures – their values, beliefs, and behaviors – aligned with GREENzone's culture. He realized that only when an individual's actual or lived culture align with the company's espoused culture was there a chance of shared work, value, success, and joy at work. When people believe in what they do, and when it matters to them, they are more likely to share their knowledge and expertise with others. Each workforce member will support the common business goal when this is the dominant culture. Norman always strove to maintain the company culture and to align it with strategy. Norman also believed that when the strategy and culture aligns, the alignment would be internally and externally significant and visible. A strong and aligned culture and strategy generate strong internal and external relational capital, increasing the company's reputation – its authenticity, trustworthiness, and loyalty to its clients and customers.

In sum, intellectual capital is generated from both formal and informal knowledge processes. It is the focal point of organizational performance. Knowledge culture drives learning and requires collaboration to be efficient. Knowledge culture is critical to enhancing knowledge processes an intellectual capital generation. All three KLC cultures are closely intertwined. A culture is a powerful tool affording any knowledge-driven company the ability to develop dynamic capabilities and to adapt effectively to internal or external changes. Knowledge flows and exchanges fuel a company's growth. Knowledge culture is the key factor in the entire company's performance and development.

Knowledge Paradox and Cultural Collision

Mabey and Zhao (2017) remind us that the more knowledge is controlled and formally managed, the less likely it is shared among workmates. The essence of the knowledge paradox is that "the more knowledge is formally managed, the less likely it is to flow and achieve its full value." It is due to the essential economic nature of knowledge capital and its fundamental differences from financial and physical capital. The more significant efforts organizations make to formalize and control knowledge flows, the less value they will realize. The effects are counter-intuitive to industrial economy management theory. Kucharska (2021) explored this paradox and explained it by contrasting management approaches best suited to formal (e.g., explicit) or informal (e.g., tacit) knowledge processes. She confidently demonstrated that intellectual capital components are created informally (i.e., human and relational) and formally (i.e., structural). Therefore, formal and informal knowledge processes must be supported for the best effects. The KLC cultures approach strongly supports both.

Mature, hierarchical, and often bureaucratic organizations tend to focus on uncertainty avoidance in the false belief that organizational success will be enhanced by formalization and control. If organizations focus on formalization and control, it jeopardizes the development of knowledge flows, relationships, and knowledge networks, workforce creativity, and essential competencies to innovate, think, and act "out of the box." Following traditional management assumptions and practices will diminish the value and impact of human capital. Strictly controlled procedures and policies are no longer suited to today's knowledge economy and dynamic markets. They do not generate the expected value in a changing business environment. They do not support the behaviors we need to develop to adapt to change in the hyperdynamic knowledge economy. Even if there is an espoused focus on knowledge capital, individuals' everyday actions, choices, and decisions will not generate the expected value. The knowledge culture will not nourish and cultivate knowledge. Rather it may impede and diminish that capital. Human, procedural, cultural, reputational, and relational knowledge capital assets are essential sources of innovation. Relying only on explicit and easily visible knowledge and its use to generate explicit structural capital by definition will limit growth to current areas of expertise and core business capabilities. These cultural paradoxes will always present a challenge to business. Knowledge culture is critical. Without learning and collaborative cultures, though, it will not effectively generate the practical value expected for a knowledge economy. Knowledge as a critical capital asset in the knowledge-driven economy should generate new value and performance improvement.

The challenge is that even if an organization develops a knowledge culture, it may not pair it with a double-loop learning culture (Argyris, 1976). Double-loop learning focuses on teaching people to examine their assumptions and beliefs. It aligns with our individual and company cultures. Double-loop learning differs from single-loop learning, which involves a simpler focus on changing methods and improving efficiency to obtain pre-defined objectives. It focuses on learning to do things "the right way." Double-loop learning allows the learner to change the objectives themselves – doing the right things, whatever they are.

Single-loop learning refers to learning that aims to maintain business operations in their current form and at current goals. Double-loop learning aims to fuel changing business operations, assets, and markets. These concepts pertain to the distinction between first-order and second-order change, a change that is vital to the hyperdynamic knowledge economy. Organizations may be performing according to expectations and striving for continuous improvements, but their internal learning culture remains focused on generating value in the same old ways. They continue to focus on the efficiency or efficacy of their traditional approach. The efficiency and efficacy improvement is valuable, to be sure. However, in a dynamic economy, this strategy will be insufficient to generate the critical organizational growth, development, and competitiveness required to survive and thrive. Organizations that favor uncertainty avoidance by mapping and controlling assets and processes risk their ability to adapt and grow. They forego the critical learning that is achieved by learning in action, learning in and on the job. Consequently, as Steiber (2018) suggests, bureaucracies do not respond well to rapid or continuous change.

The knowledge paradox occurred when the company espoused and actual cultures were in conflict. Cultural conflicts and collisions can result if priority is given to uncertainty avoidance and structural explicit information assets. These conflicts will impede the development of dynamic capabilities grounded in human, procedural, cultural, relational, and reputational capital. The conflict results because organizations fail to see knowledge as a value, to avoid taking knowledge risks, and try to control knowledge processes to avoid uncertainties and risks. Conflict can also result if an organization understands the value of collaboration and open knowledge flows but adhere to hierarchical management cultures and strictly controls collaboration and knowledge flows. The organization applies strict rules for collaboration to control knowledge flows and manage uncertainty and risks. The organization may focus on knowledge capital creation and sharing, but it applies controls to those flows to manage risks. These conflicting approaches will create conflicting business and learning cultures. Individuals must be free to create human capital – the more opportunities for individuals to invest in their human capital, the better. Knowledge capital growth will be sub-optimized when restrictions are placed on those opportunities and challenges are imposed. The same is true where challenges and impediments are imposed on the lack of smooth exchange of ideas between individuals. In the end, the knowledge paradox describes fundamental challenges to an organization's cultural infrastructure and exposes potential conflicts between a knowledge-driven business strategy and the company culture.

Case Study – DataSoft

DataSoft is a company that has operated in the market for over 20 years. Their whole business model is focused on data storage and protection. A culture of total control, management of risks, and uncertainty avoidance dominate the company. The culture is grounded in a set of detailed procedures as norms that govern business process sequences, responsibilities, entitlements, paths of escalations, and any decision regarding data security. Particular value is assigned to risk management procedures, e.g., risk control, prevention, mitigation, and crisis management. All employees strictly respect these norms and align their behaviors to suit the hierarchy. The company culture strongly resembled a military unit or organization in many ways.

Traditionally, the company has employed highly educated, intelligent, and diligent people who are satisfied and fulfilled, performing repeated sequences of actions and adhering to hierarchical norms. It is a cultural behavior that is not well-aligned with the expectations of highly educated, intelligent, creative, and innovative workers. Knowledge workers prefer to exploit their human capital by looking for new solutions. The company was intentionally hiring with knowledge and cultural competencies to "employ the best" and expose it to clients. Still, unfortunately, this was not well-aligned with the nature of the work in the company. The company expected to apply only verified, safe solutions rather than continually creating new ones. Risky and out-of-the-box ideas were not expected. So, some highly educated knowledge workers who needed an intellectual challenge at work became increasingly frustrated and left. Those who stayed repeated their everyday routines as it was expected. The culture favored those who preferred rule-following as a cultural norm rather than developing and leveraging its human and relational capital. The company's reward and recognition systems favored secure mutual trust with the company's employees, life-long employment security, and corporate loyalty. And it worked.

Lately, the company realized that DataSoft's business environment was becoming more unpredictable in the more dynamic economy. The traditional services needed by clients were changing from traditional security risks to new forms of attacks. Increasingly frequent cyberattacks forced DataSoft to change its business strategy and re-organize the company to better position itself for the new information and knowledge warfare and malicious hacking. To meet the new need, the company hired a new team with all the tacit knowledge, skills, and competencies, and personal characteristics required to meet these new challenges. There was a problem, though. The team culture suited the new business demands and security threats, but it collided with the overarching company culture. The team wanted to conduct their work in a way that aligned with the business goals, but others expected them to conform to the more traditional company rules, norms, and behaviors. Achieving the new business goals of working within a traditional work culture was not possible. The traditional work culture did not value a shared mindset, shared values, shared beliefs, attitudes, aims, and vision. The cultural infrastructure did not allow the company to adapt as quickly and deeply to the new business environment.

Management painfully realized that their continued support for a culture that prioritized explicit structural capital development and promoted bureaucratic values, norms, and behavior would ultimately block the growth of dynamic capabilities and prevent the development of critical knowledge capital assets.

Knowledge-oriented companies cultivate cultures where the cultivation of knowledge is inherent to their values, beliefs, attitudes, aims, and business priorities will realize the company's total business potential. If the company does not create a cultural infrastructure that aligns with its knowledge asset development strategies, the culture will undermine its strategies, business operations, and growth. This cultural-strategy discord may decrease the company's potential competitiveness and growth and ultimately threaten its survival. Therefore, company culture should evolve to align with and support organizational challenges and business goals.

Knowledge cultures promote a fundamental appreciation for high-level explicit knowledge, proficiency, and expertise as a basis for sound decision-making. This appreciation may be incompatible with the value of failing small and learning from mistakes. Knowledge does not exist without learning. Creating a learning culture-oriented toward dynamic capabilities, transformation, organizational reframing, continuous development, experimentation, and innovation requires a culture that values brave choices and actions. Learning culture must value mistake acceptance. Mistakes are inevitable in the new knowledge economy, where it is critical to formulate and try new approaches. The new reality of continuous change requires adaptability and innovation. Innovative activities are always risky. Organizations must constantly seek an effective balance between exploiting verified knowledge to secure organizational safety and security, exploring new methods, and creating new knowledge. All of these are dependent upon effective knowledge and learning cultures. A learning culture is dependent upon a knowledge-sharing and collaborative work culture. Finding a balance enables effective and efficient knowledge conversion, exchange, and absorption – the essence of intellectual capital development.

Intellectual capital assets are created leveraging both informal (i.e., human and relational) and formal (i.e., structural) methods. If leaders recognize that the more knowledge is formally controlled and managed by the organization, the less effective the knowledge exchange is likely at the individual or team level. Organizations must devote greater effort to informal knowledge processes that develop human and relational intellectual capital components. In essence, leaders need to develop well-aligned, espoused, and lived learning cultures to realize the organization's potential. A dominant knowledge culture is vital in building an organization's human capital in the knowledge economy. It must also, though, be supported by a well-aligned learning culture. A knowledge organization is also a learning organization. One without the other leads to suboptimal development and growth in the current economic environment. Continuous learning is essential to the knowledge economy.

Chapter Review

After reading this chapter, you should be able to:

- speak to the importance of internal knowledge cultures.
- explain how knowledge cultures work.
- explain how a knowledge culture can shape an organization's knowledge processes and knowledge work.
- explain how knowledge cultures create intellectual capital.
- define the knowledge paradox.
- discuss the interplay of knowledge paradoxes and cultural collisions.

References and Recommendations for Future Reading

Abualoush, S., Masa'deh, R., Bataineh, K., & Alrowwad, A. (2018). The role of knowledge management process and intellectual capital as intermediary variables between knowledge management infrastructure and organization performance. *Interdisciplinary Journal of Information, Knowledge, and Management, 13*, 279–309.

Agostini, L., & Nosella, A. (2017). Enhancing radical innovation performance through intellectual capital components. *Journal of Intellectual Capital, 18*(4), 789–806.

Agostini, L., Nosella, A., & Filippini, R. (2017). Does intellectual capital allow improving innovation performance? A quantitative analysis in the SME context. *Journal of Intellectual Capital, 18*(2), 400–418.

Andriessen, D. (2004). *Making sense of intellectual capital*. Routledge.

Aramburu, N., Sáenz, J., & Blanco, C. (2015). Structural capital, innovation capability, and company performance in technology-based Colombian firms. *Cuadernos de Gestión, 15*(1), 39–60.

Argyris, Ch. (1976). *Increasing leadership effectiveness*. Wiley-Interscience.

Argyris, C., & Schön, D. A. (1996). *Organizational learning II: Theory, method and practice*. Addison-Wesley.

Asher, D., & Popper, M. (2019). Tacit knowledge as a multilayer phenomenon: The 'onion' model. *The Learning Organization, 26*(3), 264–275.

Asiaei, K., Jusoh, R., & Bontis, N. (2018). Intellectual capital and performance measurement systems in Iran. *Journal of Intellectual Capital, 19*(2), 294–320.

Bedford, D., Chalphin, I., Dietz, K. and Phlypo, K. (2022). The Shifting Landscape of Organizational Communication. In *Communicating Knowledge (Working Methods for Knowledge Management* (pp. 3–21). Bingley: Emerald Publishing Limited.

Boisot, H. (2010). *Knowledge assets*. Oxford University Press.

Bontis, N. (1998). Intellectual capital: An exploratory study that develops measures and models. *Management Decision, 36*(2), 63–76.

Cameron, K. S., & Quinn, R. E. (2006). *Diagnosing and changing organizational culture: Based on the competing values framework*. Jossey-Bass.

Carayannis, E. G., & Alexander, J. (1999). The wealth of knowledge: Converting intellectual property to intellectual capital in co-opetitive research and technology management settings. *International Journal of Technology Management, 18*(3), 326–352.

Cegarra-Navarro, J. G., Martínez Caro, E., Martínez-Martínez, A., Aledo-Ruiz, M. D., Martínez-Conesa, E. (2021). Capacities, competences and capabilities as knowledge structures to build relational capital. *Kybernetes, 50*(5), 1303–1320. https://doi.org/10.1108/K-02-2020-0115

Cheng, L., & Leong, S. (2017). Knowledge management ecological approach: A cross-discipline case study. *Journal of Knowledge Management, 21*(4), 839–856.

Crane, L., & Bontis, N. (2014). Trouble with tacit: Developing a new perspective and approach. *Journal of Knowledge Management, 18*(6), 1127–1140.

García-Fernández, M. (2015). How to measure knowledge management: Dimensions and model. *VINE, 45*(1), 107–125.

Handa, P., Pagani, J., & Bedford, D. (2019). *Knowledge assets and knowledge audits*. Emerald Group Publishing.

Hussinki, H., Ritala, P., Vanhala, M., & Kianto, A. (2017). Intellectual capital, knowledge management practices and firm performance. *Journal of Intellectual Capital, 18*(4), 904–922.

Intezari, A., Taskin, N., & Pauleen, D. J. (2017). Looking beyond knowledge sharing: An integrative approach to knowledge management culture. *Journal of Knowledge Management, 21*(2), 492–515.

Jardon, M. C. (2015). The use of intellectual capital to obtain competitive advantages in regional small and medium enterprises. *Knowledge Management Research & Practice, 13*(4), 486–496.

Kianto, A. (2008). Development and validation of a survey instrument for measuring organisational renewal capability. *International Journal of Technology Management, 42*(1–2), 69–88.

Kucharska, W. (2021). Leadership, culture, intellectual capital and knowledge processes for organizational innovativeness across industries: The case of Poland. *Journal of Intellectual Capital, 22*(7), 121–141. https://doi.org/10.1108/JIC-02-2021-0047

Kucharska, W. (2022a). Tacit knowledge influence on intellectual capital and innovativeness in the healthcare sector: A cross-country study of Poland and the US. *Journal of Business Research, 149*, 869–883.

Kucharska, W. (2022b). Tacit Knowledge Awareness and Sharing as a Focal Part of Knowledge Production. Polish-US View on IT, Healthcare, and Construction Industry, AHFE 2021, S. Trzcielinski et al. (Eds.), 1–9, 2022, Springer Nature Switzerland.

Kucharska, W., & Erickson, G. S. (2023). Tacit knowledge acquisition & sharing, and its influence on innovations: A Polish/US cross-country study. *International Journal of Information Management, 71*, 102647. https://doi.org/10.1016/j.ijinfomgt.2023.102647

LaFayette, B., Curtis, W., Bedford, D., & Iyer, S. (2019). *Knowledge economies and knowledge work*. Emerald Group Publishing.

Leone, D., & Schiavone, F. (2019). Innovation and knowledge sharing in crowdfunding: How social dynamics affect project success. *Technology Analysis and Strategic Management, 31*(7), 803–816.

Mabey, C., & Zhao, S. (2017). Managing five paradoxes of knowledge exchange in networked organizations: New priorities for HRM? *Human Resource Management Journal, 27*(1), 39–57,

Nonaka, I. (1994). A dynamic theory of organizational knowledge creation. *Organizational Science, 5*(1), 14–37.

Nonaka, I., & Takeuchi, H. (1995). The knowledge-creating company: How Japanese companies create the dynamics of innovation, 29 (p. 592). Oxford University Press.

Olaisen, J., & Revang, O. (2018). Exploring the performance of tacit knowledge: How to make ordinary people deliver extraordinary results in teams. *International Journal of Information Management, 43*, 295–304.

Polanyi, M. (1966). *The tacit dimension*. University of Chicago Press.

Raudeliuniene, J., Davidaviciene, V., & Jakubavicius, A. (2018). Knowledge management process model. *Entrepreneurship and Sustainability Issues, 5*(3), 542–554.

Saint-Onge, H. (1996). Tacit knowledge the key to the strategic alignment of intellectual capital. *Planning Review, 24*(2), 10–16.

Seleim, A. A. S., & Khalil, O. E. M. (2011). Understanding the knowledge management–intellectual capital relationship: A two-way analysis. *Journal of Intellectual Capital, 12*(4), 586–614.

Steiber, A. (2018). *Management in the Digital Age. Springer Briefs in Business*.

Wang, Z., Wang, N., & Liang, H. (2014). Knowledge sharing, intellectual capital and firm performance. *Management Decision, 52*(2), 230–258.

Yang, J., Brashear, T. G., & Asare, A. (2015). The value relevance of brand equity, intellectual capital and intellectual capital management capability. *Journal of Strategic Marketing, 23*(6), 543–559.

Chapter 6

Learning Cultures Grow Minds

Chapter Summary

This chapter defines a learning culture and discusses the relationship between knowledge and learning. The authors explain why learning is essential to bringing knowledge to life and incentivizing knowledge flows and use. The chapter addresses the interplay between knowledge and learning cultures. A key point in the chapter is the value of mistakes as learning opportunities. The authors explain how mistakes are viewed in the industrial economy and how this perspective impedes critical organizational learning. Specifically, we define mistakes, explain the double cognitive bias of mistakes, explain the tendency and impact of hiding mistakes, the side effects of double mistake bias, learn to learn from mistakes, and take on the challenge of reconciling mistake acceptance and avoidance. Finally, the chapter addresses the importance of cultivating a learning climate to realize your learning culture.

Why We Care About A Learning Culture?

Organizations sustain their competitive advantage in modern markets through continuous learning, systematic improvements, and adaptation. Dynamic capabilities support this process (Teece, 2018). Dynamic capabilities are higher-level organizational competencies that enable smooth adaptability based on the internal changes brought about by continuous collective double- and triple-loop learning. These collectively developed dynamic competencies require shared organizational attitudes, e.g., openness to continuous learning, perseverance in continual learning, unlearning and re-learning, and resilience to adversities. Innovation depends on positive attitudes toward continuous learning, experimentation, risk-taking, critical thinking, boundary spanning and breaking, and making mistakes. Not only do they spur innovation, but they also enhance a company's prospects for long-term sustainability.

Learning cultures feed every organizational learning process. These learning processes, in turn, build dynamic capabilities, innovativeness, and sustainability (Klein, 2022; Romme & van Witteloostuijn, 1999). According to Kucharska and Bedford (2020), learning cultures contain components vital to building an organization's

The Cultures of Knowledge Organizations: Knowledge, Learning, Collaboration (KLC), 95–122
Copyright © 2023 by Wioleta Kucharska and Denise Bedford
Published under exclusive licence by Emerald Publishing Limited
doi:10.1108/978-1-83909-336-420231006

ability to adapt to change and develop organizational intelligence. These vital components are a learning climate and an accepting attitude toward mistakes. According to Kucharska and Bedford (2020), learning cultures contain components essential for adaptability to change and the development of organizational intelligence. The critical components in any learning culture are a learning climate and a mistake-acceptance. Such a dynamic learning culture may conflict with the cultures of knowledge organizations that focus only on exploiting static knowledge. Learning cultures are dynamic, continuously improving, and continuously looking beyond the status quo through a shared state of mind. Continuous learning cultures facilitate all the learning that happens in an organization. There is no growth without learning. It is why an organization must successfully design and implement a learning culture.

Learning Culture – Definitions and Characterizations

An organizational learning culture is described as an organization's ability to create, acquire, and exchange knowledge, modify its behaviors and choices (Garvin, 1993), and integrate that new knowledge and insights into its organizational knowledge. Islam et al. (2015) defined a knowledge culture as a set of norms and practices that secures the conditions to support the flow of knowledge across an organization. The knowledge paradox cautions that where knowledge cultures are embedded in bureaucratic and hierarchical organizational cultures, they may lead only to passive use of the existing knowledge. This alignment may not expand the minds or knowledge capital of individuals or the organization. The antidote to this problem appears in the organization's learning culture. Kucharska and Bedford (2020) found that an organizational learning climate where mistakes are accepted and used as learning opportunities has a significant positive effect on developing an organization's intelligence.

Research also reminds us that fiefs and clan cultures, and adhocracy and clan cultures (Boisot, 2010; Cameron & Quinn, 2006; Tseng, 2010) are more suitable designs for developing an organization's learning capabilities – at the individual, team, and organizational levels (Wiewiora et al., 2013, 2019). These organizational culture types are also better suited to developing more advanced levels of organizational learning. They go beyond single-loop learning (i.e., learning to do better what we have always done) to double-loop learning (i.e., learning to do what is needed now and in the future to create value), and triple-loop learning (i.e., continuously learning how to learn). Triple-loop learning cultivates learning as a core organizational capability (Argyris, 1976; Klein, 2022).

A knowledge culture is a foundation for organizational growth in a knowledge-driven economy (Powell & Snellman, 2004). But only knowledge cultures grounded in proactive and forward-looking learning cultures will achieve this result. Passive knowledge cultures alone are insufficient to foster business growth and value. In a passive knowledge culture, the real value of an organization's knowledge cannot be realized because the essential properties of knowledge are unrealized, i.e., knowledge is not exchanged and does not flow. Therefore, static knowledge or stored knowledge does not gain or generate business value. As Rothberg and Erickson (2017) stated, knowledge in action requires strategic and tactical intelligence, which derives from the organization's intellectual capital and knowledge processes. Nonaka and Takeuchi (1995, 2019) noted that continuous innovation results from a company continuously and repeatedly creating new knowledge, disseminating the knowledge, and converting the knowledge into new knowledge and action.

Knowledge is Power, But Learning is Everything

An organization's ability to learn is critical to building dynamic capabilities. Winter (2003) characterizes this organizational capability as higher-level change routines that help an organization adapt to the new economic reality. Learning cultures enable organizations to move beyond the status quo and to grow beyond their existing knowledge base. Learning cultures cannot exist in a knowledge vacuum. They must be grounded in productive knowledge cultures. Knowledge cultures facilitate the creation and distribution of knowledge (Aramburu et al., 2015). They reflect the value an organization assigns to relevant, pertinent knowledge and expertise to guide its behaviors, choices, and decisions. Where a knowledge culture predominates in an organization and is paired with a continuous learning culture actively engaged in knowledge creation and exchange, the organization will thrive in the knowledge economy. In contrast, organizations that focus on maintaining the status quo, maintaining current knowledge levels, and storing and protecting explicit knowledge will not perform as well.

Knowledge cultures are foundations for learning cultures. Where an organization is struggling to achieve the goal of transitioning to a knowledge organization, the challenge is likely an unbalanced focus on and investment in static and explicit data and information assets. These are essential elements in an organization's knowledge capital stock, but they are insufficient to realize the transition. Organizations that value and continue to invest in traditional, low-risk "proven methods" and behaviors rather than in risk-tolerant, double- and triple-loop learning will fall short. They lose the opportunity to learn from mistakes and risk thinking about new methods and solutions. Organizations that build their stocks of proven knowledge, adhere to a bureaucratic culture that limits organizational methods of acting tan follow the rules of "how things are done here," and this way give precedence to controlled, safe, well-known routines that unfortunately stunt the organization's growth and competitiveness in the new economy.

Kucharska and Rebelo (2022a) proved that organizational learning cultures facilitate novel tacit knowledge sharing and discourage tacit knowledge hiding. Knowledge cultures do not have the same direct effect but provide a foundation for encouraging the curiosity that leads to learning. This finding is in line with Webster and Pearce (2008), who highlighted the meaning of learning cultures. They stressed the importance of aligning the focus on knowledge with situational learning opportunities. Situational learning is critical because it represents daily business challenges an organization must address. Learning in the situation – learning on and off the job – will generate the most significant value for an organization. This business context is where new ideas and methods are suggested and tested, mistakes are made, learned from, and new proven solutions emerge.

In other words, it is where learning, unlearning, and re-learning occur. A dynamic business environment will generate new challenges and create new solutions. Sorting through and testing new ideas naturally produces mistakes. These mistakes create valuable learning opportunities. Where mistake tolerance and acceptance are not part of the learning culture, learning opportunities will be lost, and the effect on the organization's ability to learn will be blocked.

Learning cultures that do not accept mistakes as a part of learning process is an illusion rather than an authentic learning cultures. Can we learn without mistakes? Kucharska and Rebelo (2022b) empirically demonstrated that continuous learning culture driven by transformational leadership are vital for promoting the tacit knowledge articulation and sharing that drives an organization's ability to adapt to change. This conclusion is consistent with Kucharska's (2021a, 2022a, 2022b) research that addressed the meaning and effect of the knowledge paradox. Tacit knowledge fuels every other type of knowledge capital and is at the heart of effective knowledge exchange (Kucharska & Rebelo, 2022a). Where tacit knowledge is hidden or hoarded, every other form of knowledge capital will be sub-optimized. Creating a learning culture devoted to dynamic capabilities, transformation, organizational reframing, continuous development, experimentation, and innovation requires a risk-tolerance climate that sees mistakes as learning opportunities. Innovative activities always carry risks. Learning organizations continually strive to balance exploiting proven knowledge to ensure organizational security and safety and seeking new knowledge and methods grounded in learning and collaboration. The former is driven by a knowledge culture, whereas the latter is learning culture driven.

Achieving a balance among these three factors – knowledge, learning, and collaboration – facilitates the building and flow of knowledge assets. Each is essential to building intellectual capital (Van Wijk et al., 2012). Kucharska (2021a) discovered variations among the three but highlighted their interdependencies. Kucharska noted that tipping the balance in favor of knowledge cultures can lead to an excessive concentration on explicit knowledge, its predictable and static exploitation, and a lower valuation of risks and mistakes. New ideas and methods always come with risks. Testing and applying new ideas and methods adds another level of risk. Some organizations are risk averse, preferring to "keep things as they are." In the end, this business strategy will stifle their development. In contrast, organizations that balance cultures and adopt a risk-tolerant learning culture will lead to continuous, dynamic knowledge acquisition. It will also generate "intelligence in action" (Erickson & Rothberg, 2012).

Therefore, the culture of knowledge seems to be an essential element in building human capital in the knowledge economy context, but it also seems insufficient without a learning culture. Thus, developing a learning culture appears vital in supporting a constant circulation of knowledge across an organization. Watkins and Marsick (1996) noted that a

> learning organization must capture, share, and use knowledge so
> its members can work together to change how the organization
> responds to challenges. People must question the old, socially

constructed, and maintained ways of thinking. And the process must be continuous because becoming a learning organization is a never-ending journey. (p. 4)

In light of this definition of a learning organization, a learning culture appears to be crucial for organizational performance and development (Rebelo & Gomes, 2017). However, its effectiveness decreases without implementing a knowledge culture that provides the basis for learning.

Learning Culture and Knowledge Culture

Knowledge-oriented organizations focus more on static knowledge exploitation, whereas learning organizations focus more on dynamic, constantly breaking "the status quo." Furthermore, knowledge culture is presented here as a base for learning culture based on all stated before. It is easy to predict that if any organization is stuck in the knowledge-orientation stage, then it exists in a reality where static exploitation of knowledge dominates. In organizations, old, proven methods of cultivating acting are more appreciated than new solutions seeking and risk; consequently, mistakes tied to this risk are avoided. Organizations based chiefly on proven knowledge often prefer to "keep things as they are" and that "safe, well-known routines control-oriented" organizational attitude might block these organizations' development.

Therefore, building human capital is critical in the knowledge economy context. A pervasive and persistent learning culture is essential to developing and growing human capital in learning organizations in the current economic climate of continuous change. Knowledge is power, but learning is everything – it leads to up-to-date knowledge fitted to dynamic business environment realities. An organizational learning culture can facilitate the creation and sharing of knowledge and discourage the hoarding or hiding knowledge. By itself, a knowledge culture does not have this effect, though it is a basis for fostering curiosity and exposing knowledge gaps that lead to learning. This finding is consistent with the research of Webster and Pearce (2008), who highlighted the importance of situational learning, which is essential to active learning. Situational learning is aligned with the current context. It is especially relevant today in a dynamic and rapidly changing business environment. Acting in such a dynamic business environment might naturally cause many mistakes. And the lack of mistakes acceptance component of a learning culture can block learning from them at the organizational level. Therefore, a learning culture that does not include a mistakes acceptance component is an illusion.

Kucharska and Rebelo (2022a, 2022b), based on their explored relationships between knowledge and learning cultures, noted the difference between knowledge-oriented and learning-oriented organizations. Namely, if we assume that knowledge culture dominates in knowledge-driven organizations and the constant learning culture characterizes learning organizations, then based on the presented model, it can be assumed that a knowledge orientation is a before-stage of learning orientation.

Case Study – Medical University

Martha is a chief nurse in a university hospital. She likes her job very much. Asked about the company culture, she quickly responded that the dominant culture was a knowledge culture. "If you do not have a certain level of medical knowledge, you will not be allowed near a patient." Each morning all students – from the first to third year – must pass a short exam in their medical specialization. Whether they passed the exam yesterday or two months ago, they must pass it before beginning their rounds. Medicine is not just a science but also a practice. Through traditional passive class-based learning methods, medical students build their tacit medical knowledge from explicit sources. But the essence of medical practice is expanding the "book learning" through working with patients – expanding their tacit knowledge by solving real-world patient challenges. Martha explains, "Successful medicine is a continuous interpretation and translation – 'knowledge in action.' Even if you know the textbook explanation of how a human body reacts to a particular medication or treatment, you need to understand how a particular body will react. Each reaction is specific to a person, depending on their genetics, lifestyle, and health history. An individual's medical condition is the determining factor in their recovery. Every medical practitioner needs to leverage their knowledge and intelligence to understand that medical condition. Deriving an effective remedy for any patient means collaborating with the patient and the whole medical team on every shift. Those medical practitioners on the job at any given time affect the solutions needed. The experience with patients and the shift team's medical practices is paramount. So, in my opinion," – Martha says – "The successful hospital must develop and balance its knowledge, learning and collaboration cultures. This environment creates opportunities for better patient care, cures and remedies. Medical practice is dynamic because it must translate the generic 'all patient' tacit knowledge into practical medicine for an individual patient. Knowledge is adapted from the specific advice in each instance. I am responsible for nurses in our department, and we adapted our working methods three times last year. We are satisfied with our current practices, but I have some fresh ideas for improving them. It is how we think about our work. We want every patient to have an optimal experience."

What do we learn from this?

We learn that the essence of change and adaptability lies in the organization's capacity for double- and triple-loop learning grounded in its culture. Both knowledge and learning cultures are important, but it is the learning culture that is essential. It generates continuous growth and development. Personal knowledge growth and investment is the dominant learning motivation. Learning fosters knowledge development, and a knowledge culture strengthens employees' positive attitudes and motivation to develop their learning capacity. Kucharska and

Bedford (2020) observed that well-balanced dependencies between knowledge and learning cultures increase an organization's capacity to adapt to change. It is particularly evident where the learning climate is risk and mistake tolerant. They define a "learning climate" as a high capacity for learning across the workforce and solid organizational encouragement for individuals and teams to discover, create, and implement new ideas. The tolerance for mistakes is reflected in the fact that mistakes are treated as learning opportunities. The company workforce understands that mistakes have positive learning consequence and tolerate them within defined limits. As a result, employees feel free to admit mistakes and discuss them openly without suffering criticism or blame. Kucharska and Bedford (2020) observed that these components of a continuous learning culture are equally crucial for learning organizations.

Learning Culture "Mistakes Acceptance" Component

Mistakes are among the most common of human experiences and one of the least appreciated. Yet, they are vital for learning (Guchait et al., 2018; Simonsson & Heide, 2018). True and deep learning does not occur without mistakes (Van Dyck et al., 2005). Therefore, we assume that learning from mistakes is an opportunity to generate new tacit human capital. Saint-Onge (1996) explains that tacit knowledge and other forms of human capital are of a higher value than other forms because they are critical to developing new ideas and innovation. Human capital comprises an individual's domain knowledge, skills and competencies, intuition, personal beliefs, assumptions, attitudes, values, and lifelong and life-wide experiences.

As Polanyi (1966) observed, individuals know more than they can tell and more than they can logically explain (Dörfler & Ackermann, 2015). It is easier to sense or observe an individual's human capital than to define it, particularly during the very early stages of its development. Asher and Popper (2019) "onion" model describes the decomposition of tacit knowledge through its various layers. The onion model identifies three layers of progressive "tacitness," including (1) a hidden practical layer, (2) a tacit reflective layer, and (3) a demonstrated layer. The degree of tacitness determines an individual's awareness of their ability to articulate and share that human capital. Tacit knowledge sharing depends on many factors, particularly an individual's trust, collaborative inclinations, the overall learning climate, and the psychological safety of the environment (Andersson et al., 2020; Kucharska & Kowalczyk, 2016). The ability to make mistakes and learn from them creates ideal conditions for exposing and sharing our tacit knowledge. A rich learning culture, a foundation for mistakes, acceptance, and tolerance are vital for human capital development in a productive learning culture.

The truth is, though, that mistakes are rarely seen as learning opportunities. In an industrial economy culture, mistakes are seen as unwelcome variations from accepted quality control standards. They are to be avoided or downplayed in all instances. They are often perceived as a negative externality of human learning. Instead, they can be a valuable source of learning and growth when acknowledged. We cannot learn from mistakes if we are not aware of them. Mistakes can be overlooked as valuable learning opportunities and deliberately ignored through marginalization, suppression, and hiding. Nonaka and Takeuchi (1995, 2019) stressed that continuous innovation results when companies continuously and repeatedly create new knowledge. Multi-level organizational learning is critical for creating new knowledge and building the organization's knowledge capital. The learning culture and acceptance and tolerance are sound stimuli for learning skills development at the individual level and learning capacity development at the team and organizational levels. Mistakes occur despite all due diligence and where established knowledge procedures and policies are respected and carefully followed. A learning culture that accepts and tolerates mistakes does not result from a lack of due diligence, negligence or observance of process. Instead, it represents an intent to design a learning culture open to continuous internal reframing grounded on learning from mistakes. Errors will occur naturally if we even if rules, processes, and procedures are respected. Mistakes at every functional level tell us that "something is wrong" and change or correction is needed. In such a context, mistakes are valuable business opportunities that can't be ignored or hidden in a learning organization. The analysis of the occurrence of the mistake brings new ideas, knowledge and alternatives. Responses to mistakes create opportunities to brainstorm and engage in deep knowledge sharing. Responses provide value to the mistake maker, the functional team, and the entire organization.

What Is a Mistake?

Errors, mistakes, and failures all have unintended and varying effects. Perceiving, defining, and managing each varies with the organizational context and the economic sector (Kucharska, 2021a, 2021b, 2021c, 2021d; Kucharska & Rebelo, 2022a, 2022b). Production sector errors are seen as a deviation from norms. This term is often used in error management studies in the broader production literature (Love et al., 2018; Seckler et al., 2017). A mistake is usually associated with a wrong decision (Mangels et al., 2006). Failure is conceptualized as the lack of the desired effect, and it includes avoidable mistakes and the inevitable adverse outcomes of risk taken, such as in experiments or new venture creation (Cannon & Edmonson, 2001; Politis & Gabrielsson, 2009). In a highly dynamic networked economy, uncertainty failure can occur equally in negligence and diligence conditions. Such failures and uncertain conditions are characteristic of early-stage entrepreneurs (e.g., those launching startups) or mature entrepreneurs seeking new business opportunities.

Senders and Moray (1991) define errors as acts that are (1) unintended by the actor, (2) at variance with a set of rules, (3) undesirable to an external observer, or (4) a condition that has placed a task or system beyond its acceptable limits that may negatively affect the organization. Something unintended, though, can sometimes create new opportunities when seen from a new perspective and an open mind. Frese and Keith (2015) defined mistakes as (1) unintended variations from plans and goals, (2) a result of inadequate feedback processing, or (3) incorrect actions resulting from a lack of knowledge. These definitions are grounded in industrial economy cultures and strategies that value control and conformance to quality norms over learning and innovation. Mistakes are the perfect solution to a critical gap in our knowledge cultures. It is why mistakes should be appreciated and valued. Error management can help us to understand mistakes constructively. It is challenging to shift perspectives in organizational cultures with a negative bias for mistakes and variations from established norms. From a cultural perspective, such a negative bias and value translated to individuals' cognitive bias, assumptions and beliefs. However, the organization is made up of people, and people will adhere to established values if that is what is required to succeed in the organization.

Consequently, a learning organization is defined as an organization whose people learn. The bias against learning from mistakes inhibits learning culture development. To learn from mistakes, we must first acknowledge and accept them. The studies by Farnese et al. (2019, 2020) stressed the importance of cultural orientation in learning from errors. Vanderheiden and Mayer (2020) further highlighted the cultural factor of mistake perception.

The Double Cognitive Bias of Mistakes

There is no learning without mistakes. Accepting errors is an essential part of continuous learning. There is confusion where there is a positive attitude and belief toward learning and a negative attitude toward mistakes. This confusion can lead to bias that may affect individual, organizational, and societal learning abilities. Errors can lead to blaming. How errors are viewed can affect the personal attribution of individuals – it can affect their attitudes and behaviors (Roese & Vohs, 2012). Errors often are seen as indicators of negligence or lack of intelligence (Mangels et al., 2006). This bias is even more problematic for a society's sustainable growth. It is further compounded by the common belief that "bosses never make mistakes." Kucharska et al. (2023) empirically exposed the double cognitive bias of mistakes' impact on organizational intelligence by weakening collaborative and learning cultures and blocking tacit knowledge creation.

The mistake itself is seen negatively. And when a mistake, error or failure occurs, it may create a negative perception of the mistake maker's self-identity and social identity. The fear of being seen as "incompetent" or a "loser" might lead to counterproductive behaviors in managers. These counterproductive behaviors may include blaming others, risk avoidance, knowledge rejection, or knowledge hiding (Kucharska & Rebelo, 2020a, 2020b). Leaders' counterproductive behaviors can block organizational collaboration and learning capabilities and damage trust among organizations and society.

Organizations and their leaders have been slow to adopt error management. Dimitrova and Hooft (2021) discuss error acceptance, correction, and learning from errors. These authors suggest that, at first glance, the key challenge is the negative image created by the mistake maker. The critical question is how managers can claim their own mistakes, learn from them, and safeguard their professional images. The solution is a culture of continuous learning.

Taking a hermeneutic approach to social constructivism theory, Gergen (1985) describes social cognition as the collective coming to an understanding. Gergen describes social cognition as a dynamic, multi-directional, and multi-faceted adaptation during which society organizes world experiences. Social cognition gives meaning to particular experiences collectively through the communal interchange.

The meaning of a mistake and its actor's social identity is a collective process. Culture plays an essential role in this process as a carrier of meanings. In a nutshell, culture determines how we understand and interpret elements of reality (e.g., error, mistake, failure). As a result, the cognizant agent (e.g., error actor) independently constructs an internal image of the event that relates to all their experiences. At the same time, Lawrence (2006) tells us that error actors are culturally conditioned by the groups of reference, i.e., representatives of a particular profession, organization, sector, or nation.

Learning Culture as Organizational Antidote to the Double Cognitive Bias of Mistakes

Organizations must cultivate cultures that address mental biases and beliefs against mistakes. A culture that can overcome these biases is vital to the success of organizational learning. This double bias in organizations today addresses two critical attitudes and beliefs: (1) *Mistakes are wrong* and (2) *Bosses never make mistakes*. We learn the first bias early in our primary education. We learn the second in our work environments and organizations. These assumptions and beliefs are translated into organizational values – those who do not make mistakes are more likely to be promoted. High performance without risks and flaws will be rewarded over those who make and learn from mistakes. If we cannot demonstrate excellence, we may no longer be valued by the organization and may be considered dispensable. These biases also influence the behaviors of managers – they must maintain an image of high performance and success, an illusion that can block their learning, growth, and development.

This bias has significant consequences for experienced employees and higher-level management, whose performance is expected to meet a higher standard without flaws or errors. This mistake avoidance or mistake intolerance value system causes these individuals to fear mistakes and be risk-averse. As a result, these individuals significantly influence the company culture and value system. High-risk aversity will lead to low levels of learning. As a result, organization-wide mistake intolerance and risk aversity may lead to lower levels of learning. And lower organizational learning will affect the organization's ability to develop dynamic capabilities and adapt to change. It is a compelling argument for implementing organizational learning cultures grounded on assumptions and beliefs in the value of mistakes.

Without organizational learning, organizational innovativeness is unsustainable in the new knowledge economy (Choi & Chandler, 2020). Learning with the opportunities provided by mistakes is suboptimal (Van Dyck et al., 2005). Everyone makes mistakes, especially those who look beyond the current environment, seek new horizons, break conventions, and invest in their learning and knowledge capital. When shared, the knowledge gained from mistakes can be a valuable lesson for others. Mistakes are unavoidable – they are an element of human existence – but they have particular value in the dynamic knowledge economy. Unfortunately, this basic assumption is not widely recognized in organizations today. The strong value system of statistical management in the industrial economy and its strong quality control values makes the shift challenging for many managers.

Organizations should ensure that mistake acceptance and tolerance values are translated to mistake acceptance. And, thanks to learning, they should ensure that managing mistakes leads to improvement, mastery, and prevention. Managers must demonstrate and reinforce by example and through encouragement that mistakes are learning opportunities. They should demonstrate through their actions that seeing and managing mistakes, i.e., making all effort to anticipate and resolve them, is part of how an organization works. However, organizational cultures can create cognitive bias in assumptions and beliefs where complete mistake avoidance is both espoused and reinforced. This cognitive bias may also lead to the unconscious hiding of knowledge gained from making and learning from mistakes. As a result, the value of what has been learned may only be known to an individual and not leveraged across the workforce. It may also encourage individuals to hide the tacit knowledge they gained by making and fixing a mistake. Organizations can shift these traditional biases by encouraging workers to manage mistakes, engage in learning, and seek out and learn from mistakes; organizations can shift these traditional biases.

In a constructive learning environment, workers understand it is safe to report a mistake and discuss it without shame, blame, or fear (Ferguson, 2017). In a learning climate, they may remain open-minded, be open to learning lessons from any situation, positive or negative, and gain valuable new knowledge. Learning cultures that foster rich learning climates and accept mistakes can transform values, beliefs, attitudes, and behaviors. It is a power that learning culture offer over knowledge culture.

Accepting mistakes in a work context can be controversial because of the cognitive bias introduced by earlier industrial economy cultures. In those cultures, mistakes were unwanted variations from well-controlled and statistically managed business processes. Mistakes were often seen as the result of someone's negligence or oversight. It indicates something gone wrong rather than simply a different-than-expected effect. In a prism of a learning culture, when an unexpected result of our action occurs, it does not always signify that something went wrong. Instead, it is seen as a new learning opportunity to improve how we think and work.

When we have the cognitive capacity to see mistakes differently, we create new learning opportunities and potential innovations. Groundbreaking innovations have resulted from clear failures and failed experiments. Consider Silver's development of *sticky notes* at 3M. Silver was a chemist striving to develop solid adhesives in the aerospace industry. Instead of finding solid adhesives, he invented weak glue that could be repeatedly peeled off without leaving a trace on the surface. The research was a total failure when measured against its original goal. However, it created a whole new market around a new product with broad appeal. It was a tremendous business success that redefined the company's consumer base. We see a result as a success or a failure entirely due to our interpretation and perspective. When we can learn from every mistake, mistakes will not signal failure. A mistake is just a lesson, sometimes with near-term costs but always with long-term value. And the value is always worth the cost! Even if the immediate result's impact is insignificant, mistakes offer us an opportunity to grow our individual and collective capacity to learn and innovate. Therefore, learning from small mistakes is better than avoiding them entirely.

Hiding Mistakes – The Side Effect of the Double Cognitive Bias of Mistakes

The consequences of hiding and suppressing mistakes are exponential (Hobfoll et al., 2018). The resulting loss of knowledge can generate the loss of several other resources. First, there is an opportunity loss and resource waste when we do not learn from experience, from our own mistakes, and the mistakes of others. *Mistakes are precious, everyday human experiences. Without recognizing and accepting them, we can neither understand their meaning nor learn from them.* Therefore, it is critical to shift from a culture of "espoused perfection" (which is radical and harmful) to a culture of "authentic learning." It changes an organization's assumptions, beliefs, and values from radical and harmful to business to agile, constructive, and evolutionary. Authentic learning cultures provide opportunities to re-humanize humans by enabling mental change, allowing for interpretations and translations of personal experiences and mistakes, and developing shared frames of reference through critical reflection. This authentic learning culture creates an environment where dynamic organizational capabilities will grow. *This shift offers a high business gain.* Employees with learning mindsets are open to change. They "are ready to be wrong," as Senge (2006) explains the essence of learning. Therefore, organizations must be ready to be wrong if they hope to generate value from their employees' learning and constantly develop their human capital.

Positive Attitude Towards Learning from Mistakes

Many positive examples of learning from mistakes have emerged from entrepreneurship, i.e., entrepreneurial learning from business failures (e.g., Cardon et al., 2011; Cope, 2011; Eggers & Song, 2015; McGrath, 1999; Politis & Gabrielsson, 2009; Yamakawa & Cardon, 2015). Recent studies from the hospitality sector (Guchait et al., 2015, 2016, 2018; Jung & Yoon, 2017; Pasamehmetoglu et al., 2017; Wang et al., 2020) reduce the organizational attitude toward errors to a single question – should mistakes at work be tolerated? The research suggests that error tolerance yields positive employee outcomes, including psychological safety, self-efficacy, supportive employee behaviors, learning, and increased error reporting rates. These outcomes speak directly to essential types of tacit human, structural, and relational capital. The new advice and guidance are that errors should be tolerated. And not just tolerated but valued because they result in improved work engagement and service recovery performance.

Anderson and Abrahamson (2017) explained that simple reporting mistakes do not result in learning. Learning from mistakes must happen individually, within groups and teams, and ultimately across the organization. At all levels, it involves sharing rather than hiding knowledge, insights and lessons learned from exploring and resolving mistakes. Sharing up and across the levels generates a cumulative growth of intellectual capital. And, given the essential economic properties of knowledge capital, a cumulative increase also means an exponential increase. In complex and multi-level organizations, learning from sharing mistakes can also generate cost efficiencies, economies of scale and scope in capital creation (Argyris & Schon, 1978; Wiewiora et al., 2019). Oswald and Mascarenhas (2019) emphasize the importance of critical thinking in knowledge creation. Critical thinking is critical to transforming the experience we gain from mistakes into new knowledge. Transforming personal experience into new knowledge relies on tacit mental processes, i.e., listening, translation, interpretation, evaluation, and absorption.

Sharing the tacit knowledge inherent in the experience of making and resolving mistakes requires specific personal characteristics that can affect both formal and informal processes. These personal characteristics, i.e., human capital such as attitudes, behaviors, emotional intelligence, social competencies, and so on, can facilitate or impede the flow of new knowledge. Critical personal characteristics also include openness to new ideas and experiences (Loh et al., 2013), emotional control and metacognition (Keith & Frese, 2005), goal orientation (Heimbeck et al., 2003), and critical thinking abilities (Oswald & Mascarenhas, 2019). These characteristics are critical to shifting the perception of mistakes and how we see them.

Frese and Keith (2015) and Weinzimmer and Esken (2017) studied learning from mistakes and observed that deep organizational learning is rooted in identifying and resolving errors. It is core to the organization's approach to error management. Historically, error management is defined as an organizational strategy to minimize the negative consequences of errors through early detection and correction and to prevent errors through learning (Deming, 1981; Van Dyck et al., 2013). In this context, cultures that value the exposure and leveraging of mistakes are critical to a knowledge organization's deep learning.

Error management in the information technology sector is classified into four categories – errors in methods, errors of people, errors in tools, and errors in requirements (Anu et al., 2018; De Felice & Petrillo, 2017). In the information technology field, we focus on detecting and correcting errors by applying statistical methods (e.g., Di Sanzo et al., 2021). These methods generally build on the early quality control concepts of W. Edward Deming (Juran et al., 2005) – to identify and detect any situation that varies from a norm or acceptable degree. Software development is a knowledge-intensive process. Logically, employees' cognitive failures are the primary cause of software errors (Balaji & Murugaiyan, 2012). Learning from mistakes in this field leverages individual and collective reflections throughout the software development lifecycle. It spans every development phase, from requirements to design to coding and testing. Errors may be discovered at the desk check stage, prototype stage, test stage, and operationalization stage. One effective method for discovering errors is the V model for testing (Akinsola et al., 2020). Other methods to improve the software development process include the capability maturity model (Huang & Liu, 2017) and the agile retrospective process in the Scrum method (Annosi et al., 2020). Agile retrospective learning also requires the support of culture.

Acceptance of Mistakes and the Mistakes Avoidance Challenge

Achieving a balance between avoiding and managing mistakes is challenging. Mistakes are never welcome; logically, we all want to avoid them. A negative attitude toward mistakes is a significant cultural and mental barrier. It is what we all have been taught from childhood. Given that mistakes are culturally negative values and beliefs, there is a natural unconscious bias against seeing them positively and as a potential source of learning. It explains why learning from mistakes is problematic and why learning cultures can be crucial for breaking through this bias.

For this reason, Kucharska and Rebelo (2022a) intentionally separated knowledge culture from learning culture in exploring those mechanisms that have an essential effect on knowledge sharing and hiding. In the broader context, these findings expose a need for formal and informal practices, attitudes and behaviors. The simultaneous mistakes avoidance and acceptance facilitate the mistakes reporting frequency that matters for organizational learning from mistakes. Such a balance is needed. Accepting that people make mistakes is needed for organizational learning. Mistake avoidance is needed for high performance and safety security. It is possible, because, regarding knowledge workers, no one intentionally makes a mistake at work; if so, it is sabotage, not a mistake (it is a huge difference). So, the company culture that esteems high performance focuses on learning and growth and understands human nature – introduced in this book the KLC culture approach – is a remedy for balancing superb performance and sustainability thanks to constant human capital development focus. It can facilitate the process of learning from mistakes. Their work exposed the essential paradox of organizations today – Employees have no opportunity to grow where errors are treated as undesirable events which should be hidden. Mentally and behaviorally, individuals will devote their tacit knowledge and skills to hiding their mistakes. Instead, employees will have opportunities to discover, learn, and grow when they do not regard mistakes as expected and routine events but as essential and exceptional opportunities. The intellectual effort devoted to hiding mistakes has little value for other individuals, teams, and the whole organization. In this situation, intellectual growth will not be equal to the growth of organizational intelligence. Potentially valuable learning opportunities and organizational knowledge will be lost because it has been hidden.

Unfortunately, most learning and knowledge-intensive organizations do not tolerate on-the-job mistakes made by employees. Mistakes are efficient learning methods for those who want to learn, but their effectiveness in the learning process needs further examination. Learning lessons from our own mistakes can be costly, particularly when the consequences of those mistakes are significant. In these cases, we may pay a price for the mistake without learning from it. The essence of the mistake paradox is that people cannot learn without making mistakes, but mistakes are problematic for management. Errors are commonly perceived as a phenomenon that should be eliminated, which is why employees often conceal their mistakes. Everyone makes mistakes, and everybody hides them. The lack of mistakes contributes to an artificial culture and image – an illusion of the work environment and the organization's performance. We encourage organizations to develop internal mechanisms that will allow them to leverage mistakes to transform performance through "lessons learned." Mistakes are the best source of new knowledge. New knowledge is vital to an organization's adaptability to change and intelligence development in the knowledge economy. Mature knowledge organizations that expect to learn from mistakes must develop appropriate supporting mechanisms.

Case Study – Medical University

I asked Martha, a nurse chief working in a medical university hospital, about her hospital's best practices regarding the implementation of learning from mistakes. "It is an overly sensitive but critical issue, especially for young doctors," – Martha said. "Young doctors at the early stage of their career want to prove themselves, but they lack practical experience. So, they take their own mistakes very seriously. Some are ashamed and try to hide them, and some report them immediately. Some lose self-confidence as a result, but others can be more narcissistic. It is the narcissistic group that hides their mistakes. Sometimes their ambitions to portray an image as a 'good doctor' are greater than their actual 'good doctor' practices." We noticed that the consequences of mistakes could affect fundamental patient safety and young doctors' human capital, personalities, professional skills, and reputations. This form of human capital has value and impact on their medical careers. And it has significant implications for the safety and well-being of their future patients.

For this reason, the hospital developed an error management policy to reify that hiding mistakes were unacceptable in the hospital culture. In the hospital culture, hiding mistakes is irresponsible and immature. It does not align with the hospital's core values.

Regarding the hospital's new policy, all mistakes must be immediately reported through the channels established within the administrative structure. But, the policy is more than reporting. Immediate reporting matters because it protects patients. Whatever assistance is needed to resolve the mistake is available immediately. It is a tremendous managing mistake and fundamental value. But we need more than reporting to learn from the experience and to shape new attitudes. Self-reflection is essential to drawing lessons learned from the event and achieving mental shifts. To make it effective, the hospital established a fundamental new rule and behavioral norm – that after each shift, all reported mistakes are discussed concisely and constructively within a team working on this shift. Such an after-action review enables quick lessons learned and best practices formulation that matters for working methods improvement and entire organizational learning. If something happens, the team is informed. It ensures that complete knowledge is shared, rather than partial or incorrect knowledge that may be shared through gossip. More importantly, the entire team can learn from this particular case. The team discussion aims to understand why this particular mistake occurred – was it through negligence or diligence? Mistakes can result from both – patients can have unexpected responses to treatments or therapies. Medicine is a practice as well as a science. If a mistake occurs through diligence, it is an opportunity to learn from it and avoid this particular practice or treatment for this patient. Reflection is the goal of this stage of mistake review and analysis. Staff referred to this new behavior as a "summary of the day" and expressed it with the phrases:

I learned today....; I learned it thanks to.......; The best practice I want to implement in the future is:.......; or What others can learn from my experience today is:.......... This new practice of team reflection enables the team to adapt and change its procedures to serve its patients better and achieve its goals.

The next option for knowledge sharing was an official mistake registration system, including (a) a context description, (b) a good behavior statement, (c) the indication of the mistake cause (human such as lack of knowledge, tiredness, routine, distraction), and (d) obligatory lesson learned formulation.

Finally, the most powerful lessons are discussed monthly at meetings to ensure that knowledge is disseminated. We care about the form of these meetings. It is vital to avoid stigmatizing individuals, particularly young doctors, as "mistake makers." Instead, it is vital to encourage people to share their knowledge and to allow everyone to learn. Meetings are opened by someone from the senior staff who shares their most valuable lesson learned from a mistake to demonstrate that everyone makes mistakes and mastery is gained by learning from mistakes. Meetings close with a discussion of the most interesting case – mistakes before they were resolved. The person presenting the most interesting, successful case must share their most recent "lesson learned from a mistake." We want to promote the assumption and belief that mastery comes from a long life and sustainable learning that does "no harm." It is an assumption and belief that aligns with the Hippocratic Oath – a core medical value – "Above all, do not harm." Creating and realizing a learning culture requires inner motivation and external support. Mentally accepting the fact that you made a grave medical mistake is never easy. We are here to support human life – not to oppose it. It is against our fundamental beliefs; this is why it is never easy.

The truth is that many factors influence how we think about mistakes. Young doctors work from these fundamental beliefs and ambitions as they strive to prove themselves as doctors, experienced staff, and critical and essential experts. Instead of a "fear, blame and shame climate," we promote a "learning climate." The pressure to be perfect and free of errors can lead to narcissism and ignorance. They can be serious impediments to learning. We promote humanism to reinforce the idea that those who deal with and learn from mistakes are as valuable as those who never make a mistake. Those who learn from their mistakes become better doctors, nurses, or workmates because they are open-minded and ready to "be wrong." Our policy aims to achieve sustainable learning across the whole staff. The policy focuses on diligence at work and recognizing that we are all human. And humans sometimes make mistakes even though they strive not to.

In sum, mistakes are an interesting source of new knowledge – they are, in a way, a "call for change" in individual and organizational behaviors. The empirical evidence aligns with the scanning, interpretation, learning, and incorporation phases of the metamodel for organizational change (Maes & Van Hootegem, 2019) and the central idea that the analysis of mistakes may initiate a change. When mistakes are transformed into meaning, organizations can generate new knowledge. However, there will be little new organizational knowledge that individuals or organizations are unwilling to learn. The same is true for unprepared organizations to leverage and learn from errors.

Individuals may strive to learn effectively and grow their human capital, but the value will not accrue to the whole organization if that knowledge is not shared. Paradoxically, if an organization is unprepared to accept mistakes, its employees may learn, but the organizational intelligence will not reap the benefit and will not grow (Kucharska & Bedford, 2020). Employees learn how to bypass the system, e.g., to avoid mistakes, and when they occur – as they will because to err is human – to cover them up. Increasing individual employees' intelligence is essential, but it does not necessarily mean that organizational intelligence will grow. Employees learn how to adapt to the espoused company norms and behaviors. When an organization does not make mistakes, it cannot learn from them. When it does not learn from mistakes, organizational knowledge cannot grow.

But at the same time, if makes are accepted, individuals have no incentive to learn. *Hence, a love-hate relationship with the acceptance of mistakes exists.* Mistakes are efficient in terms of adaptability to change, but only for those who want to learn from them. The essence of the mistake paradox is that people cannot learn without making mistakes, but mistakes are never welcomed. As noted, errors are commonly perceived as something that should be eliminated, which is why employees often conceal their mistakes. Since everybody makes mistakes and covers them up, it creates an illusion. Instead, organizations should be encouraged to behave intelligently and develop internal mechanisms that acknowledge and leverage the learning opportunities of mistakes. These mistakes have often been referred to as lessons learned in the past two decades.

The Learning Culture "Climate" Component

The fear of making a mistake and revealing it can discourage employees from sharing any knowledge they gained from experimenting, breaking the rules, and finding new ways of resolving those mistakes. As a result, mistakes might sometimes be ignored or hidden (Kucharska & Rebelo, 2022a, 2022b). Instead, accepting and recognizing *mistakes* as a source of learning is most effective in organizations with a strong learning climate. Valuing mistakes and a learning climate is critical to developing an authentic learning culture.

A *learning climate* is a mental, shared motivation and disposition to develop and change mental models, assumptions, and beliefs continually. By definition, a learning climate opens up minds. The learning climate is evident in organizations that can collectively retain an open mind. A particular mental disposition favors dynamic development rather than a static state. Learning climates can be reduced to a collective passion for improvement. Authentic learning cannot exist without a fundamental change of mindset, and a change of mindset cannot occur without a call for new learning. A change of perception always gives rise to a demand for deeper understanding and actions. The learning climate is essential to continuous culture-strategy alignment.

Organizational learning and change are interconnected (Argyris, 1982; Watad, 2019). Learning fosters change, and change stimulates learning. Organizational learning efficiently and effectively drives business challenges and provides resilient adaptation for rapid growth (Vithessonthi & Thoumrungroje, 2011). It provides a chance to learn and deliver unique value to the organization – for example, via innovations (Ghasemzadeh et al., 2019). Learning enhances the efficiency of business opportunities – change management (Li et al., 2014). Dynamic and uncertain environments require a culture oriented toward continuous, productive learning, which leads to innovative approaches (Rebelo & Gomes, 2011). Change can be considered a phenomenon tied to continuous learning and adaptation (Bahrami et al., 2019; Nadim & Singh, 2019). According to Yeo (2007), organizational learning cannot exist unless a change is noted in how employees confront their daily challenges and engage in defensive routines. Organizations that continuously renew their knowledge are better positioned to adapt to changes in the business environment and respond to them more quickly (Sanz-Valle et al., 2011). Moreover, knowledge processes cannot succeed without collaboration, including discovery and creation, transfer and exchange, encoding, storage, security, distribution, usage, and re-usage (Nonaka & Toyama, 2003).

Hence, the culture of knowledge must be a driver of collaborative work. Without collaboration and cooperation, there is no context for transforming passive knowledge into active knowledge. Also, collaboration is essential for transforming knowledge into intelligence. Moreover, employees learn faster when learning together and from one another (Poell & Van der Krogt, 2010). Knowledge culture fosters intelligence via collaborative learning, as demonstrated by Kucharska and Bedford (2020).

A continuously regenerating learning culture is essential for achieving sustainability because it generates continuous improvements and innovativeness (Kucharska, 2021a, 2021b, 2021c, 2021d). People with a learning mindset are persistently open to being wrong (Senge, 20), i.e., they accept that mistakes happen and that we can learn from them. Organizational learning cultures were initially understood to promote and support continuous learning at all levels of an organization. Rebelo and Gomes (2011) observed that effective organizational learning culture has as core values (1) a focus on people, (2) concern for all stakeholders, (3) stimulation of experimentation, (4) encouraging an attitude of responsible risk, (5) a readiness to recognize errors and learn from them, (6) promotion of open and intense communication, and (7) the promotion of cooperation, interdependence, and sharing of knowledge. They suggest that a learning culture must include the acceptance of mistakes to enable people to leave their comfort zone and solve problems by developing new approaches.

Higher levels of mistake acceptance foster learning processes, as demonstrated in the levels of adaptation to continuous change (Hind & Koenigsberger, 2008;

Thomas & Brown, 2011). Indeed, change is inevitable. Accepting this fact means recognizing that we must continuously adapt and learn. Watkins and Marsick (1996) noted that the first step in building a learning organization is to create the ability to learn and change. Organizational learning and change are interconnected (Argyris, 1982; Watad, 2019). Change can be inextricably linked to continuous learning and adaptation to change (Nadim & Singh, 2019). According to Yeo (2007), organizational learning cannot be said to exist where change is not inherent to the way employees confront problems and engage in defensive (against changes) routines. Organizations that continuously renew their knowledge are better positioned to adapt to business environment change and respond more quickly (Sanz-Valle et al., 2011).

Learning fosters change, and change stimulates learning. Learning requires motivation (Heckhausen et al., 2010). Learning occurs when we can observe organizational behaviors changing (Bahrami et al., 2016). An organizational learning climate reflects the organization's readiness to change its collective mental model where necessary. The assumptions and beliefs reinforce the expectation that this organizational change will generate new value.

The organizational learning climate drives business challenges and enables the organization to become resilient and adaptable for rapid growth (Vithessonthi & Thoumrungroje, 2011). It allows the organization to learn and deliver unique value through innovation. Learning enhances the efficiency of business opportunities change management. Dynamic and uncertain environments require a culture oriented toward continuous, productive learning. This continuous, productive learning leads to innovative approaches (Rebelo & Gomes, 2011). For these reasons, a learning culture is essential for knowledge organizations' continuous improvement, survival, and development (Van BredaVerduijn & Heijboer, 2016; Scott-Ladd & Chan, 2004). There is no better way to lead the company through a hyperdynamic economy with high uncertainty than through shared learning. The more agile organizational learning is, the better.

Case Study – Residential Development

Gabriela, a residential developer and the CEO of the Happy Future Company, noticed how people envisioned their dream properties had changed significantly pre- and post-COVID-19. Post-COVID, people prefer multifunction living spaces where they can live, work, and raise children. Those places and spaces with extensive gardens and terraces were in higher demand. In contrast, the market had become more challenging because consumers' purchasing power had decreased simultaneously. As a result, the distinctions in property market segments increased sharply. Developers in the property market must know which segments they want to target. Gabriela knew that property investments are long-term, and she must look beyond today to envision the market in five years. Her business success would be dependent upon her ability to project and predict.

Gabriela has operated in this market for over twenty years, so she understood the real estate adage – "Location, location, location." She decided to balance the risk and invest in a location with long-term stable value – the city center, which offers multifunction living in green spaces and places. The challenge was that buildings in these areas were costly, and the high price of properties must be offset by the value of perfect designs to attract sophisticated buyers. To hedge her post-pandemic risk, she decided to invest in properties in the second set of locations that resembled the city center properties but were much cheaper in the current market. Having well-located parcels, Happy Future could align its property offerings with the current market segments and demand.

To do this alignment well, she needed to continuously grow her knowledge about consumers and clients. It required a supportive learning climate. Gabriela noticed that the best attitude her employees could take in working with clients was to understand and accept their expectations and visions. So, Happy Future Company taught the sales force team to listen rather than speak and to observe rather than assume clients' expectations. Meanwhile, The Happy Future Analysts Division followed the market trends to understand changes in market segments. The challenge with market analysis is that the observed statistical trends tend to reflect earlier market conditions. Therefore, they may not be a vital source of current knowledge. However, the Happy Future Company understood it was only one part of the larger picture. Another critical part is the tacit knowledge from the customer-facing sales force team derived from their client interactions. It is tacit knowledge because it is individual observations and interpretations of clients' physical expressions and reactions – an unspoken language that tells real estate agents more about a client's reaction than their spoken words. Gabriela wanted her team to "feel the market." It was why employees working in investments and design divisions were obligated to spend one day per month working at the front desk in the Sales Department to listen and learn directly from clients. They summarized the "lessons learned" in a report.

Additionally, the most interesting "lessons learned" were interactively discussed and shared one day per quarter across all divisions. The most valuable lessons were discussed first within teams and divisions. Gabriela expected that the effects of these discussions would result in changes in procedures, policies, and behaviors. She wanted her organization to think critically about its actions and to make decisions that would lead to continuous improvement. "There is no future in this business without constant learning" – Gabriela says – "It is why all my people need to be open-minded every day if they want to be part of my team."

In sum, an organizational learning culture can facilitate the sharing of existing and new tacit knowledge and discourage the hiding of that tacit knowledge. An organizational learning climate can stimulate human capital growth. Knowledge culture has this potential and a basis for fostering the curiosity that will lead to learning. In and of itself, though, a knowledge culture is an essential but not a sufficient catalyst for organizational growth. Leaders seeking to foster organizational growth should support the design and implementation of knowledge cultures that drive authentic learning cultures. Authentic learning cultures nurture a learning climate and encourage a mistake-acceptance value system that supports human capital growth.

Assuming that human capital development is central to learning organizations, everything supporting this development has value. An organization's ability to implement a learning culture with both a learning climate and a mistakes acceptance value system as a source of learning has significant business value.

Internal policies supporting innovation should be rooted in the authentic learning culture, where the organizational climate motivates individuals to learn continuously and share the knowledge they gain from success and failure.

The learning culture approach presented in this book has two primary components – mistake acceptance and a learning climate. These critical components break with the conventions of "exaggerated excellence" and traditional pedagogical methods. These methods may call out those who make mistakes when learning. Pedagogy reflects the methods we use to teach children. A learning culture approach is more aligned with andragogy – the teaching and learning of adults. Mistakes have always been a part of human life and a common source of learning, creativity and innovation. This behavior is pervasive in human societies. It will persist whether organizations are comfortable with it or not. It is up to organizations to perceive mistakes as an opportunity for developmental change or to see them as a burden and concern. Based on the findings presented in this study, a love-hate relationship with accepting mistakes is recommended. Love them as an opportunity to learn and grow, and hate them when this opportunity is lost.

Chapter Review

After reading this chapter, you should be able to:

- define a learning culture.
- discuss the relationship between knowledge and learning.
- explain why learning is essential to bringing leveraging and achieving the value of knowledge.
- explain the interplay between knowledge cultures and learning cultures.
- describe the value of mistakes as learning opportunities.
- explain how mistakes are viewed in the industrial economy and how this perspective impedes critical organizational learning.
- define mistakes.
- explain the double cognitive bias of mistakes.
- explain the tendency and impact of hiding mistakes.

- explain the side effects of double mistake bias.
- define how to learn from mistakes.
- explain why it is essential to reconcile mistake acceptance and avoidance.
- why it is vital to cultivate a learning climate.

References and Recommended Future Readings

Akinsola, J. E. T., Ogunbanwo, A. S., Okesola, O. J., Odun-Ayo, I. J., Ayegbusi, F. D., & Adebiyi A. A. (2020). Comparative analysis of software development life cycle models (SDLC). In R. Silhavy (Ed.), *Intelligent algorithms in software engineering. CSOC 2020. Advances in Intelligent Systems and Computing* (Vol. 1224). Springer. https://doi.org/10.1007/978-3-030-51965-0_27

Anderson, J. G., & Abrahamson, K. (2017). Your health care may kill you: Medical errors. *Studies in Health Technology and Informatics, 234*, 13–17.

Andersson, M., Moen, O., & Brett, P. O. (2020). The organizational climate for psychological safety: Associations with SMEs' innovation capabilities and innovation performance. *Journal of Engineering and Technology Management, 55*, 101554. https://doi.org/10.1016/j.jengtecman.2020.101554

Annosi, M. C., Martini, A., Brunetta, F., & Marchegiani, L. (2020). Learning in an agile setting: A multi-level research study on the evolution of organizational routines. *Journal of Business Research, 110*, 554–566. https://doi.org/10.1016/j.jbusres.2018.05.011

Anu, V., Hu, W., Carver, J. C., Walia, G. S., & Bradshaw, G. (2018). Development of a human error taxonomy for software requirements: A systematic literature review. *Information and Software Technology, 103*, 112–124. https://doi.org/10.1016/j.infsof.2018.06.011

Aramburu, N., Sáenz, J., & Blanco, C. (2015). Structural capital, innovation capability, and company performance in technology-based Colombian firms. *Cuadernos de Gestión, 15*(1), 39–60. https://doi.org/10.5295/cdg.130427na

Argyris, C. (1976). *Increasing leadership effectiveness.* Wiley-Interscience.

Argyris, C. (1982). How learning and reasoning processes affect organizational change. In Goodman et al. (Eds.), *Change in organizations* (pp. 47–86). Jossey Bass.

Argyris, C., & Schön, D. A. (1997). Organizational learning: A theory of action perspective. *Reis, 77/78*, 345–348. https://www.jstor.org/stable/40183951?seq=1

Asher, D., & Popper, M. (2019). Tacit knowledge as a multilayer phenomenon: The 'onion' model. *The Learning Organization, 26*(3), 264–275. https://doi.org/10.1108/TLO-06-2018-0105

Bahrami, M. A., Kiani, M. M., Montazeralfaraj, R., Zadeh, H. F., & Zadeh, M. M. (2016). The mediating role of organizational learning in the relationship of organizational intelligence and organizational agility. *Osong Public Health and Research Perspectives, 7*(3), 190–196. https://doi.org/10.1016/j.phrp.2016.04.007

Balaji, S., & Murugaiyan, M. S. (2012). Waterfall vs V-model vs agile: A comparative study on SDLC. *International Journal of Information Technology and Business Management, 2*(1), 26–30.

Boisot, H. (2010). *Knowledge assets.* Oxford University Press.

Cameron, K. S., & Quinn, R. E. (2006). *Diagnosing and changing organizational culture: Based on the competing values framework.* Jossey-Bass.

Cannon, M. D., & Edmondson, A. C. (2001). Confronting failure: Antecedents and consequences of shared beliefs about failure in organizational work groups. *Journal of Organizational Behavior, 22*(2), 161–177. https://doi.org/10.1002/job.85

Cardon, M. S., Stevens, C. E., & Potter, D. R. (2011). Misfortunes or mistakes?: Cultural sensemaking of entrepreneurial failure. *Journal of Business Venturing, 26*(1), 79–92. https://doi.org/10.1016/j.jbusvent.2009.06.004

Choi, T., & Chandler, S. M. (2020). Knowledge vacuum: An organizational learning dynamic of how e-government innovations fail. *Government Information Quarterly, 37*, 101416. https://doi.org/10.1016/j.giq.2019.101416

Cope, J. (2011). Entrepreneurial learning from failure: An interpretative phenomenological analysis. *Journal of Business Venturing, 26*(6), 604–623. https://doi.org/10.1016/j.jbusvent.2010.06.002

De Felice, F., & Petrillo, A. (2017). *Theory and application on cognitive factors and risk management – New trends and procedures.* IntechOpen.

Deming, W. E. (1981). Improvement of quality and productivity through action by management. *National Productivity Review, 1*(1), 12–22.

Di Sanzo, P., Avresky, D. R., & Pellegrini, A. (2021). Autonomic rejuvenation of cloud applications as a countermeasure to software anomalies. *Software Practice and Experience, 51*(1), 46–71. https://doi.org/10.1002/spe.2908

Dimitrova, N. G., & van Hooft, E. A. J. (2021). In the eye of the beholder: Leader error orientation, employee perception of leader, and employee work-related outcomes. *Academy of Management Discoveries, 7*(4). https://doi.org/10.5465/amd.2019.0184

Dörfler, V., & Ackermann, F. (2015). Understanding intuition: The case for two forms of intuition. *Management Learning, 43*(5), 545–564. https://doi.org/10.1177/1350507611434686

Eggers, J. P., & Song, L. (2015). Dealing with failure: Serial entrepreneurs and the costs of changing industries between ventures. *Academy of Management Journal, 58*(6), 1785–1803. https://doi.org/10.5465/amj.2014.0050

Erickson, G. S., & Rothberg, H. (2012). *intelligence in action: Strategically managing knowledge assets.* Springer.

Farnese, M. L., Fida, R., & Picoco, M. (2020). Error orientation at work: Dimensionality and relationships with errors and organizational cultural factors. *Current Psychology.* https://doi.org/10.1007/s12144-020-00639-x

Farnese, M., Zaghini, F., Caruso, R., Fida, R., Romagnoli, M., & Sili, A. (2019). Managing care errors in the wards: The contribution of authentic leadership and error management culture, *The Leadership and Organization Development Journal, 40*(1), 17–30. https://doi.org/10.1108/LODJ-04-2018-0152

Ferguson, C. C. (2017). The emotional fallout from the culture of blame and shame. *JAMA Pediatrics, 171*(12), 1141. https://doi.org/10.1001/jamapediatrics.2017.2691

Frese, M., & Keith, N. (2015). Action errors, error management, and learning in organizations. *Annual Review of Psychology, 66*(1), 661–687.

Garvin, D. A. (1993). Building a learning organization. *Harvard Business Review, 71*(4), 78–91.

Gergen, K. J. (1985). The social constructionist movement in modern psychology. *American Psychologist, 40*(3), 266–275.

Ghasemzadeh, P., Nazari, J. A., Farzaneh, M., & Mehralian, G. (2019). Moderating role of innovation culture in the relationship between organizational learning and innovation performance. *The Learning Organization, 26*(3), 289–303. https://doi.org/10.1108/TLO-08-2018-0139

Guchait, P., Lee, C., Wang, C. Y., & Abbott, J. L. (2016). Impact of error management practices on service recovery performance and helping behaviors in the hospitality industry: The mediating effects of psychological safety and learning behaviors. *Journal of Human Resources in Hospitality and Tourism, 15*(1), 1–28. https://doi.org/10.1080/15332845.2015.1008395

Guchait, P., Paşamehmetoğlu, A., & Lanza-Abbott, J. (2015). The importance of error management culture in organizations: The impact on employee helping behaviors during service failures and recoveries in restaurants. *Journal of Human Resources in Hospitality and Tourism, 14*(1), 45–67. https://doi.org/10.1080/15332845.2014.904175

Guchait, P., Zhao, X., Madera, J., Hua, N., & Okumus, F. (2018). Can error management culture increase work engagement in hotels? The moderating role of gender. *Service Business, 12*(4), 757–778.

Heckhausen, J., Wrosch, C., & Schulz, R. (2010). A motivational theory of life-span development. *Psychological Review, 117*(1), 32–60. https://doi.org/10.1037/a0017668

Heimbeck, D., Frese, M., Sonnentag, S., & Keith, N. (2003). Integrating errors into the training process: The function of error management instructions and the role of goal orientation. *Personnel Psychology, 56*, 333–361. https://doi.org/10.1111/j.1744-6570.2003.tb00153.x

Hind, M., & Koenigsberger, J. (2008). Culture and commitment: The key to the creation of an action learning organization. *Action Learning: Research and Practice, 4*(1), 87–94. https://doi.org/10.1080/14767330701233939

Hobfoll, S. E., Halbesleben, J., Neveu, J.-P., & Westman, M. (2018). Conservation of resources in the organizational context: The reality of resources and their consequences. *Annual Reviews, 5*, 103–128. https://doi.org/10.1146/annurev-orgpsych-032117-104640

Huang, F., & Liu, B. (2017). Software defect prevention based on human error theories. *Chinese Journal of Aeronautics, 30*(3), 1054–1070. https://doi.org/10.1016/j.cja.2017.03.005

Islam, M. Z., Jasimuddin, S. M., & Hasan, I. (2015). Organizational culture, structure, technology infrastructure and knowledge sharing. *VINE Journal of Information and Knowledge Management Systems, 45*(1), 67–88. https://doi.org/10.1108/VINE-05-2014-0037

Jung, H. S., & Yoon, H. H. (2017). Error management culture and turnover intent among food and beverage employees in deluxe hotels: The mediating effect of job satisfaction. *Service Business, 11*(4), 785–802. https://doi.org/10.1007/s11628-016-0330-5

Juran, J., Taylor, F., Shewhart, W., Deming, E., Crosby, P., Ishikawa, K., Feigenbaum, A., Taguchi, G., & Goldratt, E. (2005). Quality control. *M. Juran: Critical Evaluations in Business and Management, 1*, 50.

Keith, N., & Frese, M. (2005). Self-regulation in error management training: Emotion control and metacognition as mediators of performance effects. *Journal of Applied Psychology, 90*(4), 677–691. https://doi.org/10.1037/0021-9010.90.4.677

Klein, J. T. (2022). Building capacity for transformative learning: Lessons from crossdisciplinary and cross-sector education and research. *Environmental Development and Sustainability, 24*, 8625–8638. https://doi.org/10.1007/s10668-021-01802-5

Kucharska, W. (2021a). Leadership, culture, intellectual capital and knowledge processes for organizational innovativeness across industries: The case of Poland. *Journal of Intellectual Capital, 22*(7), 121–141. https://doi.org/10.1108/JIC-02-2021-0047

Kucharska, W. (2021b). Do mistakes acceptance foster innovation? Polish and US cross-country study of tacit knowledge sharing in IT. *Journal of Knowledge Management, 25*(11), 105–128. https://doi.org/10.1108/JKM-12-2020-0922

Kucharska, W. (2021c). Wisdom from experience paradox: Organizational learning, mistakes, hierarchy and maturity issues. *Electronic Journal of Knowledge Management, 19*(2), 105–117. https://doi.org/10.34190/ejkm.19.2.2370

Kucharska, W. (2021d). Tacit knowledge awareness and sharing as a focal part of knowledge production. Polish-US View on IT, Healthcare, and Construction Industry. In S. Trzcielinski, B. Mrugalska, W. Karwowski, E. Rossi, & M. Di Nicolantonio (Eds.), *Advances in manufacturing, production management and process control. AHFE 2021. Lecture Notes in Networks and Systems* (Vol. 274). Springer. https://doi.org/10.1007/978-3-030-80462-6_20

Kucharska, W. (2022a). Tacit knowledge influence on intellectual capital and innovativeness in the healthcare sector: A cross-country study of Poland and the US. *Journal of Business Research, 149*, 869–883. https://doi.org/10.1016/j.jbusres.2022.05.059

Kucharska, W. (2022b). Tacit knowledge awareness and sharing as a focal part of knowledge production. In S. Trzcielinski et al. (Eds.), *Polish-US View on IT, Healthcare, and Construction Industry, AHFE 2021* (pp. 1–9). Springer Nature Switzerland. https://doi.org/10.1007/978-3-030-80462-6_20

Kucharska, W., & Bedford, D. A. D. (2020). Love your mistakes! – They help you adapt to change. How do knowledge, collaboration and learning cultures foster organizational intelligence?*Journal of Organizational Change Management, 33*(7), 1329–1354. https://doi.org/10.1108/JOCM-02-2020-0052

Kucharska, W., Bedford, D. A. D., & Kopytko, A. (2023). The double bias of mistakes – A measurement method. In *Proceedings of the 22nd European Conference on Research Methodology for Business and Management Studies* 6 September, Lisbon, Portugal (in press).

Kucharska, W., & Kowalczyk, R. (2016). Trust, collaborative culture and tacit knowledge sharing in project management – A relationship model. In *Proceedings of the 13th international conference on intellectual capital, knowledge management and organisational learning* (ICICKM), Ithaca, NY (pp. 159–166).

Kucharska, W., & Rebelo, T. (2022a). Knowledge sharing and knowledge hiding in light of the mistakes acceptance component of learning culture-knowledge culture and human capital implications. *The Learning Organization Journal.* https://doi.org/10.1108/TLO-03-2022-0032

Kucharska, W., & Rebelo, T. (2022b). Transformational leadership for researcher's innovativeness in the context of tacit knowledge and change adaptability. *International Journal of Leadership in Education.* https://doi.org/10.1080/13603124.2022.2068189

Lawrence, B. S. (2006). Organizational reference groups: A missing perspective on social context. *Organization Science, 17*(1), 80–100.

Li, Y., Chen, H., Liu, Y., & Peng, M. W. (2014). Managerial ties, organizational learning, and opportunity capture: A social capital perspective. *Asia Pacific Journal of Management, 31*(1), 271–291. https://doi.org/10.1007/s10490-012-9330-8

Loh, V., Andrews, S., Hesketh, B., & Griffin, B. (2013). The moderating effect of individual differences in error management training: Who learns from mistakes? *Human Factors: The Journal of the Human Factors and Ergonomics Society, 55*, 435–448. https://doi.org/10.1177/0018720812451856

Love, P. E. D., Smith, J., & Teo, P. (2018). Putting into practice error management theory: Unlearning and learning to manage action errors in construction. *Applied Ergonomics, 69*, 104–111. https://doi.org/10.1016/j.apergo.2018.01.007

Maes, G., & Van Hootegem, G. (2019). A systems model of organizational change. *Journal of Organizational Change Management, 32*(7), 725–738. https://doi.org/10.1108/JOCM-07-2017-0268

Mangels, J. A., Butterfield, B., Lamb, J., Good, C., & Dweck, C. S. (2006). Why do beliefs about intelligence influence learning success? A social cognitive neuroscience model. *Social Cognitive and Affective Neuroscience, 1*(2), 75–86.

McGrath, R. G. (1999). Falling forward: Real options reasoning and entrepreneurial failure. *Academy of Management Review, 24*(1), 13–30. https://doi.org/10.5465/amr.1999.1580438

Nadim, A., & Singh, P. (2019). Leading change for success: Embracing resistance. *European Business Review, 31*(4), 512–523. https://doi.org/10.1108/EBR-06-2018-0119

Nonaka, I. (1994). A dynamic theory of organizational knowledge creation. *Organizational Science, 5*(1), 14–37. https://doi.org/10.1287/orsc.5.1.14

Nonaka, I., & Takeuchi, H. (1995). *The knowledge-creating company: How Japanese companies create the dynamics of innovation.* Oxford University Press. https://doi.org/10.1016/0024-6301(96)81509-3

Nonaka, I., & Takeuchi, H. (2019). *The wise company: How companies create continuous innovation.* Oxford University Press.

Nonaka, I., & Toyama, R. (2003). The knowledge-creating theory revisited: Knowledge creation as a synthesizing process. *Knowledge Management Research and Practice, 1*(1), 2–10. https://doi.org/10.1057/9781137552105_4

Oswald, A. J., & Mascarenhas, S. J. (2019). The ethics of corporate critical thinking. In A. J. Oswald & S. J. Mascarenhas (Eds.), *Executive response to market challenges.* (pp. 285–293) Bingley: Emerald Publishing Limited.

Pasamehmetoglu, A., Guchait, P., Tracey, J. B., Cunningham, C. J. L., & Lei, P. (2017). The moderating effect of supervisor and coworker support for error management on service recovery performance and helping behaviors. *Journal of Service Theory and Practice, 27*(1), 2–22. https://doi.org/10.1108/JSTP-06-2015-0130

Poell, R. F., & Van der Krogt, F. J. (2010). Individual learning paths of employees in the context of social networks. In S. Billett (Ed.), *Learning through practice: Models, traditions, orientations and approaches* (pp. 197–221). Springer.

Polanyi, M. (1966). *The tacit dimension.* University of Chicago Press.

Politis, D., & Gabrielsson, J. (2009). Entrepreneurs' attitudes towards failure: An experiential learning approach. *International Journal of Entrepreneurial Behavior & Research, 15*(4), 364–383. https://doi.org/10.1108/13552550910967921

Powell, W. W., & Snellman, K. (2004). The knowledge economy. *Annual Review of Sociology, 30*(1), 199–220.

Rebelo, T., & Gomes, A. D. (2011). Conditioning factors of an organizational learning culture. *Journal of Workplace Learning, 23*(3), 173–194. https://doi.org/10.1108/13665621111117215

Rebelo, T., & Gomes, A. D. (2017). Is organizational learning culture a good bet? An analysis of its impact on organizational profitability and customer satisfaction. *Academia Revista Latinoamericana de Administración, 30*(3), 328–343. https://doi.org/10.1108/ARLA-10-2015-0275

Roese, N. J., & Vohs, K. D. (2012). Hindsight bias. Perspect. *Psychology Science, 7,* 411–426.

Romme, A. G. L., & van Witteloostuijn, A. (1999). Circular organising and triple loop learning. *Journal of Organizational Change Management, 12*(5), 439–454.

Rothberg, H. N., & Erickson, G. S. (2017). Big data systems: Knowledge transfer or intelligence insights? *Journal of Knowledge Management, 21*(1), 92–112. https://doi.org/10.1108/JKM-07-2015-0300

Saint-Onge, H. (1996). Tacit knowledge the key to the strategic alignment of intellectual capital. *Planning Review, 24*(2), 10–16. https://doi.org/10.1108/eb054547

Sanz-Valle, R., Naranjo-Valencia, C. J., Jim_enez-Jim_enez, D., & Perez-Caballero, L. (2011). Linking organizational learning with technical innovation and organizational culture. *Journal of Knowledge Management, 15*(6), 997–1015. https://doi.org/10.1108/13673271111179334

Scott-Ladd, B., & Chan, C. C. A. (2004). Emotional intelligence and participation in decision-making: Strategies for promoting organizational learning and change. *Strategic Change, 13,* 95–105. https://doi.org/10.1002/jsc.668

Seckler, Ch., Gronewold, U., & Reihlen, M. (2017). An error management perspective on audit quality: Toward a multi-level model. *Accounting, Organizations and Society, 62,* 21–42.

Senders, J. W., & Moray, N. P. (1991). *Human error: Cause, prediction, and reduction.* CRC Press, Taylor & Francis Group.

Senge, P. M. (2006). *The Fifth Discipline: The art & practice of the learning organization.* Crown Business.

Simonsson, C., & Heide, M. (2018). How focusing positively on errors can help organizations become more communicative: An alternative approach to crisis communication. *Journal of Communication Management, 22*(2), 179–196. https://doi.org/10.1108/JCOM-04-2017-0044

Teece, D. J. (2018). Business models and dynamic capabilities. *Long Range Planning, 51*(1), 40–49.

Thomas, D., & Brown, J. S. (2011). *A new culture of learning: Cultivating the imagination for a world of constant change.* CreateSpace.

Tseng, S. (2010). The correlation between organizational culture and knowledge conversion on corporate performance. *Journal of Knowledge Management, 14*(2), 269–284. https://doi.org/10.1108/13673271011032409

Van Breda-Verduijn, H., & Heijboer, M. (2016). Learning culture, continuous learning, organizational learning anthropologist. *Industrial and Commercial Training, 48*(3), 123–128. https://doi.org/10.1108/ICT-11-2015-0074

Van Dyck, C., Dimitrova, N. G., de Korne, D. F., & Hiddema, F. (2013). Walk the talk: Leaders' enacted priority of safety, incident reporting, and error management. *Leading in Health Care Organizations: Improving Safety, Satisfaction and Financial Performance (Advances in Health Care Management,* Vol. 14, pp. 95–117). Bingley: Emerald Group Publishing Limited. https://doi.org/10.1108/S1474-8231(2013)0000014009

Van Dyck, C., Frese, M., Baer, M., & Sonnentag, S. (2005). Organizational error management culture and its impact on performance: A two-study replication. *Journal of Applied Psychology, 90*, 1228–1240. https://doi.org/10.1037/0021-9010.90.6.1228

Van Wijk, R., Jansen, J. J., Van Den Bosch, F. A., & Volberda, H. W. (2012). How firms shape knowledge to explore and exploit: A study of knowledge flows, knowledge stocks and innovative performance across units. *Technology Analysis and Strategic Management, 24*(9), 929–950. https://doi.org/10.1080/09537325.2012.718666

Vanderheiden, E., & Mayer, C.-H. (2020). *Mistakes, errors and failures across cultures.* Springer.

Vithessonthi, C., & Thoumrungroje, A. (2011). Strategic change and firm performance: The moderating effect of organizational learning. *Journal of Asia Business Studies, 5*(2), 194–210. https://doi.org/10.1108/15587891111152348

Wang, X., Guchait, P., & Paşamehmetoğlu, A. (2020). Tolerating errors in hospitality organizations: Relationships with learning behavior, error reporting and service recovery performance. *International Journal of Contemporary Hospitality Management, 32*(8), 2635–2655. https://doi.org/10.1108/IJCHM-01-2020-0001

Watad, M. (2019). Organizational learning and change: Can they coexist?*Business Process Management Journal, 25*(5), 1070–1084. https://doi.org/10.1108/BPMJ-12-2016-0240

Watkins, K. E., & Marsick, V. J. (1996). *In action: Creating the learning organization.* American Society for Training and Development.

Webster, J., & Pearce, G. (2008). Crossfire: Knowledge sharing should focus on learning culture, rather than the generation of knowledge. *Waterlines, 27*(2), 97–103. https://doi.org/10.3362/1756-3488.2008.012

Weinzimmer, L. G., & Esken, C. A. (2017). Learning from mistakes: How mistake tolerance positively affects organizational learning and performance. *The Journal of Applied Behavioral Science, 53*(3), 322–348. https://doi.org/10.1177/0021886316688658

Wiewiora, A., Smidt, M., & Chang, A. (2019). The 'How' of multilevel learning dynamics: A systematic literature review exploring how mechanisms bridge learning between individuals, teams/projects and the organization. *European Management Review, 16*, 93–115. http://dx.doi.org/10.1111/emre.12179

Wiewiora, A., Trigunarsyah, B., Murphy, G., & Coffey, V. (2013). Organizational culture and willingness to share knowledge: A competing values perspective in Australian context. *International Journal of Project Management, 31*, 1163–1174. http://dx.doi.org/10.1016/j.ijproman.2012.12.014

Winter, S. G. (2003). Understanding dynamic capabilities. *Strategic Management Journal, 24*, 991–995. https://doi.org/10.1002/smj.318

Yamakawa, Y., & Cardon, M. S. (2015). Causal ascriptions and perceived learning from entrepreneurial failure. *Small Business Economics, 44*(4), 797–820. https://doi.org/10.1007/s11187-014-9623-z

Yeo, R. K. (2007). Change in(ter)ventions to organizational learning: Bravo to leaders as unifying agents. *The Learning Organization, 14*(6), 524–552. https://doi.org/10.1108/09696470710825132

Zappa, P., & Robins, G. (2016). Organizational learning across multi-level networks. *Social Networks, 44*, 295–306. https://doi.org/10.1016/j.socnet.2015.03.003

Zhao, B., & Olivera, F. (2006). Error reporting in organizations. *Academy of Management Review, 31*(4). https://doi.org/10.5465/amr.2006.22528167

Chapter 7

Collaborative Culture Enhances the Network of Minds

Chapter Summary

Chapter 6 focuses on cultures of collaboration and explains how collaborative cultures are essential to developing networked intelligence in any organization. The authors explain how collaborative cultures relate to three critical business processes: trust, risk, and critical thinking. The chapter addresses how important collaborative cultures are to developing these capabilities in knowledge organizations and the knowledge economy. How collaborative cultures help organizations to become more resilient and adaptable to the hyperdynamic change at the core of the knowledge economy is also explained. And how collaborative cultures help organizations to maintain and sustain their business performance in chaotic environments is also addressed.

Why We Care about Collaborative Culture?

Collaborative culture constitutes an organization. An organization is a set of people who act together to achieve the aim that none can achieve alone. To do this, people need to collaborate. Organizational collaborative culture facilitates all internal processes and increases trust for knowledge sharing (Kucharska, 2017; Kucharska et al., 2017) that is needed for collective learning and new knowledge development, its acceptance, usage, and re-usage. Trust makes it easier to overcome mental barriers in breaking beaten paths and patterns of acting and thinking, which is needed for innovativeness. A culture of collaboration and mutual accountability provides an opportunity to effectively learn and end the blame-game cycle, as claimed by Wallace and Mello (2015).

Moreover, collaborative culture is a culture that facilitates social capital development in the entire organization. Its development is critical because it impacts tacit knowledge. Since tacit knowledge is the primary source of any novelty needed for value creation in a constantly changing world, and social capital is a base for it (Kucharska & Erickson, 2022). Social capital is created more efficiently if collaborative culture facilitates it. Therefore, today's businesses cannot afford to live without collaborative culture development. So, we care about the collective culture because it

The Cultures of Knowledge Organizations: Knowledge, Learning, Collaboration (KLC), 123–135
Copyright © 2023 by Wioleta Kucharska and Denise Bedford
Published under exclusive licence by Emerald Publishing Limited
doi:10.1108/978-1-83909-336-420231007

empowers in synergy with learning and knowledge cultures (the KLC approach) and all organizational capabilities.

Collaborative Culture and Networked Intelligence

What is better than opening up a brilliant mind to knowledge and learning? Or the network of minds that results from effective collaboration? A network of brilliant collaborative minds is the best source of wealth for teams, organizations, and society in the twenty-first-century knowledge economy.

Collaboration among workmates is the core competency that enables knowledge organizations to create social and relational components of intellectual capital. Relational capital has always been a critical business asset, but it has been understood as the "connections" of senior leaders. Today we understand relational capital as an asset of every individual. The ability to collaborate is vital to business growth and performance. A collaboration culture is the "software of the organizational shared mindset" that facilitates cooperation. Shared values and beliefs are at the heart of a collaborative culture. These shared values and beliefs include an organization's open communication, norms of respect, trust, teamwork, adaptability, risk-taking, and diversity (Barczak et al., 2010; Pinjani & Palvia, 2013). In a collaborative culture, we find favorable climate for knowledge dissemination, critical thinking, reflection, smooth interactions, and communications that foster employee learning. The collaborative culture enhances trust among workmates. The organization's values shape collaborative cultures, attitudes, and behaviors and foster competitive performance (Muneeb et al., 2019). Collaborative culture supports the creation of a relational component of intellectual capital that builds competitive advantage and business performance (Chowdhury et al., 2019). A collaborative culture is a base for organizational existence and development in the hyperdynamic knowledge economy.

Learning at work requires interaction – it is the essence of procedural capital, where groups and teams act together. Employees learn faster when they collaborate and collectively discuss new experiences to gain the best lesson from them— moreover, shared mental and practical challenges foster solutions development. According to Julien-Chinn and Lietz (2019), the decision-making process is supported through group dialog, and the ideas of collaboration and shared decision-making are consistent with a learning culture. The collaboration broadens our perception of events and conditions and fosters deeper understanding. In addition, collaboration enables an individual to shift their mindset as a result of the interaction and to reify the shift with others (Senge, 2006).

Organization-wide collaboration fosters learning and has the potential to shift organizational attitudes, aims, and behaviors (Garvin et al., 2008). Hence, collaborative culture will positively influence learning routines. Those organizational cultures that reflect an appreciation for knowledge, learning, and collaboration (KLC) will naturally, efficiently, and effectively develop their intellectual capital components. In addition, they will adapt to changes more naturally, which is the critical ingredient for developing dynamic capabilities. Dynamic capabilities determine the organization's "mastery" to adapt continuously to changes. Also, organizations will adapt in a way that will always bring real value to consumers, clients, society, and the organization itself consistently and sustainably.

Knowledge culture shifts every knowledge process at all life cycle stages and flows, i.e., identification, creation, encoding, storage, security, sharing, communication, distribution, use, re-usage, and new knowledge production. Every stage leads to learning and, by definition, brings change. The moment we learn something new, our knowledge capital changes – we absorb it, which changes our existing knowledge. It changes our perception of things, and perception shapes attitude. Attitudes shape behavior. For these reasons, knowledge culture is essential as it drives the learning culture. A knowledge culture is influential, but a learning culture is fundamental for growth. Collaborative culture enables us to grow collectively. An organization of individuals exists and functions to achieve a complex goal the individuals could not achieve alone. Collaboration culture enables organizations to become an organization in the truest sense of the word. In essence, a collaboration culture creates a network of collaborating minds.

An organization's capability to change and adapt is a proxy for organizational intelligence (Feuerstein et al., 1979). Organizational intelligence is reflected in its employees' shared intelligence, a product of the company's shared mind culture. This culture demonstrates a shared appreciation of KLC. As Rothberg and Erickson (2017) observe, shifting from knowledge to intelligence in any organization depends on its culture. Thus, collaborative culture will determine the efficiency and effectiveness of a shift from focusing on individuals to focusing on the collective and the exponential value of the communal level. The shared mindset is critical to any company's success. It is why the collaborative culture is so vital.

Human interactions foster learning and knowledge dissemination (Su & Vanhaverbeke, 2019). The innovation process is supported through group dialog, ideas sharing, and decision-making consistent with a learning culture. Sharing ideas and collaboration expands our perception and helps us to understand an issue at a deeper level than we might individually. Exposure to other perspectives in the network fosters a shared perception and deep understanding. Collaboration throughout the organization enables learning and mental and behavioral adjustments whose effects are visible in organizational actions and behaviors. Hence, it is why Kucharska and Bedford (2020) claimed that collaborative culture driven by knowledge culture positively influences learning culture and adaptability to change. It is why knowledge culture is so vital for organizational intelligence. It is why collaborative culture is a base for collective, networked intelligence building. The reality of the networked knowledge economy highlights the value of networked intelligence as a determining factor in the wealth of societies. Therefore, collective intelligence can't be developed without collaborative culture. Therefore, the collaborative culture is the missing link that bridges organizations' knowledge and learning climates as they grow dynamic capabilities. It is the optimum effect of collective intelligence. Dynamic capabilities enable organizations to respond to the reality of dynamically changing networked economy. The confluence of these factors suggests that a company culture grounded in a shared mindset focused on collaboration, learning, and knowledge will be well suited to face the inevitable changes successfully.

As noted in Chapter 4, knowledge assets in the knowledge economy matter, but passive knowledge consumption does not necessarily produce value. Hence, active, shared, and continuously new and regenerated knowledge is needed.

Organizations need collaborative learning practices as dynamic as the changes occurring around them. Organizations must learn to systematically strive for, acquire and leverage "up-to-date" and pertinent knowledge. The culture of learning shapes an organization's incentive to broaden minds systematically. Knowledge culture is fundamental to developing intelligence. But it is only those motivated to learn and change, who appreciate the knowledge, develop pro-knowledge attitudes and behaviors and can collaborate who will achieve mastery in building dynamic capabilities. The ability to collectively adapt to or drive change reflects collective intelligence at the organizational, unit, group, and individual levels. A network of brilliant collaborative minds is the best source of creating new business wealth for teams, organizations, and societies.

Case Study – LAP MAP

Andrea is the CEO and owner of LAP MAP (LM), a company that developed an application that maps "intelligent life learning and satisfaction" to daily activities. The LAP application monitors daily routines such as the time users spend on public transport, in traffic jams, in the kitchen, at the desk, partying, shopping, watching television, walking, sleeping, reading, and other physical activity. Users report the "activities taken" and "satisfaction achieved." Users also report general "life satisfaction." LAP helps users gain a higher-level self-awareness and understanding of how they correlate. To gain this self-awareness, LAP users must also define their daily, monthly, and life-long life goals. Life-long goals are broken down into subgoals to make monitoring easier. Users also report their goals and achievements. They report whether their daily aims were achieved, and if not, why not. Users also record their "lessons learned" daily. The LAP asks about the source of the lesson. LAP leverages the data collected – managerial, sociological, psychological – to provide users with the knowledge they need to assist users in life planning and organizing. It builds users' self-awareness and supports self-motivation. Users gain this higher-level self-awareness because LAP makes visible their life goals and the events that support their achievement.

Recognizing the value of all life experiences – good and bad – also contributes to users' self-awareness. LAP also motivates students to see and learn from all their experiences and to define and achieve their life goals in an attractive, entertaining, and gaming way. The application is designed for a particular group of people who highly value self-development. For the LAP application to be successful for users with different self-development goals, it must accommodate different gamification strategies, different-motivation systems, graphics, sounds, interfaces, and other features. In addition, different groups of users will have different life aims to reflect different domains or professions, ages, gender, or where they live. To be successful and to ensure LAP is always up to date with people's changing goals, the LM team must continuously learn and adapt the application. Maintaining personal and private data security in a dynamic environment with evolving threats is of particular concern. Security protocols are strict and continuously improved because safety and trust reflect the product's core values. Andrea's company prioritizes continuous improvement of dynamic capabilities and skills development to keep pace with these dynamic consumer expectations.

As CEO and owner, Andrea created a continuous learning system for LM based on social sciences sources of quality scientific information and data. LM monitors current social science sources to identify trends based on big data collected from social platforms. LM data scientists also continuously analyze big data collected from LAP users. Taken together, these sources enable LM to grow and develop. Cultures of KLC strongly support these efforts. LM employs people who want to understand what they do and why and to see the value of their work reflected in the effects achieved by the entire company. "Let's do the LAP we are proud of and want to use ourselves daily!" – Andrea says. It is the essence of the collective intelligence inherent in the company's hundred people strong team. "We all are crazy about learning; we sincerely like what we have achieved so far together, and we want to support and motivate one another to do something that brings us satisfaction and value to society. We care about the quality of our databases and sources. We continuously improve our algorithms to ensure they adapt to a dynamic technology environment and new trends in human perception of value and behaviors.

Additionally, the team continuously shares new targeted and functional knowledge across small teams. New lessons that change perceptions are shared broadly across the entire organization. There are dedicated 'knowledge sharing meetings' where the most exciting lessons are shared in a particular context. The workforce believes that context is everything. The company creates an organizational climate that focuses on learning. Andrea describes examples of the learning focus, including to log out properly from the system every day, we need to accomplish....; or a sentence that begins with: I learned today...., or I believe it matters to be consistent in what we dream about, belief is reasonable, and do – this brings happiness."

"Finally, what I am most proud of in my company is what we have achieved and continuously do together. We appreciate each other's contribution to the collective success. We support and motivate one another. Because they care about this company's improvement, we share their best knowledge naturally and communicate freely. We discuss successes and failures. We all look for the best solution when we have a problem. The agility of our collective intelligence impresses me every day. I am working in an authentic network of brilliant and continuously developing minds. It is what I have always wanted. Lucky me!" – Andrea summarizes with a smile.

In today's aggressive and complex business environment, organizations must continuously evolve their collective, networked intelligence and adapt to change with agility. Company cultures that value and support KLC will succeed in growing that collective, networked intelligence. Attitudes of trust, critical thinking, and risk-taking are intensely personal but are shaped by national and home cultures.

Organizational culture can sustain it or destroy it. Bureaucracies and hierarchies neutralize it, whereas markets, clans, and fiefs sustain them.

Collaborative Culture and Trust, Risk and Critical Thinking

Trust among co-workers ensures successful collaboration and vice versa (Kucharska, 2017). Both increase knowledge sharing, team creativity, and performance (Kucharska et al., 2017). At the same time, knowledge sharing supports trust-building among knowledge workers (Thomas et al., 2009). So, knowledge sharing then creates trust that promotes collaboration. Collaboration supports learning that is a source of new knowledge (Nugroho, 2018). So, knowledge (especially if shared) creates trust. But at the same time, team members share knowledge when they can trust each other (Park & Lee, 2014). So, the knowledge-sharing act then is an act that has a bidirectional power to create trust. So, following this line, organizational learning is also affected by trust among employees (Swift & Hwang, 2013). Based on the above, there is an assumption that there is a spiral of KLC culture that supports the development of critical thinking, risk, and trust attitudes that, due to their interchangeable influence, are a source of sustainable knowledge creation, leads to development. The logic of this assumption is more in-depth presented below.

Thomas et al. (2009) define trust as a relationship between people involving voluntary acceptance of risk based on the other party's actions. So, in this context risk-taking attitude supports trust and collaboration. Indeed, it sounds encouraging – we trust those who trust us. Therefore, the essence of starting cooperation is to find the one party who is ready as the first to take the risk and show trust to the other and vice versa. But to sustain this cooperation, trust, risk, and critical thinking are the base. Therefore, the nature of the sustainably cooperating intelligence network is determined by trust and risk circulating among the network of competent, credible, and critically thinking minds. Critical thinking as a skill fostering knowledge awareness and sharing (Kucharska, 2021) is next to trust and risk focal for the sustainable cooperation of the networked intelligence (Kucharska & Bedford, 2023). The essence of the sustainably collaborated network is the selection of competent and credible brilliant minds thinking critically, ready to take a risk to trust all network actors and gain this trust from others and, as a result, smoothly collaborate with them.

By supporting knowledge sharing, knowledge culture fosters learning and collaboration, thanks to trust. Moreover, trust is built thanks to professional competency and credibility and social skills perception, e.g., the personal warmth perceived by workmates. So, professional and personal social skills matter for the collaboration quality in networked intelligence systems (Kucharska, 2022).

A collaborative network of minds depends on trust. Trust sustains a network of minds. Organizations are composed of people. Therefore, organizational success depends on people. A company's sustainability increasingly depends on employees' well-being. Kucharska and Bedford (2019) proved that job satisfaction factors that affect knowledge sharing influence company performance. Also, the concept of negative resource spirals (Hobfoll et al., 2018) – namely, the loss of one resource causes the loss of others – helps to expose the relationship of company culture to company performance. An organizational culture that favors KLC will shape the personal and shared attitudes of trust, risk-taking, and critical thinking and will build dynamic capabilities. If such a culture is lost, it could result in losing other resources. Without knowledge of culture, this spiral does not happen. Therefore, the company's ability to adapt to a hyperdynamic economy will be problematic.

Case Study – Financial Services Company

Stephan is working for a financial services company that employs 3,000 people. To be successful, each accountant must be well-versed in professional knowledge of financial practices and standards and must keep abreast of and learn about changes in financial law. Collaboration among workmates is essential to keeping up to date. Each accountant carries a substantial personal responsibility for producing financial reports. Trust in co-workers' work and knowledge is the most significant knowledge deficit, not because co-workers are not seen as trustworthy but because of the personal accountability and responsibility each carries for their reports. Employees respect one another deeply. There is extensive discussion of the most "problematic cases" and sharing opinions to derive the best solution. In the end, the responsibility for the report and its effects is personal. To reduce personal risk, they check and double-check themselves. When working in teams, when the project and its report are complex, they check, double-check, and even triple-check their contributions and those of their colleagues. It is a good business practice. The company is successful. People are satisfied, and operations go smoothly. The accounting department is characteristically knowledge and learning-oriented, where critical thinking and trust matter.

Stockbrokers are working in different conditions. A different pattern of behaviors is observed in the investment department, where a risk-taking attitude is an inherent aspect of the role and value of time. "There is time pressure – sometimes you need to make the decision 'now or never,' so you must trust your judgments first" – Stephan says. "There is no time to double or triple-check your decisions and actions. You must think critically and quickly if you need to second-guess your ideas. In this case, you can ask more experienced colleagues for their opinions on your choices and reduce uncertainty. You might receive the best advice because the final effect of your work affects the entire department. Everybody cares about the effect of our individual choices on the group" – Stefan admits. "Stockbrokers and investment analysts are, by nature, more networked than accountants. Stockbrokers understand that final department figures depend on the whole department. There are strong dependencies for everyone. We care about whom we work with and how we work," – Stephan says. "So, yes, the culture of knowledge, learning and collaboration are strong and important to socially coherent professionals who are ready to take a risk, trust and still think critically. These cultures matter for our sustainability."

In sum, a powerful interdependency spiral of KLC cultures is critical to developing critical thinking, risk, and trust attitudes. They are a source of sustainable development due to their interchangeable influence. Personal attitudes of trust, risk, and critical thinking skills can determine how the network of brilliant minds functions. In a hyperdynamic networked economy, knowledge creation facilitated by collaboration and learning will determine the capabilities of the network of brilliant minds contribute smoothly to the dynamic capabilities' development.

Collaborative Culture for Change Management and Sustainability

We have argued that sustainable organizational development depends on the well-being of employees. Therefore, company culture matters for workforce well-being. Most company cultures and business goals align with individual and business goals. Employees have a better chance of achieving their individual performance goals where the collective psychological well-being, professional competency and credibility are supported. The smooth operation of a collaborative network of brilliant minds is a source of competitive advantage. We also have argued that company culture is vital to determining whether a company achieves its strategy. Undoubtedly, organizational culture is the key driving force of any organization. Therefore, company culture is a vital asset of any organization today. While shaping it is challenging, it should be the center of management's attention.

We also argued that the national culture affects the culture of employees and will shape the company culture. A company's culture is the unique and cumulative product of all its employees. The national culture of the company's culture, as well as the national cultures of each individual, shapes the overall culture. Employees' national culture dimensions affect company culture (Bedford & Kucharska, 2020). Kucharska and Bedford (2019) examined which national culture dimensions (Hofstede, 1980) most support job satisfaction and how it influences knowledge sharing and performance. They observed that (1) lower power distance (*hierarchy*), (2) higher uncertainty avoidance (*risk avoidance through more and more precise processes, procedures, policies – bureaucracy*), (3) higher collectivism (*efficient network*), (4) the more masculine style of management (*leadership*), (5) longer term orientation (*sustainability perspective*) of the organization; and (6) higher job satisfaction. It can directly increase knowledge sharing and company performance. These national dimensions influence personal and collective performance. Every organization is a network of people, and each person is a network hub. The more efficient the network, the better the organization performs. Collectivism as a cultural dimension is focused on a collaborative culture. An efficient network reinforces the quality of business performance. The collectivism and collaborative culture that reinforces it should be seen as a paradigm for higher-level performance. If there is no collectivism – there is no efficient network.

In such a context, the networked alliance of brilliant minds is a critical sustainable growth paradigm in a hyperdynamic, networked knowledge economy. The essence of sustainability is to manage resources for the long term. We argue that a company culture that supports collective intelligence is essential to developing an organizationally and socially sustainable system. Skare and Porada-Rochon (2022) noted that sustainable growth requires constant technological innovation. Knowledge, learning, and dynamic capabilities are necessary for innovation and change adaptability. To do it sustainably, a long-run perspective is essential. Seeing business from a long-run perspective requires intelligence. A collectivist perspective is essential to a long-run perspective. To achieve sustainability, we need a well-coordinated and cooperating network of minds at all levels – micro, meso, and macro. We argue that a company culture that sustains a spiral of KLC and develops critical thinking, risk, and trust attitudes will achieve sustainable development.

Both dimensions of culture – collectivism and a long-run perspective – are fundamental to supporting knowledge sharing and learning within a particular intelligence network. It is a source of competitive advantage in the knowledge-driven hyperdynamic network economy. Employees often learn both these dimensions at the national level (society). They are inherently embedded in employees' "software of minds." They strongly affect organizations composed of employees who bring different national cultures. It is why national cultures strongly affect nations' wealth (societies) and determine their sustainability.

Case Study – IT B2B Software Services Company

Amanda worked as a service desk team leader in an IT B2B software services company. She liked her job. Her position is strong, she is good at it, and she is self-confident about her work after five years of doing it. Her job is easy, well paid and predictable, which she always appreciated. It is easy to excel and perform her work largely without error – "perfectly." Amanda appreciated this situation. She grew up in a society and home that was well organized and valued security and stability. She grew up in a home where daily routines and traditions were celebrated. Her parents cared deeply about her education, friends, hobbies, and leisure time. They did everything to make her life perfect. As a result, she felt safe living in a perfectly defined "frame."

The company she is working for is significant in the market. So naturally, there are a lot of detailed procedures and policies. Processes are transparent and perfectly defined. After five years of working for the same company, Amanda was a champion of all these rules and protocols. She always followed the rules and strictly managed her team, and others who worked with them behaved similarly. "Policy is policy" – she often cut discussions at work. Recently, Amanda realized she was facing a problematic situation. It was the first time she faced a new situation where neither policy nor procedure provided clear guidance. She was clever, though, so she found a solution. After the crisis had passed, she developed a new procedure that worked in a similar situation. These situations became increasingly frequent over time. She was constantly confronted with new challenges where established policies blocked options for a quick resolution. She knew policies must be respected but did not see the harm in breaking some. If she breaks some, though, it does not mean there will not be consequences or harm in other areas of the organization. It directly affected Amanda's sense of security and her sense of security as a person in a position of control. Her self-confidence dropped, and her work performance began to suffer. It led to personal aggravation and frustration. Unable to tolerate the situation, one day, she quit.

Sometimes even highly educated people have a problem with uncertainty, whereas others might not. A high level of education may suggest a high level of knowledge and confidence, but our cultures – mental assumptions, beliefs, and values – can significantly affect how we deal with everyday uncertainty.

Kucharska and Bedford (2019) observed that higher job satisfaction is often associated with lower power distance (*hierarchy*), higher uncertainty avoidance (*risk avoidance through more and more precise processes, procedures, policies – bureaucracy*), higher collectivism (*efficient network*), more masculinity styles of management (*leadership*) and the longer term orientation (*sustainability perspective*), higher knowledge sharing and performance. Given what we know about company culture and dynamic capabilities development, their findings suggest significant management problems may be generated where *uncertainty avoidance* is dominant. This dimension is visible in attitudes that avoid shared risk-taking and are characterized by high numbers of detailed procedures and other forms of control. On the other hand, where uncertainty avoidance is low, a company may prefer cultural solutions that deal with uncertainty, risk, experimentation, and mistakes rather than rely solely on bureaucracy and control. It is the root cause of the contradiction between employees with different work culture preferences. Those employees prefer a predictable environment that offers an illusion of safety, security, and *job satisfaction*. The dynamic work environment offers less sense of work security and safety because it carries long-term risks. But thanks to the constant need for learning and adaptability, the dynamic work environment is essential to creating those internal and external innovations that support long-run sustainability.

It is why the collaborative culture is so vital for sustainability. Collaborative culture contributes to long-term sustainability if combined with knowledge and learning cultures. It contributes to long-term sustainability and the common good by encouraging critical thinking, supporting risk and trust attitudes to leave personal comfort zones, and bringing into question the "safe" status quo. Long-run perspectives and sustainability require intelligence. A healthy functioning collaborative intelligence network exists only where the company culture is a spiral of KLC. This spiral grows critical thinking, risk, and trust attitudes and supports sustainable development.

Chapter Review

After reading this chapter, you should be able to:

- describe a culture of collaboration.
- explain how collaborative cultures develop networked intelligence.
- explain the relationship of collaborative cultures to trust, risk, and critical thinking.
- explain how collaborative cultures develop dynamic business capabilities.
- explain how collaborative cultures contribute to resilience and adaptability.
- describe how collaborative cultures help organizations to maintain and sustain their business performance in chaotic environments is also addressed.

References and Recommended Future Readings

Argyris, C. (1982). How learning and reasoning processes affect organizational change. In P. S. Goodman et al. (Eds.), *Change in organizations* (pp. 47–86). Jossey Bass.

Bahrami, M. A., Kiani, M. M., Montazeralfaraj, R., Zadeh, H. F., & Zadeh, M. M. (2016). The mediating role of organizational learning in the relationship of organizational intelligence and organizational agility. *Osong Public Health and Research Perspectives*, 7(3), 190–196. https://doi.org/10.1016/j.phrp.2016.04.007

Barczak, G., Lassk, F., & Mulki, J. (2010). Antecedents of team creativity: An examination of team emotional intelligence, team trust and collaborative culture. *Creativity and Innovation Management*, 19(4), 332–345. https://doi.org/10.1111/j.1467-8691.2010.00574.x

Bedford, D., & Kucharska, W. (2020). *Relating information culture to information policies and management strategies*. IGI Global.

Chowdhury, M. M. H., Quaddus, M., & Agarwal, R. (2019). Supply chain resilience for performance: Role of relational practices and network complexities. *Supply Chain Management*, 24(5), 659–676. https://doi.org/10.1108/SCM-09-2018-0332

Feuerstein, R., Feuerstein, S., Falik, L., & Rand, Y. (1979). *Dynamic assessments of cognitive modifiability*. ICELP Press.

Garvin, D. A., Edmondson, A. C., & Gino, F. (2008). Is yours a learning organization? *Harvard Business Review*, 109–116.

Ghasemzadeh, P., Nazari, J. A., Farzaneh, M., & Mehralian, G. (2019). Moderating role of innovation culture in the relationship between organizational learning and innovation performance. *The Learning Organization*, 26(3), 289–303. https://doi.org/10.1108/TLO-08-2018-0139

Hobfoll, S. E., Halbesleben, J., Neveu, J.-P., & Westman, M. (2018). Conservation of resources in the organizational context: The reality of resources and their consequences. *Annual Review of Organizational Psychology and Organizational Behavior*, 5, 103–128.

Hofstede, G. (1980). *Culture's consequences: International differences in work-related values*. Sage.

Julien-Chinn, F. J., & Lietz, C. A. (2019). Building learning cultures in the child welfare workforce. *Children and Youth Services Review*, 99, 360–365. https://doi.org/10.1016/j.childyouth.2019.01.023

Kucharska, W. (2017). Relationships between trust and collaborative culture in the context of tacit knowledge sharing. *Journal of Entrepreneurship, Management and Innovation, 13*(4), 61–78. https://doi.org/10.7341/20171344

Kucharska, W. (2021). Do mistakes acceptance foster innovation? Polish and US cross-country study of tacit knowledge sharing in IT. *Journal of Knowledge Management, 25*(11), 105–128. https://doi.org/10.1108/JKM-12-2020-0922

Kucharska, W. (2022). *Personal branding in the knowledge economy: The inter-relationship between corporate and employee brands.* Routledge. https://doi.org/10.4324/9781003178248

Kucharska, W., & Bedford, D. A. D. (2019). Knowledge sharing and organizational culture dimensions: Does job satisfaction matter? *Electronic Journal of Knowledge Management, 17*(1), 1–18. http://dx.doi.org/10.2139/ssrn.3406496

Kucharska, W., & Bedford, D. A. D. (2020). Love your mistakes! – They help you adapt to change. How do knowledge, collaboration and learning cultures foster organizational intelligence? *Journal of Organizational Change Management, 33*(7), 1329–1354. https://doi.org/10.1108/JOCM-02-2020-0052

Kucharska, W., & Bedford, D. A. D. (2023). The KLC Cultures, Tacit Knowledge, and Trust Contribution to Organizational Intelligence Activation. In *Proceedongs of the 24th European Conference on Knowledge Management*, 7–8 September, Lisbon, Portugal. (in press).

Kucharska, W., & Erickson, G. S. (2022). Social capital, human capital, tacit knowledge, and innovations, A Polish-US cross-country study. In *Proceedings of the 23rd European Conference on Knowledge Management*, Naples, Italy. https://doi.org/10.34190/eckm.23.1.402

Kucharska, W., Kowalczyk, R., & Kucharski, M. (2017). Trust, Tacit Knowledge Sharing, Project Performance and their Managerial Implications. In *Proceedings of the 18th European Conference on Knowledge Management*, Barcelona (Vol. 1, pp. 532–539).

Li, Y., Chen, H., Liu, Y., & Peng, M. W. (2014). Managerial ties, organizational learning, and opportunity capture: A social capital perspective. *Asia Pacific Journal of Management, 31*(1), 271–291. https://doi.org/10.1007/s10490-012-9330-8

Muneeb, D., Khong, K. W., Ennew, C., & Avvari, M. (2019). Building an integrated conceptual model of competitive learning capability: A strategic management perspective. *Asia-Pacific Journal of Business Administration, 11*(3), 267–287. https://doi.org/10.1108/APJBA-02-2019-0042

Nadim, A., & Singh, P. (2019). Leading change for success: Embracing resistance. *European Business Review, 31*(4), 512–523. https://doi.org/10.1108/EBR-06-2018-0119

Nonaka, I., & Toyama, R. (2003). The knowledge-creating theory revisited: Knowledge creation as a synthesizing process. *Knowledge Management Research and Practice, 1*(1), 2–10. https://doi.org/10.1057/9781137552105_4

Nugroho, M. A. (2018). The effects of collaborative cultures and knowledge sharing on organizational learning. *Journal of Organizational Change Management, 31*(5), 1138–1152. https://doi.org/10.1108/JOCM-10-2017-0385

Park, J. G., & Lee, J. (2014). Knowledge sharing in information systems development projects: Explicating the role of dependence and trust. *International Journal of Project Management, 32*(1), 153–165.

Pinjani, P., & Palvia, P. (2013). Trust and knowledge sharing in diverse global virtual teams. *Information and Management, 50*, 144–153.

Poell, R. F., & Van der Krogt, F. J. (2010). Individual learning paths of employees in the context of social networks. In S. Billett (Ed.), *Learning through practice: Models, traditions, orientations and approaches* (pp. 197–221). Springer.

Rebelo, T., & Gomes, A. D. (2011). Conditioning factors of an organizational learning culture. *Journal of Workplace Learning*, *23*(3), 173–194. https://doi.org/10.1108/13665621111117215

Rothberg, H. N., & Erickson, G. S. (2017). Big data systems: Knowledge transfer or intelligence insights? *Journal of Knowledge Management*, *21*(1), 92–112. https://doi.org/10.1108/JKM-07-2015-0300

Sanz-Valle, R., Naranjo-Valencia, C. J., Jiménez-Jiménez, D., & Perez-Caballero, L. (2011). Linking organizational learning with technical innovation and organizational culture. *Journal of Knowledge Management*, *15*(6), 997–1015. https://doi.org/10.1108/13673271111179334

Senge, P. M. (2006). *The fifth discipline: The art & practice of the learning organization.* Crown Business.

Skare, M., & Porada-Rochon, M. (2022). The role of innovation in sustainable growth: A dynamic panel study on micro and macro levels 1990–2019. *Technological Forecasting and Social Change*, *175*, 121337. https://doi.org/10.1016/j.techfore.2021.121337

Su, Y.-S., & Vanhaverbeke, W. (2019). How do different types of interorganizational ties matter in technological exploration? *Management Decision*, *57*(8), 2148–2176. https://doi.org/10.1108/MD-06-2018-0713

Swift, P. E., & Hwang, A. (2013). The impact of affective and cognitive trust on knowledge sharing and organizational learning. *The Learning Organization*, *20*(1), 20–37. https://doi.org/10.1108/09696471311288500

Thomas, G. F., Zolin, R., & Hartman, J. L. (2009). The central role of communication in developing trust and its effects on employee involvement. *Journal of Business Communication*, *46*(3), 287–310.

Vithessonthi, C., & Thoumrungroje, A. (2011). Strategic change and firm performance: The moderating effect of organizational learning. *Journal of Asia Business Studies*, *5*(2), 194–210. https://doi.org/10.1108/15587891111152348

Wallace, N., & Mello, J. (2015). Collaborative culture: The new workplace reality. *Foresight: The International Journal of Applied Forecasting*, *39*, 31–35.

Watad, M. (2019). Organizational learning and change: Can they coexist? *Business Process Management Journal*, *25*(5), 1070–1084. https://doi.org/10.1108/BPMJ-12-2016-0240

Yeo, R. K. (2007). Change in(ter)ventions to organizational learning: Bravo to leaders as unifying agents. *The Learning Organization*, *14*(6), 524–552. https://doi.org/10.1108/09696470710825132

Section 3

KLC and The Complex Cultures of the Public Sector

Chapter 8

Public Sector Cultures

Chapter Summary

This chapter addresses the potential for knowledge, learning, and collaboration (KLC) cultures in public sector organizations. Public sector organizations are among the most complex for introducing or nourishing a KLC approach because there are multiple levels of cultures with varying levels of influence. We describe these complex cultures as tiers. First, we define public sector organizations' business goals, purpose, and strategies. Then, the authors translate and interpret all five levels of culture for public sector organizations. The chapter also details the nature of cultural complexity, namely the four tiers of public sector cultures: (1) the company culture (Tier 1); (2) the public service culture (Tier 2); (3) the culture of the external environment (Tier 3); and (4) the internal KLC cultures (Tier 4). This chapter establishes a framework for describing an organization's complex culture and determining the best KLC approach for the context.

Why we Care about the Cultures of Public Sector Organizations?

Public sector organizations exist in every society. They persist over time though their form may change. They are essential to the functioning of any society and the well-being of society. Public sector organizations appear to be the simplest, but the simplicity is deceiving. They are a rich source of study of cultural dynamics in any economy. The industrial economy was complex – with a confluence of organizational cultures, functional cultures, and competing economic sectors. To this complexity, we must now add a new and hyperdynamic knowledge economy and knowledge society. Understanding the layers of culture in public sector organizations is then critical because they influence society's well-being and impact society's standards development.

This chapter sets the stage for exploring how the cultures described in Section 2 may play out in some of the most complex organizational cultures – public service cultures. We care about public sector cultures for two reasons. First, these organizations are critical players in every economic sector in any state.

The Cultures of Knowledge Organizations: Knowledge, Learning, Collaboration (KLC), 139–166
Copyright © 2023 by Wioleta Kucharska and Denise Bedford
Published under exclusive licence by Emerald Publishing Limited
doi:10.1108/978-1-83909-336-420231008

Their cultures can have beneficial or adverse effects on strategies in both the private and the public sectors. By building strong KLC cultures in these organizations, we may influence the cultures of the other organizations they work with. Second, although their cultures appear at first glance to be one-dimensional and straightforward, there are four levels at play. Except for one – the fundamental public service culture – each layer varies with the essential company culture and the culture of the external environment. For this reason, they are among the most challenging research context we can identify for learning more about what works and what does not work for designing and operationalizing KLC cultures.

Public Sector Organizations – Goals, Purpose, and Strategy

The public sector plays a vital role in ensuring the smooth functioning of our society. In contrast, the primary purpose of the private sector is to generate profits. Similar to the voluntary sector, organizations in the public sector do not seek to generate a profit. Instead, public sector organizations provide products and services which are either of little market value (e.g., they have a high investment cost but low payback value) or there is a universal need for them to be available to the entire public community. The nature of the products and services means that there is a limited market for them (one or two consumers), or their distribution and provision to the general public would significantly reduce any potential profits. Generally, there is little expectation (i.e., assumptions) of those supporting these cultures of personal or independent profit or rewards.

They promote economic growth and stability, serve the public, and safeguard public resources. The primary purpose of the public sector is to provide services that are considered essential for the well-being of society. These organizations must put the public interests first but operate within the national and functional cultures of the location and the domain. Public sector organizations have equivalent organizations in the private, non-profit, and academic sectors. In addition to being aligned with a government entity, they each function within a particular economic sector. Within each sector, they provide essential services necessary for the well-being of communities. There are a wide variety of public sector organizations, each with its unique mandate and purpose. Some common examples of public sector organizations include:

- Administration of *justice*
- *Educational services and institutions*
- *Emergency and disaster management* services
- *Environmental protection* and *natural resource* services and regulations
- *Healthcare* facilities and services
- *Law enforcement* and *protective* services
- *Mail* and postal services
- *Military* and national security services
- Public *buildings and infrastructure*
- *Social services*
- *Telecommunications* networks and regulatory regimes

- *Transportation* infrastructure
- Urban *planning* and *zoning*
- *Utilities.*

Public sector organizations are typically funded by taxpayers, while private sector organizations are typically funded by shareholders, investors, or business owners. Funding for public services is usually raised through various methods, including taxes, fees, and financial transfers from other levels of government (e.g., from a federal to a provincial or state government). Public services are typically provided free of charge or at a subsidized rate. Moreover, public services are supported by public funds, which are collected through the levying of taxes and fees. In non-profit organizations, services and products are often supported by voluntary contributions, donations, and endowments.

Public sector organizations are grounded on the economic concepts of economies of scale and scope. Where essential services or activities are required by the broad population, striving for economies of scale and scope is essential. The challenge is that not all segments of a population may require the same form of service or activity – a challenge of public sector organizations is to identify the core elements of those services and to allow the private sector to allow any extended aspects of those services.

Public sector organizations provide public services. A public service is any service intended to address specific needs pertaining to the aggregate members of a community. Public services are available to people within a government jurisdiction as provided directly through public sector agencies or via public financing to private businesses or voluntary organizations (or even as provided by family households, though terminology may differ depending on context). Other public services are undertaken on behalf of government's residents or in the interest of its citizens.

Public service describes doing something valuable or worthwhile for society and a specific sector of the economy and labor force. In this book, the authors use public service to refer to the sector of the economy and its labor force. This focus is relevant because it suggests a specific organizational culture grounded in values, ethics, beliefs, and behaviors. We can expect organizations in this sector to have distinct organizational cultures. And we can expect managers and the workforce to exhibit particular behaviors.

Public Service – The Public Sector Strategy

Public service is grounded in the social consensus that certain services should be available to all, regardless of income, physical ability or mental acuity. And to ensure these services are apportioned and administered to meet the community's needs, they are usually subject to regulation going beyond that, applying to most economic sectors for social and political reasons. A public service may sometimes have the characteristics of a public good (being non-rivalrous and non-excludable). However, most are services that may (according to prevailing social norms) be under-provided by the market. In most cases, public services are services, i.e., they do not involve manufacturing goods. They may be provided by local or national monopolies, especially in sectors that are natural monopolies. They may involve outputs that are hard to attribute to specific individual efforts or hard to measure in terms of key characteristics such as quality. They often require high levels of training and education. They may attract people with a public service ethos who wish to give something to the broader public or community through their work.

Thomas Jefferson enunciated the basic principle of public service: "When a man assumes a public trust, he should consider himself as public property." Numerous others have expressed this sentiment over time, becoming the familiar principle – public service is a public trust. A public service is any service intended to address specific needs pertaining to the aggregate members of a community. Public services are available to people within a government jurisdiction as provided directly through public sector agencies or via public financing to private businesses or voluntary organizations (or even as provided by family households, though terminology may differ depending on context). Other public services are undertaken on behalf of government's residents or in the interest of its citizens. The term is associated with a social consensus (usually expressed through democratic elections) that certain services should be available to all, regardless of income, physical ability, or mental acuity.

A public service may be delivered by organizations in the public sector, private sector, or third sector. When the private or third sector is involved, a procurement process is generally in place. The involvement of these different sectors further introduces additional goals, strategies, and cultures that influence fundamental public service goals, strategies, and cultures. Public services can be constructed, coordinated, and operated in many ways or forms. They include government agencies, independent state-funded institutes, government-coordinated organizations, civil society, militaries, and volunteers. In addition, public services are often delivered through various intergovernmental organizations and across levels of government.

There are three levels of government in the public sector: federal, state, and local. Each level of government has different responsibilities, and they all interact with each other to some degree. There is also a hierarchy of authority between the three levels of government. Federal or National is responsible for national defense, foreign policy, printing money, and regulating interstate commerce. Regional, state, and provincial are often responsible for education, transportation, prisons, and welfare. Local, municipal, and country are often responsible for police and fire departments, zoning, and trash collection.

The Structure and Complex Nature of Public Service Cultures

Public sector cultures are the most complex of all the organizational cultures we may explore. Public sector organization cultures have multiple layers. There are four layers of interpretation of culture within any public sector organization (Fig. 1). The first tier focuses on a public sector organization's essential goals and purpose. Tier 1 culture focuses on the essential structure of the organization and its essential operating culture. Tier 2 culture represents the fundamental public service culture – the essential assumptions, beliefs, values, behaviors, and artifacts involved in designing and delivering public services. Tier 3 represents the external environments in which public sector organizations function – aligned with the sector and domain of their services and products. Finally, Tier 4 represents those three cultures essential to the knowledge economy – KLC approach.

A public sector organization delivers public services to sectors and domains supplementary to the private sector. The work context is the public sector, and the deliverables are public services. However, each organization must also function in economic sectors and domains (i.e., military, education, health, economics, international relations, transportation, space exploration, and so on). At this level, we see a range of organizational business structures and cultures, i.e., bureaucracy, fief, market, and clan. There is no clear pattern of organizational structure or business culture across public sector organizations – they all exist. The public sector organizational culture is a blending of public interest culture and the domain culture – this means synthesizing the domain or functional culture of its stakeholders with the organizational cultures they bring from the for-profit sector, the academic sectors,

The first layer describes an organization's foundational administrative structure and company culture (Tier 1). It represents the foundation layer which concentrates on the essential business structure and culture. Public service structure and culture are bureaucratic at their highest level.

The second layer represents an organization's internal public service culture (Tier 2) tailored to the nature of the services it provides, e.g., military, education, labor, health, and diplomacy. We find a culture that aligns with the essential

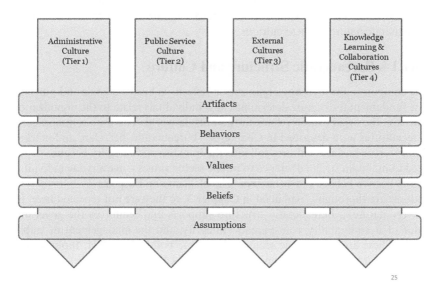

Fig. 1.   Four Tiers of Public Sector Cultures.

values, norms, and ethics of public service but adapts that culture to achieve the organization's particular public service goals and objectives.

The third layer represents the cultures of the external environment (Tier 3) and all those other entities involved in the general sector or market related to the organization's particular service. The two previous layers will be influenced by the domain or sector in which they operate. The actual complexity is observed at the functional level because public sector organizations work with all the other sectors to deliver domain-based services and products.

To these three layers, the authors add a fourth (Tier 4) focused on the organization's KLC cultures. We consider how the complex cultures of public sector organizations affect the design and implementation of their KLC cultures. The authors suggest we cannot assume that a one-size fits all approach will be effective for all public sector organizations.

In any given public sector organization, the four tiers will produce a unique culture grounded in public service but adapted to perform in diverse external environments. While there is a persistent bureaucratic administrative culture, that culture will be influenced by the goals and motives of the political leadership. This leadership is transitory representing the current government leadership in place at the time. We have positioned the KLC cultures at Tier 4, but in fact they play out in the day-to-day public service behaviors and decisions of the organization.

To navigate the culture of any public service organization, we must understand the confluence of all these cultures in a dynamic knowledge economy. The remainder of this chapter is devoted to exploring the fundamental nature of each of the four cultures. The heart of any public service culture, though, is those assumptions, beliefs, values, behaviors, and artifacts that define public service. We examine each of the five levels of public service culture in detail below. In Chapters 9–12, we select specific public sector organization to better understand the dynamic nature of these cultures.

Tier 1 – Bureaucratic Structure and Culture

The company culture of any organization reflects its business goals and purpose. The fundamental structure determines how individuals relate to the organization and how the organization relates to the outside world. The four common company cultures were described in Chapter 3 – bureaucratic, fief, clan, and market. Public sector business cultures fall into the bureaucratic category because of the need to maintain strict adherence to public sector values – in everyday individual and collective beliefs and behaviors. The elements and aspects of bureaucratic cultures are thoroughly explained in Chapter 3, so they are not repeated here. By its very nature, a bureaucratic structure supports and reinforces the governing value of accountability, transparency, integrity, and the management of public funds. These are core public sector values. One point of conflict, though, is in the empowerment and involvement of individuals. In public sector organizations, empowerment of individuals is less important than it is in the private sector. Public sector values are there for a reason – they are essential to building support for the independent institutions of government. Without these institutions, there can be no public services. Public sector organizations have established codes of conduct. These codes of conduct affect how the organization is managed. And, in some cases, the codes of conduct have been translated into regulations.

The bureaucratic structure tends to be more autocratic in its management style. In addition, the fundamental organizational culture is heavily influenced by leaders' management style and organizational practices. This presents a paradox for public sector organizations. The bureaucratic structure and culture are least likely to promote and encourage the individual styles of top and line managers. Managers are rewarded for the collective achievements of their teams, rather than their individual efforts and styles. Public sector managers cultivate employee commitment, belief in the business goals, adherence to collective and espoused ethics, values, and norms, and a commitment to work group cohesion. While public sector organizations are generally bureaucratic in nature, their fundamental cultures tend to contradict these tendencies. It presents a first example of the cultural complexity of public sector organizations (Angle & Perry, 1981; Baladwin, 1987; Choudhry, 1989; Kline & Peters, 1991; Mishra & Kasim, 2021; Morrow & Goetz, 1988; O'Reilly, 2008; Odom et al., 1990).

In the case of public sector organizations, though, the bureaucratic structure is tempered by the public sector purpose and goals. The moderating influence of public sector cultures allows for employee participation and involvement within the bureaucracy. Supporting some degree of participation and involvement is critical to higher levels of employee commitment. It explains how public sector cultures can thrive within a bureaucratic structure. The bureaucratic structure and culture are essential to managing public funds, engendering trust, and ensuring full accountability of public sector organizations to citizens.

Tier 2 – Public Sector Cultures

The second level of culture in public sector organizations reflects public service assumptions, beliefs, values, behaviors, and artifacts. While every culture is comprised of five levels (Fig. 2), public sector cultures are strongly anchored on the third or middle-level which focuses on values. The peer-reviewed literature strongly supports this idea. Research suggests that public sector values, norms, and ethics are taught to the entire workforce, reinforced through rewards and recognitions, integrated into performance assessment processes, and evident in artifacts in any public sector facility (Anderson, 2012; Kernaghan, 2000, 2003; Peters & Waterman 1984; Schein, 1993; Tait, 1997; Van Wart, 2013).

Every public sector organization has published codes of ethics (e.g., values), codes of conduct (e.g., behaviors), and artifacts that reflect these core values. The core tier is common to public sector organizations. The assumptions and beliefs that individual's act upon every day are grounded in these values. Their behaviors will be guided by adherence to these values. And, the reward or punishment of those behaviors will be designed to support these values (e.g., whistleblowers, internal audits, compliance regimes, censure, punishment, and dismissal).

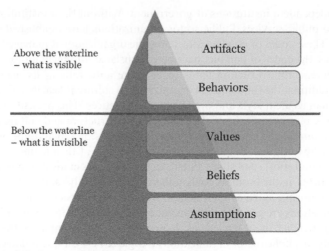

Above the waterline
– what is visible

Below the waterline
– what is invisible

Artifacts

Behaviors

Values

Beliefs

Assumptions

Fig. 2.   Public Sector Culture Focus on Values.

In this section, we offer a high-level comparison of private and public sector values. The comparison illustrates the cultural paradox experienced by public sector organizations. The bureaucratic structure and culture typically favor private sector values. We gain a deeper understanding of public sector values by contrasting them with private sector values. Larson (1997) provides a side by side comparison of private and public sector values (Fig. 3).

An important caveat in some contexts is the influence that transitory political leadership may have on public sector cultures. Political leadership may tend to favor some values over others, or to downplay them in favor of the bureaucratic culture. The literature suggests this variation in values, though, is likely to influence the top levels of the organization rather than the whole workforce. In those contexts where political leadership changes on a frequent basis, we can expect cultural adjustments. There is a tendency to see this top management shift as a cultural fragility. History has shown, though, that the mechanisms in place to support and reinforce values tend to maintain a balance to the public sector culture. They help to ensure that behaviors remain within the range of codes of conduct.

Values, Norms, and Ethics Common Across Public Sector Organizations

Cultural research defines several types of values including espoused, lived and actual, and aspirational. In public sector organizations, the most obvious values are espoused values, norms, and ethics. These are the values promoted by the organization. The public and community service nature of public sector work, and the core values of transparency and accountability, tend to give greater visibility to espoused values. The public visibility of public sector espoused values in published codes, in behavioral standards and in artifacts is designed to engender trust and

Private Sector Values	Public Sector Values
Seize opportunity	Avoid danger
Take risks	Eliminate risk
Least cost	Least danger
Speed	Due process
Efficiency	Transparency
Effectiveness	High technical standards
Empower the individual	Accountability
Bottom line	Public good
Market niche	Equality of access
Customer focus	Order taker
Market price	Rationed access
Selection on best fit	Equal opportunity
Value added	Control
Pay market price	Fair pay
Pay for performance	Pay for level

Fig. 3.   Larson's Comparison of Public and Private Sector Values.

equitable treatment of the customer base (Argyriades, 2003; Bellante & Link, 1981; Blank, 1985; Georgel & Jones, 1997; Van der Wal et al., 2008). It is essential to the functioning of any public sector organization. The espoused values are grounded in a state's founding documents and values. Examples of widely espoused values for democratic states include:

- the avoidance or minimization of *danger*,
- the elimination or minimization of *risk*,
- ensuring *due process*,
- striving for *transparency*,
- respect for objectivity,
- setting and achieving *high standards*,
- ensuring *accountability* of actions,
- maintaining *control* to ensure accountability,
- serving the *public good*,
- affording *equality* of access,
- taking and fulfilling requests and *orders from constituents*,
- providing *rationed access*,
- affording *equal opportunity*,
- *fair rewards* and pay,
- pay for level of *qualification*.

Espoused values are defined to influence how we behave at work, and to influence what we believe when we are at work (Baldwin, 1987, 1990; Barney, 1986; Barzelay, 2001; Boore & Scarbrough, 1998; Rifkin, 1995; Staats, 1988). And, they influence the assumptions we make when we take actions or make decisions at work. In some organizations, espoused values may be at variance with the actual or lived values of employees. This is the case in many private sector organizations where individual work is promoted for the collective work of the workforce (Buchanan, 1975; Crewson, 1995; Gabris & Simo, 1995; Christensen, Paarlberg, & Perry, 2017; Perry, 1997; Perry & Wise, 1990; Rainey, 1982).

Public sector organizations tend to have a relatively close alignment of espoused and lived or actual values. Research suggests that this set of values is different from private sector organization cultures. The primary and unique grounding of public sector espoused values is in democratic principles, public institutions, and the public interest (Christensen, Paarlberg, & Perry, 2017; Perry, 1997; Perry & Wise, 1990; Rainey, 1979). Research also suggests that individuals in these organizations are predisposed to perform public service in any area of society and in all aspects of their lives. Furthermore, the literature suggests that there is a strong alignment of values and beliefs across the public sector workforce.

Values are often closely aligned with an individual's core beliefs. We would expect this to be the case where there is a close alignment of espoused and actual values. Individuals with highly aligned values and beliefs may be attracted to public service as a means of living their values. Kernaghan (2003) provides deeper insights into the full set of public sector values (Table 1). The breakdown of values may also be seen as common beliefs. This suggests that there may be a close alignment of espoused and actual values in public sector cultures.

The professional values identified by Kernaghan are closely aligned with ethical values. The alignment explains how core values may influence behavior. Public administrators must act with integrity in all of their doings to earn public trust. Integrity means always being honest and fair, whether it is with neighbors, friends, or businesses. Everything a public administrator does and says can be looked

Table 1.   Kernaghan's Characterization of Public Sector Values.

Ethical Values	Democratic Values	Professional Values	People Values
Integrity	Rule of law	Effectiveness	Caring
Fairness	Neutrality	Efficiency	Fairness
Accountability	Accountability	Service	Tolerance
Loyalty	Loyalty	Leadership	Decency
Excellence	Openness	Excellence	Compassion
Respect	Responsiveness	Innovation	Courage
Honesty	Representativeness	Quality	Benevolence
Probity	Legality	Creativity	Humanity

upon by the public. Many public administrators have been caught deceiving the public or acting unethically, and it often ruins their careers. Public administrators must always show integrity and be mindful of laws and regulations. They must not use their power in the wrong way.

There is also a moral dimension to public service (Frederickson & Hart, 1985) which includes patriotism and benevolence. Public servants guard espoused values, including ensuring that all citizens are ensured of their basic rights.

Beliefs of Public Service Organizations

What is a public service belief? What is a public service assumption? In Chapter 1, we defined an assumption as something we accept as true without question or proof. Assumptions are thoughts we take for granted and believe to be true. They aren't based on facts; they are based on past experiences. Assumptions describe how people perceive situations and make sense of events, activities, and human relationships. What does the public sector workforce assume about the world? Beliefs are underlying assumptions about the world and how it works. Beliefs held for a long time without being violated or challenged may be taken so much for granted that we are no longer aware of them. Beliefs are our brain's way of making sense of and navigating our complex world. They are mental representations of how our brains expect things in our environment to behave and how things should be related – the patterns our brain expects the world to conform to. A belief is an attitude that something is the case or that some proposition about the world is true.

As a desk check of complex cultures, we take public sector organizations from the United States. The examples and the effects of culture will vary in other governance structures in other countries. We can, though, lay out a framework for analysis using these examples. American democracy is based on a belief in the core values on which the country was founded. Jiao, Richards, and Zhang (2011) calls out the extensive and active care and respect for others as a primary belief and motivator. The belief in self-sacrifice (Christensen, Paarlberg, & Perry, 2017) is another motivator. Burns (2007) calls out other fundamental belief as a heroic love for the public good, a devotion to justice, a willingness to sacrifice comfort and riches for the public well-being. Another core belief is the importance of making a difference in society means more to me than personal achievements.

Research that suggests that individuals are drawn to public service primarily by a unique set of altruistic assumptions and beliefs. Such assumptions and beliefs may include wanting to serve the public interest, to effect social change, and shape policies that benefit society as a whole (Frederickson & Hart, 1985; Perry & Porter, 1982; Perry & Wise, 1990). This perspective views public service as a distinct profession or calling to which certain types of people are morally drawn.

Public service values are translated to attitudes, beliefs, and assumptions at the individual level (Gelissen, 2008; Kaase et al., 1997; Ohr et al., 2017). Beliefs and assumptions may be visible in the form of personal motivations. Motivations in turn lead to work actions and behaviors. Work values are a form of motivation. They are a critical link between values and beliefs. They explain both how espoused values are internalized, and how individual beliefs are adapted to align with espoused values. Work values are generalized beliefs about the desirability of certain attributes of work (e.g., pay, autonomy, and working conditions), and work-related outcomes (e.g., accomplishment, fulfillment, and prestige). Like general values, work values act as the criteria that an individual uses in selecting appropriate work-related behaviors and goals (Elizur & Sagie 1999; Sagie & Elizur, 1999). Work values are derived from broader general values (George & Jones, 1997; Roe & Ester, 1998). The literature also suggests that public sector organizations have peculiar work values, including (1) extrinsic work values; (2) intrinsic work values; (3) altruistic work values, (4) prestige work values; and (5) social work values. Work values also translate to and influence work behaviors.

Intrinsic work values include aspects related to the nature of one's work, such as intellectual stimulation, creativity, and challenge. The theory of occupational choice suggests that people who value intrinsic rewards highly will seek employment in the sector that best fulfills that value. The research also suggests that public sector workers have a stronger desire to help others and to be useful to society. Research suggests that public sector employees were more likely to seek jobs that offered job security, interesting work, opportunities to help others, to be useful to society rather than personal empowerment and high salaries.

Altruistic work values (Perry & Wise, 1990) suggest that people who seek work in the public sector are fundamentally motivated to serve the public interest. Past research that has examined altruistic work values has consistently found that public servants value helping others and making a contribution to society more than private sector employees (Frank & Lewis, 2004; Karl & Sutton, 1998; Lewis & Frank, 2002).

The only *prestige work value* to be included in prior research is advancement opportunities, and the research is inconclusive. Frank and Lewis (2004) found that private sector employees value advancement opportunities more than public sector employees. However, Khojasteh (1993) found that public sector managers value advancement opportunities significantly more than private sector managers. And, Karl, and Sutton (1998) found no significant difference between the two sectors for this value.

Social work values were examined by Rawls et al. (1975). They found that public sector employees place greater importance on personal relations than did private sector employees. However, Khojasteh (1993) found no significant difference between public sector employees and private sector employees with respect to the value of interpersonal relations.

Public Sector Behaviors and Codes of Conduct

In the construction of cultures, there are dependencies between values and behaviors. Just as it is impossible to understand our values outside of our beliefs, so is it difficult to understand our behaviors without knowing our values. As we noted in Chapter 1, behaviors and habits are what an external observer can see. Individuals, communities, and societies demonstrate their values in their everyday behaviors and work practices (Alonso & Lewis, 2001; Liou & Nyhan, 1994;

Moshabaki et al., 2013; Newstrom et al., 1976; Schermerhorn Jr. et al., 2011; Vasu et al., 2017; Young et al., 1998; Zeffane, 1994). Behaviors are represented in the language we use, how we communicate, how we dress or present ourselves, how we make decisions, how we reward others, our relationships, and even how we respond to change or crises. Individuals tailor their behaviors to suit the context. Organizations have codes of conduct that instruct individuals how to dress, how to conduct yourself, to interact with and communicate with others when you are in a work environment, how to behave in a faith or spiritual context, the gym or exercise context, the maker space, a college classroom, or an open public space, or on public transport. Each of these behavioral adaptations is grounded in our value systems – and each of these different environments causes us to adapt and translate to meet the expectations of others around us.

The behaviors of interest to the authors are work behaviors, learning styles, knowledge-sharing practices, and willingness to work with others. How do public sector organizations turn values into behaviors? And, how do they maintain and reinforce them? Do public service employees follow espoused values in their behavior? Or, are there indications of actual, lived, or individual values in their behaviors? Public sector espoused behaviors describe how public servants interact with others in their organizations and with the public. They address how public servants should view their work and its importance to their communities. It also speaks to how they behave when they are serving their communities, cities, states, and nation. Public servants' behaviors speak to the essence of how public services are delivered and administered.

The most obvious representation of public service behaviors are organizational codes of conduct. Codes of ethics and codes of conduct are often translated to measure the public uses to assess the effectiveness and efficiency of these public sector organizations. At the core of any public sector code of conduct is a simple instruction – public servants must conduct themselves in a manner that shows the public that they are trustworthy. This means adhering to the core values of the organization. The core values essentially reflect Kernaghan's four categories – professional, democratic, ethical, and human. By way of example, we offer a summary of the behavioral guidelines specified in the US Federal Government Executive Order 12674 below:

- Public service is a public trust, requiring you to place loyalty to the constitution, the laws, and ethical principles above private gain.
- You shall not hold financial interests that conflict with the conscientious performance of duty.
- You shall not engage in financial transactions using non-public government information or allow improper use of such information to further any private interest.
- You shall not, except pursuant to such reasonable exceptions as are provided by regulation, solicit or accept any gift or other item of monetary value from any person or entity seeking official action from, doing business with, or conducting activities regulated by your agency, or whose interests may be substantially affected by the performance or nonperformance of your duties.

- You shall make no unauthorized commitments or promise of any kind purported to bind the government.
- You shall put forth honest effort in the performance of your duties.
- You shall not engage in outside employment or activities, including seeking or negotiating for employment, that conflict with your official government duties and responsibilities.
- You shall disclose waste, fraud, abuse, and corruption to appropriate authorities.
- You shall satisfy in good faith your obligations as citizens, including all just financial obligations, especially those such as federal, state, or local taxes that are imposed by law.
- You shall adhere to all laws and regulations that provide equal opportunities for all Americans regardless of race, religion, color, sex (including pregnancy, gender identity, and sexual orientation), parental status, national origin, age, disability, family medical history or genetic information, political affiliation, and military service.
- You shall not use your public office for private gain.
- You shall act impartially and not give preferential treatment to any private organization or individual.
- You shall protect and conserve federal property and shall not use it for other than authorized activity.
- You shall endeavor to avoid any actions creating the appearance that you are violating the law.

The code of conduct defined in Executive Order 12674 focuses on behaviors that are not acceptable for public servants. The codes of individual organizations take the Executive Order as a foundation, but go beyond to address what types of behaviors are expected. These behaviors all have clear and obvious links to public sector espoused values (Table 2). Public servants are expected to follow the behaviors described in Column 1. Column 2 traces the behavior to one or more espoused public service values.

While the Executive Order is a foundation, every public sector organization adds behavior and conduct guidelines that are specific to the services they provide. For example, military services will have codes of conduct that speak to the well-being and security of the team or corps. Diplomatic services will speak to the importance of ensuring full and true representation of the country's interests over an individual's beliefs. Each of these behavioral guidelines is grounded in an ethic or value discussed in the previous section. These are espoused behaviors grounded in espoused values and beliefs. It is not unreasonable to expect that cultural conflicts will emerge where partners or other stakeholders collaborating with public servants have variant values and beliefs. It is difficult, though, for individuals with different actual or lived values and assumptions to work and succeed in an environment because the espoused values are strictly enforced.

Table 2. Mapping of Public Sector Behaviorss to Values.

Public Service Code of Conduct	Public Service Values
Safeguard public funds	• Accountability • Control • Minimization of danger • Risk avoidance • Transparency
Be accountable for your actions	• Accountability • Risk avoidance • Transparency
Be professional in carrying out your duties	• Transparency • Objectivity • Constituent services • Equal opportunity
Provide service to all	• Equality of access
Prohibit expression of personal opinions	• Minimization of risk • Objectivity
Avoid conflicts of interest	• Objectivity • Transparency • Constituent services
Provide public access to information	• Equality of access • Constituent services
Provide public access to services	• Equality of access • Constituent services
Support access to training and learning	• Qualification and competence • Equal opportunity • Equality of access
Ensure respect for law	• Due process
Ensure equal treatment before the law	• Due process • Equality of opportunity • Equal access • Constituents
Treat everyone with equal respect	• High standards • Constituents • Due process • Public good
Provide service to the public	• Public good • Equality of access • Constituents • Rationed access
Ensure equity in compensation	• Fair rewards and pay • Qualification and competence
Ensure equity in treatment and classification	• Equal opportunity • Equal access
Ensure support and care for the whole Person – well-being, education, due process	• Equal opportunity • Fair rewards and pay

Behavior is also influenced by motivation. A motivation is a fundamental belief that determines how an individual will behave and the choices they will make. Beliefs are rational, norm-based, and affective motives. A rational motive or belief is one that serves to maximize an individual's self-interest. Research suggests that public service workforce believe less in self-interest than in the community welfare and the public good. Normative motives reflect a commitment to serving the public interest, achieving social justice and carrying out one's civic duty (Gawthrop, 1998). A common belief held across the public sector workforce is a commitment to the public interest, social justice and a desire to ensure that those who lack resources are not disadvantaged (Christensen, Paarlberg, & Perry, 2017).

The public service workforce is likely to hold individual beliefs that are aligned with an organization's espoused values, including: (1) a belief in the importance of ethics; (2) a belief in the good of the community over the good of the individual; (3) a belief in accountability; (4) a belief in transparency; (5) a belief in equality; (6) a belief in universal access; (7) a belief in universal access (8) a belief in universal rights; and (9) a belief in objectivity. Perry and Wise (1990) defined public service employees norm-based motives as grounded in a desire to pursue the common good and further the public interest, in patriotism, duty, and loyalty.

Another element of the behavioral level of public sector culture is those processes designed to ensure accountability of public service behaviors and actions. There are formal mechanisms, e.g., hiring and firing actions, whistleblower reports, internal audit processes, policies and procedures that favor risk aversity and avoidance, and a strict safeguarding of public funds. We note the federal code of conduct specifically states "...as a condition of public service, you are expected to adhere to these fundamental principles of ethical behavior." In other words, if you are unable to adhere to these principles of ethical behavior, there will be consequences. Public sector cultures also include reinforcing mechanisms as part of the organization's behavior.

The codes of conduct and acceptable behaviors are important guidelines for hiring, promotion, and firing actions. Internal audit units, inspector general offices, oversight, and whistleblowers are independent mechanisms that guarantee fairness and merit. Public sector behaviors also include formal mechanisms for addressing grievances. To these formal enforcement mechanisms, there is another informal mechanism – governance in the public interest. Informal mechanisms are enforced through behavioral examples – behaving in a way that is consistent with the foundational values. It is this tight alignment of four levels of culture that make public sectors such an interesting source of learning and research.

The explicit espoused codes of conduct and the formal reinforcement processes of public sector organizations create strong organizational cultures. Because these behaviors are grounded on espoused values, ethics, norms, and beliefs, they also promote strong organizational citizenship (Erkutlu, 2011; Ghorbani & Ghaempanah, 2014; Korsgaard et al., 2010; Koning & Van Kleef, 2015; Mohanty

& Rath, 2012; Soltani & Maupetit, 2015). The research suggests that public sector cultures serve to achieve the organization's business goals and objectives. The challenge, though, is how might these strong cultures adapt to working with other conflicting cultures. And, how well can they integrate the new knowledge, learning, and collaborative cultures essential to the knowledge economy?

As the codes of conduct examples suggest, public servants are charged with making our communities and our society better by fostering citizenship, making cities safer, educating youth, healing the sick, protecting the vulnerable, and keeping the country and the world clean, safe, and prosperous. They work with partners, elected officials, business leaders, citizens, world leaders, and others to achieve these goals. It is at this level that behaviors can reflect different underlying values and beliefs of those other partners.

Organizational behavior in the public sector is the sum of interactions and influences across all of the cultures of its stakeholders – whether partners, the general public, stakeholders, or competitors. It is the product of a complex set of interactions among individuals, groups, organizational factors, and the public environment. In part because of the complexity of these interactions, the management of behavior in organizations always will be complex, somewhat unpredictable, and challenging. This further explains why it is important for behaviors to be grounded in values, and values to be reflected in individual beliefs and assumptions.

Public Sector Artifacts

The fifth and most visible form of any culture is its artifacts. Artifacts take many forms, including logos and insignia, statues, medals and awards, building architectures, and work environment designs. A cursory review of symbols and architectures demonstrates the consistency of what is visible and what is invisible in public sector cultures. The architectures of most public sector buildings resemble historical monuments and architectures of ancient Greece – the home of democratic principles (Fig. 4). The architecture of public buildings is simple, not ornate – reflecting the focus on service to the broader community rather than showcasing or promoting individual styles. Because of the basic architectures, it is easy for citizens to recognize a public building. These architectural styles are found at all levels of the public sector. Each public sector building flies the flag of the organization as well as the broader governing entity. Symbols or insignia are often carved into the buildings. The consistent and unchanging nature of public sector architecture also reinforces the value of persistence, dedication, and stability. The designs also reinforce the idea of accessibility to the public.

Additionally, each public sector organization has its own symbol and insignia. The designs tend to reinforce fundamental values and beliefs, augmented by symbols representing the particular service of an organization. Fig. 5 provides a sample of organizational insignia for defense services, justice, diplomacy,

Fig. 4.   Sample Public Sector Buildings.

agriculture, space exploration, and agriculture. Each includes some form of the national culture – in this case – and tailors that symbol to reflect the services provided by the organization.

For example, the insignia of the Department of State derives from the Official Seal of the United States, which symbolizes independence and self-government. It is affixed to official documents such as proclamations, treaties, and communications issued by the President to heads of foreign governments. The Department of Defense insignia positions rays and stars above the eagle to signify glory. The three arrows in the eagles talons are symbolic of the three branches of service – Army, Navy, and Air Force. The laurel stands for honors received in combat defending the peace represented by the olive branch. The defense sector of any public sector has an extensive repertoire of artifacts to represent an individuals' rank and achievements. In this way, artifacts are a clear and obvious cultural award for high performance. The three insignia at the bottom of Fig. 5 focus on the missions and purpose of those organizations, rather than build on the symbols of the national culture. For example, the Department of Agriculture insignia communicates a modern organization focused on the future while respecting historical traditions. The center image is a representation of the land – the foundation of agriculture. NASA's insignia represents the environment and context in which the organization – its focus. Finally, the insignia of the Department of Health and Human Services represents the people sheltered in the wing of the

Fig. 5. Sample Insignia of Public Sector Organizations.

American Eagle, suggesting a concern and responsibility for the welfare of the people – another core value of the public sector.

We could select and explain many other artifacts of public sector organizations. However, we make the argument that public sector cultures are well aligned and reinforced across all five levels. As we move into Tier 3 of the larger culture, though, the coherence at Tiers 1 and 2 can lead to paradoxes in all levels. And, the paradoxes differ depending on the external environment, the stakeholders and the nature of the service.

Tier 3 – Cultures of the External Environment

The third tier of public sector cultures focuses on the cultures of the external environment. As noted earlier, public services may be developed and delivered through a variety of mechanisms and with a variety of partners. The paradox is that those organizations that partner with public sector organizations may have very different internal cultures. The beliefs, values, and behaviors of individuals in those organizations may be at variance with public sector organizations. In most cases, the basic assumption (e.g., a critical culture level) is that public service culture will prevail in the face of differences to ensure the safeguarding and accountability values are respected. There are three sources of external influence, including: (1) the political environment and the transitory leadership culture assigned to the organization; (2) the external environment and the cultures of partners and stakeholders; and (3) the nature of the service and its commercial value.

Every public sector organization has private sector, non-profit, and not-for-profit partners and stakeholders. In the larger market, public services are a subset of the full production and delivery system. For example, public defense services and branches work with the weapons industry, the telecommunications industry, the equipment industry, the food sector, the medical sector, and the education sector. Each of these partners has their own business structure and culture. Those cultures may vary from public sector cultures at any or at all levels of the culture. The same may be said of public sector health and medical organizations. Stakeholders include medical education, medical research, pharmaceutical industries, medical practices, Therapies, and social work.

There are many sources of influence in the external environment (Fig. 6). Looking across the public sector landscape, the most common external partners and stakeholders include (1) business and private sector organizations; (2) research organizations and institutes; (3) non- and not-for-profit entities; (4) other organizations in the same subject domain; and (5) education, learning, and training partners. In working with other organizations, variations in cultures will become evident.

The alignment of business goals and cultures may vary significantly. When there are cultural variations, there may be cultural conflicts. Where the conflicts are constructive, both cultures may benefit from adaptation. Where the conflicts are not constructive, though, the public service culture must prevail for the public sector workforce. In some cases, the conflict may be external and not directly affect the internal culture of the organization. In other cases, though, the conflicts are internal to the organization. In these cases, serious paradoxes may exist.

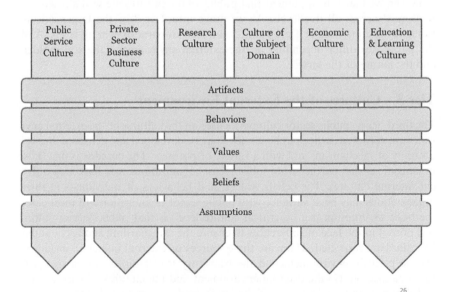

Fig. 6.   Complex Cultures of the Public Sector.

The most serious public service culture conflicts occur when political actors exert undue influence to ignore, adapt or rescind the strong internal culture. As the leader of the organization, the influence on the culture can be significant. Where leaders do not accept or align their behaviors with the organizational culture, doubt will be case over the espoused culture. In some cases, where the espoused culture is also the lived and actual culture, there may be a reaction to leadership. When culture is in conflict or even in doubt, we know from Chapter 3 that the organization's strategy and performance will be at risk. Aligning and adapting cultures to achieve a goal may affect strategy and performance in different ways. In the following chapters, the authors discuss how shifts in cultural values lead to significant accidents. Over the past 40 years, political leadership has advocated for introducing some core business values – risk taking, cost efficiency, empowerment of individuals – into public sector cultures.

While grounded in bureaucratic and public sector cultures, the cultures of individual public sector organizations are unique. In order to understand the historical or future effects of potential external influences, we must examine each organization. It is necessary to analyze each institutional culture to understand the role these other cultures play, and how they influence the Tier 1 values. And to understand how this complex cultural environment may be further influenced by the cultures of transient political leadership.

It is important for the public service workforce to have a good understanding of culture and the effect it can have on beliefs, values, behaviors, and performance. The deeper their understanding, the better prepared they will be to make wise choices to fulfill their responsibilities and still honor the public service culture. Earlier, we suggested that there was a close alignment of espoused and actual values in the public sector. That may change if the balance and integration of the public service workforce changes. The greatest discrepancy is at the values level – an actual clash of values between private and public sector values – without reconciliation or synthesis.

Tier 4 – KLC Cultures of Public Services Organizations

As discussed in Chapters 3, 4, and 6, the synergies generated by the three cultures are essential to surviving and thriving in a hyperdynamic knowledge economy, including (1) a knowledge culture; (2) a learning culture; and (3) a collaboration culture. Working together these three cultures ensure that there is awareness of the value of knowledge and a recognition of the value of the human source of knowledge, that there is continuous generation of knowledge through learning, and that knowledge flows through collaboration. These chapters, though, also exposed the challenges and paradoxes we encounter when we build these functional cultures into hierarchies – bureaucracies, adhocracies – fief, markets, or clan cultures.

How does the KLC approach apply to public service with dominating hierarchies? Is it different from the KLC approach in the private sector? How might the complex, multilayer culture of the public sector hierarchies affect how knowledge is created, preserved, curated, and shared? How might the complex culture of the public sector affect how the organization and the workforce learn? How might the complex culture of the public sector affect collaboration?

We have found that public service cultures are deceptively simple at first glance. We suggest that public service cultures provide an important environment for understanding all of the ways that different cultural sources and factors may affect KLC cultures. We can learn much by examining these complex cultures, and thus provide more rigorous guidance for managers across all types of organizations,

While we can say that generally, a public service organization has a bureaucratic business or company culture (Tier 1), it may not represent the business or company culture of the whole organization. All public service organizations may be bureaucratic at the very top level, but as we will see in our examples – some have market and clan cultures at levels below the company leadership level. This means that we may find varying KLC cultures across the organization. It is generally not the case in private sector organizations where company leaders have more power to define the culture. The bureaucratic – hierarchical culture is more representative of the strategic level of a public sector organization rather than the workforce of those organizations. In many countries, the leadership of these organizations is transitory, changing with each new governing administration. The bureaucratic – hierarchical culture tends to provide a level of stability at a level which tends to be more dynamic and unpredictable.

One element of public service culture tends to reduce complexity. It is the clear and consistent espoused public service culture (Tier 2) that exists across the full governance landscape. This espoused public service culture is also a lived culture where it reflects and reinforces national cultures. This is the case where national cultures stress the values of public well-being and knowledge, sharing, and access. Where discrepancies exist, we may find espoused but not lived values. The alignment will determine how knowledge is created, how and with whom it is shared, and whether and with whom we collaborate.

Each public service organization has a unique external environment (Tier 3), even though they are formally part of a single government. The nature of the external environment will affect what knowledge is created, whether it is shared or protected, with whom it may or may not be shared; what is learned, from whom and with whom we learn; and whether collaboration is possible.

In the four chapters that follow, the authors explore how company cultures (Tier 1), public service cultures (Tier 2), and the cultures of external stakeholders (Tier 3) may influence the KLC cultures of public sector organizations. In our preliminary review – which provides the groundwork for further research and exploration – we find that the effects vary across public sector organizations. For example, while the public service culture may support knowledge creation and sharing, learning, and collaboration, it will be tempered or enhanced by the nature of the organization's mission and the economic environment in which it functions. In other words, each public sector organization provides a rich opportunity to see how different factors may affect the KLC orientation. These opportunities may lead to insights into the design and implementation of the KLC approach in other complex cultural contexts.

Knowledge Cultures

As we learned in Chapter 4, knowledge capital comes in several forms – human capital, structural capital, and relational capital. Organizations with bureaucratic structures and cultures tend to emphasize uncertainty avoidance, formalization, and control. These values, though, can jeopardize the development of knowledge flows, relationships and knowledge networks, workforce creativity, and the growth of essential competencies to innovate, think, and act out of the box. Moreover, in a bureaucratic culture, following traditional management assumptions and practices will diminish the value and impact of human capital.

It is a fundamental challenge for public service cultures. To be faithful to the values of accountability, transparency, and trust, it is crucial to maintain formal processes and control those processes. Public sector organizations are fundamentally bureaucratic at the base. Public service cultures at Tier 2, though, introduce a paradox. The paradox lies in those other core public service beliefs and values at odds with the spirit of a bureaucratic culture – public welfare, access to services, equity, and education. These beliefs and values align more closely with knowledge's basic economic properties and behaviors. This paradox may work in favor of introducing and sustaining a knowledge culture.

In addition to the business culture, we must also consider the influence of external cultures on a knowledge culture. In external environments where knowledge is subject to national security or intellectual property constraints, there may be effects on a knowledge culture. What an organization can achieve in those environments may be less than others simply because the stock of knowledge available is restricted. The restrictions may be imposed by public sector organizations (i.e., defense, national security, or intelligence organizations) or by private sector partners (i.e., pharmaceutical companies and medical practitioners protecting patients). There may be more significant incentives to create and share knowledge where the public sector organization's mandate is to conduct, promote, and disseminate research and applied knowledge (e.g., agriculture, education, and labor) or where external partners are primarily non- and not-for-profit organizations. Ultimately, though, the public service codes of ethics support a culture of learning and development of the whole individual. This aspect of public sector cultures bodes well for developing and sustaining a knowledge culture.

Learning Cultures

In Chapter 5, we defined a learning culture as an organization's ability to (Garvin, Edmondson, & Gino, 2008) create, acquire, and exchange knowledge, modify its behaviors and choices, and integrate that new knowledge and insights into its organizational knowledge. It is a set of norms and practices that secures the conditions to support the flow of knowledge across an organization. Learning cultures in bureaucratic and hierarchical business cultures presented one of our earliest cultures. Where knowledge cultures are embedded in bureaucratic and hierarchical organizational cultures, they may lead only to passive use of the existing knowledge. This alignment may not expand the minds or knowledge capital of individuals or the organization.

An antidote to this paradox is to create a learning climate across the organization where mistakes are accepted and used as learning opportunities. Where this is possible, we can significantly positively affect the development of an organization's intelligence. However, while the public service cultural values and beliefs may support an individual's learning and growth, the acceptance of mistakes as learning opportunities may be challenging. The challenge is reconciling mistakes with accountability, transparency, and public sector-wide performance guidelines and classifications.

Also, the cultures of the external environment will set expectations for the learning culture based on the learning climate of the broader field. External tolerance for mistakes and encouragement for multiple forms of learning will further support the development of an internal learning culture in public sector organizations.

Collaboration Cultures

A core tenet of any learning organization or culture is collaboration. Collaboration is the core competency that enables knowledge organizations to create relational knowledge capital. Relational capital has always been a critical business asset, but it has been understood as the "connections" of senior leaders. Today we understand relational capital as an asset of every individual. The ability to collaborate is vital to organizational growth and performance. Collaboration cultures create shared mindsets. They are grounded on shared values and beliefs. These shared values and beliefs include an organization's open communication, norms of respect, trust, teamwork, adaptability, risk-taking, and diversity (Pinjani & Palvia, 2013). In a collaborative culture, we find a favorable climate for knowledge dissemination, critical thinking, reflection, smooth interactions and communications that foster employee learning. The organization's essential values shape collaborative cultures, attitudes and behaviors and foster competitive performance. A collaborative culture can be created and sustained to the extent that public sector values predominate in any public sector organization. To the extent that the bureaucratic culture or the cultures of the external environment predominate, there may be obstacles.

One of the possible paradoxes for this internal culture may be whether collaboration is understood to involve both implicit and explicit knowledge capital. Most public sector organizations are mandated to make explicit information available to the public and to conduct research or investigations to produce explicit information. Established information policies will meet the fundamental requirements of collaboration. However, they are not sufficient for creating a collaborative culture among people. They are not sufficient for creating relational capital or exchanging other forms of implicit knowledge capital. Developing internal collaborative cultures for any specific public sector organization will depend upon which cultures are dominant and the sensitivity or protective nature of knowledge.

General Observations

The KLC approach represents groundbreaking research. It provides a rich agenda for future research. The authors begin to expand the application of the

KLC approach in four selected public service cultures, specifically the cultures of diplomatic services, defense services, space exploration, and agricultural services. Two of these are state-oriented, and two are constituent-oriented. They provide a good initial test of the KLC approach. However, these examples are not representative of all public service cultures. The comprehensive research caused us to examine our assumptions and beliefs about public sector cultures. We learned to see the complexity of the environments. And we learned to see the paradoxes within and across public service cultures.

Chapter Review

After reading this chapter, you should be able to:

- describe the business goals, purpose, and strategies of public sector organizations.
- explain how public service is the core public sector strategy.
- translate and interpret all five levels of culture for public sector organizations.
- explain the structure and complex nature of public service cultures.
- describe the complex nature of the four tiers of public service cultures.

References and Recommended Future Readings

Alonso, P., & Lewis, G. B. (2001). Public service motivation and job performance: Evidence from the federal sector. *The American Review of Public Administration, 31*(4), 363–380.

Anderson, S. (2012). Public, private, neither, both? Publicness theory and the analysis of healthcare organisations. *Social Science & Medicine, 74*(3), 313–322.

Angle, H. L., & Perry, J. L. (1981). An empirical assessment of organizational commitment and organizational effectiveness. *Administrative Science Quarterly, 26*(1), 1–14.

Argyriades, D. (2003). Values for public service: Lessons learned from recent trends and the Millennium Summit. *International Review of Administrative Sciences, 69*(4), 521–533.

Baldwin, J. N. (1987). Public versus private: Not that different, not that consequential. *Public Personnel Management, 16*(2), 181–193.

Baldwin, J. N. (1990). Public versus private employees: Debunking stereotypes. *Review of Public Personnel Administration, 11*(1–2), 1–27.

Barney, J. B. (1986). Organizational culture: Can it be a source of sustained competitive advantage? *Academy of Management Review, 11*(3), 656–665.

Barzelay, M. (2001). *The new public management: Improving research and policy dialogue* (Vol. 3). Univ of California Press.

Bellante, D., & Link, A. N. (1981). Are public sector workers more risk averse than private sector workers? *ILR Review, 34*(3), 408–412.

Blank, R. M. (1985). An analysis of workers' choice between employment in the public and private sectors. *ILR Review, 38*(2), 211–224.

Borre, O., & Scarbrough, E. (Eds.). (1998). *The scope of government* (Vol. 3). New York, NY: Oxford University Press.

Buchanan, B. (1975). Red-tape and the service ethic: Some unexpected differences between public and private managers. *Administration & Society, 6*(4), 423–444.

Burns, C. P. (2007). Self-sacrificial love: Evolutionary deception or theological reality? *CrossCurrents*, 102–115.

Choudhry, S. (1989). Occupational level and job satisfaction: A comparative study of public and private sector organisations. *Indian Journal of Applied Psychology, 26*(2), 1–5.

Christensen, R. K., Paarlberg, L., & Perry, J. L. (2017). Public service motivation research: Lessons for practice. *Public Administration Review, 77*(4), 529–542.

Crewson, P. E. (1995). *The public service ethic.* American University.

Elizur, D., & Sagie, A. (1999). Facets of personal values: A structural analysis of life and work values. *Applied psychology: an international review, 48*(1), 73–87.

Erkutlu, H. (2011). The moderating role of organizational culture in the relationship between organizational justice and organizational citizenship behaviors. *Leadership & Organization Development Journal.*

Frank, S. A., & Lewis, G. B. (2004). Government employees: Working hard or hardly working? *The American Review of Public Administration, 34*(1), 36–51.

Frederickson, H. G., & Hart, D. K. (1985). The public service and the patriotism of benevolence. *Public Administration Review, 45*(5), 547–553.

Gabris, G. T., & Simo, G. (1995). Public sector motivation as an independent variable affecting career decisions. *Public Personnel Management, 24*(1), 33–51.

Garvin, D. A., Edmondson, A. C., & Gino, F. (2008). Is yours a learning organization?. *Harvard Business Review, 86*(3), 109.

Gawthrop, L. C. (1998). The human side of public administration. *PS: Political Science & Politics, 31*(4), 763–769.

Gelissen, J. P. T. M. (2008). European scope-of-government beliefs: The impact of individual, regional and national characteristics. In W. van Oorschot, M. Opielka, & B. Pfau-Effinger (Eds.), *Culture and the welfare state: Values and social policy in comparative perspective* (pp. 247–267). Edward Elgar.

George, J. M., & Jones, G. R. (1997). Organizational spontaneity in context. *Human Performance, 10*(2), 153–170.

Georgel, J. M., & Jones, G. R. (1997). Experiencing work: Values, attitudes, and moods. *Human Relations, 50*(4), 393–416.

Ghorbani, R., & Ghaempanah, B. (2014). An investigation on the effect of organizational citizenship behavior on perceptions of service quality. *Management Science Letters, 4*(5), 937–940.

Jiao, C., Richards, D. A., & Zhang, K. (2011). Leadership and organizational citizenship behavior: OCB-specific meanings as mediators. *Journal of Business and Psychology, 26,* 11–25.

Kaase, M., Newton, K., & Scarbrough, E. (1997). Beliefs in government. *Politics, 17*(2), 135–139.

Karl, K. A., & Sutton, C. L. (1998). Job values in today's workforce: A comparison of public and private sector employees. *Public Personnel Management, 27*(4), 515–527.

Kernaghan, K. (2000). The post-bureaucratic organization and public service values. *International Review of Administrative Sciences, 66*(1), 91–104.

Kernaghan, K. (2003). Integrating values into public service: The values statement as centerpiece. *Public Administration Review, 63*(6), 711–719.

Khojasteh, M. (1993). Motivating the private vs. public sector managers. *Public Personnel Management, 22*(3), 391–401.

Kline, C. J., & Peters, L. H. (1991). Behavioral commitment and tenure of new employees: A replication and extension. *Academy of Management Journal, 34*(1), 194–204.

Koning, L. F., & Van Kleef, G. A. (2015). How leaders' emotional displays shape followers' organizational citizenship behavior. *The Leadership Quarterly, 26*(4), 489–501.

Korsgaard, M. A., Meglino, B. M., Lester, S. W., & Jeong, S. S. (2010). Paying you back or paying me forward: understanding rewarded and unrewarded organizational citizenship behavior. *Journal of Applied Psychology, 95*(2), 277.

Lewis, G. B., & Frank, S. A. (2002). Who wants to work for the government? *Public Administration Review, 62*(4), 395–404.

Liou, K. T., & Nyhan, R. C. (1994). Dimensions of organizational commitment in the public sector: An empirical assessment. *Public Administration Quarterly, 18*, 99–118.

Mishra, S. S., & Kasim, J. J. (2021). Team culture, employee commitment and job performance in public sectors: A multi-level analysis. *International Journal of Organizational Analysis, 31*(2).

Mohanty, J., & Rath, B. P. (2012). Influence of organizational culture on organizational citizenship behavior: A three-sector study. *Global Journal of Business Research, 6*(1), 65–76.

Morrow, P. C., & Goetz Jr, J. F. (1988). Professionalism as a form of work commitment. *Journal of Vocational Behavior, 32*(1), 92–111.

Moshabaki, A., Madani, F., & Ghorbani, H. (2013). An investigation of the role of human resource diversity management on organisational citizenship behaviour from organisational justice and commitment point of view in automotive industry in Iran. *International Journal of Management and Enterprise Development, 12*(4–6), 331–348.

Newstrom, J. W., Reif, W. E., & Monczka, R. M. (1976). Motivating the public employee: Fact vs. fiction. *Public Personnel Management, 5*(1), 67–72.

Odom, R. Y., Boxx, W. R., & Dunn, M. G. (1990). Organizational cultures, commitment, satisfaction, and cohesion. *Public Productivity & Management Review, 14*, 157–169.

Ohr, S., Jeong, S., & Saul, P. (2017). Cultural and religious beliefs and values, and their impact on preferences for end-of-life care among four ethnic groups of community-dwelling older persons. *Journal of Clinical Nursing, 26*(11–12), 1681–1689.

O'Reilly, C. (2008). CMR Classics: Corporations, Culture, and Commitment: Motivation and Social Control in Organizations. *California management review, 50*(2), 85–101.

Perry, J. L. (1997). Antecedents of public service motivation. *Journal of Public Administration Research and Theory, 7*(2), 181–197.

Perry, J. L., & Porter, L. W. (1982). Factors affecting the context for motivation in public organizations. *Academy of Management Review, 7*(1), 89–98.

Perry, J. L., & Wise, L. R. (1990). The motivational bases of public service. *Public Administration Review, 50*, 367–373.

Peters, T. J., & Waterman, R. H. (1984). In search of excellence. *Nursing Administration Quarterly, 8*(3), 85–86.

Pinjani, P., & Palvia, P. (2013). Trust and knowledge sharing in diverse global virtual teams. *Information & Management, 50*(4), 144–153.

Rainey, H. G. (1979). Perceptions of incentives in business and government: Implications for civil service reform. *Public Administration Review*, 440–448.

Rainey, H. G. (1982). Reward preferences among public and private managers: In search of the service ethic. *The American Review of Public Administration, 16*(4), 288–302.

Rawls, J. R., Ullrich, R. A., & Nelson Jr, O. T. (1975). A comparison of managers entering or reentering the profit and nonprofit sectors. *Academy of Management Journal, 18*(3), 616–623.

Rifkin, J. (1995). *The end of work: The decline of the global labor force and the new post-market era.* Jeremy P.

Roe, R. A., & Ester, P. (Eds.). (1998). *Values and work* (Vol. 48, No. 1). Taylor & Francis.

Sagie, A., & Elizur, D. (1999). Achievement motive and entrepreneurial orientation: A structural analysis. *Journal of Organizational Behavior: The International Journal of Industrial, Occupational and Organizational Psychology and Behavior, 20*(3), 375–387.

Schein, E. H. (1993). How can organizations learn faster?: The problem of entering the Green Room. *Sloan Management Review, 35* (2), 85–92.

Schermerhorn Jr, J. R., Osborn, R. N., Uhl-Bien, M., & Hunt, J. G. (2011). *Organizational behavior.* John Wiley & Sons.

Soltani, B., & Maupetit, C. (2015). Importance of core values of ethics, integrity and accountability in the European corporate governance codes. *Journal of Management & Governance, 19*(2), 259–284.

Staats, E. B. (1988). Public service and the public interest. *Public Administration Review*, 601–ii.

Tait, J. (1997). A strong foundation: Report of the task force on public service values and ethics (the summary). *Canadian Public Administration, 40*(1), 1–22.

Van der Wal, Z., De Graaf, G., & Lasthuizen, K. (2008). What's valued most? Similarities and differences between the organizational values of the public and private sector. *Public Administration, 86*(2), 465–482.

Van Wart, M. (2013). *Changing public sector values*. Routledge.

Vasu, M. L., Stewart, D. W., & Garson, G. D. (2017). *Organizational behavior and public management*. Routledge.

Young, B. S., Worchel, S., & Woehr, D. J. (1998). Organizational commitment among public service employees. *Public Personnel Management, 27*(3), 339–348.

Zeffane, R. (1994). Patterns of organizational commitment and perceived management style: A comparison of public and private sector employees. *Human Relations, 47*(8), 977–1010.

Chapter 9

The KLC Approach and Public Sector Diplomacy

Chapter Summary

This chapter describes the business goals, purpose, and strategy of public diplomatic services. It reinforces diplomatic organizations' fundamental bureaucratic administrative culture (Tier 1). The bureaucratic culture of diplomacy is deconstructed, and each of the five layers is described in detail. The authors also explain why focusing on the artifacts and behavior layers are the dominant and essential starting points for analysis in diplomatic cultures. The public service culture (Tier 2) overlays and mediates the bureaucratic culture.

Additionally, the authors describe the influence that political appointees as leaders may play in shaping public service cultures. Next, the authors explain how diplomatic cultures reflect the core values of a state's culture. Next, the chapter outlines the landscape of external influencing cultures (Tier 3) in diplomacy. Finally, the knowledge, learning, and collaboration (KLC) culture of diplomacy is considered, with opportunities for future growth.

Why We Care About Diplomatic Cultures?

Diplomacy is an essential process of the international system. It is how states talk to one another. It is essential to maintaining peace among states. As such, it is an essential function of states. Moreover, it is a primary function of the public sector. The world of diplomacy has been tightly controlled for the last thousand years, but the diplomatic environment is changing. The changes coming from the external environment affect the fundamental company culture of diplomacy. New technologies, increased standards of living, and travel are all contributing to the growth of a new world of public diplomacy.

We find an interesting mix of cultures and cultural paradoxes in diplomacy. The paradoxes provide a vibrant context to explore how the new KLC approach can be supported and its effects. Moreover, the paradoxes in diplomacy may create challenges and opportunities for implementing the KLC approach. For example,

The Cultures of Knowledge Organizations: Knowledge, Learning, Collaboration (KLC), 167–192
Copyright © 2023 by Wioleta Kucharska and Denise Bedford
Published under exclusive licence by Emerald Publishing Limited
doi:10.1108/978-1-83909-336-420231009

public diplomacy culture may be more welcoming to the KLC approach than traditional diplomacy. Do we pose three primary questions, including to what extent are diplomatic cultures (1) knowledge oriented; (2) learning oriented; and (3) collaboration oriented? What cultural factors encourage or impede their growth? And, can we best introduce the KLC approach?

Diplomatic Organizations – Goals, Structures, and Strategies

Today, diplomats are the official representatives of their states. They communicate on behalf of their states and maintain contacts and relationships so those communications can occur. There are protocols for their communications and relationships. Diplomats do not act on their own but act only based on the instructions of the states they represent. Diplomats tend to be located in the same place in a country, enabling them to observe some basic protocol rules.

Diplomacy and diplomatic culture evolved over centuries from European missions in the Renaissance and personal appointees of kings and rulers to today's public officials (Berridge & Lloyd, 2012; Freeman, 2010; Constantinou et al., 2016; Kappeler, 2004; Lewis, 2010). While the nature of the state may have changed with time, the protocols and knowledge base of diplomacy have remained relatively stable over the centuries. Diplomacy today requires knowledge of laws, social structures, economic systems, languages, and most importantly, cultures of other states. The profession's protocols also require knowledge of behaviors, conventions, and communication styles. Today, diplomatic service falls largely in a governmental or public service context. Consequently, diplomats tend to be career public servants.

States can only communicate with one another through humans acting as representatives. These state-level communications are conducted through a diplomatic system. The diplomatic system is the network of embassies, consulates, and corps that have evolved over the last thousand years. The first step in any communication is establishing and agreeing to diplomatic relations. The idea of diplomatic relations is at the core of regular and routine contact between states. Diplomacy as a process focuses on overcoming estrangement or conflicts in the international system (Grossman, 2010; Henökl, 2016; Kilcullen, 2006). Diplomacy is the mediation of difference and establishing relationships across alien boundaries (Der Derian, 1996). Diplomacy recognizes but strives to reduce the effects of differences and separation (Sharp, 2004, 2013). Diplomacy is often characterized as a set of practices within international relationships (Reynolds, 2006b).

At its core, diplomacy is about the translation of cultures. Diplomacy is grounded on shared assumptions, beliefs, values, and behaviors to accomplish its goals. The essential behavior is a common language. A common language does not simply mean linguistically but a diplomatic vocabulary or linguistic register grounded on shared beliefs and attitudes about the world. At a diplomatic level, linguistic practices are not just instrumental to communication, but they define the worlds within which we live. Through a common language, we see the role of materials, practices, visual representations, spaces, and knowledge in cultures of translation. Diplomatic culture is at the heart of what diplomats do.

Tier 1 – The Company Culture of Diplomacy

At its core, diplomatic culture results from interactions between representatives of states and international institutions. Diplomats are embedded in the culture of the institution or state that employs them. By its nature, diplomatic culture imposes constraints and restrictions on diplomats' actions and expressions. Diplomats must adopt the espoused attitudes, beliefs, and values of the state or institution they represent. In official diplomatic activities, there can be no gap between personal actual and lived values and beliefs and officially espoused values and beliefs. Bull (1977) suggested that diplomatic culture is at the heart of today's international state system.

Der Derian (1987, 1996) and Sharp (2004, 2013) argues that diplomatic culture comprises three concentric circles. The outmost circle represents the world and the broader set of values that humans espouse to share. Within this circle is the realm of the modern interstate system's "international political culture." The innermost circle is where we find the diplomatic culture. Sharp (2004) defines diplomatic culture as the common stock of ideas and values possessed by the official representatives of states (Bull, 1977). It represents explicit knowledge of other states and the common stock of rhetoric and manners that defines diplomatic relations and actions.

While there is a common culture across states, each has its own diplomatic culture. For example, in most democratic states, diplomatic culture aligns with the culture of the state rather than an individual. In democracies, diplomatic culture typically reflects republican ideals and democratic values. These diplomatic cultures introduce some interesting paradoxes because the egalitarian foundation allows other cultures to surface depending on the external environment, i.e., citizen diplomacy, celebrity diplomacy, military or intelligence diplomacy, economic diplomacy or even environmental diplomacy.

Official diplomatic culture aligns with bureaucratic company culture. Diplomacy is high risk and uncertainty averse. As noted earlier, bureaucracies operate on the "need for knowledge" or "the need to know principle." Bureaucratic cultures control the diffusion of explicit knowledge from and to selected roles in the administrative hierarchy and per their levels of authority. The control of knowledge is part of the risk-averse culture. Control is often the solution to managing uncertainty. It is entirely consistent with official diplomatic relationships and communications. The authority of state officials is transferred to diplomats as empowered subordinates. Relationships are transactional and impersonal. There is hierarchical coordination of processes. Shared values and beliefs are presumed, but they come from the organization and are adopted and lived by individuals in the diplomatic service. Diplomacy is a culture where we expect to find high levels of alignment between espoused and lived values and between values and conforming behaviors.

By definition, the culture can constrain the growth of the company's knowledge assets. It has been observed in the recent past when diplomatic focused on "official communications" from other states at the expense of seeing and trusting knowledge from the larger populations (e.g., Arab Spring). A diplomatic culture, like a bureaucratic culture, is characterized by high power distance and uncertainty avoidance, given the alternative consequences (Moonen, 2017). In diplomatic and bureaucratic cultures, innovation and asset development are neither strengths nor desirable goals. By definition, diplomacy is about managing and maintaining existing power relationships and control. It is consistent with a bureaucratic culture. We suggest that military and intelligence diplomacy also resembles a bureaucratic culture.

The Pivotal Layer in Diplomatic Cultures

Diplomatic cultures represent peculiar business goals and strategies, behaviors and processes, roles and responsibilities. We can see all five layers of culture within diplomatic cultures. However, the nature of the business or company culture and the strict controls over diplomats' actions suggests that the focal point for analysis and understanding is the behavior layer. It is through diplomatic behaviors that we see diplomatic values. Diplomats' behaviors, such as reflection and reflection in action, demonstrate the espoused values. And in many cases, it is the behavior – communications, negotiations, resolutions, translation, shared cultures – that are the output and outcome of diplomacy.

While diplomatic behavior and artifacts are the most pivotal of the five layers, all five layers are anchored in values (Fig. 1). Values influence behavior and are deeply engrained in beliefs. It is also unusual to see such tightly managed

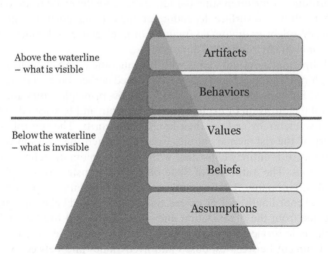

Fig. 1.   Areas of Emphasis in Diplomatic Cultures.

espoused and lived beliefs and assumptions. It ties back to the essential values and assumptions of a diplomatic culture. Diplomatic values are the simplest of any work culture, yet they form the core of every diplomatic behavior.

Diplomatic Values

Most diplomatic values will reflect national values (Rathbun, 2014). For this reason, we expect diplomatic values to align with public sector values. It is the case for most states. However, across states, values may differ. Finding a common or core set of values across states is challenging. We would likely discover that common values describe principles and platitudes. There is one core value of diplomacy, though, which is loyalty. Today's diplomats use the core value and principle of loyalty as their grounding. Bjola and Murray (2016) identify three principles of diplomatic loyalty – loyalty to a sovereign, to a state, and to people. These three loyalties also call out the ethical challenges diplomats may face in their work. At times, these three loyalties may conflict. Loyalty to the state is a primary value. It is inherent to the role and the work. Loyalty to the people is an extension of diplomatic ethics to those they represent.

Similarly, another value is a suspicion of divided loyalties. These three loyalties are the normative basis of diplomats' ethical judgments and actions. Each loyalty imposes imitations for moral judgment. Diplomats reconcile the needs of the task with their loyalties through self-reflection and reflection-in-action. The process of reflection in action allows diplomats to reconcile their three loyalties and their lived and espoused values.

Historically, diplomats acted under moral protection. An aristocratic code of honor guided diplomacy. Today, diplomatic ethics considers whether and, if so, how diplomats can be held morally accountable for their actions. Diplomats generally have limited agency because of their work because others direct their actions. Diplomats are, though, morally accountable as they exercise power through representation, information-gathering and negotiation.

Diplomatic Behaviors

Diplomatic behaviors are best understood in the context of a diplomatic practice performed in an international context. Diplomacy is practiced daily by diplomats as they represent their states in international contexts. Diplomacy and foreign policy have an intimate relationship (Nicolson, 1939). Foreign policy and diplomacy are interlinked components in a foreign policy process (Bozeman, 2017; Buzan & Little, 2000; Dittmer & McConnell, 2015; Friedman, 1999; Gellner, 1983). Diplomacy is also the day-to-day practice of international relations and negotiation of war and peace. Diplomatic action is highly controlled, scripted, and often invisible (Artzi, 2000; Bolewski, 2008). Diplomatic behaviors derive from a well-defined and developed a set of practices. To address these complex problems, diplomatics employ many methods. These methods may include communication, negotiation, translation, mediation, and summitry.

Diplomatic behaviors also include acting as a remote interface to the populations of the states in which they reside. These often include many common requests and services associated with bureaucratic functions.

Communication is essential to diplomacy. Without communication, there is neither diplomacy nor negotiation (Berridge, 2021; Bjola & Kornprobst, 2013; Constantinou, 1996; James, 1980; Jönsson & Hall, 2005; Watson, 2013). Diplomatic communication must consider communication styles and practices of other states. Diplomatic communication is an art form. Diplomats leverage two languages when communicating – a linguistic language that is common to the parties and a diplomatic language that leverages and references diplomatic protocols (Carvalho, 2011; Haslett, 1989; Hofstede et al., 2005; Slavik, 2004). Diplomacy is commonly linked to linguistic skills (Eban, 1983). Diplomats leverage language and linguistics to "do" diplomacy. Language and linguistics are inherent to oral statements, remarks, speeches, and conversations layered with written communiqués, demarches, notes, non-papers, readouts, and press releases. Finding a common linguistic language is a matter of negotiation. Diplomats must be able to communicate with their peers to communicate a state's messages. Professional diplomatic language is characterized by courtesy, non-redundancy, and constructive ambiguity. Both words and silences send messages in diplomatic communication. Diplomatic language is instrumental: it allows diplomats to form and maintain relationships with those who manage international relations (Baldi & Gelbstein, 2004; Oglesby, 2016; Reynolds, 2006a).

Diplomatic communication includes verbal and nonverbal actions, silence, and inactivity. Diplomatic language comprises signals, codes, and conventions constructed over time by diplomats to smooth and soothe the communication process between states and the organizations created by states in the international political realm. Diplomatic body language ranges from personal gestures, via meeting and travel logistics, to manipulating military forces. Protocols provide a convenient medium for nonverbal signaling. Both actions and non-actions send messages in diplomacy. Diplomats send signals intended to convey messages subject to decoding and interpretation. Diplomats choose words to be precise enough to communicate clearly with diplomatic interlocutors yet elastic enough to plausibly suggest the alternative meanings the diplomat's political masters need to manage their domestic politics. It explores the balance diplomats attempt to achieve between ambiguity and precision in producing diplomatic texts. And it considers how the expanded and increasingly diverse cast of actors affects and increases language challenges.

Negotiations are the core diplomatic process – to pursue, prevent, manage, resolve, and transform conflicts among states (and other parties), overcome problems, and instill cooperation (Cohen, 1991; Munn, 1998; Sebenius, 2017). Communication depends upon communication. Negotiation operates under an unspoken assumption of equality (Fisher, Ury & Patton, 2011; Stein, 1988). Equal status, equal treatment, reciprocity, and justice are common core beliefs in the diplomatic culture. While parties are never equal in power, a sense of equality is helpful to productive negotiation (Zartman, 2016; Zartman & Kremenyuk, 1995).

Diplomacy is about *translating cultures* to increase understanding and encourage transmitting, sharing and transforming values, beliefs and narratives. Translation occurs in every diplomatic exchange when two distinct entities enter into relations. However, translation is particularly complex in the field of diplomacy because of the scale and scope – from the scale of the individual to the scale of the nation.

International *mediation* includes a broad range of methods and practices. In mediation, we may find contrasting assumptions about leverage, resources, power, strategy, entry, and outcome (Aggestam, 2002). In addition, diplomatic mediation must take into consideration (1) potential resistance to negotiation and mediation; (2) quest for timing; and (3) management of devious objectives. Diplomatic mediation ranges from low to high forms of intervention.

Improved communications have increased the opportunity for *summitry*. Diplomacy conducted on behalf of the state rather than a single ruler means that others with a role in managing the state may also be involved in diplomacy, i.e., politicians. Historically, summits were infrequent due to the difficulty of travel and security concerns. Summits have moved from the most powerful states addressing substantive issues to leaders of all nations meeting for various purposes. Summits have increasingly become institutionalized (Dunn & Lock-Pullan, 2016). Today, summits are frequent and have superseded many more traditional forms and methods of diplomacy, especially as politics has become more critical in the summit processes. Summits have also increasingly become institutionalized.

Younger diplomats, reflecting the outlook of their peers in society at large, are much more likely than their elders to agree with the proposition that "people say all sorts of stuff." Diplomatic practice, therefore, might evolve in the direction of not holding diplomats so tightly to their words or, perhaps, specifying when their public or revealed utterances are interpreted as meaningful when they should be regarded as harmless.

Diplomatic Beliefs

The beliefs of official and credentialed diplomats are tightly aligned with the espoused values of the state. A vital belief is a belief in the state. Another is the belief in the importance of the people and broader community over the self. Finally, those in diplomatic service must believe in the role of the service in the international community and discourse among states. These beliefs are at the core of diplomatic values and the state's definition. Where those in diplomatic service do not internalize these beliefs, there may be a risk to the state.

Diplomatic Assumptions

Diplomatic culture rests on norms, rules, and institutions devised to improve relations and avoid war between states (Wiseman, 2005). These norms, rules, and institutions include core religious values, a preference for peace, intellectualism, everyday habits, fundamental assumptions of the equality of states and the accumulated wisdom and prudence of earlier generations. The core assumption of diplomacy is equality. Relations among states are grounded on the presumed equality of those states. While this is never true, it must be assumed that diplomacy takes place.

Diplomatic Artifacts

Diplomatic artifacts are all about the representation of the state. Artifacts are designed to reinforce the official and easily recognized states engaged in diplomacy. Artifacts include buildings such as embassies and consulates, diplomatic corps and diplomats as official physical representatives, dress codes, symbols and insignia, flags, official events, celebrations and meetings. The most important artifact is the physical representation of the state in another state's environment. The most prominent diplomatic artifacts are embassies in other states, foreign missions, consulates, and the diplomatic corps.

Countries will always need agents to build trust and pursue relationships with widening circles of state and non-state actors, working in varied circumstances beyond the formal settings of the past. Each of these artifacts reflects the espoused values of the state and the protocols of the diplomatic culture. Artifacts of diplomacy are buildings or the individuals who serve in those buildings. These buildings, the staff who work in them, the flags and the insignia on the buildings are the primary artifacts of the state.

Embassies and missions, permanent and special missions. In essence, embassies and missions represent the image and presence of the state in another environment (Rana, 2004, 2011). The resident embassy symbolizes the international system. Embassies address demands common to public services worldwide: to deliver value and be measured in their performance. Resident embassies provide enhanced value in our globalized world of instant communication, volatility of international affairs, and information overload. Today, bilateral embassies have a more prominent role than before in the formulation of policy and in its execution, which adds to its work demands. They also interact with state and non-state actors in the home country and the country of assignment. Diplomatic missions embedded in international and regional organizations dealing with a wide range of subjects in a dynamic and volatile environment, calling for high professional skills. Their numbers are likely to grow.

Consulates are old institutions (Pasarín, 2016). Consular institutions are artifacts and behaviors (i.e., a subfield of diplomacy). The consular corps is members of the consular services who provide services at the consulate in a city. In contrast to the embassy diplomatic corps, a consular corps is more easily identifiable in non-capital cities. Consular functions including border security policy advice, natural and manmade disaster response, visa support, and citizens' protection and assistance. In addition, consulates address customer service-oriented administrative issues. The increased demand for these services has highlighted the strategic role of consulates. Often they are the public image of a state in another environment. Today, consulates reflect the increased pressure for enhanced intergovernmental cooperation, public–private partnerships, and the use of technology from the external environment. The *diplomatic corps* refers to the diplomats of different sovereign states resident in the capital city of another sovereign state (Sharp & Wiseman, 2007). The principal members of the diplomatic corps at any capital or international organization headquarters are the heads of mission. The ambassador represents the corps to the host government, usually on practical matters but occasionally on policy questions. The informal powers and influence of the dean depend on their personal qualities (e.g., behaviors). In addition, the diplomatic corps may provide opportunities for contact between the diplomats of states which do not enjoy diplomatic relations.

Tier 2 – The Public Service Culture of Diplomacy

The state's core values are visible when we overlay the bureaucratic culture of diplomacy with the public service culture. In particular, two fundamental values are at the heart of a diplomatic culture – promoting national security and ensuring economic health (Fig. 2). The primary client of a public service culture is the state and, indirectly, the people the state represents. As noted earlier, we observe a tight alignment between espoused and lived values, espoused and lived beliefs, and espoused and lived behaviors. Strong loyalty to the state is inherent to the promotion of national security.

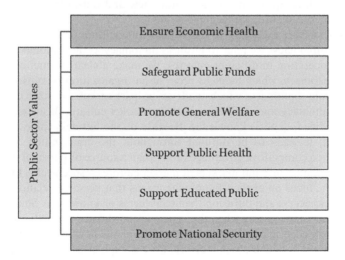

Fig. 2. Diplomatic Culture – Core Values.

The exception to the tight alignment of espoused and lived beliefs, values and behaviors may be found in two groups of actors. One group may represent the political leadership of the organization. Depending on the political culture, they may be more or less invested in public service cultures. The second groups are those in the diplomatic core and their support teams, who do the work of diplomacy and representation every day. The second group is vested in the culture, whereas the first may not be.

Tier 3 – Complex and Competing Diplomatic Cultures

In contrast, emerging public diplomacy is conducted by citizens as non-official diplomats and outside of official channels. We suggest that the underlying company culture of unofficial public diplomacy resembles a clan culture. Public diplomacy may include various forms of diplomatic practice such as environmental, celebrity, religious, and other more closely resembling clan cultures. These cultures are grounded in shared experiences and heavily dependent upon human capital (e.g., tacit knowledge, skills, and competencies) and relational capital (e.g., existing relationships and reputations). Because human and relational capital is intangible, it is diffused throughout a community through face-to-face interactions or synchronous digital connections. Relationships in clan cultures are personal and equal rather than hierarchical, a contrasting horizontal version of vertical official state diplomacy. Communication protocols may not be standardized but reflect the community's shared practices, values, and beliefs. In these contexts, unofficial diplomats leverage negotiation and revolutionary thinking to discover and develop shared values and beliefs across cultures. The common "unofficial" cultures are highly collective (Moonen, 2017). Clan cultures create an environment for generating new and out-of-the-box ideas that may lead to crucial cutting-edge innovations.

Perhaps another exception to the bureaucratic culture of official diplomacy is business diplomacy. We refer to business diplomacy as the diplomacy between businesses operating in different cultures. We make a clear distinction between business diplomacy, which tends to occur at an organization or subsector level, and economic diplomacy, which tends to be part of official state diplomacy. Business diplomacy may have an underlying market culture. Businesses tend to leverage codified, explicit knowledge. Because of the business value of explicit information, it tends to be diffused throughout the organization. Access to knowledge is a competitive advantage rather than a source of personal power. We find self-regulating internal markets in market cultures – specifically, knowledge markets. The focus on explicit knowledge means that personal relationships are less critical to access and diffusion than tacit forms of knowledge. Shared values and beliefs are unnecessary when the system is coordinated through impersonal, internal knowledge markets. Moonen (2017) explains how low power distance, low uncertainty avoidance, high individuality and high masculinity can predominate in market cultures.

By design and definition, diplomacy is about engaging with the external environment. Diplomats function in an increasingly complex international system and an increasingly complete set of problems. In the twenty-first century, many other non-state actors are doing some form of diplomacy. In the twenty-first century, we see an increased democratization of diplomacy. Globalization and accessible communication channels have expanded the actors, issues, and instruments of diplomacy. It means that the relationships to be managed are more complex, and the boundaries and protocols are less clear. The new global media ecology has disrupted diplomatic dialogue and taken on a less scripted, decorous tone. The interface between diplomacy and governance is populated by various actors performing in different languages from different scripts, for different audiences and with varying intent.

Twenty-first century official and unofficial public diplomacy is a new type of complexity. Traditionally, diplomats had few competitors and were in control of the environment. Today, there is increasing competition from a rich set of non-state-supported actors (Fig. 3). There are also non-state actors with a stake in diplomacy who exert influence over foreign policy and, thus, diplomacy. As a result, foreign policy has profoundly changed agendas and the arenas in which it is conducted. Given the linkages between them, these changes in the constitution of foreign policy have significant implications for diplomacy. We also observe a shift in power – with the rise of social power –affecting the nature of diplomacy.

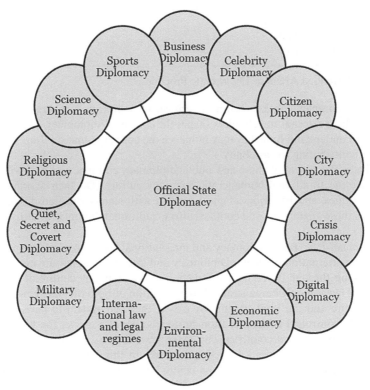

Fig. 3.   External Actors in the Landscape of Diplomacy.

The increased democratization of diplomacy means that the external environment will be complex, with potential conflicts. The new world of competitive and collaborative public diplomacy can significantly affect official diplomatic cultures. So who are the new non-state actors? And how does their form of diplomacy influence the traditional culture of diplomacy? A review of the diplomatic literature suggests there are 14 other diplomatic actors in the external environment (Fig. 4).

- Business Diplomacy
- Celebrity Diplomacy
- Citizen Diplomacy
- City Diplomacy
- Crisis Diplomacy
- Digital Diplomacy
- Economic Diplomacy
- Environmental Diplomacy
- international law and legal regimes
- Military Diplomacy
- Quiet, Secret and Covert Diplomacy
- Religious Diplomacy
- Science Diplomacy
- Sports Diplomacy

Fig. 4.   Extended Areas of Diplomatic Practice.

In this complex context, culture is critical to achieving a coherent strategy. Each of these external stakeholders shapes the culture of diplomacy. Therefore, it is vital to understand how they may influence the core diplomatic culture and the factors contributing to variability.

What is the nature of these new public diplomacy cultures, and how will they influence the traditional bureaucratic company culture? Do their assumptions, beliefs, values, and behaviors align or conflict with state-sponsored diplomacy? How do these alignments and conflicts affect traditional diplomatic culture?

International Law. Both diplomacy and international law are central components of the international system. Diplomacy and international law are essential to working through differences and disputes. The company culture of international law is highly bureaucratic. It is a reflection of both the state government structure and the legal system. We expect the legal system to have in place tightly controlled communication protocols. We also expect the network to include people and countries who make laws, lawyers, judges, judicial staff, and courts. What does knowledge look like in this community? There is a knowledge barrier you must cross before becoming part of this community: knowledge of international laws and the laws of specific states. While laws are codified, their application is continually tested. Learning is continuous, through practice and based on relationships with other people in the network.

It is a networked area of practice. Every member of the network is creating some form of new knowledge that builds the base. The primary form of new knowledge creation is in the form of brief filed and court decisions. New knowledge creation and sharing are grounded in precedent and existing knowledge. Continuous monitoring and learning are essential to survival in this network. An important form of learning is collective learning at the state level. Those who make international law or enforce international law, such as international organizations, international courts, and states, also learn through filings and decisions. While learning is continuous and collective, what is learned is limited in scope. The diplomatic corps benefit from the learning of this community by gathering and ingesting new knowledge. Collaboration is between state representatives, international organizations, and external stakeholders. The opportunities to introduce a KLC culture here are limited. The opportunities will come from the external environment – the external stakeholders bringing cases to courts or engaging in advocacy. Knowledge will come from the outside and will represent a viewpoint.

Foreign policy possesses a clear agenda, heavily focused on military security. It reflects policy processes distinct from those associated with the domestic policy sphere. The concern with territorial defense implies "national" interest, marking off one community from another and symbolically expressed in geographical borders. The demands of the new international security agenda (e.g., climate change, global pandemics, global terrorism, international crime, and fragile states) push foreign policy concerns beyond the traditional integrity and stability of the state and the physical, psychological, and economic security and welfare of the citizen within it. The company culture of foreign policy is bureaucratic. The people will shape foreign policy knowledge within the state or foreign affairs office of each state. Knowledge will be specific to the state's foreign policy. This knowledge may be dynamic with leadership changes. We expect much of the new knowledge to come from external investment. Knowledge is drawn into the foreign policy community. Foreign policymakers are learning from the new knowledge and sharing it with the diplomatic corps. Learning may be event-specific and long-term.

Quiet and secret diplomacy involves a conscious desire to leave activities unadvertised or to hide certain forms of engagement from scrutiny (Maley). This diplomatic practice provides a safe and controlled space for complex negotiations. Secrecy may be essential in facilitating engagement with groups with whom state actors do not want to appear to be engaged. This community has a robust bureaucratic culture. Control is critical to this area of practice. But much push is going to be coming from the outside. Who creates the knowledge in this? What kind of knowledge is being created here. This diplomatic practice places barriers to knowledge for all but a select few. This practice may also be a barrier to learning from experience where the experience is unknown or cannot be shared. Additionally, it is difficult to learn from this practice as secret diplomacy militates against comprehensive analysis since critical cases (or data points) are likely to be missing. Furthermore, secrecy may prevent leaders from learning important lessons for the future. Finally, it may cause rumors to spread, with detrimental consequences for those who opted for secrecy. Well, it depends on the nature of the specific event. And I would say that the chances of learning here are a little on the low side. So KLC cultures are low.

Crisis diplomacy comes into play in an international crisis. An international crisis is a sequence of interactions between governments involving a dangerously high probability of war (Snyder, 2013) or an acute conflict between two or more states associated with a specific issue and involving perception by decision-makers of a serious risk of war (Avenell & Dunn, 2016; Richardson, 1994). Diplomats play a vital role in resolving conflicts between and among states. Crises are no longer restrained to armed conflicts between states but can emerge from every arena, financial, medical, and natural. And the impact of these crises has become much more significant, with some able to affect every corner of the globe quickly. Crisis diplomacy leverages a market company culture. Market culture is best suited to supporting multiple stakeholders with varying specializations and knowledge bases. This culture resembles that of disaster and emergency response teams. Learning is specific to the event. By and large, it will be experiential and situational. Learning is also cross-cultural and cross-domain. This community offers essential opportunities to introduce a KLC approach. Given the knowledge and information sharing level, it is a good practice example. Because it is focused on resolving a crisis, the community behaves in a knowledge pooling and review mode. All stakeholders will collaborate as each stakeholder shares, applies, and adapts their knowledge. Collaboration is the norm.

City diplomacy is grounded in a clan culture. It is the practice of mediated international relations by local governments (Acuto et al., 2017; Clark & Moonen, 2016). Cities and urban areas have gained stature in world affairs. Cities are increasingly popular actors on several fronts, from the environment to security and health. City diplomacy helps us see a broader landscape of international relations. City diplomacy highlights the networked patterns that cities are creating in international affairs. Knowledge creation is a synthesis of the knowledge and culture of the city. It is synthesized to share with other cities. This community demonstrates culture-to-culture learning. The learning potential is high. The opportunity for collaboration is also high. It presents an external opportunity to introduce a KLC approach, which will also affect the diplomatic culture.

Citizen diplomacy can be defined either as citizen-led citizen diplomacy or the use of citizens in state-led citizen diplomacy (Bishop, 2015; Henrikson, 2006; Kuznetsov, 2014; Pamment, 2012; Riordan, 2002; Tyler et al., 2016). The essential question today is, who can be considered a citizen diplomat? And when are they official and unofficial diplomats? The official diplomatic corps has resembled a club or a fief culture. The increased presence of citizen diplomacy has shifted the culture to a market or clan culture. Communication can now be people-to-people between citizens. These communications have benefits, including forming deep and long-lasting authentic relationships. But, they can also take the form of "rogue" communications and the formation of networks that may not represent the interests of states. There are several examples of state-sanctioned citizen involvement in official diplomacy where citizens assist the state with their expertise. This external community is comprised of official citizen diplomacy. The company culture of official citizen diplomacy resembles a clan with extensive information exchange and lower levels of command and control. It is a citizen-centered culture. Each citizen brings a different knowledge base to the task. Each has a small effect on the diplomatic culture, but it is a notable effect cumulatively. The potential for new knowledge creation is significant. Collaboration is pervasive, though it is mainly invisible. The effect of collaboration and learning is also cumulative and long-term.

Celebrity diplomacy is a logical result of the democratization of foreign policy (Wheeler, 2011). Celebrity diplomacy has been associated with international governmental organizations IGOs (e.g., United Nations, UNICEF, and World Bank) and non-governmental organizations (NGOs) (e.g., Amnesty, Greenpeace, and Human Rights Campaign) have developed corps of ambassadors. Additionally, freelance celebrity diplomats (e.g., Bono and Geldof) have launched charitable records, global concerts, and their presence to engage in international decision-making. Celebrity diplomacy is an example of the soft power of unofficial diplomacy. Celebrity diplomacy resembles a market or fief culture, depending on the celebrity and the official or unofficial status. The celebrity's knowledge is likely focused on specific issues relevant to their talents. We expect the knowledge dissemination and broadcast value will be high to raise awareness of an issue. Learning will be among audiences or listeners. Learning may also come in the form of advocacy and influence. There is some small opportunity for collaboration. If it's a role like that of Bono or John Stewart, or people of influence advocating for an issue, there may be more widespread learning. We expect that the learning will resemble awareness rather than deep understanding.

Digital diplomacy leverages new information and communication technologies (ICTs) to do diplomacy (Danziger & Schreiber, 2021). It reshapes traditional diplomatic communication from in-person exchanges, passive emails, and websites to communications through hyper-interactive media. Diplomats can use digital communications to reach and engage three audiences: internal, domestic, and foreign. It gives diplomats more opportunities leverage and influence public opinion. It introduces risks that personal values, beliefs, and assumptions may become part of what is generally perceived as less formal communication channels. This new media also leverages less formal language than that of diplomatic languages. The challenge is preserving the communication values, protocols, and codes of conduct in these new digital spaces. This diplomatic practice has created new paradoxes for the diplomatic corps because it requires fast responses, which could be careless and counterproductive. It offers opportunities to establish innovative mechanisms for diplomacy that would support knowledge sharing, learning, and collaboration.

Digital diplomacy will follow a market culture because of the practice's open community and innovative nature. There is a significant potential for knowledge dissemination, though perhaps not for direct exchange and understanding. Digital capabilities can increase learning and collaboration activities, though the technology alone will not accomplish this. Nonetheless, digital diplomacy provides a significant opportunity for introducing and nourishing a KLC approach. Digital technologies indeed offer diplomats the ability to reach broader populations beyond their official state networks.

The evolving nature of *economic diplomacy* is driving change in domestic and multi-lateral institutions, including new ways of decision-making (Okano-Heijmans, 2011; Kremenyuk & Sjöstedt, 2000; Lee & Hudson, 2004; Russell, 1990; Lang, 1992; Tyler et al., 2016). The state continues to be the primary actor in economic diplomacy. Globalization and shifting power balances highlight the diplomatic role that economic institutions can play in foreign affairs. Economic diplomacy is becoming more comprehensive as it addresses trade and investment promotion (commercial diplomacy), economic agreements (trade diplomacy), and development cooperation. Trade and investment promotion is the most traditional form of economic diplomacy. Regional and bilateral negotiations around international trade rules are increasing. Many non-state actors – including the private sector and civil society organizations (CSOs) – have a stake in economic diplomacy, though not always a role. Decision-making in economic diplomacy is a complex issue because there is a diversity of state and non-state stakeholders aiming for different economic and political outcomes. Economic diplomacy leverages a market culture. The critical issue for this external stakeholder is whose knowledge is being leveraged. There are many economic players with diverse economic goals and perspectives. These actors are potential new sources of knowledge and learning for diplomats. The potential lies in the knowledge of the economic environment and conditions of people engaged in it. It can also be an essential source of economic intelligence about the state of interest. Because external actors may closely hold economic knowledge, sharing will occur in collaboration.

Business Diplomacy

In a changing business environment, multinational organizations (MNCs) are now engaged in *business diplomacy*. Doing business successfully in today's international business environment requires MNCs to move away from one-sided shareholder models and become active members of stakeholder networks instead. Globalization has changed the roles and relationships between MNCs, governments, NGOs, local pressure groups, and society (Ruël & Wolters, 2016). MNCs must engage in long-term relationships with foreign governments and NGOs to create legitimacy and build trust. They create legitimacy by interacting and building positive relationships with all stakeholders. Business diplomacy is broader in scope than economic diplomacy because more individual company players are involved. The stakeholders in this practice are companies and the government structures of the foreign state. Business diplomacy more closely resembles a typical bureaucratic culture or a fief culture, depending on the nature of the business. Learning in this contest is limited to the business's goals and the interests of the foreign state. There is an opportunity for extensive collaboration and networking between the business and the population of the country where the business is established. For example, in times of conflict, businesses may continue to function in a foreign state and provide a source of knowledge and learning. Or they may be recalled in a conflict. At a diplomat level, there is some learning. In collaboration, though, we see the most significant opportunity.

Religious or faith-based diplomacy may be practiced by religious institutions, religiously affiliated NGOs, and individual religious practitioners (Wellman, 2016). We have addressed the first in our discussion of public service cultures grounded in universal values and beliefs. Religious diplomacy will follow either a fief or a bureaucratic culture, depending on the role and the nature of the religious community in diplomacy. Knowledge creation and sharing are more likely to come from the religious community than from the diplomatic corps or foreign states. The nature of religious diplomacy may be including religious tenets or beliefs in the diplomatic conversation or shaping the conversation around religious beliefs. The learning potential depends on religious organizations engaged in lending wisdom or perspective to a situation or if they engaged in promoting their particular beliefs and values.

Military diplomacy involves the peacetime cooperative use of military assets and resources as a means of a country's foreign and security policy (Tan, 2016). Its goals are conservative or pragmatic, such as building capacity and interoperability and enhancing mutual understanding among countries and militaries, and transformative, such as resolving conflicts and developing democratically accountable armed forces (Muthanna, 2011; Natsios, 2005; Zartman & Kremenyuk, 1995). Additionally, non-state actors are increasingly involved in the production and supply – equipment trainers, strategic and tactical trainers, peacekeeping forces, investigators, inspectors, mercenaries, and volunteer combatants. However, military actors and institutions have not always contributed to enhancing strategic trust and improving relations between and among states – an essential element of successful diplomacy. Military cultures will be discussed in detail in Chapter 10. They represent a bureaucratic company culture of strict command and control. From a knowledge perspective, they will be an essential source of external knowledge for diplomacy. In addition, they will be an important source of learning from the military, as they are trusted partners. Collaboration, though, will be strictly controlled and encouraged at particular levels of the hierarchy.

Environmental diplomacy has evolved to encompass interactions on natural resource governance between nation-states and conflict resolution and peacebuilding around the environment more broadly (Lang, 1992). While international relations remain the dominant arena for environmental diplomacy, grassroots environmental groups have taken up community-based conflict resolution. This community resembles a market or a clan culture (Ali &

Vladich, 2016). Ecosystems transcend geopolitical boundaries; hence, diplomacy has been essential to managing environmental resources most efficiently and effectively. The external knowledge is extensive. Knowledge exchange is likely to be in one direction – from the external community to the diplomatic corps. There may be some knowledge conflicts where the two communities do not agree on how to address problems. In this case, external knowledge is both hard and soft science. There is also a social, political, and economic element of the knowledge that may be at odds with official diplomatic roles. Environmental scientists have essential roles to play in diplomatic arbitration and negotiation on climate issues. Environmental issues are often at the heart of state conflicts, which may bring diplomacy into the discussion. Learning is likely to be outside as well. However, what is learned may not be added to the diplomatic knowledge base if considered outside the current foreign policy borders. Collaboration is more likely when environmental degradation is presented as a concern, and environmental sustainability is a shared value. Environmental diplomacy requires an understanding of the broader underpinnings of environmental conflicts. Environmental diplomacy often uses core diplomatic methods and behaviors, mediation, communication, and summitry.

Traditional *sports diplomacy* is a tool that governments occasionally use to achieve foreign policy goals (Murray, 2013, 2018). Where sport serves a diplomatic purpose beyond the game, governments often exploit it. In the twenty-first century, fields of sport, clubs, and individual sports celebrities can play an influential, non-state diplomatic role. Sports diplomacy emphasizes government partnerships with non-state actors such as CSOs, intergovernmental organizations (IGOs), sports personalities, and sports corporations. States may leverage sports events as public diplomacy opportunities. In contrast to these diplomatic events, sports diplomacy is regular, inclusive and embraces the amateur levels of the sport. In a traditional, bilateral sense, sporting matches can create leadership summit opportunities for engagement beyond entrenched foreign policy positions. Sports diplomacy resembles a clan or a market culture. This type of diplomacy is similar to celebrity diplomacy when a sports figure is called upon to engage in official diplomacy. In other contexts, though, states may leverage sporting events to create an environment for discourse and bring cultures into closer contact. There is a significant opportunity for learning in the latter case, where populations from different states can meet and learn directly from one another. Collaboration is also possible in planning, staging, and implementing sporting events and in the network relationships built due to the events. Again, the diplomatic corps may benefit from this knowledge and learning through ingesting rather than dissemination.

Science diplomacy will play a critical role in solving problems, reducing inequality, resolving differences and advancing security and development prospects. The world's most pressing threats and challenges to peace and prosperity are rooted in science and driven by technology (Copeland, 2016). Science diplomacy resembles a clan culture – the exchange and flow of knowledge among scientists is the core process of this practice. Science diplomacy may be carried out at two levels – expert and novice. Expert-level diplomacy is knowledge-rich as it encourages sharing expert scientific advice in international policy development. At the novice level, science diplomacy may involve citizen scientists from around the globe to share knowledge, learn together, and create new networking and collaborative opportunities. Again, this area of external practice provides essential external knowledge for the diplomatic corps. Again, it will likely be a one-way sharing – ingest from external stakeholders to the diplomatic corps.

General Observations on Cultures of External Partners and Competitors

The diplomatic landscape has expanded significantly in the past 80 years. The external environment is redefining what diplomacy is and how we do diplomacy. Today, we have many different actors engaged in and represented by diplomatic practice. Each of these external actors brings a unique company culture, which affects both the public service cultures and the potential for a KLC approach. There is diplomatic practice at work in all of these cases. All four types of company cultures are represented at the company culture level (Tier 1). It makes for a complex KLC culture for diplomacy. External actors' influence will pressure diplomacy to adapt to new cultures. In some cases, the external pressure will ease the strict control of the bureaucratic company culture and create opportunities for greater KLC culture. Paradoxically, the KLC cultures of the external actors may be pivotal in shaping the new KLC culture of public service diplomacy.

The critical level of diplomatic culture is behavior. Today, diplomatic actors represent a broader external environment. They may be involved as state- or non-state actors. Regardless of their status, their behaviors will affect the conduct of diplomacy, its language, communication, and protocols. In some cases, the expanded scope of actors may change the focus of diplomacy from the state to a state's population. In other cases, the expanded actors may introduce more selfish economic or business goals. The cultures of external actors profoundly affect the culture of diplomacy.

Tier 4 – KLC Cultures of Diplomatic Organizations

The cultures described above were analyzed from a multifaceted perspective to understand their organizational knowledge processes, support for collaboration, the power distances in their relationships, and uncertainty avoidance behaviors. All of these are critical cultural dimensions that support knowledge creation and sharing. Clan and fief cultures seem to be the most inclined toward dynamic knowledge creation and learning, specific intangible knowledge capital assets. Bureaucracy and market cultures seem more inclined toward static knowledge consumption, e.g., explicit and encoded knowledge capital assets. Dynamic knowledge creation leads to dynamic capabilities development in organizations.

Dynamic capabilities are responsible for organizational change adaptability to hyperdynamic knowledge-economy reality. Dynamic capabilities are higher-level competencies that determine the organizational response to a changing environment (Teece, 2018). Learning is at the center of such capabilities (Uhl-Bien & Arena, 2018). Organizations exposing bureaucracy and market cultures tend to focus less on learning than do fief and clan cultures. The result may be that they are less able to optimize opportunities and continuously adapt to new challenges.

In contrast to the common cultures, the external actors of local and domain-based communities tend to be clan, market, or even fief cultures. We are less likely to see bureaucratic cultures at play for these external actors. Nevertheless, these external cultures may hold promise for building a KLC culture into the foundational bureaucratic culture.

Cultures with a high disposition for social collaboration generally have shorter power distance in their relationships. They also tend to have a greater tolerance for uncertainty avoidance. These characteristics support knowledge creation and sharing, allowing these organizations to adapt to change more rapidly and effectively. National culture is the shared, national software of the mind. When national cultures are both espoused and shared in assumptions, beliefs, values, and behaviors, countries may be able to adapt to change more effectively. Where we find gaps in nationally espoused and fundamental assumptions, beliefs, values, and behaviors, it may be more challenging for a country to transition to the new economy. These cultures may face challenges in retaining values in a transition, particularly where there is little awareness or reconciliation of values. Culture is deeply embedded and long-lived. Cultural transformation is slow and complex. These cultures can significantly affect the cultures of multinational companies, particularly where cultural differences among employees are not recognized, valued, and aligned. Having an espoused or "official company culture" does not address the actual and lived "software of many minds" problem. Multinational companies must learn to see, value, and align these individual variant cultures to construct a lived organizational knowledge-rich culture.

Successful knowledge-driven organizations are highly dependent on the capability of their employees to produce, acquire, and apply knowledge to create value. Therefore, the free and easy flow of knowledge among employees and interactions that enable them to create this value is critical. The fundamental values, procedures, and rules of human interactions at work matter for organizational success – they are the essence of the company culture. However, because they are intangible, they are less visible, and their effects are difficult to see.

Knowledge Culture of Diplomacy

At its core, traditional official state diplomacy leverages all forms of knowledge capital. It is about information messaging, cultural projection and international reputation management (Cornago et al., 2016). Diplomacy is about building relations through dialogue and networking activities. The emerging twenty-first-century public diplomacy involves many actors within and beyond official state roles and channels. The role of non-state actors has become more prevalent. There is an increased awareness of the roles that domestic citizens may play. The expanded field of diplomacy addresses relationships below the international level and across states. The changing actors and expanded focus of this emerging public diplomacy are now and will continue to affect the traditional diplomatic culture.

Diplomats use their knowledge, skills, and competencies to represent the states in other environments. Among their less visible roles, though, is knowledge and intelligence gathering from the environment for the state. It presents a challenge for knowledge sharing, as the flow is expected to be primarily from external to internal. The sharing of internal knowledge with external actors is highly constrained. There is a good reason for the constraints, but they can also create significant risks and intelligence gaps. There have been significant failures in diplomacy over the past century that would recommend we consider a new KLC approach.

The implications for building a knowledge culture are significant. Diplomats must have extensive knowledge of a country, its languages, culture, and legal and social protocols. They gain this through formal study and absorption of explicit knowledge. However, the behavioral protocols required to do the job are learned on the job and in the country. A diplomat may come to the job with some relationships in the country, but the real task once in the country is building relational capital–cultivating a network of trusted sources. From these trusted sources, much of the intelligence about state affairs is collected. The most significant value is tacit knowledge – about the country's current state and future affairs. This type of knowledge is highly perishable. Diplomats must also have finely tuned skills and competencies for judging authenticity and trustworthiness. The source knowledge they gather will carry the perspective of its custodian. These perspectives must be exposed and assessed, and knowledge weighed where sources are neither authentic nor trustworthy.

Knowledge is an essential component of diplomatic communication and representation. Diplomatic communication is about acquiring and diffusing knowledge in the most diverse domains. It is about trans-cultural communication, discovery and understanding, and the negotiation of identity. The fundamental knowledge of diplomacy is statecraft – it is about procedural knowledge. Therefore, knowledge is essential to the diplomatic corps' competencies and capabilities.

Diplomatic knowledge is gained and learned over decades – it is expansive for individuals, the corps, and subject knowledge generally. Over time, the diplomatic practice has also contributed to the knowledge of geography, medicine, biology, anthropology, architecture, engineering, administration, and information sciences. Today, given a broader landscape of actors, the knowledge of diplomacy is expanding in both its scale and scope. It is expanding in every aspect of diplomatic practice and behavior. We see a socialization of diplomatic knowledge beyond professional diplomacy. Adapting public service diplomacy from traditional bureaucratic cultures to a blend of KLC cultures is critical.

The public service cultures (Tier 2) also temper the traditional bureaucratic company cultures. Public service cultures emphasize public access, access to information, knowledge and services, support for well-being and opportunities such as education, and public funds and resources to generate new knowledge. Public service cultures often mandate shared public ownership of publicly funded research and knowledge. It can also respect but mitigate the exclusionary effects of intellectual property regimes.

Learning Cultures of Public Service Diplomacy

In a diplomatic culture, learning takes place on the job and in the job (Korshuk, 2004). Diplomats and embassy staff learn from others who are doing the job well. Diplomatic learning is more about absorption and observation than book learning. Diplomats are expected to come to the job with a wealth of knowledge and experience about a country, its cultures, and its legal and governance environment. What diplomats must learn on and off the job is how to detect, see, and interpret environmental signals. Learning takes place in person and the environment. As sources and signals are increasingly digital, they also need to learn to access, interpret, and forward what they are learning to others in the corps.

We noted earlier in the chapter that diplomatic company cultures tend to be risk and uncertainty averse. The preference is for mistake avoidance. There may be some learning from mistakes, but the effect of a mistake, depending on its consequences, is generally felt by the individual making a mistake. This culture focuses on being cautious and conservative in one's actions – learning from other good behaviors. Learning from mistakes is an after-action event, generally focused on how the mistake varied from established knowledge, protocols, and practice. Mistakes may also generate feedback which is given one on one. Hence, mentoring or correcting individual actions, but generally, diplomats do not have many opportunities to be innovative or take risks.

A clear example of the consequences of a mistake-avoidance culture is the missed signals of the Arab Spring and the missed opportunities to engage earlier in the process with Ukrainian forces in the country's defense. Often these failures are attributable to the choice of knowledge sources and the nature of the diplomatic network. One of the most critical learning opportunities in diplomatic cultures is cultivating networks. Historically, diplomatic networks have been restricted to official actors of other state embassies, consulates, and diplomatic corps. However, the expanding landscape of diplomacy presents opportunities to learn from a more extensive slate of state and non-state diplomatic actors.

In addition to exploring the effect of external cultures on public service cultures, we must also consider the nature of knowledge creation and sharing, learning, and collaboration within the diplomatic corps. We suggest the primary learning culture is based on (1) expert to novice teaching and mentoring; and (2) role-based need-to-know value. These are reinforced by the bureaucratic company culture and may be justified by the public service culture of security and accountability values. How would the diplomatic culture benefit from the influence of cultures of emerging external actors?

Collaborative Cultures of Diplomatic Organizations

Diplomacy is more about knowledge gathering than it is about sharing. A diplomat's second most important role is to collect and remit intelligence back to the state to feed into foreign policy. The state leadership will control collaboration outside the diplomatic corps with diplomats from other countries. Collaboration with other actors or representatives in the resident country is coordinated with the country's government. Some socialization may occur at official or embassy events, but this could only be considered collaboration in creating or reaffirming relationships. The traditional culture of diplomacy provides little opportunity for collaboration. Collaboration is limited to the resident country corps, home state intelligence services, and possibly with academics in the state. Collaboration is generally within the hierarchy and span of control.

The expanding scope and scale of diplomatic culture create opportunities to increase collaboration. There is a growing collaboration among non-state diplomatic actors, which is influencing the practice of diplomacy. The opportunities to collaborate with official state diplomats are slowly growing, but collaboration is still a tightly controlled practice. The core belief of diplomats is that their training, experience, and knowledge make them the most competent actors in diplomacy. There is no incentive to collaborate or learn from non-state actors until this belief is adjusted. Collaboration today tends to be more one-directional, from the state to the non-state actors regarding diplomatic protocols and behavior.

Observations on Advancing a KLC Approach in Diplomatic Organizations

Changes to the expanding landscape of diplomacy may positively or negatively affect diplomatic knowledge. Understanding these different cultures is worth noting because the design and development of the KLC approach may vary. Given the importance of diplomacy generally to healthy relationships among states, ensuring that the KLC approach is in place and supported in both environments is essential.

Chapter Review

After reading this chapter, you should be able to:

- describe the company cultures of diplomacy organization.
- explain how public service cultures affect the company cultures.
- describe the cultures of the external environment of diplomacy.
- explain the KLC cultures of diplomacy.
- discuss the opportunities and challenges of developing a KLC approach in diplomatic organizations.

References and Recommended Future Readings

Acuto, M., Morissette, M., & Tsouros, A. (2017). City diplomacy: Towards more strategic networking? Learning with WHO healthy cities. *Global Policy*, *8*(1), 14–22.

Aggestam, K. (2002). Mediating asymmetrical conflict. *Mediterranean Politics*, *7*(1), 69–91.

Ali, S., & Vladich, H. (2016). Environmental diplomacy. In C. Constantinou, P. Kerr, & P. Sharp (Eds.), *The SAGE handbook of diplomacy* (pp. 601–616). Newbury Park, CA: Sage.

Artzi, P. (2000). The diplomatic service in action: The Mittani file. In R. Cohen & R. Westbrook (Eds.), *Amarna diplomacy: The beginnings of international relations* (pp. 205–211). Johns Hopkins University.

Avenell, E., & Dunn, D. H. (2016). Crisis diplomacy. In C. M. Constantinou, P. Kerr & P. Sharp (Eds.), *SAGE handbook of diplomacy* (p. 470). Newbury Park CA: Sage.

Baldi, S., & Gelbstein, E. (2004). Jargon, protocols and uniforms as barriers to effective communication. *Intercultural Communication and Diplomacy*, *20*, 225–240.

Berridge, G. (2021). *Diplomacy: Theory and practice*. Springer Nature.

Berridge, G., & Lloyd, L. (2012). *The Palgrave Macmillan dictionary of diplomacy*. Springer.

Bishop, D. M. (2015). Public diplomacy: Time to debate change, continuity, and doctrine. *American Diplomacy*, *1*, 1–15.

Bjola, C., & Kornprobst, M. (2013). *Understanding international diplomacy: Theory, practice and ethics* (Vol. 105). Routledge.

Bjola, C., & Murray, S. (Eds.). (2016). *Secret diplomacy: Concepts, contexts and cases*. Routledge.

Bolewski, W. (2008). Diplomatic processes and cultural variations: The relevance of culture in diplomacy. *Whitehead Journal of Diplomacy and International Relations*, *9*, 145.

Bozeman, A. B. (2017). *Politics and culture in international history: From the ancient Near East to the opening of the modern age*. Routledge.

Bull, H. (1977). Diplomacy and International Order. In R. Little, & J. Williams (Eds.). (2006). *The anarchical society in a globalized world* (pp. 226–232). New York: Palgrave Macmillan.

Buzan, B., & Little, R. (2000). International systems in world history: Remaking the study of international relations. New York, NY: Oxford University press.

Carvalho, E. M. D. (2011). Diplomatic discourse. In *Semiotics of international law* (pp. 37–56). Springer.

Clark, G., & Moonen, T. (2016). *World cities and nation states*. John Wiley & Sons.

Cohen, R. (1991). *Negotiating across cultures: Communication obstacles in international diplomacy* (No. 31). United States Institute of Peace.

Constantinou, C. M. (1996). *On the way to diplomacy* (Vol. 7). U of Minnesota Press.

Constantinou, C. M., Kerr, P., & Sharp, P. (Eds.). (2016). *The SAGE handbook of diplomacy*. Sage.

Copeland, D. (2016). Science diplomacy. In C. M. Constantinou, P. Kerr, & P. Sharp (Eds.), *The SAGE handbook of diplomacy* (pp. 628–641). SAGE.

Cornago, N., Constantinou, C., Kerr, P., & Sharp, P. (2016). Diplomatic knowledge. In C. Kerr & P. Sharp (Eds.), *The SAGE handbook of diplomacy* (pp. 133–141), Sage.

Danziger, R., & Schreiber, M. (2021). Digital diplomacy: Face management in MFA Twitter accounts. *Policy & Internet*, *13*(4), 586–605.

De Carvalho, E. M. (2010). *Semiotics of international law: Trade and translation* (Vol. 91). Springer Science & Business Media.

Der Derian, J. (1987). *On diplomacy a genealogy of western estrangement*. Oxford University Press.

Der Derian, J. (1996). Hedley Bull and the idea of diplomatic culture. In R. Fawn & J. Larkin (Eds.), *International society after the Cold War: Anarchy and order reconsidered* (pp. 84–100). Macmillan.

Dittmer, J., & McConnell, F. (2015). *Diplomatic cultures and international politics*. Taylor & Francis.

Dunn, D. H., & Lock-Pullan, R. (2016). Diplomatic summitry. In *The SAGE handbook of diplomacy* (pp. 231–241).

Eban, A. (1983). *The new diplomacy: International affairs in the Modern Age* (Vol. 321). Random House,.

Fisher, R., Ury, W. L., & Patton, B. (2011). *Getting to yes: Negotiating agreement without giving in*. New York, NY: Penguin.

Freeman Jr, C. W. (2010). *Diplomat's dictionary*. 2nd edition. Washington, DC: United States Institute of Peace Press.

Friedman, T. (1999). *The Lexus and the olive tree: Understanding globalization Farrar*. Straus & Giroux.

Gellner, E. (1983). *Nations and nationalism*. Basil Blackwell.

Grossman, M. (2010). Diplomacy before and after conflict. *Prism, 1*(4), 3–14.

Haslett, B. (1989). Communication and language acquisition within a cultural context. *Language, Communication, and Culture*, 19–34.

Henökl, T. E. (2016). Conflict and continuity in European diplomatic cultures: Accountability, scrutiny and control in EU external affairs. *International Relations and Diplomacy*, *4*(5), 324–340.

Henrikson, A. K. (2006). *What can public diplomacy achieve?* Netherlands Institute of International Relations Clingendael.

Hofstede, G., Hofstede, G. J., & Minkov, M. (2005). *Cultures and organizations: Software of the mind* (Vol. 2). McGraw-Hill.

James, A. (1980). Diplomacy and international society. *International Relations, 6*(6), 931–948.

Jönsson, C., & Hall, M. (2005). *Essence of diplomacy*. Springer.

Kappeler, D. (2004). The birth and evolution of a diplomatic culture. In H. Slavik (Ed.), *Intercultural Communication and Diplomacy* (pp. 353–359). Malta, Geneva: DiploFoundation.

Kilcullen, D. (2006). Twenty-Eight Articles Fundamentals of company-level counterinsurgency. *Marine Corps Gazette*, *90*(7), 50.

Korshuk, A. (2004). On intercultural training of diplomats. *Intercultural Communication and Diplomacy*, 405–415.

Kremenyuk, V. A., & Sjöstedt, G. (Eds.). (2000). *International economic negotiation: Models versus reality*. Edward Elgar Publishing.

Kuznetsov, A. (2014). *Theory and practice of paradiplomacy: Subnational governments in international affairs*. Routledge.

Lang, W. (1992). Diplomacy and international environmental law-making: Some observations. *Yearbook of International Environmental Law*, *3*(1), 108–122.

Lee, D., & Hudson, D. (2004). The old and new significance of political economy in diplomacy. *Review of International Studies*, *30*(3), 343–360.

Lewis, R. (2010). *When cultures collide* (pp. 171–211). Nicholas Brealey Publishing.

Mazzucelli, C. (2008, July). The importance of the European Union's Strategic and Diplomatic Cultures. Jean Monnet/Robert Schuman Paper Series, Vol. 5 No. 16.

Moonen, P. (2017). The impact of culture on the innovative strength of nations: A comprehensive review of the theories of Hofstede, Schwartz, Boisot and Cameron and Quinn. *Journal of Organizational Change Management*.

Munn, J. (1998). Negotiating across cultures. *Journal of International Peacekeeping*, *5*(3), 187–188.

Murray, S. (2013). Sports diplomacy. *The Hague Journal of Diplomacy*, *8*(3–4), 191–195.

Murray, S. (2018). *Sports diplomacy: Origins, theory and practice*. Routledge.

Muthanna, K. A. (2011). Military diplomacy. *Journal of Defence Studies*, *5*(1), 1–15.

Natsios, A. S. (2005). The nine principles of reconstruction and development. Agency for International Development Washington DC.

Nicolson, H. (1939). *Diplomacy*, Thornton Butterworth Ltd. London.

Oglesby, D. M. (2016). Diplomatic language. *The SAGE Handbook of Diplomacy*, 242–254.

Okano-Heijmans, M. (2011). Conceptualizing economic diplomacy: The crossroads of international relations, economics, IPE and diplomatic studies. *The Hague Journal of Diplomacy*, *6*(1–2), 7–36.

Pamment, J. (2012). *New public diplomacy in the 21st century: A comparative study of policy and practice*. Routledge.

Pasarín, A. M. F. (2016). Consulates and consular diplomacy. In C. M. Constantinou, P. Kerr & P. Sharp (Eds.). *The SAGE Handbook of* (p. 161). Newbury Park, CA: Sage.

Rana, K. S. (2004). Diplomatic culture and its domestic context. In H. Slavik (Ed.), *Intercultural Communication and Diplomacy* (pp. 391–290). Malta, Geneva: DiploFoundation.

Rana, K. S. (2011). *21st-century diplomacy: A practitioner's guide*. Bloomsbury Publishing USA.

Rathbun, B. C. (2014). 1. The value and values of diplomacy. In B. C. Rathbun (Ed.), *Diplomacy's value creating security in 1920s Europe and the Contemporary Middle East Book* (pp. 1–21). Cornell University Press.

Reynolds, D. (2006a). Culture, diplomacy and language: Some further thoughts. *Cultural and Social History*, *3*(4), 490–495.

Reynolds, D. (2006b). International history, the cultural turn and the diplomatic twitch. *Cultural and Social History*, *3*(1), 75–91.

Richardson, J. L. (1994). *Crisis diplomacy: The great powers since the mid-nineteenth century* (No. 35). Cambridge University Press.

Riordan, S. (2002). *The new diplomacy*. Cambridge University Press.

Ruël, H., & Wolters, T. (2016). Business diplomacy. In C. M. Constantinou, P. Kerr, & P. Sharp (Eds.), *The Sage handbook of diplomacy* (pp. 564–576). SAGE.

Russell, B. (1990). *Sunshine, negotiating for international development: A practitioner's handbook*. Martinus Nijhoff Publishers.

Sebenius, J. K. (2017). Caveats for cross-border negotiators. In R. Tomasic & L. Wolff (Eds.), *Commercial Law in East Asia* (pp. 231–244). London: Routledge.

Sharp, P. (2004). The idea of diplomatic culture and its sources. *Intercultural Communication and Diplomacy*, 361–379.

Sharp, P. (2013). Diplomacy in international relations theory and other disciplinary perspectives. In P. Kerr & G. Wiseman (Eds.), *Diplomacy in a globalizing world* (p. 54). Oxford University Press.

Sharp, P., & Wiseman, G. (Eds.). (2007). *The diplomatic corps as an institution of international society*. Basingstoke: Palgrave Macmillan.

Slavik, H. (Ed.). (2004). *Intercultural communication and diplomacy*. Diplo Foundation.

Snyder, J. (2013). *The United States and the challenge of public diplomacy*. Springer.

Stein, J. G. (1988). The wrong strategy in the right place: The United States in the Gulf. *International Security*, *13*(3), 142–167.

Tan, S. S. (2016). Military diplomacy. In C. M. Constantinou, P. Kerr & P. Sharp (Eds.). *The Sage handbook of diplomacy* (pp. 591–600). Newbury Park, CA: Sage.

Teece, D. J. (2018). Business models and dynamic capabilities. *Long Range Planning*, *51*(1), 40–49.

Tyler, M. C., Beyerinck, C., Constantinou, C., Kerr, P., & Ps, S. (2016). Citizen diplomacy. In C. M. Constantinou, P. Kerr & P. Sharp (Eds.). *The SAGE handbook of diplomacy* (pp. 521–529). Newbury Park, CA: Sage.

Uhl-Bien, M., & Arena, M. (2018). Leadership for organizational adaptability: A theoretical synthesis and integrative framework. *The Leadership Quarterly*, *29*(1), 89–104.

Watson, A. (2013). *Diplomacy: The dialogue between states*. Routledge.

Wellman, D. J. (2016). Religion and diplomacy. In C. M. Constantinou, P. Kerr & P. Sharp (Eds.). *The Sage handbook of diplomacy* (pp. 577–590). Newbury Park, CA: Sage.

Wheeler, M. (2011). Celebrity diplomacy: United Nations' goodwill ambassadors and messengers of peace. *Celebrity Studies*, *2*(1), 6–18.

Wiseman, G. (2005). Pax Americana: Bumping into diplomatic culture. *International Studies Perspectives*, *6*(4), 409–430.

Zartman, I. W. (2016). Diplomacy and negotiation. In C. M. Constantinou, P. Kerr & P. Sharp (Eds.). *The Sage handbook of diplomacy* (pp. 207–219). Newbury Park, CA: Sage.

Zartman, I. W., & Kremenyuk, V. A. (Eds.). (1995). *Cooperative security: Reducing third world wars*. Syracuse University Press.

Chapter 10

The KLC Approach and Public Sector Military

Chapter Summary

This chapter describes the business goals, purpose, and strategy of public defense and military services. It reinforces defense and military organizations' fundamental bureaucratic administrative culture (Tier 1). The authors describe the influence that political appointees as leaders may play in shaping public sector cultures. The bureaucratic culture of diplomacy is deconstructed, and each of the five layers is described in detail. Additionally, the authors explain why focusing on the beliefs layer is the dominant layer and the essential starting point for analysis in military cultures. The public service culture (Tier 2) is a mediating and grounding culture for the military. It is firmly grounded in the foundational values of the state. The chapter outlines the landscape of external influencing cultures (Tier 3) in the defense and military landscape. Finally, the potential value and challenges of developing internal knowledge, learning, and collaboration (KLC) cultures are explored.

Why We Care About the Cultures of Military Organizations?

In the twenty-first century, defense and military services are changing to address the new arenas in which conflict occurs and how the state- and non-state actors engage in conflict. State-affiliated military and defense services have an expanding scope of roles and responsibilities to fulfill their states' security, safety, and protection. The advance in technology has dramatically increased the sophistication of combat. The advance of communications technologies has increased the ability of non-state actors to engage in conflict. Warfare and combat are shifting from the physical and personal to wars of information, knowledge, and intelligence. The role of KLC is now a critical success factor in any state-supported defense organization. Given the consequences of mistakes, they are also among the most risk-averse. Uncertainty is not a knowledge gap that presents learning

The Cultures of Knowledge Organizations: Knowledge, Learning, Collaboration (KLC), 193–212
Copyright © 2023 by Wioleta Kucharska and Denise Bedford
Published under exclusive licence by Emerald Publishing Limited
doi:10.1108/978-1-83909-336-420231010

opportunities – instead, it is a significant threat. The challenge is that military and defense cultures are among the most rigid bureaucratic cultures – they may not be conducive to knowledge creation, sharing, and learning. They are though naturally collaborative. This area of public service presents several challenges for introducing the KLC approach.

Military Services – Business Goals, Structures, and Strategies

The military services exist to defend the nation, protect vital national interests, support national security, develop and carry out defense strategies, fulfill national military responsibilities, support ongoing peacekeeping operations, maintain the security of country borders, maintain coastlines, maintain intelligence sources, conduct surveillance and reconnaissance, search and rescue, and in some cases to assist law enforcement in enforcing national laws. The military services also often support civil authorities in times of emergency. These business goals are adapted to the arena or environment in which each service operates. For example, these goals would be adapted to reflect strategies and security on land (e.g., army), on water (e.g., navy, marine corps, and coast guard) and in the air (e.g., air forces) (Fig. 1).

To complete its goals, the military services also ensure fair pay and entitlements, provide training, and have the equipment they need, including weapons, systems, and supplies. In addition, military service requires specialized education and training in the classroom and on the job. Each military service maintains dedicated academies and universities to support learning in the classroom. They also maintain training facilities at most bases and ports.

Tier 1 – Company Culture of the Military

Military and defense cultures are, by definition, bureaucratic (Brim, 2013; Center for Deployment Psychology, 2018; Collins, 1998; Department of Defense, 1994, 2010, 2011, 2018, n.d.; Dunivin, 1994; Hall, 2013; Hamaoka et al., 2014; Hillen, 1999; Soeters et al., 2003; Straub et al., 2002; Wilson, 2008). Bureaucracy provides the control, accountability, risk, and uncertainty management critical for survival and success. The company culture of any military – whether state or non-state – is command and control. The highest levels of the organization are responsible for understanding the whole theater, seeing the risks and controlling them to ensure its forces' safety. Communications generally flow from top to bottom.

In some cases, particularly among corps and in theater, communication flows within a team or a mission. Social structures and relationships are tightly knit and interdependent to support the team. Learning takes the form of official and service-defined training. Competencies are assessed and certified. Learning may occur on the ground in the job and on the job. It is generally shared

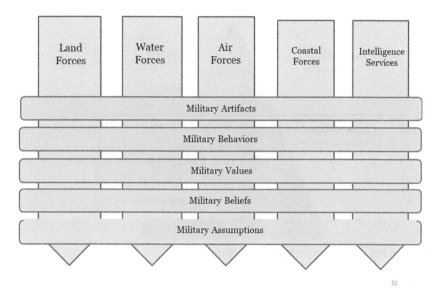

Fig. 1.   Areas of Practice of Military Services.

within the team rather than up or across the chain. Innovative and independent thinking may be considered a risk, representing non-conformity. Conformity to norms is understood as predictable and low-risk behaviors.

Beliefs reflect values. Military beliefs reflect military values. They are internalized by every individual to ensure the safety of the collective. The team's safety and survival depend upon individuals' actions and decisions. Therefore, individuals must act in conformity and a predictable way. Individual behaviors must be grounded in deeply held beliefs. Situations requiring split-second decisions will be grounded in deeply held beliefs and assumptions. Beliefs reflect values – military and public sector – but they are internalized values – a belief. For this reason, we suggest that this service's primary level of analysis is the belief layer.

When beliefs are deeply internalized, they become assumptions – individuals can act quickly without thinking (Howard, 2006). Beliefs motivate and guide behaviors. It means that the starting layer for analysis is below the water line – it is invisible (Fig. 2). In the case of the public sector military, these "invisible layers" are made visible to support transparency, accountability, and trust – all core public service values. To understand the company culture of defense and military services, we must begin with what is visible – explicit and espoused beliefs and creeds. Then, we can better understand their transformation into individual beliefs and assumptions from the collective level of values. We can better understand how they are taught, learned, and reinforced. We can also understand the consequences of gaps in espoused and actual values and non-conformity of beliefs.

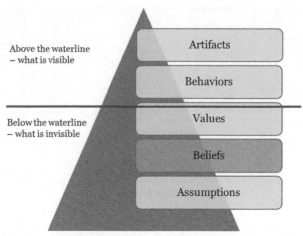

Fig. 2.   Primary Level of Military Cultures.

Military Beliefs and Assumptions

Military beliefs are the primary level of military culture because beliefs are where values are interpreted and lived (Stoddard et al., 2021). Further evidence of the importance of beliefs is that every service has a "creed" – the army has a soldier's creed (Boringa & Wubs, 2018; Griffith, 2008; Howard, 2013; Lancaster et al., 2018; Winslow, 2000), navies have seaman creeds (Evered, 1980; Jenks, 2006), air forces have an airman's creed (Duncan, 2010; Machoian, 2004), and the marine corps has a warrior creed (Barrett, 2018; Pollman, 2018; Terriff, 2006a, 2006b). By definition, creed or credo is something we believe in – an individual belief. These creeds tell us both the espoused core values and how each soldier or seaman internalizes those values as individual beliefs. Beliefs are critical to military service because the service and the team must be able to expect that each soldier will act in conformity. Each creed strongly reflects the values of the state and the nation. Each creed is a clear blending of the military and public service cultures.

In the military, there must be a close alignment of lived and espoused beliefs because conformity and predictability are critical to success. These creeds clearly refer to the team, the service, the country – but stresses that it is up to each soldier based on these beliefs to conform with them. Each individual internalizes these values as beliefs so that a whole team will act in conformity. In the case of military services, the input to any military or peacekeeping operation is the full strength of the team. When individuals can be expected to have a core set of beliefs, the team's effort will be predictable, and the overall risk will be reduced. When an individual internalizes the core values, the risk to the team and the service is reduced.

Army creeds call out loyalty, duty, respect, selfless service, honor, integrity, and
personal courage. In addition, soldiers are expected to: bear true faith and
allegiance to the US Constitution, the Army, their unit and other soldiers, to

fulfill their obligations, to treat people as they should be treated, to put the welfare of the nation the army, and your subordinates before your own, to live up to army values, do what's right – legally and morally, and to face fear, danger, physical or moral adversity.

Air Force creeds call out integrity first, service before self, and excellence in all they do. Airmen are expected to act with integrity, courage, and conviction, give precedence to professional over personal duties, and continually improve themselves and the service.

Navy creeds call out honor, courage, and commitment. Seamen are expected to bear true faith and allegiance, support and defend their country, the service and the team, and obey orders.

Similarly, *Marine creeds* refer to honor, courage, and commitment. The Marines believe that personal integrity and honor will guide them to do the right thing when no one is looking. In addition, they believe in mental, physical, and ethical strength and the spirit of determination.

The *Coast Guard creeds* call out honor, respect, and devotion to duty. Integrity is a behavioral standard demonstrated through uncompromising ethical conduct and moral behavior in all personal actions. Coast Guard creeds also speak to core national values of fairness, dignity, and compassion. They also believe in seeking responsibility and accepting accountability. Finally, the Coast Guard creed is grounded in a strong belief in service.

Military Values

Military values are embedded in their creeds. Espoused values are evident in creeds and beliefs (Coker, 2007; Eighmey, 2006; Feaver & Kohn, 2000; Koivula, 2009; McCormick et al., 2019; Parrott et al., 2018; Siebold, 2006; Williams, 2010). In texts on military values, we find intermingled references to assumptions, beliefs (Kasurak, 1982; Riccio et al., 2004), virtues (Currier et al., 2018; Jinkerson, 2016; Shay, 2014), and values. It is a testament to how tightly integrated the levels of military culture are. Sometimes, a value, e.g., hierarchy and command, may be translated into a distinct Field Manual that describes communication, decision-making, and behaviors. It tells us that the values are not just slogans or words posted on a wall. These values are part of what makes a military member. They should be incorporated into the member's belief system. They become a part of the member's character. Army values describe who soldiers are. Each service has a set of "core values" the service has identified as essential principles for its members to follow. These core values are taught during basic or officer training and are reinforced throughout a member's service. It is interesting to compare the values of citizen-based military and defense services and those of professional armies and defense organizations. The former espouse values that are tied to those of the nation, whereas the latter espouse values related to the effectiveness of a military professional (e.g., efficiency, effectiveness, performance, etc.). In researching military and defense values across all the services, we found 19 common values (Fig. 3).

- Accountability
- Adaptability
- Camaraderie, Spirit, Esprit de corps
- Commitment
- Courage
- Discipline
- Excellence
- Hierarchy
- Honor means
- Humility
- Integrity
- Leadership
- Loyalty
- Loyalty
- Mission
- Respect
- Respect
- Unity
- Unselfishness-selfless service

Fig. 3.   Core Common Values of Military and Defense Cultures.

Core values are all designed to shape an individual service member's behavior – a standard to judge behavior. Each individual can look in the mirror and affirm that they have served the corps by doing things the right way, the best way they knew how. It is a fundamental assumption, a grounding belief, and a guiding behavior. We can expect that service members will honor their values because they expect them of themselves. This essential standard of behavior is represented in the nineteen core and shared values, as described below.

- *Accountability* means instilling some valuable behaviors and ingrained habits.
- *Adaptability* means to adapt and innovate, be self-critical, and adopt the good practices of others.
- *Humility* means a humble service member is a willing learner, maintains accurate self-awareness, and seeks out others' input and feedback.
- *Loyalty* means to the country, the service, and other service members, treating others as they would be treated, trusting others to do their jobs.
- *Respect* means working as a team, treating others with fairness, dignity, and compassion, respecting the chain of command, looking out for the welfare of others.
- *Camaraderie, Spirit or Esprit de corps* means teamwork, corps and regiment spirit, comradeship, pride, flexibility.
- *Commitment* means total dedication to the service and the country, never giving in or giving up, never accepting the second best, selfless determination, relentless

dedication to excellence, devotion to duty, existing to serve, and serving others with pride.

- *Courage* means a military virtue, preparing for the hardships of combat, doing the right thing, personal courage, enduring physical stress, facing moral fear, and personal risk safety.
- *Discipline* sometimes means oblique and implicit; explicit form is the relationship with hierarchy.
- *Excellence* means care of resources, technical competence to accomplish the mission.
- *Hierarchy* means the style of command, leadership, and nature of command.
- *Honor* means never doing anything that reflects poorly on the reputation of their service, honesty, truthfulness, integrity, accountability, uncompromising ethical conduct, moral behavior, respect, duty, loyalty, selfless service, integrity, and personal courage.
- *Integrity* means honor, doing the right thing at all times, being honest with yourself, being honest with others, doing the right thing legally, doing the right thing morally, doing the right thing materially, and self-disinterested service.
- *Leadership* means ethos and ethical basis, leadership by example.
- *Loyalty* means an internal version of respect, an object of the soldier's loyalty, loyalty to the state, loyalty to the service, loyalty to the team, loyalty to service values.
- *Mission* means the mission is sacred. The mission is an absolute, primary justification of any fighting force, sacrifice, selfless service, allusive, the responsibility of the citizen in uniform.
- *Respect* means an external version of loyalty, respect for others, bearing arms and using lethal force mandates appropriate behavior under law, the highest standards of decency, a sense of justice for all people, a sense of justice all the time, ethical aspects of respect for the enemy.
- *Unity* means unity within the corps, unity across all ranks.
- *Unselfishness* and *selfless service* mean going beyond an expectation, a way of life, putting the nation, their service branch, their units, and their fellow service members and their families before themselves.

The challenge for military cultures has always been to reshape individual values to conform with the public service military values to ensure the safety of a team and to ensure the mission is accomplished. It means that aligning individual cultures with the public service military culture must be done at "intake." It is why basic training involves "breaking and remaking" the cultures of individuals in preference for the cultures of teams. Where individual values are allowed to predominate as lived values, the service values will remain espoused.

It is essential that core values be translated to core beliefs and that individual beliefs be consistent with espoused beliefs. Where there are gaps, there are risks and vulnerabilities. Every individual has a value system. Values help us identify those things that are important in our lives. Values are taught by parents, family, friends, teachers, our society and its institutions. Values are multifaceted – they come from our religious teachings, economic training, political ideation, and many other sources. Some values are superficial and may change over time as a person grows or matures. But a person's core values reflect what is deeply important to them and will usually stay with a person for life.

Each recruit comes into the military service with their core values, beliefs, and assumptions. Each service teaches its military service values to recruits during basic training. Officers are taught these values during the commissioning process. Core values are taught as a transition from individual to collective military service values. They allow recruits to relate and adapt their values to the collective values of the service. Their behavior is thus shaped, and they are prepared to complete a mission.

The reality is that when individuals adapt their values to the service values, interpretation may vary. For example, an individual may assign greater weight to the value of loyalty over discipline and standards. Not seeing and internalizing the values as a whole set of beliefs can lead to ethical failures. For example, ethical conflict may arise when loyalty is more highly valued than service. It is an important consideration when we discuss Tier 3. At Tier 3, we find visible differences in value systems across stakeholders. Depending on how closely service members work with stakeholders, there may be an imbalance in their core values.

Military service members encounter many genuinely complex ethical challenges during their careers. Unfortunately, these challenges may also conflict with their personal beliefs. It is particularly true when mission values and behaviors conflict with individual religious and moral beliefs.

Military Behaviors

Any military service's core mission and function are to prevent or engage in combat or, more recently, in keeping the peace, as such behaviors are defined around the battlefield or zones of conflict. There is an extensive body of research on military behaviors (Hall, 2011; Jones et al., 1975; Kelty et al., 2010; Koenig et al., 2014; Kuehner, 2013; Moore, 2011; Pease et al., 2016; Redmond et al., 2015; Savitsky et al., 2009; Soeters et al., 2006; Wong, 2005; Woodruff et al., 2006; Yamada et al., 2013). They are also related to the appropriate or inappropriate use of force. By definition, the military and defense services act – they "do." Their behaviors define their actions. These behaviors include combat methods, but they also go beyond including how service members conduct themselves when not in combat. Military and defense behaviors also include language, naming, and forms of address (e.g., formal titles, respect), military dress and uniforms, and military etiquette and codes of conduct.

Citizen-based military personnel are held to a stricter standard of allegiance than other citizens or non-citizen forces. This standard is evident in the "oath of allegiance" that each service member takes upon entering the service. These behaviors are defined in codes of conduct: honor codes and codes of justice. They are strictly enforced and tightly tied to values and beliefs. Citizen-based military services develop regulations that define expected behaviors. They incorporate the laws of combat. Military codes of conduct identify prescriptions and proscriptions grounded in values and ethics. Essentially, military regulations and codes of conduct address the value of force and the use of force. These codes and regulations reflect the ethical system at the core of the state's values.

Military Artifacts

Artifacts are the most visible aspect of culture. Military artifacts are among the most well-defined and widely recognized. Categories of artifacts are common across all of the services, including attire, mottos and insignia, mascots, symbols of rank, medals, and even architecture. In the design of every artifact, we find the core values of the service. Mottos reflect both the underlying national and the service values. Dress and attire conform with the value of selflessness and dedication to others. Buttons carry the insignia of the service. Every service has a hat, but they vary across services – consider the Green Beret, the seaman's cap, the armed services cap, and the airman's cap. Medals are awarded for service, dedication to duty, courage, and advancement due to increased responsibility, duty, and earning. Each service has an official mascot, just as sports teams have mascots. These artifacts reinforce the team spirit and esprit de corps. At the architectural level, any military base or building is designed for functionality, minimal personalization, and a clear reflection of sparseness and frugality. Consider also the Pentagon building in Washington, DC – a wing to symbolize the five services. We are hard-pressed to find personalization of any military officer not focused on an individual's service and record of service.

In total, citizen-based military and defense cultures are among the most tightly integrated and coordinated cultures we can find. The challenge for introducing a KLC culture approach is understanding how to relax or augment some of the core values to enable knowledge, learning and collaboration. Building a KLC culture in the military services would encourage broader sharing, knowledge socialization, small risk and mistake acceptance, to learn beyond the immediate situation, and to redefine learning as more than skills training. At its foundation a KLC culture implies relaxing the hierarchical structure to allow for more networked collaboration across ranks, missions, and services (Canfield & Weiss, 2015).

Tier 2 – Public Service Cultures of the Military

We have presented a citizen-based military as our example of a Tier 1 culture. There are Tier 1 cultures of non-citizen military and defense forces whose company culture more closely resembles a fief or a market culture. Where this is the case, we suggest the most significant difference will be found at the values level. Mercenary services may be market-based structures, and the core value may be profit or power. Military contractors may have a fief structure where a core value is a loyalty to the company. We can continue this analogy also to examine the cultures of terrorist or revolutionary forces. However, the point is that the culture of a citizen-based military is different from these because its values – the core layer

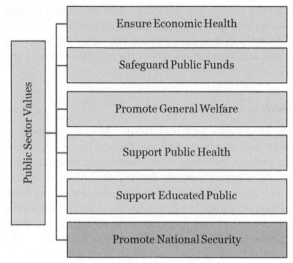

Fig. 4.   Seeing the Public Service Culture in Military Cultures.

of culture – are highly aligned with the values of the state. Consider how closely the values, beliefs, and behaviors described above align with the core values of public service organizations in general. Those values specific to military service reflect those public service values – accountability, high standards, others before self, equality, respect, honor, and transparency.

Citizen-based military service is grounded in the ethical systems defined in a state's founding documents. Military professionals adhere to the ideals of constitutional ethics as a consequence of their oath to protect and defend the country (Fig. 4). The national culture will heavily influence the public service culture, which will be tightly interwoven with the military culture. Chapter 2 discussed how national cultures could shape culture through its individuals. National cultures affect how and when we communicate, with whom we communicate, how we think about learning, how we work together, and how we think about rewards. Public service values aligned with democratic state values provide important tempering of military cultures. In particular, the values of the public service culture provide a vital tempering of using force.

These are essential considerations in the twenty-first century, where we see a growing use of multinational forces for peacekeeping and combat situations. National cultures may also determine the core company culture of a military. Rather than bureaucracy grounded on national values, it may resemble a fief, a clan, or a market culture. It may also affect whether there is or is not a public service military and whether it is a state's primary defense source. The national culture may also influence how the military is structured – around individual forms of service or a single entity, and whether those services share knowledge, learn together, or collaborate.

Tier 3 – External Cultures of Military and Defense Services

An economic sector is constructed around defense forces – it is often referred to as the "defense industry." It is a complex sector with many players, some serving and supporting the state military services, some competing with it, and others working in conflict. In addition, private sector military agents (i.e., contractors, manufacturers, think tanks, training, and education services) have different business goals and values.

Each of these external stakeholders has its own cultures, some of which are aligned with and others in conflict with the citizen-based state military culture. We can see significant differences in public and private military service cultures – in goals, stakeholders, beliefs, values, and behaviors. It is a challenging environment for military and defense services to navigate. It is also a rich KLC environment. The challenge, though, is understanding each stakeholder's company, KLC cultures to gain the most significant value. What is the nature of the company, KLC culture of each of these stakeholders?

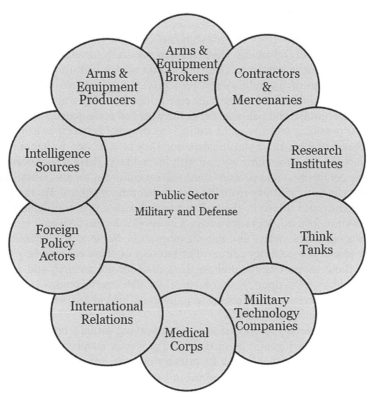

Fig. 5.   How Military Stakeholder Culture May Conflict or Align.

Arms and military equipment manufacturers exhibit market or fief company cultures. Their business goals are profit based, and their work is industrial production. Because they are also concerned with engineering and design, they have a higher tolerance for mistakes, risk, and uncertainty. They are looking for new approaches and ideas, inventions, and creative solutions. Their teams exhibit clan cultures in their scientific and engineering work. They generally have a single customer – the state military – who defines the market and the products. This stakeholder exhibits high learning levels and learning cultures. At the team level, there is significant collaboration. There is also a collaboration with the military partner.

Contractors and mercenary cultures generally take the form of a fief culture. The focus and value are on the individual soldier. Beliefs are focused on the individual's role rather than the team's. In recent years, we have observed contracted individuals being left alone to negotiate a safe exit from a situation. Generally, these soldiers act for themselves rather than the country, service, or team. Loyalty is to who is paying for service. Values and behaviors may vary with and reflect those of the entity paying. Ethics may be an anti-value. It is a risk preferring – or perhaps risk-ignorant culture. There is little incentive to learn and improve performance as the team's longevity is uncertain. There are varied knowledge bases within a mission.

Military-oriented think tanks tend to exhibit fief cultures. Their business is strategy formulation and consulting. They are often politically focused and motivated. The core value is influence. Their interaction is with high-ranking individuals in and out of the military service. Knowledge of international relations, politics, economics, and business are core values. Learning is also a core value. They are mistake and risk-tolerant as there are few consequences to researchers for providing bad advice. Learning is an essential behavior as it speaks to the heart of what these stakeholders do. They offer advice. Collaboration is limited to within the company and with the military. There is significant academic competition and perhaps some market culture in the specializations.

Technology industry cultures resemble a market company culture. We rarely find a bureaucratic culture in the tech industry because it is too dynamic and innovation-focused. Working within a controlled hierarchy would introduce unnecessary time delays and impede innovation. Some tech companies also may resemble a celebrity culture. The business of these companies, particularly those supporting the military, is state-of-the-art research and security. The military relies upon these companies for stable performance and deployment. These company cultures tend to focus on individuals, which is consistent with an innovation culture.

Medical corps generally leverage clan cultures working within a bureaucratic culture. The primary goal is on medical care to service members who may have been injured in conflicts. Like its primary domain, medical science, knowledge, and learning are highly valued in these cultures. The challenge is that knowledge produced in for-profit organizations may not be shared with public service military cultures. Learning and collaboration are critical behaviors. Risk acceptance is grounded in need to address and solve new problems.

Mistake acceptance as a learning opportunity reflects common medical and scientific practice to learn from experimentation. We expect to see learning on the job, on the job, and from traditional sources. We also expect high levels of collaboration with other medical experts. The values of the medical corps are closely aligned with core military values.

As discussed in the previous chapter, the cultures of *international relations, foreign policy, and diplomacy* are well-controlled bureaucratic cultures. International relations experts, foreign policy officials, and diplomats have critical roles in defining military missions. There is close collaboration at the top levels of all these organizations. But, there is little collaboration at the corps level. There is a clear overlap with military diplomacy. There is another natural link between these players in their cultural alignment with state- or national cultures.

The *intelligence community* might be characterized as a clan culture at its operational levels. The nature of the work requires continuous learning. And knowledge is the most highly valued product. Collaboration is encouraged within a closely defined team. There are controlled knowledge flows from the intelligence to the military. The flows, though, tend to be at higher levels of the military and intelligence organizations. Intelligence cultures are risk-averse because mistakes can mean lives. Uncertainty is the critical problem they are trying to solve. The values of the intelligence culture are consistent with those of the military.

Tier 4 – KLC Cultures of Public Service Military

Knowledge organizations are grounded on three embedded cultures: KLC cultures. What are military and defense services' natural knowledge creation and sharing tendencies? What are the learning practices? And how does collaboration fit into the military culture? We know that the company culture of any organization will affect what the KLC cultures look like, what form they take, and how they affect behaviors. In this section, we consider how these three cultures take form in a military company culture context.

Can we say that military and defense services are knowledge organizations? If so, how can we strengthen those tendencies? If not, how can we augment the company, public sector and external cultures to move toward a KLC approach? There are rarely absolutes when it comes to culture, so perhaps the better question is – in this complex culture, where do we see opportunities for knowledge creation and sharing, learning, and collaboration? And what impediments might we need to overcome?

Knowledge Cultures of Military Services

The military's KLC cultures are unlike diplomacy. However, diplomacy is more predictable and consistent than the military, so managing and shaping diplomatic cultures may be more predictable. In the military, creating and sharing knowledge daily, learning continuously, and collaborating intensely are necessary. Military knowledge creation and sharing, learning, unlearning, relearning, and collaborating depend on the context. We expect there to be intense knowledge creation and sharing on the battlefield. Knowledge improvization and adaptation will be intense in that environment. Having a baseline from which to adapt and improvise is why the military relies heavily on basic training and learning at onboarding. It is an intense form of situational and experiential learning. Troops on the ground leverage knowledge of the terrain, methods and tactics, and team knowledge. Relationships and relational capital are critical. Procedural knowledge is critical. Knowing the culture of the environment is critical – the physical, the cultural, and the social environment. Situational and experiential knowledge becomes tacit human capital.

Military cultures are, by necessity, knowledge cultures, but the knowledge is directly related to the nature of the business and the organization. As was noted in Chapter 5, there is no knowledge organization without knowledge workers. They are the producers who transform existing, explicit knowledge into new knowledge. We also noted that knowledge workers do not need to be directed or led but prefer to be inspired. These basic assumptions present some challenges for knowledge cultures in the military. The knowledge workers are all service members. The nature and type of knowledge depend on the context and the mission.

Knowledge creation and sharing will be intense in theater or on the field. There is an assumption that every soldier, seaman, or airman has the baseline knowledge required to perform for the team. It is the purpose of basic training, officer training, or training for specialized roles. However, the work of the military is to apply this knowledge to resolve a situation in a specific context. Critical knowledge is interpreting the environment, determining what knowledge is available, quickly designing a solution, and then assessing the situation. It is the tacit knowledge of individuals. The skills and competencies of scanning, detecting, designing, acting, and assessing are the core knowledge of the military – these must all be learned over time and in the field. Soldiers, seamen, and airmen learn from observing each other every day. They learn by building procedural knowledge – working together to design solutions.

Individual service members learn from their experiences and share them through their immediate networks, but it is unclear whether it goes beyond that level. Traditionally, we would have said it did not. Today's citizen-military, though, sees decision-making and direction moving to lower levels in the hierarchy. It means the distance knowledge must travel before being recognized and sanctioned is shortening. The nature of the task is team-based – individuals cannot lead themselves and follow their inspiration without significant consequences to the service. While the military may not be able to redefine the roles of individuals, they can create a knowledge climate where new knowledge is considered, evaluated, tested, and adopted. In an increasingly competitive world of conflict, the military must be able to out-think, out-smart, and out-guess their adversaries. It only happens in a knowledge culture.

An individual's and a team's reputation is critical knowledge capital. One's reputation reflects their performance and behavior. Military beliefs are grounded in high performance, integrity, and honor. These are all attributes of reputational capital. If we hope to build a mistake-tolerant culture in the military, we must find a way to build this into reputations – positively and constructively. Currently, the most highly valued reputations are those of individuals who avoided mistakes. One's reputation is also tied to visible artifacts such as rank, promotions, and medals. Medals speak – they signal an individual's reputation. In the current culture, medals signal "mistake-avoiding" or "mistake-free" performance.

Learning Culture of Military Services

Where we see a significant possibility for growth, though, is in the learning culture. There is a rich tradition of learning and training in military services based on the needs of the mission and the service members' roles and specializations. For many service members, the military is their primary source of domain-based learning – they develop their skills and competencies from the training they receive in the military. Training for specialized roles often leads to new careers after military service. It is formal training leading to certification and credentialing. It does not speak directly to learning in and on the job. This type of learning occurs daily – in the form of "fixing" trouble-shooting, making do, meeting a challenge, or just problem-solving. Every situation faced by military services will be unique. Every situation requires new learning.

The learning culture of the military is like that of the diplomatic corps. They are both representatives of the state. The knowledge they need is fulfill their role is defined by the state. There is a persistent knowledge foundation for each agency. And there is a core knowledge across agencies and departments anchored national values. The critical learning, though, occurs every day when diplomats and military personnel must interpret and operationalize that knowledge. Learning in this context is vital to survival of individuals and to the well-being of the state. The challenge is that these environments are dynamic and what is learned is perishable. Situational learning is essential in this context.

The challenge for defense and the military is to capture and integrate the knowledge learned on the ground into the formal knowledge base. Given the need to maintain high quality and rigorous information quality, tacit human capital must make its way through the formal hierarchy and channels to become part of the knowledge base to train the new workforce. A knowledge risk to the military is to allow individuals without experiential knowledge or with poor experiential knowledge to advance through the hierarchy. Learning in the environment is learning from mistakes – small mistakes. Given the nature of the risk, mistakes must be small. The size of the failure and the impact of the failure are essential. After-action reviews may be a form of tacit knowledge capture, assuming an opportunity to expose and share mistakes. The knowledge of mistakes may not be shared beyond the core troops. The military has a mistake-avoidance culture for a good reason. Ideally, a mistake-avoidance culture will ensure that a minimum of errors in judgment are made, avoiding any adverse consequences to service men and women.

When mistakes are made in teams and units, there is considerable personal after-action review. The challenge is whether these reviews take the form of lessons learned and lead to new learning opportunities or rather to blame, downgrading or dismissal. Mistakes are not valued because of the potentially high cost to human life. Learning from experience and resolving mistakes are highly valued in an unspoken way. However, this learning can often not be acknowledged because of the military value of high performance. Servicemen and women advanced through the ranks based on their high performance. Mistakes can hold them back from advancing or even lead to dismissal.

It is, though, critical that mistakes made and learned from being transparent and accessible to others to ensure they are not repeated, or if repeated, are recoverable. A significant challenge with the high-performance value is the opportunity to hide mistakes, not learn from them, and as a result, advance in the ranks. Having said this, we acknowledge that learning must be focused on small failures. Large failures have significant consequences and should be avoided. However, learning from mistakes should also be a critical criterion for advancement. As such, it should be made more transparent and rewarded in the military style – through awards and advances in rank. It will be a challenging cultural change to achieve, in any case.

Given the tight integration of mistake and uncertainty avoidance in the core values of the services, this shift will come gradually. The change needs to occur at all levels of the hierarchy. We suggest there might be more significant mistake denial and avoidance at the higher levels of the hierarchy than at the lower. Establishing a learning climate throughout the hierarchy would be a critical success factor.

Cultures of Collaboration in Military Services

A core value and belief in citizen-military forces is the team over the individual. The critical concept to understand is – how the military defines a team. A team may be a new group of officers, a team deployed to a theater or service members with a common specialization. Collaboration is a kind of structural capital – it revolves around processes, methods, and learning how to do something as a team. It is a vital source of knowledge capital building in every military team. Closely aligned with procedural knowledge is relational and reputational capital. Collaboration builds relationships. Given the short-term and frequent deployments, service members build enduring relationships throughout their careers. Collaboration is also where individuals build their reputational capital. Collaboration within a team is well-developed and intense. The strength of military cultures is that collaboration and learning are closely tied to core values and beliefs. They are essential starting points for building a KLC culture and shaping a military service into a knowledge organization.

Perhaps the most challenging of the three elements of the KLC approach is collaboration within the larger hierarchy – across levels. Collaboration thrives where there are short power distances. Authority and command are essential values and behaviors in military cultures. Shortening power distances may occur as power shifts to younger generations more comfortable with social collaboration. However, there is an impediment to collaboration that is unlikely to change – the free flow of sensitive military knowledge and intelligence – across unsecured human networks. Within the service, though, a culture of collaboration can be nourished within trusted sources.

Military cultures, like diplomatic cultures, are grounded in the state's core values. Where these values highlight service, respect, accountability, transparency, high performance, and community over self, there is a greater probability of integrating and sustaining a knowledge, learning and collaboration culture. The public service cultures can play a decisive and critical role in transforming military and defense services into knowledge organizations.

An individual's and a team's reputation is critical knowledge capital. One's reputation reflects their performance and behavior. Military beliefs are grounded in high performance, integrity, and honor. These are all attributes of reputational capital. If we hope to build a mistake-tolerant culture in the military, we must find a way to build this into reputations – positively and constructively. Currently, the most highly valued reputations are those of individuals who avoided mistakes. One's reputation is also tied to visible artifacts such as rank, promotions, and medals. Medals speak – they signal an individual's reputation. In the current culture, medals signal "mistake-avoiding" or "mistake-free" performance.

In the past half-century, military collaboration has been affected by the development of professional citizen defense forces and for-profit contracted defense sources. Anecdotally evidence that requires further research suggests that for-profit contracted defense forces have a significantly different set of values that affect collaboration. Whereas a citizen-based defense force values the team and operates on the assumption that "no one is left behind," contracted defense forces may be left on their own or left behind. Similarly, honor, integrity, and loyalty may be of secondary importance to that profit and military success. The value assigned to the safety and defense of others may be lower.

Additionally, the two cultures may have significantly different tolerances for mistakes. While a state military is mistake averse, the for-profit military may have a high threshold for mistakes. Mistakes may not only be tolerated. They may be entirely ignored. The risk may fall on the individual rather than on the team. Often citizen forces and contracted forces operate in the same theater. When this is the case, assumptions, beliefs, and behaviors may be significant differences. We do not know how these conflicts might affect either party's KLC culture. However, we know that it is an important topic to consider for future research. In these situations, will there be less collaboration and more individual and independent actors? Will the for-profit culture influence the behaviors of the public service culture?

Chapter Review

After reading this chapter, you should be able to:

- describe the company cultures of military organizations.
- explain how public service cultures affect the company cultures.
- describe the cultures of the external environment of military service.
- explain the KLC cultures of military organizations.
- discuss the opportunities and challenges of developing a KLC approach in military organizations.

References and Recommended Future Readings

Barrett, S. (2018). *Always faithful, always forward: Marine corps culture and the development of marine corps forces special operations command.* Naval Postgraduate School Monterey United States.

Boringa, T., & Wubs, B. (2018). A Soldier's Creed. Retrieved December 1, 2022, from https://www.ausa.org/soldiers-creed

Brim, W. L. (2013). Impact of military culture on the clinician and clinical practice. In B. A. Moore, & J. E. Barnett (Eds.), *Military psychologists' desk reference* (pp. 31–36). Oxford University Press.

Canfield, J., & Weiss, E. (2015). Integrating military and veteran culture in social work education: Implications for curriculum inclusion. *Journal of Social Work Education, 51,* S128–S144.

Center for Deployment Psychology. (2018, March 1). Military cultural competence. Retrieved December 1, 2022, from http://deploymentpsych.org/online-courses/military-culture

Coker, C. (2007). *The warrior ethos: Military culture and the war on terror.* Routledge.

Collins, J. J. (1998). The complex context of American military culture: A practitioner's view. *Washington Quarterly, 21*(4), 213.

Currier, J. M., Farnsworth, J. K., Drescher, K. D., McDermott, R. C., Sims, B. M., & Albright, D. L. (2018). Development and evaluation of the Expressions of Moral Injury Scale – Military version. *Clinical Psychology & Psychotherapy, 25*(3), 474–488.

Department of Defense. (1994). Mission Statement 1994 April 14, 2014. Retrieved December 1, 2022, from http://govinfo.library.unt.edu/npr/ library/status/mission/mdod.htm

Department of Defense. (2010). *Demographics 2010: Profile of the Military Community.* Department of Defense.

Department of Defense. (2011). *Demographics 2011: Profile of the Military Community.* Department of Defense.

Department of Defense. (n.d.). *About the Department of Defense (DOD).* Retrieved December 1, 2022, from http://www.defense.gov/about/

Department of Veterans Affairs. (2018, March 1). PTSD 101: Military Culture. Retrieved December 1, 2022, from https://www.ptsd.va.gov/professional/continuing_ed/military_culture.asp

Duncan, K. D. (2010). *Wingman, Warrior, Airman Branding the US Air Force.* University of Missouri-Columbia.

Dunivin, K. O. (1994). Military culture: Change and continuity. *Armed Forces & Society, 20*(4), 531–547.

Eighmey, J. (2006). Why do youth enlist? Identification of underlying themes. *Armed Forces & Society, 32*(2), 307–328.

Evered, R. (1980). *The language of organizations: The case of the Navy.* Naval Postgraduate School.

Feaver, P., & Kohn, R. (2000). The gap: Soldiers, civilians and their mutual misunderstanding. *The National Interest,* (61), 29–37.

Griffith, J. (2008). Institutional motives for serving in the US Army National Guard: Implications for recruitment, retention, and readiness. *Armed Forces & Society, 34*(2), 230–258.

Hall, L. K. (2011). The military culture, language, and lifestyle. In R. B. Everson & C. R. Figley (Eds.), *Families under fire: Systemic therapy with military families* (pp. 31–52). Routledge/Taylor & Francis Group.

Hall, L. K. (2013). Military culture. In B. A. Moore & J. E. Barnett (Eds.), *Military psychologists' desk reference* (pp. 22–26). Oxford University Press.

Hamaoka, D., Bates, M. J., McCarroll, J. E., Brim, W. L., Lunasco, T. K., & Rhodes, J. E. (2014). An introduction to military service.

Hamaoka, D., Bates, M. J., McCarroll, J. E., Brim, W. L., Lunasco, T. K., & Rhodes, J. E. (2014). An introduction to military service. In S. J. Cozza, M. N. Goldenberg, & R. J. Ursano (Eds.), *Care of military service members, veterans, and their families* (pp. 3–21). American Psychiatric Publishing, Inc.

Hillen, J. (1999). Must US military culture reform? *Parameters, 29*(3), 9.

Howard, J. L. (2006). The role of culture in shaping perceptions of discrimination among active duty and reserve forces in the US military. *Employee Responsibilities and Rights Journal, 18*(3), 171–187.

Howard, M. (2013). A military tradition institutionalized: Rhetorical personification and anthropomorphism in "The Riflemen's Creed". *Journal of Military Experience, 3*(2), 8.

Jenks, T. (2006). *Naval engagements: Patriotism, cultural politics, and the royal navy 1793–1815.* Oxford University Press.

Jinkerson, J. D. (2016). Defining and assessing moral injury: A syndrome perspective. *Traumatology, 22*, 122–130.

Jones, A. P., James, L. R., & Bruni, J. R. (1975). Perceived leadership behavior and employee confidence in the leader as moderated by job involvement. *Journal of Applied Psychology, 60*(1), 146.

Kasurak, P. C. (1982). Civilianization and the military ethos: Civil-military relations in Canada. *Canadian Public Administration, 25*(1), 108–129.

Kelty, R., Kleykamp, M., & Segal, D. R. (2010). The military and the transition to adulthood. *The Future of Children, 20*(1), 181–207.

Koenig, C. J., Maguen, S. Monroy, J. D., Mayott, L., & Seal., K. H. (2014). Facilitating culturecentered communication between health care providers and veterans transitioning from military deployment to civilian life. *Patient Education and Counseling, 95*, 414–420.

Koivula, T. (2009). Toward an EU military ethos. *European Foreign Affairs Review, 14*(2), 171–190.

Kuehner, C. A. (2013). My military: A Navy nurse practitioner's perspective on military culture and joining forces for veteran health. *Journal of the American Association of Nurse Practitioners, 25*(2), 77–83.

Lancaster, S. L., Kintzle, S., & Castro, C. A. (2018). Validation of the warrior identity scale in the Chicagoland veterans study. *Identity, 18*(1), 34–43.

Machoian, R. G. (2004). Looking skyward: The emergence of an air-minded culture in the US Army. Air Command and Staff Coll Maxwell Air Force Base, Alabama.

McCormick, W. H., Currier, J. M., Isaak, S. L., Sims, B. M., Carroll, T. D., Hammer, K., & Albright, D. L. (2019). Military culture and post-military transitioning among veterans: A qualitative analysis. *Journal of Veterans Studies, 4*(2), 287–298.

Moore, B. A. (2011). Understanding and working within the military culture. In B. A. Moore & W. E. Penk (Eds.), *Treating PTSD in Military Personnel: A clinical handbook* (pp. 9–22). The Guilford Press.

Parrott, S., Albright, D. L., Dyche, C., & Steele, H. G. (2018). Hero, charity case, and victim: How US news media frame military veterans on Twitter. *Armed Forces & Society.* https://doi.org/10.1177/0095327X18784238

Pease, J. L., Billera, M., & Gerard, G. (2016). Military culture and the transition to civilian life: Suicide risk and other considerations. *Social Work, 61*(1), 83–86.

Pollman, M. A. (2018). Framing marine corps culture. *Proceedings Magazine-June, 144*(6/1,384), 2.

Redmond, S. A., Wilcox, S. L., Campbell, S., Kim, A., Finney, K., Barr, K., & Hassan, A. M. (2015). A brief introduction to the military workplace culture. *Work, 50*(1), 9–20.

Riccio, G., Sullivan, R., Klein, G., Salter, M., & Kinnison, H. (2004). *Warrior Ethos: Analysis of the concept and initial development of applications.* Wexford Group International Inc.

Savitsky, L., Illingworth, M., & DuLaney, M. (2009). Civilian social work: Serving the military and veteran populations. *Social Work, 54*(4), 327–339.

Shay, J. (2014). Moral injury. *Psychoanalytic Psychology, 31,* 182–191.

Siebold, G. L. (2006). Military culture and values: A personal view. In T. W. Britt, A. B. Adler, & C. A. Castro (Eds.), *Military life: The psychology of serving in peace and combat: Military culture* (Vol. 4, pp. 3–10). Praeger Security International.

Soeters, J. L., Poponete, C.-R., & Page, J. T. J. (2006). Culture's consequences in the military. In T. W. Britt, A. B. Adler, & C. A. Castro (Eds.), *Military life: The psychology of serving in peace and combat: Military culture* (Vol. 4, pp. 13–34). Praeger Security International.

Soeters, J. L., Winslow, D. J., & Weibull, A. (2003). Military culture. In G. Caforio (Ed.), *Handbook of the sociology of the military* (pp. 237–254). Springer Science & Business Media.

Soeters, J. L., Winslow, D. J., & Weibull, A. (2006). Military culture. In G. Caforio & M. Nuciari (Eds.), *Handbook of the sociology of the military* (p. 63). New York, NY: Springer.

Stoddard, J., Hodges, D., Huston, D., Johnson, M., Underwood, J., Durnil, D., & Morgan, H. (2021). True Warrior Ethos – The Creed of Today's American Warrior. *The Journal of Character & Leadership Development.* article2_TrueWarriorEthos.pdf

Straub, D., Loch, K., Evaristo, R., Karahanna, E., & Srite, M. (2002). Toward a theory-based measurement of culture. *Journal of Global Information Management (JGIM), 10*(1), 13–23.

Terriff, T. (2006a). 'Innovate or die': Organizational culture and the origins of maneuver warfare in the United States Marine Corps. *Journal of Strategic Studies, 29*(3), 475–503.

Terriff, T. (2006b). Warriors and innovators: Military change and organizational culture in the US Marine Corps. *Defence Studies, 6*(2), 215–247.

Williams, K. R. (2010). An assessment of moral and character education in initial entry training (IET). *Journal of Military Ethics, 9*(1), 41–56.

Wilson, P. H. (2008). Defining military culture. *Journal of Military History, 72*(1), 11–41.

Winslow, D. (2000). *Army culture.* OTTAWA UNIV (ONTARIO). DTIC.

Wong, L. (2005). Leave no man behind: Recovering America's fallen warriors. *Armed Forces & Society, 31*(4), 599–622.

Woodruff, T., Kelty, R., & Segal, D. R. (2006). Propensity to serve and motivation to enlist among American combat soldiers. *Armed Forces & Society, 32*(3), 353–366.

Yamada, A. M., Atuel, H. R., & Weiss, E. L. (2013). Military culture and multicultural diversity among military service members: Implications for mental health providers. In F. A. Paniagua & A. M. Yamada (Eds.), *Handbook of multicultural mental health* (pp. 389–410). Academic Press.

Chapter 11

The KLC Approach and Public Sector Space Exploration

Chapter Summary

This chapter describes public space exploration services' business goals, purpose, and strategy. It reinforces space exploration organizations' fundamental bureaucratic administrative culture (Tier 1). The authors describe the influence that political appointees as leaders may play in shaping public sector cultures. Next, the public service culture (Tier 2) is deconstructed, and each of the five layers is described in detail. Additionally, the authors explain why focusing on the beliefs layer is the dominant layer and the essential starting point for analysis in space exploration cultures. Next, the chapter outlines the landscape of external influencing cultures (Tier 3) in the space exploration landscape. Finally, the potential value and challenges of developing internal KLC cultures are explored.

Why We Care about Public Sector Space Exploration Cultures?

Public service space exploration is a primary source of theoretical and practical knowledge generation for a relatively new area of science and engineering. One of the roles of the public sector is to support research and development where there is little or no incentive for other market sources to invest. And, where the value of the investment may benefit the general population, Public service also plays a critical integrating role in a field that leverages human, structural, and relational capital from several fields. Public service space exploration ensures that innovations, discoveries, and new knowledge are available to the public to develop new economic and business opportunities. By definition, we note that public service space exploration is KLC oriented. Therefore, there are significant opportunities to operationalize a KLC approach in this area of public service.

The Cultures of Knowledge Organizations: Knowledge, Learning, Collaboration (KLC), 213–230
Copyright © 2023 by Wioleta Kucharska and Denise Bedford
Published under exclusive licence by Emerald Publishing Limited
doi:10.1108/978-1-83909-336-420231011

Public Service Space Exploration – Goals, Structures, and Strategies

By its very nature, space exploration is multidisciplinary. The level of effort required to conduct space exploration is of such a scale that for most of its history, it could only be funded by national-level governments. The economics of space exploration is like knowledge economics – the upfront sunk costs are high, whereas the recurring costs are insignificant. It is consistent with one of the rationales for public sector organizations referenced in Chapter 8. The sunk costs required to create the knowledge up front will be recouped many times over as its products and services are realized. However, there is little direct financial profit to be achieved by the public sector investors. Additionally, because of the equipment's scale, texting and complex engineering required were beyond any sector. Therefore, it would require collaboration across several sectors and types of organizations.

Only national governments with significant financial resources can fund the new fundamental theoretical space exploration research that was needed. One of the goals of public sector organizations is to create new economic opportunities. In this case, the economic opportunity was an entirely new cross-industry sector. It also involved bridging research to practice to market. And there was no existing synthesized knowledge base. Achieving all these results would require significant upfront sunk costs. And, there was little expectation of any near-term profit that could offset an essential investment. In the twentieth century, the public sector assumed the lead role in fundamental theoretical space exploration research from universities, private institutes, and foundations, because the new knowledge would advance the population's health, security, and quality of life – core public service values.

The results had to serve extensive interests to justify the significant up-front investments in new knowledge and capabilities. In the last 80 years, public sector space exploration has been mandated to increase knowledge, advance national status and prestige, enhance national security and strength, and benefit citizens in their everyday life. As we see in fundamental knowledge economics, knowledge is not a capital asset that can be controlled in a traditional market economy. Instead, the knowledge that would be created was a quintessential public good – it provided new knowledge for citizens, scientists, engineers, technologies, and private sector organizations to leverage to build other new products and services. In the twenty-first century, the knowledge generated by the early public service agencies and departments is now available to private sector organizations. The level of financial investment to "get in the business of space" is now affordable to those organizations. We have seen the beginning of commercial space travel for non-scientists, engineers, and technologists.

Space exploration is multifaceted. There are two main disciplines in space sciences which is the fundamental discipline of space exploration – astronomy and astronautics. Astronomy includes astrophysics, cosmology, planetary science, astrochemistry, astrobiology, space biology, space chemistry, astrobotany, archeoastronomy, space archaeology, space archaeology, forensic astronomy, astrometry, photometry, spectroscopy, radio astronomy, optical astronomy, high-energy astronomy, etc. Astronautics include aerospace engineering, space technology, space architecture, space flight, bioastronautics, planets, and life in space. In addition, we can see how many other fields have subfields pertinent to space sciences – biology, botany, chemistry, archeology, forensic sciences, communications, physics, and technology. By definition, space exploration will always span multiple fields and encounter many other fundamental company cultures.

Tier 1 – Company Cultures of Space Exploration

Over its history, the knowledge generated by public sector space exploration has given rise to many new fields of study and business opportunities. Today, we have vastly richer communications, weather observation and tracking services, navigation systems, positional location, and more precise timing capabilities. We can also point to the development of satellites for the relay of voice, video, and data. Satellite telecommunications today is a multibillion-dollar business that would not have been possible with the initial upfront investment of the public sector. The knowledge from this early work was quickly handed off to the private sector. In this case, the private sector could generate profits by provisioning telecommunications services and backbones, which are the foundation of today's communications products and services.

The company culture of any space exploration organization will be relatively young. While the field has roots in military air services and air transportation, its predominant culture is scientific. Because it is a new field of research and practice, science culture came first. Management cultures evolved from the successful construction and grounding of the new field. Scientific and engineering cultures tend to be cultures of excellence (Roberts, Rousseau, & LaPorte, 2019; Roberts et al., 1994). The mission culture of space exploration reflects military behavior. As we saw in Chapter 8, military cultures also value high standards and performance. The origin of space travel in the military air corps reinforces this value in science. The military aspect of the culture is further reinforced by international competition across states to succeed. A culture of excellence is ingrained in space exploration cultures' values, behaviors, and artifacts. A culture of excellence is reflected in expertise and knowledge creation, a realization that exploration would not happen without tested hands-on strategies, a clear awareness of risk and failure, and the open and free flow of communications. An aspect of a company culture that varies across states is the value placed on human safety. Space exploration is about putting people into high-risk and unknown environments. Like other transportation cultures, safety is often a core value of the science culture.

Given the complexity of the twenty-first-century space exploration field, we expect to see various company cultures in place. A science, engineering, and technology foundation tends to favor a market culture. Space exploration cultures need the flexibility to change direction and resources as they learn. A market-like, competitive, performance-focused culture is critical to ensuring the organization has the expertise and infrastructure it needs at any point in time. A more flexible, information-based market culture is also vital to innovation. Market-like company culture will also support knowledge and technology exchange with industry and universities. We might find clan cultures at the individual team or project level. Space exploration organizations only adopt a bureaucratic culture once it has reached a particular state of maturity. As the new field stabilizes, there is something to manage. A bureaucratic company culture tends to value production, efficiency and effectiveness over innovation, creativity, learning, and safety. These potential conflicts can introduce significant new risks and dangers.

Given the history of space exploration in some public sector environments and the interplay of industry, business, research, and teaching, we suggest the more predominant company culture is a blend of bureaucracy, market, and clan. We suggest bureaucracy is dominant at the top leadership level to ensure accountability, trustworthiness, public welfare, risk aversity and management, and transparency values (Roberts & Libuser, 1993; Weick & Sutcliffe, 2001). These cultures tend to be "knowing" rather than "learning." At the lower levels, though, where science, engineering, and technology are done each day, we see a blend between a market and a clan culture.

Market cultures represent mission management levels that must collaborate and coordinate their work with external partners. These cultures tend to have low power distance, a higher tolerance for uncertainty, and high levels of individuality (Argyris, 1957). These cultures leverage codified explicit knowledge and exhibited higher levels of diffusion. In these cultures, access to knowledge is not a tool of power and control. Instead, they behave like self-regulating internal markets – checking, cross-checking, testing, mistake-making, and mistake management (Farson & Keyes, 2006; Kramer, 2003; Langewiesche, 2003; Mitroff & Pearson, 1993; Vaughan, 1996). Market cultures resemble scientific cultures in that relationships remain impersonal and competitive. In these cultures, there is an implicit set of shared values and beliefs grounded in the norms of science (Mason, 2004).

Clan cultures are more characteristic of the project research team or the mission team. Clan cultures are prevalent in smaller organizations with greater access to other individuals – at the lower levels, these organizations tend to be teams working on parts of specific missions. These cultures are grounded in shared experiences. Relationships are personal and equal rather than hierarchical. Respect and relationships are based on the nature of knowledge rather than power. Horizontal coordination and knowledge exchange predominate. Negotiation and resolution among members afford opportunities to share values and beliefs. Human capital, e.g., tacit knowledge, skills and competencies, and relational capital, is the foundation of clan cultures. Clan cultures are highly collective. They are effective environments for generating new and out-of-the-box ideas. The clan culture is well suited to a space exploration organization.

The bureaucratic company culture is dominant at the leadership level of a center or location. The mission, program, and project cultures, though, will vary with the work of the teams and functions. If we consider space exploration in an academic college, university, or research institution, the business culture will tend toward a market or a clan culture. Market cultures leverage codified and explicit knowledge but in a diffused and shared way throughout the organization.

Clan cultures are defined around shared experiences. When we consider the nature of space science and engineering, much of the work is trial and error-based and requires large teams working in collaboration, learning from mistakes, and correcting mistakes as quickly as possible. In contrast, though, where space exploration is the goal of a private sector for-profit organization, the market or clan culture may still exist, but it will be secondary to the bureaucratic culture, which will define the goals, not as scientific advancement and contributions to the field of science, but to make a profit and to offer products to the open market.

Analyzing the Layers of Company Culture

Space exploration is about science, engineering, and technology research and testing, whether in a private, public, non-, or not-for-profit context (Resnick, 1985). Because of the solid aperspectival assumptions and beliefs at the heart of science cultures, we suggest the beliefs layer (Fig. 1) is the starting point for understanding the company culture.

Space Exploration Beliefs

Scientific rationalism is the dominant assumption across the whole structure of modern society (Swartz, 1998). Moreover, it is close to being the source of cognitive authority (Gieryn, 1983). Rationalism is grounded in a core belief of any scientific culture: aperspectival objectivity (Daston, 1992; Daston & Galison, 1992). Aperspectival objectivity is independent from individual and social influences and reliance on explicit, quantitative data, and analysis. The goal of aperspectival objectivity is to eliminate the subjective and the role of the human observer (Daston & Galison, 1992; Feldman, 2004; Novick, 1988; Pool, 1997). Aperspectival objectivity eliminates the individual's view and idiosyncrasies from interpreting scientific experimentation and results (Bloor, 1984; Daston, 1992; Galion, 1987;

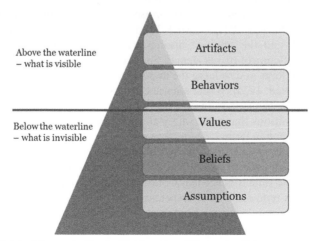

Fig. 1.   Critical Layer in Space Exploration Company Cultures.

Novick, 1988). Aperspectival objectivity greatly restricts our moral sense. It values goals and the means to achieve them over safety, caution, and consideration for the person. Objectivity requires we disregard what is unique and focus on the collective (Merton, 1969). Experience is reduced to laws or regularities and is brought under control. This results in a tendency toward gross or aggregate moral decision-making. This belief can lead to disregarding qualitative data, over-reliance on quantitative data, and reifying safety standards, leading to underestimating uncertainty and risk.

Space Exploration Assumptions

The belief in objectivity suggests that knowledge can exist independently of a knowing subject (Popper, 1972, 1983). If knowledge is objective, it stands apart from (and above) culture and the biases of particular social groups. Beliefs in objectivity can encourage other beliefs and assumptions. For example, they create an environment where the decision-making of a bureaucratic culture may tend to support power roles. The power invested in the bureaucratic hierarchy may prevail over the flexibility of scientific knowledge (Foucault, 1977). Scientific knowledge is open to interpretation because it is tacit in nature (Polanyi, 1958, 1962, 1966, 1969, 2012). It rests on implicit background assumptions that cannot be entirely explicit (Longino, 1990, 1996). Power can grow in an environment of assumed uncertainty and force a decision and closure (Biagioli, 1995). Similarly, hubris or an assumed pride or self-confidence results from excessive admiration of oneself, a series of previous successes, uncritical acceptance of accolades and a belief that one is exempt from the rules. In the end, hubris is eventually rewarded with disaster and comeuppance.

Space Exploration Values

Merton's (1957) "norms of science" – universalism, communalism, disinterestedness, and organized skepticism – comprise any scientific culture's core values (Longino, 1996; Mason, 2004; Turner & Mccreery, 2007; Weber, 2013). The value of universalism and the value of disinterestedness or detachment suggest an emphasis on self-control or self-denial. Science and the scientific mindset have been the critical force in devaluing the importance of the past in moral decision-making (Whitehead, 1925). Where science cultures are utilitarian and focused on cost–benefit analysis and the consequences of a decision, it devalues moral traditions. Moral traditions that value safety and prudence, for example, are reduced to or are interpreted in terms.

Science cultures assign a high value to quantitative, explicit knowledge and expertise. There is a value to sharing knowledge and ensuring it is accessible where it is needed at the time it is needed. Contrary or annoying ideas are embraced. Decision-makers require diverse perspectives and information. It involves iterative review, decision-making, and balancing hierarchical command-and-control bureaucracies with flatter market and clan cultures. Science cultures also place a high value on open communication, transparency, and access to information.

Silence, confidentiality, cover-up, and tendencies to protect a reputation are afforded lesser value.

Space Exploration Behaviors

Values are often reflected in behaviors. In a scientific culture, behaviors may reflect a value of self-image and self-actualization, a focus on the outcome, training and learning, performance, communication, rewards tied to performance, and a preference for participatory and people-oriented management (Pelz, 1967; Straw, 1976; Vollmer et al., 1964; Vroom, 1994). People prefer to work in groups and teams where there is interaction. Interaction with those outside the immediate team is also valued for knowledge sharing. The work environment is project-, mission-, and goal-oriented.

Science involves practice, and it is in human practice that results must prove themselves. Detailed studies of scientific practice have demonstrated a constitutive role for contingency in the particular closures that are arrived in particular experiments or investigations (Pickering, 1993, 1995). Moreover, the practice of science has its full-blown historicity. That is, it creates meaning in response to its problems and struggles. Meaning is not just a derivative of cultural consensus. Indeed, cultural standards themselves are subject to change in practice.

In scientific practice, most ideas will initially fail. Success is worked out by continuous adjustments and changes, what Pickering (1993, 1995) calls the "mangle of practice." Understanding evolves. Failure means running into resistance; resistance is situated concerning goals. They arise unpredictably. Scientists have to make accommodations to deal with them. Accommodations are relative to goals (Fleck, 2012). This dialectic between resistance and accommodation has its historical character, creating its facts and theories in real-time scientific practice. The closures (i.e., knowledge) result from this dialectical struggle and reflect the mangling of cultural standards, interests, and material obstructions in pursuing practical goals. From this view, the notion of "objectivity" must be understood in terms of the mangle of practice and the process of knowledge creation that emerges from it.

Space Exploration Artifacts

The company culture of space exploration includes two types of artifacts – military culture and science culture. Like the military culture, work environments are sparse, economic, and objective, with few, if any, office embellishments. Some artifacts from the early military cultures include heroes, rank, awards, and achievements. These reflect a close alignment with the air force and army air corps. Astronauts are equivalent to military heroes. We can see the influence of an academic and research culture in the artifacts of every day space exploration. These artifacts include business casual or informal dress, collections of journals, papers and books in offices, open physical office designs to encourage conversations and knowledge exchange, miniature models, and scientific awards. However, the symbols and insignia of space exploration cultures are future-focused. They describe what is new and innovative rather than traditional or fundamental.

Tier 2 – Public Service Culture of Space Exploration

The naturally dominant company culture in any space exploration organization will be the culture of science, engineering, and technology (Andrews & Pelz, 1966; Bourdieu, 1975; McCurdy, 1989; Resnick-West & Von Glinow, 1990). However, a public sector organization must consider transparency, accountability, and safeguarding of funds. This means overlaying market and clan cultures with a bureaucratic leadership and decision-making culture. A scientific and engineering culture is grounded in fundamental beliefs, which are reflective of values. It will, though, be heavily influenced by bureaucratic company culture.

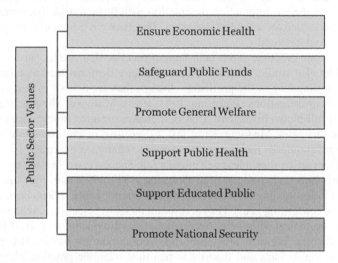

Tier 3 – Competing and Complex Cultures in Space Exploration

The external environment resembles a military culture but with a broader scope and larger scale of stakeholders. The upfront public sector investments in sunk costs have achieved the goal of establishing an advanced, cross-disciplinary field of research and practice. These state-level investments achieved the goal 60 years ago – establishing the foundation from which a healthy and thriving private, non-, and not-for-profit sector can grow. Space technology is no longer a monopoly at the state level. As a result, space exploration's external and internal landscape has been shifting and will continue to shift. The growth of a new field and research topic demands new approaches to problem-solving and innovation. Additionally, the external landscape has become more competitive. New stakeholders are generating a wealth of new knowledge, capabilities, and competencies. Private space companies have emerged. And well-funded national space agencies now create a globally competitive environment.

The external political environment has also shifted, leading to critical roles and responsibilities being contracted out. The expanded use of contractors brings in new knowledge and introduces new and potentially conflicting value systems. Value conflicts can arise where a community and state service motivation for knowledge creation, learning, and collaboration comes into close contact with for-profit value systems. These competing value systems can lead to knowledge hoarding and exclusion. However, close collaboration can also promote on-the-job and in-the-job learning and the exchange of competencies across stakeholders (Reid et al., 2022).

In 2022, the landscape of space exploration included professional associations, scientific research companies, colleges and universities, research institutes, private space exploration companies, national space agencies, the aerospace industry, aeronautics associations, contractors, politicians, scientific researchers, aerospace associations, and the military equipment industry. We briefly describe stakeholders' business goals, company culture, KLC cultures to understand how they affect public service space exploration.

Military Industry comprises individuals who have left military service and private
   sector, business executives. The company culture is bureaucratic, with some
   market cultures at the research, development, and production levels. The goal
   of these organizations is profit and sustainable business, as they have a limited number of consumers. The knowledge culture is responsive, specifications,
   and requirements-based, rather than innovative. Knowledge is held close as it
   is power in bidding for public sector contracts. Knowledge is often tightly held
   by non-disclosure agreements. There is little incentive to innovate as it may not
   align with consumer demands. Knowledge sharing likely occurs when individuals leave one company and join another. Learning occurs at lower levels

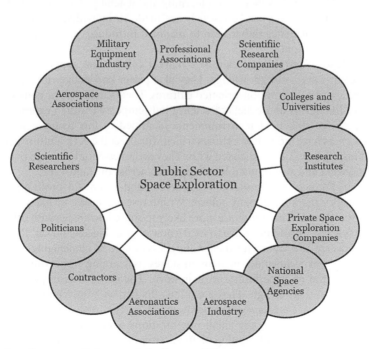

Fig. 2.   Company Cultures of the External Environment.

of development and production within the company. Collaboration with space exploration likely occurs through networks of air services and corps and astronautics. Collaboration also likely occurs at the person-to-person level.

Professional Associations often exhibit a clan company culture. The intent is to share knowledge across the community. Professional associations provide critical knowledge-sharing opportunities for astronautics and aeronautics as they represent both the field's traditional and new research. Professional associations also provide learning activities for members. It is another important channel for knowledge to travel from public service space exploration to the core disciplines. We are more likely to see collaboration with these external actors than with most others.

Colleges and Universities exhibit a *clan company culture*. They are closely aligned with public service space exploration. They contribute to and draw from public service and external knowledge bases. They focus on theoretical and applied research but do not take on formal development or large-scale testing unless an affiliated research institute with significant facilities exists. Colleges and universities are highly networked organizations. An example of an extended knowledge network might be the relationship between the University of California Berkeley, Lawrence Livermore Laboratory, Sandia National Laboratory, and NASA's Jet Propulsion Laboratory. This external stakeholder provides a safe environment for investigating high-risk issues which will result in small failures. They move the failure factor out of public service into academics. These stakeholders are heavy knowledge creators and sharers. Their work is focused on learning and teaching. There is a tempered collaboration culture, where rewards are made to individual academics for scientific performance rather than to teams. It introduces an element of academic competition.

Scientific Researchers prefer a clan or a market culture that supports the open flow of and access to knowledge. They also prefer knowledge-rich, learning-focused, and collaboration-oriented cultures. Their values will be consistently tied to the norms and beliefs of science but tempered through experience in some of the stakeholder environments identified in this section. Scientific researchers have individual cultures which will affect the KLC cultures of any organization they are associated with. They are an essential leverage point for introducing and sustaining a KLC approach across the landscape.

Research Institutes and Laboratories are generally non- or not-for-profit organizations with a market company culture. Within research areas, we likely see clan cultures. Research institutes are more likely to share knowledge with others as there is a lower profit incentive to treat knowledge as bidding power. Research institutes are also valued for their willingness to take on challenging research, learn from experimentation, treat mistakes as learning opportunities, and expect a level of uncertainty in their work. The collaboration potential of research institutes is high. They are often affiliated with universities.

Scientific Research Companies commonly exhibit a clan or a market company culture. They are generally small organizations whose support depends on government grants and funding or funds from high-net-worth individuals in the private sector. The research knowledge generated by private sector funds will not likely be shared with public service space organizations. The research knowledge generated by public sector funding is mandated to be shared back. These stakeholders take on specific research and development challenges that may be too high risk for public service and for which there is no private sector market. They exhibit high knowledge use, generation, and sharing rates within research teams. They are risk and uncertainty tolerant because it is in the gaps that new knowledge is produced. They demonstrate high rates of learning and collaboration within the organization. And they have varying levels of sharing, learning, and collaboration in the external landscape.

Private Space Exploration Companies have emerged in the past decade, often leveraging public service organizations' knowledge, infrastructure, and resources to create new commercial opportunities. After eight decades of public sector investment, commercial space travel is now a reality. These companies have a strong market company culture to define and respond to market forces. They can effectively leverage a market culture because the workforce tends to be smaller, with less need for a bureaucratic culture. Knowledge sharing within the company is likely very high and reciprocal. Outside the company, though, it is more likely that knowledge will be ingested from other sources than that knowledge will be disseminated to others. Learning will be high-paced, with some tolerance for minor mistakes and learning from those mistakes. A learning climate is essential to these companies. Collaboration is likely strictly controlled within the company.

National Space Agencies leverage bureaucratic company cultures at the leadership level. There may be clan or market cultures at the research levels. They are knowledge creators and sharers within the organization. The level of risk and uncertainty tolerance will vary with the state and the state's position in the world order. The national values will also influence it. The spectrum of values extends from risk-preferring in favor of business performance to risk-averse in favor of human safety and life (Roberts & Libuser, 1993; Weick & Sutcliffe, 2001). Some state agencies are more performance drive than others. There is some collaboration across agencies and some joint missions and research. There is some cross-agency learning in agencies whose states are allied. A KLC approach exists where countries are generally aligned and collaborate in other endeavors. A KLC approach will be challenging to achieve where there is greater competition across agencies.

Aerospace Industry leverages a *bureaucratic culture* at the leadership level. At the development and production levels, a market culture is more prevalent. There is extensive knowledge sharing within teams, but research has not yet determined whether it is cross-organization. There is sharing with public service organizations, mainly where financial incentives and contracts are in place. However, there is little sharing with private sector competitors. These stakeholders are risk and mistake-averse. Given the nature of the work, engineering knowledge is more highly valued. The bureaucratic culture is focused on production – the knowledge to produce is most highly valued. Learning is aligned with business goals. Work and production time are valued. There is little value in investing in off-goal learning. Collaboration is strictly controlled within the team and within the organization. These stakeholders are often aligned with military cultures and military equipment producers.

Aeronautics and Astronautics Professional Associations leverage clan and market cultures. These stakeholders tend to have more KLC-focused business goals. They draw members from all stakeholders in the external landscape. Aeronautics and astronautics are where networks form and individuals establish relationships that are important for learning and collaboration. Professional associations have a close alignment with academic and research organizations. As a result, there is significant knowledge creation, sharing, and flow through association networks.

Contractors have two company cultures in play. We find a bureaucratic culture at the leadership level reflecting the profit goal. And a clan culture at the team level where the work is performed. Knowledge must be shared with the contracting agency but is generally not shared outside the work environment. Knowledge is viewed as a high-value asset and a source of market power. As such, it is highly guarded and protected. It is protected to the point of requiring employees to sign non-disclosure agreements. Public service organizations gain all forms of knowledge capital from contracts or as much as the contractor is required to share. Project employees' human capital is often the most valued commodity. The nature of the contract determines to learn. Where there are awards and rewards, the contractor will allow more time for learning. Where there are not, time will not be made available. Contractors are generally very risk-averse and mistake-intolerant. Collaboration is strictly controlled within the team and at the leadership levels of the public sector and contract managers only. It is not an encouraging environment for introducing or sustaining a KLC approach except for cost-plus award fee contracts. There are, though, pervasive opportunities for knowledge theft.

In summary, there are opportunities and challenges for building a cross-landscape KLC culture. A closer look at each culture will build an understanding of the approach that will work in each context.

Tier 4 – Knowledge Cultures of Space Exploration Organizations

Space exploration is a particularly interesting example for several reasons to consider for a twenty-first century KLC culture. First, they have a built-in "learning from mistakes" and "mistake management" culture at the research level but a "mistake avoidance" and "mistake denial" culture at the leadership level. Second, research-level cultures are, by definition, KLC oriented. However, depending on the prevailing political environment, the leadership culture may focus on risk-averse, cost efficiency, and branding rather than knowledge and learning. Finally, we find conflicts in goals and strategies with stakeholders in the external environment. The space exploration culture provides opportunities to leverage and challenges to be met.

The challenge to nourishing a KLC approach in a space exploration organization is determining how the different company cultures interact in the ordinary course of events. We can "see" this in particular historical events such as major accidents or critical decisions of leadership. We can also see which culture is dominant at any time and what factors have elevated it over others.

Knowledge Cultures of Space Exploration

Space exploration draws knowledge from many fields of science. It draws many types and forms of scientific and engineering knowledge. It draws upon explicit and encoded scientific knowledge is a complex object. It draws many forms of scientific and engineering knowledge, both implicit and explicit. It draws from all types of human capital, including tacit knowledge, skills and competencies, and procedural knowledge (Restivo, 1994). The knowledge sharing capability is extensive in the academic and research contexts – colleges, universities, research institutes, and companies (Pinch & Bijker, 1984). We find experimentation, exploration, explanation, translation, interpretation, and negotiation in scientific contexts. While objectivity is the espoused norm, in practice, scientific communities are dominated by a limited number of people leveraging their competencies and credentials to establish new knowledge (Pinch & Bijker, 1984; Restivo, 1994). Knowledge growth and development are continuous – there is little stability in a field like space exploration. Finally, scientific knowledge is socially constituted (Pinch & Bijker, 1984; Restivo, 1994). Perhaps the earliest reference to a knowledge culture derives from the study of the sociology of scientific knowledge by Knorr-Cetina (1999).

There is a large, well-established body of scientific knowledge in published papers, books, grey literature, procedures, manuals, experiment videos, specifications, and design documents. The challenge with explicit knowledge is that it is rarely a complete and true representation of the human and structural capital that created it. Therefore, it is crucial to look beyond that explicit body of knowledge to the knowledge of individuals engaged in space exploration. Additionally, high-pressure experimental science projects leave little time to record or share mistakes. Historically, the purpose of laboratory notebooks was to record the complete knowledge creation process, successes, and failures. Unless scientists and engineers record mistakes and trials daily, we lose a significant amount of knowledge. The Apollo mission is a classic example of the loss of knowledge in space exploration. Time pressures and the pressure to succeed allowed little time for scientists and engineers to record how they developed the cutting-edge knowledge that enabled the Apollo mission to succeed. In the twenty-first century, the agency had to re-create that fundamental knowledge.

Explicit scientific knowledge is like an iceberg. At best, 10% of the science we know or learn is articulated and recorded. The other 90% is still in the minds of individuals and groups. The methods, trials, successes, and failures that a scientist or an engineer went through to realize the results are rarely published. Scientists and engineers experiment, make mistakes and learn from their mistakes. However, publishers and professional associations are reticent to report on any failures. Peer review guidelines allow for some noting of lessons learned, but they must be part of a larger successful research effort or project. failures. There is no value in broadcasting our mistakes. As a result, scientists and engineers sometimes repeat the mistakes of others. It results in inefficient learning. If a scientist or engineer is part of a subject or practice network, knowledge of mistakes and their causes may be shared from individual to individual. It further proves the importance of looking beyond the visible and explicit body of knowledge.

Learning Cultures of Space Exploration Organizations

Science is the practice of learning from mistakes and failures. Ideally, a learning culture that accepts and treats mistakes as opportunities is endemic to space exploration. Learning in science is a continuous process of learning, unlearning, and relearning. We find this in the clan cultures at the workforce level. We are less likely to find it in the bureaucratic cultures at the leadership level. The bureaucratic culture determines what is valued and will be rewarded. This learning culture reinforces mistake avoidance or devaluation at the knowledge level. When space exploration company cultures shifted from discovery and exploration to management and control, the pressure to avoid mistakes increased significantly. Rather than reward or even recognize small rewards, they were suppressed.

Space exploration grew out of a vision. We needed a body of knowledge from which to draw and build to realize the vision. That body of knowledge did not exist. The body of knowledge of space exploration grew in two primary areas – aeronautics and astronautics. These fields are highly interdisciplinary. They draw from or contribute to astronomy, chemistry, biology, botany, medicine, physics, engineering, and computer science. The knowledge of those related disciplines was adapted by continuous and vigorous human learning. Learning was collaborative, interactive, exploratory, in the job and on the job. Learning was motivated by public service values of security and education.

Over time space exploration has shifted from a risk preferring, learning from mistakes, and uncertainty-expecting culture to a risk and uncertainty avoidance and mistake-denial culture. This culture has permeated the learning culture across public service space exploration. Unfortunately, the learning culture was devalued for several decades in favor of a bureaucratic performance culture. The bureaucratic culture suppressed the clan cultures. The major failures of those decades are now attributed to a culture of risk and mistake denial.

It is essential to understand the spectrum of failures in space exploration. Learning from small mistakes and failures over time and through controlled tests is preferable to learning. Small mistakes occur daily and are tolerated because they are invisible. Significant failures in space exploration often result from a chain of small failures and missed learning opportunities. Significant failures often occur when leaders make decisions outside the scientific culture, e.g., politicians and non-scientific leaders. For example, the Space Shuttle Columbia and the Challenger accidents were big mistakes resulting from the devaluation of scientific and engineering knowledge and increased personal reputation and performance valuation. Failure factors in space exploration include higher valuation of delivery timelines, management knowledge, hubris, and confidence. They also include a devaluation of safety, risk levels, scientific competencies and knowledge, small mistakes, cross-organization communication, and the social aspects of scientific knowledge. Systemic failures in human processes also exacerbate technical failures.

Collaboration Cultures of Space Exploration

The fundamental values associated with knowledge across stakeholders are an impediment to learning and collaboration. Private sector stakeholders see the knowledge acquired and enhanced as their private property. They may see sharing with other partners and competitors as a poor business strategy – giving away a comparative advantage. There may be limits to knowledge sharing in the new landscape – which is now competitive with a growing private sector. The early years' broad and open learning and sharing are shifting to reflect the new external landscape. In the new landscape, knowledge sharing, learning, and collaboration has limits. Learning and collaboration continue in the non-, not-for-profit research, and academic organizations. The challenge surfaces as we move out of the research landscape and into the private sector.

There is significant collaboration within organizations, across space centers, and with external stakeholders at the research and development level (e.g., market and clan cultures). Collaboration is less evident, though, at the leadership levels of those organizations (e.g., the bureaucratic culture). Those in bureaucratic cultures engage less in learning and collaboration, presenting a "knowing" rather than a "learning" image. Public service space exploration organizations have been responsible for establishing the knowledge base from which all other stakeholders draw. When the workforce's KLC culture is valued less than the management culture, the entire landscape will feel the effects.

Advancing the KLC Approach in Public Service Space Exploration

In the final analysis, learning and collaboration climates and cultures are human. The human capital, the structural capital, and the relational capital are critical to ensuring that knowledge is created, shared, flows, and is rigorously tested and revised. Learning does not occur among documents – learning occurs among humans. Collaboration is fundamentally human. People and their intellectual capital are essential to a KLC approach. To achieve a KLC approach in space exploration, we must address the scientific belief in aperspectival objectivity. To achieve the synergies of a KLC culture, we must put the human element back into science. It means addressing the beliefs level. We must build a new scientific belief in the human element of knowledge.

Chapter Review

After reading this chapter, you should be able to:

- describe the company cultures of space exploration organization.
- explain how public service cultures affect the company cultures.
- describe the cultures of the external environment of space exploration.
- explain the KLC cultures of space exploration.
- discuss the opportunities and challenges of developing a KLC approach in space exploration organizations.

References and Recommended Future Readings

Andrews, F. M., & Pelz, D. C. (1966). *Scientists in organizations*. University of Michigan, Institute for Social Research.

Argyris, C. (1957). *Personality and organization: The conflict between system and the individual*. Harper.

Biagioli, M. (1995). Tacit knowledge, courtliness and the scientist's body. In S. L. Foster (Ed.), *Choreographing history* (pp. 69–81). Indiana University Press.

Bloor, D. (1984). A sociological theory of objectivity. In S. C. Brown (Ed.), *Objectivity and cultural divergence* (pp. 229–245). Cambridge University Press.

Bloor, G., & Dawson, P. (1994). Understanding professional culture in organizational context. *Organization Studies, 15*(2), 275–295.

Bourdieu, P. (1975). The specificity of the scientific field and the social conditions of reason. *Social Science Information, 14*, 19–47.

Daston, L. (1992). Objectivity and the escape from perspective. *Social Studies of Science, 22*, 597–618.

Daston, L., & Galison, P. (1992). The image of objectivity. *Representations, 40*, 81–128.

Farson, R., & Keyes, R. (2006). The failure-tolerant leader. In Mayle, D. (Ed.), *Managing Innovation and Change* (pp. 249–257). Newbury Park, CA: Sage.

Feldman, S. P. (2004). The culture of objectivity: Quantification, uncertainty, and the evaluation of risk at NASA. *Human Relations, 57*(6), 691–718.

Fleck, L. (2012). *Genesis and development of a scientific fact*. University of Chicago Press.

Foucault, M. (1977). A preface to transgression. M. Foucault & D. F. Bouchard (Eds.), *Language, counter-memory, practice: Selected essays and interviews*, (pp. 29–52). Cornell University Press.

Galison, P. (1987). *How experiments end*. University of Chicago Press.

Gieryn, T. F. (1983). Boundary-work and the demarcation of science from non-science: Strains and interests in professional ideologies of scientists. *American Sociological Review, 48*(6), 781–795.

Knorr-Cetina, K. (1999). *Epistemic cultures: How the sciences make knowledge*. Harvard University Press.

Kramer, R. M. (2003). The harder they fall. *Harvard Business Review*, October (10), 58–66.

Langewiesche, W. (2003). Columbia's last flight. *The Atlantic Monthly, 292*(4), 58–87.

Longino, H. E. (1996). Cognitive and non-cognitive values in science: Rethinking the dichotomy. In L. H. Nelson & J. Nelson (Eds.), *Feminism, science, and the philosophy of science* (pp. 39–58). Dordrecht: Springer.

Longino, H.E. (1990). *Science as social knowledge: Values and objectivity in scientific inquiry*. Princeton University Press.

Mason, R. O. (2004). Lessons in organizational ethics from the Columbia Disaster: Can a culture be lethal? *Organizational Dynamics, 33*(2), 128–142.

McCurdy, H. E. (1989). The decay of NASA's technical culture. *Space Policy, 5*(4), 301e310.

Merton, R. K. (1957). Priorities in scientific discovery: A chapter in the sociology of science. *American Sociological Review, 22*(6), 635–659.

Merton, R. K. (1969). Behavior patterns of scientists. *The American Scholar, 38*(2), 197–225.

Mitroff, I. I., & Pearson, C. M. (1993). *Crisis management: A diagnostic guide for improving your organization's crisis-preparedness*. Jossey-Bass.

Novick, P. (1988). *That noble dream: The 'objectivity question' and the American historical profession* (Vol. 13). Cambridge University Press.

Pelz, D. C. (1967). Creative tensions in the research and development climate: Technical achievement of scientists and engineers was high under conditions that seemed antithetical. *Science, 157*(3785), 160–165.

Pickering, A. (1993). The mangle of practice: Agency and emergence in the sociology of science. *American Journal of Sociology, 99*(3), 559–589.

Pickering, A. (1995). *The mangle of practice: Time, agency and practice*. University of Chicago Press.

Pinch, T. J., & Bijker, W. E. (1984). The social construction of facts and artefacts: Or how the sociology of science and the sociology of technology might benefit each other. *Social Studies of Science, 14*(3), 399–441.

Polanyi, M. (1958). *Personal knowledge*. University of Chicago Press.

Polanyi, M. (1962). Tacit knowing: Its bearing on some problems of philosophy. *Reviews of Modern Physics, 34*(4), 601.

Polanyi, M. (1966). The logic of tacit inference. *Philosophy, 41*(155), 1–18.

Polanyi, M. (1969) *Knowing and being*. University of Chicago Press.

Polanyi, M. (2012). *Personal knowledge*. Routledge.

Pool, R. (1997). *Beyond engineering: How society shapes technology*. Oxford University Press on Demand.

Popper, K. R. (1972). *Objective knowledge* (Vol. 360). Oxford University Press.

Popper, K. R. (1983). *Objective knowledge*. Clarendon Press.

Resnick, S. M. (1985). Pride in Xerox: A study of employee attitude and morale. Technical Report. Xerox Corporation.

Resnick-West, S., & Von Glinow, M. A. (1990). Beyond the clash: Managing high technology professionals managing complexity. In M. A. Von Glinow & S. A. Mohrman (Eds.), *Managing complexity on high technology organizations* (pp. 237–254). Oxford University Press.

Restivo, S. P. (1994). *Science, society, and values: Toward a sociology of objectivity*. Lehigh University Press.

Roberts, K. H., & Libuser, C. (1993). From Bhopal to banking: Organizational design can mitigate risk. *Organizational Dynamics, 21*(4), 15–26.

Roberts, K. H., Rousseau, D. M., & La Porte, T. R. (2019). The culture of high reliability: Quantitative and qualitative assessment aboard nuclear-powered aircraft carriers. In G. Mars & D. Weir (Eds.), Risk Management (pp. 239–259). Routledge.

Straw, B. (1976). *Intrinsic and extrinsic motivation*. General Learning Press.

Turner, S., & Mccreery, G. (2007). Scientific norms/counternorms. In G. Ritzer, J. M. Ryan & B. Thorn (Eds.), *The Blackwell encyclopedia of sociology* (1st Ed.). John Wiley & Sons.

Vaughan, D. (1996). The Challenger launch decision: Risky technology, culture, and deviance at NASA. University of Chicago Press.

Vollmer, H. M., LaPorte, T. R., Pedersen, W. C., & Langton, P. A. (1964). *Adaptations of scientists in five organizations a comparative analysis.* Stanford Research Institute.

Vroom, V. H. (1994). *Work and motivation.* Jossey-Bass.

Weber, G. F. (2013). Dynamic knowledge: A century of evolution. *Sociology Mind, 3*(04), 268.

Weick, K. E., & Sutcliffe, K. M. (2001). *Managing the unexpected* (Vol. 9). Jossey-Bass.

Whitehead, A. N. (1925). *Science and the modern world.* Macmillan.

Chapter 12

The KLC Approach and Public Sector Agriculture

Chapter Summary

This chapter describes public agriculture services' business goals, purpose, and strategy. It reinforces agriculture organizations' fundamental bureaucratic administrative culture (Tier 1). The authors describe the influence that political appointees as leaders may play in shaping public sector cultures. The bureaucratic culture of agriculture is deconstructed, and each of the five layers is described in detail. Additionally, the authors explain why behavior is the dominant layer and the most critical starting point for understanding agriculture cultures. The public service culture (Tier 2) brings an essential element of leveling, access, and equity to the larger context. It brings the focus back to service to the people and community rather than performance. It also gives greater emphasis to the role of safety and well-being. The chapter lays out the landscape of external influencing cultures (Tier 3) in agriculture. Finally, the potential value and challenges of developing internal knowledge, learning, and collaboration (KLC) cultures (Tier 4) are explored.

Why We Care about the Cultures of Public Sector Agricultural Organizations?

We care about the cultures of public sector agriculture because agriculture is fundamental to sustaining life. Agriculture touches every aspect of our lives and impacts society in many ways, including supporting livelihoods through food, habitat, and jobs; providing raw materials for food and other products; and building strong economies through trade (Baker, 1963; Benedict, 1950; Cochrane, 1979; Danbom, 1986; Karami & Keshavarz, 2010; Nelson, 1990; Rasmussen, 1975). It also represents a significant percentage of any state's economy and is central to economic development. Agriculture also impacts global trade. Countries with solid agricultural sectors experience employment growth in other sectors. Agriculture is the second highest source of employment around the world.

The Cultures of Knowledge Organizations: Knowledge, Learning, Collaboration (KLC), 231–244
Copyright © 2023 by Wioleta Kucharska and Denise Bedford
Published under exclusive licence by Emerald Publishing Limited
doi:10.1108/978-1-83909-336-420231012

Agriculture also plays a central role in meeting consumer and business market demand in a world with interconnected economies. Here are different types of products derived from agriculture.

Public Sector Agricultural Organizations – Business Goals, Structures, and Strategies

The scope of public service agriculture is broad. Public service agriculture is essential in mediating and balancing in a world of asymmetric economic development. Agriculture encompasses forests (Mitchell, 1997), fisheries (Donatuto & Harper, 2008), land management, rural and urban poverty, food production, dairy production, nutrition and diet (Ahuja et al., 2013; Bleich, 2021; Dupont & Beecher, 2017; Hopkins & Gunther, 2015; Ralston et al., 2017; Salvador & Bittman, 2020), water systems conservation (Wallander, 2017), plant science (Griesbach & Berberich, 1995; Salter, 1951), crop farming (Arcury et al., 2015; Benedict, 1966; Cochrane & Ryan, 1976; DeWalt, 1985; Gardner, 1996; Inwood et al., 2013; Lichtfouse, 2010; Orden & Zulauf, 2015; Sumner, 2007; Tyler & Moore, 2013; Vanclay et al., 1998; Weltz et al., 2020), animal and livestock husbandry, food quality and safety (Gillen et al., 2002), biofuels, hunting and wildlife conservation (Fagerstone & Keirn, 2012), and agricultural support services, including transportation. Additionally, agriculture provides inputs for many other sectors, including lumber for construction, herbs for food production, corn for biofuels, and plants for adhesives, coatings, and paints.

Realizing a KLC culture is critical to twenty-first-century agriculture. Moreover, twenty-first-century public service agriculture addresses some of the most critical global challenges, such as poverty, nutrition, food security (Kennedy, 1999; Nikolaus et al., 2022; Rhone, 2021; Ziegelman & Coe, 2016), economic stability among others (IAASTD, 2003, 2008).

The business goal of a public sector agricultural organization is to build and sustain modernized farms and fisheries, a diversified rural economy that is dynamic, technologically advanced and internationally competitive. Its transformation is guided by the sound practices of resource sustainability, the principles of social justice, and substantial private-sector participation. Public sector agricultural organizations have a broad scope of operations. Fig. 1 identifies all of the common areas of operations in any public sector agricultural organization. The information for this figure was collected by reviewing national agriculture agencies' visions, missions, and mandates worldwide.

Tier 1 – Company Culture of Agriculture

The business culture of public agriculture services is complex and multifaceted, because the company culture of each area of practice reflects the company culture of its private sector counterparts. Public service agriculture touches every aspect of the agriculture sector – from raw materials, agricultural production, food production and safety, human consumption, policy formulation, laws, education, research and information dissemination.

- Agricultural development and policy
- Agricultural knowledge and information systems
- Agricultural laws
- Agricultural marketing service
- Agricultural policy development
- Agricultural producers' market and risk management support
- Agricultural research service
- Agricultural science
- Agricultural statistics service
- Animal and plant health inspection service
- Animal feed production
- Biofuels
- Business and cooperative programs
- Commercial farming support and promotion
- Community facilities for tribal communities
- Competitive and sustainable agriculture and fisheries support
- Cotton for clothing
- Crop and food sales
- Economic opportunity promotion
- Economic research service
- Environmental justice
- Extreme poverty reduction
- Farm income and work promotion
- Food affordability and security
- Food and agriculture research
- Food and nutrition service
- Food health and nourishment promotion
- Food safety and inspection service
- Foreign agricultural service
- Fruits and vegetable production.
- Industrial products and products derived from biomass
- Natural resources preservation and protection
- Natural rubber production
- Pharmaceutical products derived from plants
- Poverty reduction
- Regional tribal food systems, financing, and technical assistance
- Regulatory, service, and educational activities
- Rural business cooperative services
- Rural communities support
- Rural housing services
- Rural utilities services
- Tribal communities support
- Utilities development.

Fig. 1.   Scope of Operations in Public Sector Agricultural Organizations.

Within the public sector agricultural agencies and departments, the bureaucratic culture may predominate, particularly at the leadership level. However, each area of practice is tightly embedded with its external partners and markets. The agency or department culture will reflect the dominant culture of the external agriculture environment, which may include market, fief and clan cultures. Most external agriculture company cultures will resemble a market culture. A market culture allows for different points of emphasis on values and the open exchange of encoded information throughout the network. It is a promising foundation for promoting the KLC approach.

Bureaucratic company cultures predominate in several areas of agricultural practice, including agricultural laws, agricultural policy development, agricultural statistics service, animal and plant health inspection service, extreme poverty reduction, food safety and inspection service, foreign agricultural service, natural resources preservation and protection, poverty reduction, regional tribal food systems, financing and technical assistance, regulatory, service and educational activities, rural housing services, rural utilities services, tribal communities support, utilities development, and agricultural development and policy,

Market company cultures predominate in several areas, including agricultural marketing service, agricultural producers market and risk management support, animal feed production, biofuels, commercial farming support and promotion, competitive and sustainable agriculture and fisheries support, cotton for clothing, crop and food sales, economic opportunity promotion, food affordability and security, food and nutrition service, food health and nourishment promotion, fruits and vegetables production, industrial products and products derived from biomass, and pharmaceutical products derived from plants, and farm income and work promotion.

Clan company cultures predominate in several areas: business and cooperative programs, agricultural knowledge and information systems, agricultural research service, agricultural science, economic research service, environmental justice, food and agriculture research, rural business cooperative services, and rural community support. Finally, a *fief company culture* may predominate in the community facilities development for tribal communities.

Agriculture has a well-established and extensive body of knowledge. To maintain a healthy agriculture sector – private, public, non-, and not-for-profit sectors – this knowledge must be shared, absorbed, improved, adapted, and extended. Given a traditional- and future-focused agricultural sector, it is also critical that cultures support learning, unlearning, and relearning. As the KLC approach suggests, knowledge revitalization and refresh do not happen without human learning. At base, knowledge is a science culture. Learning through mistakes, unlearning and relearning are established behaviors in agriculture.

The challenge is to find a common layer of culture across multiple company cultures (Fig. 2). It means identifying the pivotal layer of culture that provides a common point of leverage across company cultures and areas of practice.

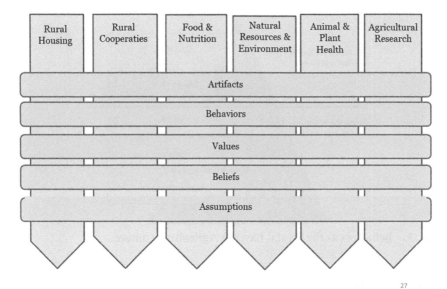

Fig. 2.   Scope of Areas of Operation in Public Service Agriculture.

Analyzing the Company Culture of Public Sector Agriculture

The authors' research suggests a common point of cultural leverage emerges at the behavior level – around the practice (Fig. 3). Behaviors are the pivotal level of culture for public service agriculture. We describe these organizations' mandate and mission with action verbs – promote, support, provide, develop, protect, and so on. The common layer of culture focuses on turning what we know into what we do. Performance is based on results and getting new knowledge and results to stakeholders. The activities common to all these practice areas are knowledge creation, learning, and collaboration. The challenge is understanding the behavioral level sufficiently well to develop a suitable KLC approach. What does behavior look like in bureaucratic, market, and clan cultures? And how do the other layers of culture influence behavior?

Agricultural Behaviors

Agricultural behavior produces, protects, promotes, safeguards, and sustains. Public service agriculture's role differs from private sector agribusiness, farmers, fishermen, forester, food producers, and food distributors. The private sector focuses on production and industrial performance, as defined by producers, businesses, and investors. Private sector behaviors reflect private sector values. In contrast, public sector behaviors focus on regulating business behaviors, setting regulatory policies, defining and distributing information, educating, promoting good practices, protecting consumers, protecting resources, serving special populations, and promoting economic well-being.

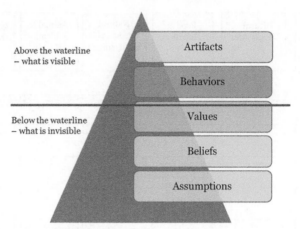

Above the waterline
– what is visible

Below the waterline
– what is invisible

Artifacts

Behaviors

Values

Beliefs

Assumptions

Fig. 3.   Behaviors as the Pivotal Layer in Agriculture Cultures.

Agricultural Values

Behaviors reflect values, and agricultural values reflect the economic and business context. There can be significant discrepancies between private, public, non-, and not-for-profit sector companies. There can also be significant variations across practice areas, for example, different value structures in crop farming, food safety, and nutrition. The conflict of values may cause conflicts at the individual and team levels, mainly because individuals may move from one sector to another over their careers. The leadership values and the influence of political and business actors will determine which values will predominate or how they are integrated.

In summary, public service agriculture values include: focus on the customer or community, quality of performance, transparency, participation, collaboration, accountability, professionalism, and stewardship. Espoused values are aligned with foundational public service values. Further research is needed to determine under what circumstances individual lived values differ from espoused values. Given documented examples in the past 50 years, there is an expectation that espoused and lived values will vary. And the variation will be due to conflicts in values at an individual level.

Agricultural Assumptions and Beliefs

We may see discrepancies between assumptions and beliefs across economic sectors and practice areas. The discrepancies will be visible at an individual level. Individuals come into the field with a basic level of agricultural knowledge. That knowledge, though, is tempered by their experience. Agriculture is about experiential and situational learning. We expect that individuals will move across economic sectors. As a result, there will be a blending of assumptions and beliefs.

Agricultural Artifacts

Agriculture focuses on serving the community rather than the state. The focus is evident in insignia and logos. Insignia, logos, and symbols represent actions and practices rather than core principles. Other artifacts, such as dress, also reflect the nature of behaviors. In some cases, the dress suits operations and the nature of work (e.g., research, marketing and promotion, fieldwork, planting and harvesting, outreach and collaboration). Language also reflects the area of practice, as each area will have a domain-specific vocabulary. The challenge with artifacts is the sheet scope of coverage of the field. As a result, we will find many rather than single styles and forms of artifacts.

Tier 2 – Cultures of Public Sector Agricultural Organizations

We've described a complex company culture. To this complex business culture foundation, we overlay public sector agricultural cultures. The public service culture (Tier 2) brings an essential element of leveling, access, and equity to the agriculture sector. It brings the focus back to service to the people and community rather than performance. It also gives greater emphasis to the role of safety and well-being.

Public service cultures span internal areas of practice and external temper areas of practice. The mission and mandate of a public service agriculture company are broader than that of the military. While public service military cultures are grounded in public service cultures, agricultural cultures appear to be tempered by public sector cultures. Further research is required to understand where the public sector values a unifying force and where they contribute to conflicts with other company goals and cultures.

The authors' research suggests that agricultural public service cultures reinforce four core values (Fig. 4), including ensuring economic health, promoting the general welfare, supporting public health, and supporting an educated public.

Public service cultures are unifying and stabilizing across agricultural areas of practice. They focus the company cultures of internal practices on the community and population. They focus the company cultures of external practices on safety, quality, trust, transparency, and accountability.

Tier 3 – Public Service Culture of Agriculture

The external agricultural environment is almost entirely under private sector ownership. It is comprised of millions of actors working in many areas. It includes everything from farmers to restaurants to food manufacturing, processing, transportation, and storage. In the diplomatic, military and space exploration examples, the external environment was defined as actors outside the public service companies. In agriculture, though, it is often difficult to identify what is internal and external because of the deep integration of public and private companies.

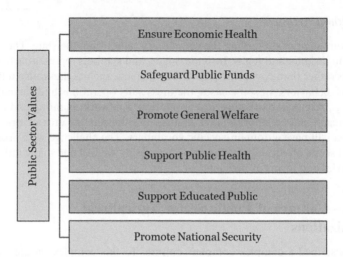

Fig. 4.   Public Service Cultural Areas of Emphasis in Agriculture.

For example, consider the area of practice we defined for Tier 1 (Fig. 5) and how closely it resembles the actors in Tier 3 (Fig. 5).

To discover the dominant company cultures of external actors, we can look to the cultures we described for comparable practice areas. Making these cultures visible is both more accessible and more complex. It is easier in their consistency. But on the other hand, it is more challenging in the scope and scale of the challenge.

Tier 4 – Knowledge Cultures of Agriculture Organizations

Agriculture provides a clear example of where KLC synergies can produce critical new business capabilities and lead to innovative practices. However, these synergies can be challenging to achieve, given the complex internal and external environments.

Knowledge Cultures of Agriculture

The stated goal of public service agriculture is to be a source of knowledge integration, safeguard people, support consumers, and provide oversight of the sector. To achieve this goal, public sector agriculture ensures wide dissemination of tacit knowledge, skills and competencies, explicit encoded knowledge, and procedural knowledge (Rivera-Ferre, 2008; Scoones, 2009). Public service agriculture produces all eight forms of intellectual capital. Of the eight, the most vital for the sector are procedural knowledge (i.e., reflecting the behavioral layer of culture), human capital such as tacit knowledge, skills and competencies, and relational capital (i.e., networks and relationships).

The knowledge challenge for public sector agriculture is the breadth and scope of the mandate. It covers many disciplines, each with its own theoretical

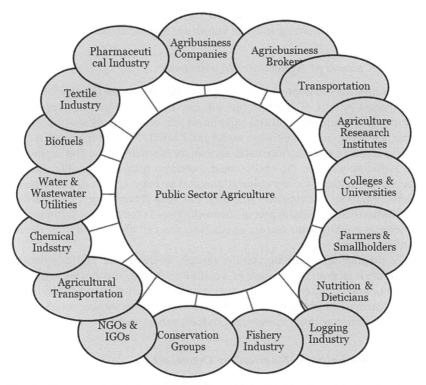

Fig. 5.   External Actors in the Public Service Agriculture Landscape.

and practical knowledge. The disciplines in scope are scientifically grounded. They espouse the same objectivity beliefs as public sector space exploration. It is not, though, science for the sake of science. Instead, science supports health, well-being, prosperity, and employment. Public sector agriculture focuses on the community and the population rather than the state. The knowledge component of agriculture is firmly grounded in agricultural values and beliefs. These values and beliefs are grounded in the values and beliefs of the state. Another important source of agricultural KLC is the emerging homesteading movement. It is a community of non-state actors who are highly networked, continuous learners, and highly knowledgeable producers and consumers.

Agricultural knowledge is a broad and complex landscape. Public service agriculture is the broadest source of knowledge. Agricultural knowledge is highly valued and protected across the landscape. Within the agriculture sector we find many different business and company cultures. Each of these cultures values agricultural knowledge differently. The commodities market has an extreme market structure, and views knowledge as a source of competition. The local homesteading groups follow a clan culture which treats knowledge as a shared asset. Industrial agriculture is either bureaucratic or market-based, which treats knowledge both as a valued asset to leverage and a competitive asset to protect.

The national culture and its grounding in an agricultural society is a mediating force which tends toward agricultural knowledge and exchange.

Learning Cultures of Agriculture Organizations

Agriculture strives to improve practice. The culture is mistake tolerant. Mistakes are expected as part of the scientific process. Learning from mistakes is part of experimentation. Agricultural experiment stations are dedicated to testing, trying new ideas, and seeing what works and doesn't. Mistake tolerance is built into the learning culture. Successful agriculture has many risks and dependencies, including weather, the environment, access to resources, wildlife, and the behavior of markets for agricultural goods. Surviving in this dynamic sector means continuous learning and adapting. Learning is continuous, and learning by mistakes is an essential aspect of the work. The challenge is not learning. The challenge is holding some factors constant so you can understand what factors of influence are.

The predominant learning culture, though, is situational and experiential. Agriculture is an excellent example of a culture where the synergies between KLC occur. The knowledge generated through experimentation, exploration, and experiential learning is most highly valued. Conversely, learning without collaboration and collaboration without knowledge produces suboptimal results.

Collaboration Cultures of Agriculture Organizations

Collaboration is natural in agriculture, from local farmers, local farming communities, extension agents, academic research institutes, and university students working as interns for large food producers. Many farmers collaborate with universities and colleges to ensure the exchange of theoretical and practical knowledge. Collaboration is excluded only in the large agribusiness arena. Agriculture is a highly networked sector where new knowledge comes from colleagues and connections. The KLC approach can thrive in the public service arenas.

Agriculture is among the oldest economic systems. Agricultural is an essential component of the national culture. From its earliest days of small farms, agriculture has been collaborative. Farmers relied on each other to survive. Farmer networks were the main source of knowledge and learning. Today, this collaboration includes agricultural researchers, practitioners, agricultural stations, extension offices, farmers, homesteaders, environmentalists, public health experts, nutritionists, gardening societies, urban and backyard gardeners, and many others. Collaboration is strong within and sometimes across these groups. The main impediment to collaboration, though, surfaces when the economic goals of the groups differ. For profit groups may see collaboration as a form of knowledge leakage or loss, and therefore decline to engage.

Additionally, this trend has implications for knowledge creation and sharing. There is a tendency to patent agricultural knowledge and to hide knowledge from the public view to ensure revenue and future products. It includes knowledge about food, the food itself, and the seeds to prevent others from sharing and using. It is a form of extreme knowledge hoarding. It is knowledge exclusion.

Agricultural knowledge is predisposed to grow and flow. Private sector agriculture is critical to production. It can threaten public service values, knowledge creation, and sharing.

Another dimension of agriculture collaboration is a collaboration between knowledge-rich and knowledge-poor stakeholders. Due to agriculture's predominant private sector culture, some knowledge- and resource-poor stakeholders have been marginalized from collaboration. Marginalized stakeholders tend to represent traditional rather than industrialized agriculture knowledge and practices. Meeting the global challenge of feeding billions of people sustainably requires full use and sharing of all types of knowledge among all stakeholders.

Collaboration should also be expanded to include stakeholders from hard and soft sciences. Social science can mitigate the adverse effects of industrialized agriculture (Barnes, 1971; Bonano, 1991; Bonano et al., 1994; Buttel & Larson, 1979; Coughenour, 1984; Dunlap & Martin, 1983; Friedland, 1978; Friedmann & McMichael, 1989; Goodman, 1999; McMichael, 1994; Molnar & Kinnucan, 1989; Pimentel et al., 1973). The collaboration will expand my understanding of the impact of agriculture on society.

Advancing the KLC Approach in Public Service Agriculture

Public service agriculture is closely aligned with and deeply embedded in private sector vertical markets. Public sector agriculture both influences and is influenced by external stakeholders. We can assume there will be robust knowledge cultures in all company cultures. The challenge arises in learning and collaboration. It is vital that knowledge sharing and deep learning take place across and among stakeholders. Like military cultures, the impediment is in the values layer of a culture where there is a fundamental difference. The difference is between a substantial profit value and a strong state and community service value. There is a good reason for both value systems to exist. The opportunity is to bring those two value systems into closer alignment. When they are aligned, cross-stakeholder learning and collaboration are part of how we work. Where there is a commonly espoused value system, individuals moving across the verticals over their career may become KLC pollinators. The KLC approach provides a critical method for achieving a closer alignment. It is vital since many of the world's most significant challenges pertain to agriculture.

Chapter Review

After reading this chapter, you should be able to:

- explain how culture can vary at the business level within a single agency.
- explain what might happen when there are variant business cultures.
- describe how public sector cultures can be a unifying force across business cultures.
- consider how the cultures of external stakes can influence a public sector culture.
- Explain how public sector values may be a good anchor point for KLC cultures of the future.

References and Recommended Future Readings

Ahuja, J. K., Moshfegh, A. J., Holden, J. M., & Harris, E. (2013). USDA food and nutrient databases provide the infrastructure for food and nutrition research, policy, and practice. *The Journal of Nutrition, 143*(2), 241S–249S.

Arcury, T. A., Kearney, G. D., Rodriguez, G., Arcury, J. T., & Quandt, S. A. (2015). Work safety culture of youth farmworkers in North Carolina: A pilot study. *American Journal of Public Health, 105*(2), 344–350.

Baker, G. L. (1963). Century of service: The first 100 years of the United States Department of Agriculture. Centennial Committee, US Department of Agriculture.

Barnes, P. (1971). Vanishing small farmer. *New Repub, 164*, 21–24.

Benedict, M. R. (1950). The Trend in American Agricultural Policy 1920-1949. *Zeitschrift für die gesamte Staatswissenschaft/Journal of Institutional and Theoretical Economics,* (H. 1), 97–122.

Benedict, M. R. (1966). Farm policies of the United States, 1790–1950: A study of their origins and development, 546 pp.

Bleich, S. (2021, October). USDA efforts to promote food and nutrition security. In *APHA 2021 Annual Meeting and Expo*. APHA.

Bonanno, A. (1991). The restructuring of the agricultural and food system: Social and economic equity in the reshaping of the agrarian question and the food question. *Agriculture and Human Values, 8*, 72–82.

Buttel, F. H., & Larson, O. W. (1979). Farm size, structure, and energy intensity: An ecological analysis of US agriculture. *Rural Sociology, 44*(3), 471.

Cochrane, W. W. (1979). *The development of American agriculture: A historical analysis.* U of Minnesota Press.

Cochrane, W. W., & Ryan, M. E. (1976). *American Farm Policy: 1948–1973.* U of Minnesota Press.

Cooper, M. D. (2000). Towards a model of safety culture. *Safety Science, 36*(2), 111–136.

Coughenour, C. M. (1984). Social ecology and agriculture. *Rural Sociology, 49*(1), 1.

Danbom, D. B. (1986). The agricultural experiment station and professionalization: Scientists' goals for agriculture. *Agricultural History, 60*(2), 246–255.

DeWalt, B. R. (1985). Anthropology, sociology, and farming systems research. *Human Organization, 44*(2), 106–114.

Donatuto, J., & Harper, B. L. (2008). Issues in evaluating fish consumption rates for Native American tribes. *Risk Analysis: An International Journal, 28*(6), 1497–1506.

Dunlap, R. E., & Martin, K. E. (1983). Bringing environment into the study of agriculture: Observations and suggestions regarding the sociology of agriculture. *Rural Sociology, 48*(2), 201–218.

Dupont, J. L., & Beecher, G. R. (2017). History of Human Nutrition Research in the U. S. Department of Agriculture. Agricultural Research Service. Government Printing Office. Retrieved December 1, 2022, from HistoryofHumanNutritionResearch.pdf (usda.gov).

Fagerstone, K. A., & Keirn, G. (2012). Wildlife Services – A leader in developing tools and techniques for managing carnivores. USDA National Wildlife Research Center – Staff Publications.

Friedland, W. H. (1978). *Manufacturing green gold: the conditions and social consequences of lettuce harvest mechanization: a social impact analysis.* Department of Applied Behavioral Sciences, California Agricultural Policy Seminar, College of Agriculture and Environmental Studies, University of California.

Gardner, B. L. (1996). The federal government in farm commodity markets: Recent reform efforts in a long-term context. *Agricultural History, 70*(2), 177–195.

Gillen, M., Baltz, D., Gassel, M., Kirsch, L., & Vaccaro, D. (2002). Perceived safety climate, job demands, and coworker support among union and nonunion injured construction workers. *Journal of Safety Research, 33*(1), 33–51.

Goodman, D. (1999). Agro-food studies in the 'age of ecology': Nature, corporeality, bio-politics. *Sociologia Ruralis, 39*(1), 17–38.

Griesbach, R. J., & Berberich, S. M. (1995). The early history of research on ornamental plants at the US Department of Agriculture from 1862 to 1940. *HortScience, 30*(3), 421–425.

Hopkins, L. C., & Gunther, C. (2015). A historical review of changes in nutrition standards of USDA child meal programs relative to research findings on the nutritional adequacy of program meals and the diet and nutritional health of participants: Implications for future research and the Summer Food Service Program. *Nutrients, 7*(12), 10145–10167.

Inwood, S., Clark, J. K., & Bean, M. (2013). The differing values of multigeneration and first-generation farmers: Their influence on the structure of agriculture at the rural-urban interface. *Rural Sociology, 78*(3), 346–370.

Karami, E., & Keshavarz, M. (2010). Sociology of sustainable agriculture. In E. Lichtfouse (Eds.), *Sociology, organic farming, climate change and soil science* (pp. 19–40). Dordrecht: Springer.

Kennedy, D. M. (1999). *Freedom from fear: The American people in depression and war, 1929–1945.* Oxford University Press.

Lichtfouse, E. (2010). *Sociology, organic farming, climate change and soil science* (Vol. 3, p. 478). Springer.

Miller, D. (2017). Methods for Evaluating Environmental Justice: Approaches to implementing US Executive Order 12898. In D. Patassini & D. Miller (Eds.), *Beyond benefit cost analysis: Accounting for non-market values in planning evaluation.* (pp. 25–44). Routledge.

Mitchell, J. (1997). Forest Service national resource guide to American Indian and Alaska Native relations. *USDA Forest Service, Washington DC, 136.*

Molnar, J. J. (2019). *Biotechnology and the new agricultural revolution.* Boca Raton, FL: CRC Press.

Nelson, J. (1990). Culture and agriculture: The ultimate simulacrum. *Border/Lines,* (18).

Nikolaus, C. J., Johnson, S., Benally, T., Maudrie, T., Henderson, A., Nelson, K., Lane, T., Segrest, V., Ferguson, G.L., Buchwald, D., Jernigan, V. B., & Sinclair, K. (2022). Food insecurity among American Indian and Alaska Native People: A scoping review to inform future research and policy needs. *Advances in Nutrition, 13*(5), 1566–1583.

Orden, D., & Zulauf, C. (2015). Political economy of the 2014 farm bill. *American Journal of Agricultural Economics, 97*(5), 1298–1311.

Pimentel, D., Hurd, L. E., Bellotti, A. C., Forster, M. J., Oka, I. N., Sholes, O. D., & Whitman, R. J. (1973). Food production and the energy crisis. *Science, 182*(4111), 443–449.

Ralston, K., Treen, K., Coleman-Jensen, A., & Guthrie, J. (2017). *Children's food security and USDA child nutrition programs* (No. 1476-2017-2076).

Rasmussen, W. D. (1975). *Agriculture in the United States: A documentary history* (No. 630.973 RAS. CIMMYT).

Rhone, A. (2021). Updated food access research atlas now maps changes in low-income and low-supermarket access areas in 2019. *Amber Waves: The Economics of Food, Farming, Natural Resources, and Rural America* (1490-2021-1194).

Rivera-Ferre, M. G. (2008). The future of agriculture: Agricultural knowledge for economically, socially and environmentally sustainable development. *EMBO Reports, 9*(11), 1061–1066.

Salter, R. M. (1951). Report of the Chief of the Bureau of Plant Industry, Soils and Agricultural Engineering. *Report of the Chief of the Bureau of Plant Industry, Soils and Agricultural Engineering.*

Salvador, R., & Bittman, M. (2020). Opinion: Goodbye, USDA, Hello, Department of Food and Well-Being. *The New York Times.*

Scoones, I. (2009). The politics of global assessments: The case of the International Assessment of Agricultural Knowledge, Science and Technology for Development (IAASTD). *The Journal of Peasant Studies, 36*(3), 547–571.

Sumner, D. A. (2007). Farm subsidy tradition and modern agricultural realities. *AEI Project on Agricultural Policy for the 2007 Farm Bill and Beyond.*

Tyler, S. S., & Moore, E. A. (2013). Plight of black farmers in the context of USDA farm loan programs: A research agenda for the future. *Professional Agricultural Workers Journal, 1*(1), 6.

Vanclay, F. (2004). Social principles for agricultural extension to assist in the promotion of natural resource management. *Australian Journal of Experimental Agriculture, 44*(3), 213–222.

Vanclay, F., Mesiti, L., & Howden, P. (1998). Styles of farming and farming subcultures: Appropriate concepts for Australian rural sociology? *Rural Society, 8*(2), 85–107.

Wallander, S. (2017). USDA water conservation efforts reflect regional differences. *Choices, 32*(4), 1–7.

Weltz, M. A., Huang, C. H., Newingham, B. A., Tatarko, J., Nouwakpo, S. K., & Tsegaye, T. (2020). A strategic plan for future USDA Agricultural Research Service erosion research and model development. *Journal of Soil and Water Conservation, 75*(6), 137A–143A.

World Bank Independent Evaluation Group. (2003). *International assessment of agricultural science and technology for development.* Washington, DC, USA.

World Bank Independent Evaluation Group. (2008). *International assessment of agricultural science and technology for development.* Washington, DC, USA.

Ziegelman, J., & Coe, A. (2016). *A square meal: A culinary history of the great depression.* HarperCollins Publishers.

Appendix A: Pulling It All Together

Chapter Summary

This appendix contains a template for a project plan to guide an organization by thinking about intelligent ways of thinking and working. The appendix explains how the plan is organized. Suggestions for how to use the project plan are also provided.

Explaining the Project Plan

This chapter is comprised of a project plan. A project plan is a simple aid for managing a complex set of tasks. Project plans are intended to help the reader plan and track progress toward establishing an organization-wide intelligence capability.

Following the project plan can help you identify stakeholders, raise awareness of crucial topics, communicate the importance of organizational culture, and define your organization's business, knowledge, learning, and collaboration cultures, as well as its current and potential cultural capacity. The project plan presented in this appendix is a synopsis of the issues and topics that have been discussed throughout the book. An organization might begin its journey by using the project plan as a roadmap. Each task in the project plan refers back to an individual chapter – as a reference for further study and consideration. The project plan is designed to be used over time and as needed to ensure an organization continues to move its strategy forward and ensure it continues to be relevant to and supportive of business goals. The project plan is designed to be adapted to your organization and adapted to include what you learn as you move forward.

The project plan is ordered logically into eight tasks. Each task is broken down into subtasks or steps that align with the individual chapters' topics.

- Tasks 1–3 are intended to help you raise awareness of culture, organizational cultures, and the effect of cultures on strategy and business performance.
- Task 4 is designed to help you determine your organization's core business structure and culture.
- Task 5 can help you determine your organization's knowledge culture.
- Task 6 focuses on determining your organization's learning culture.
- Task 7 is designed to help you discover your organization's collaboration culture.
- Task 8 is designed to assess your organization's cultural capacity.

	Start	Finish	Predecessors	Assigned To	% Complete	Status	Comments
Activity 1. Raise Awareness of Culture							
Task 1. Raise awareness of the nature and elements of culture							
Task 2. Message how to see our cultures							
Task 3. Prepare a short presentation on the five essential elements of culture							
Task 4. Explain to managers why and how an organization's culture is unique							
Task 5. Explain to managers the factors that influence any culture							
Task 6. Learn why it is hard to change an organization's culture							
Activity 2. Raise awareness of organizational culture							
Task 7. Define culture at an organizational level							
Task 8. Explain to managers the critical role culture plays in any organization							
Task 9. Identify the factors that influence each level of an organization's culture							
Task 10. Explain to managers how global, national, team, and individual cultures influence organizational culture							

(*Continued*)

Task 11. Explain to managers how these factors affect organizational capabilities

Activity 3. **Raise awareness of the role of culture in the knowledge economy**

Task 12. Explain to managers how the knowledge economy will affect corporate cultures in the future

Task 13. **Raise managers' awareness of culture as a key intangible asset**

Task 14. **Raise managers ability to see invisible de facto organizational cultures**

Task 15. **Raise managers awareness of the four types of business cultures, bureaucracy, market, clan, and fief**

Task 16. Explain to managers why it is important to align culture and strategy

Task 17. Explain to managers why culture beats strategy in any conflict

Activity 4. **Define your organization's business cultures and strategies**

Task 18. Identify your organization's business goals, purpose, and strategies

Task 19. Identify your organization's baseline business structure and culture

	Start	Finish	Predecessors	Assigned To	% Complete	Status	Comments
Task 20. Define your organizations espoused and actual/lived values							
Task 21. Define your organizations espoused and actual/lived beliefs and assumptions							
Task 22. Determine how organizational behaviors reflect espoused and actual/lived values							
Task 23. Identify the external cultures that affect your culture							
Activity 5. Define your organization's internal knowledge culture							
Task 24. Define your internal knowledge cultures							
Task 25. Determine how your knowledge cultures work							
Task 26. Determine how your knowledge culture shapes knowledge processes							
Task 27. Determine if and how your knowledge cultures create intellectual capital							
Task 28. Determine if the knowledge paradox is present in your organization							

(Continued)

Task 29. Determine how knowledge paradoxes and cultural collisions may interact in your organization

Activity 6. Define your organization's internal learning culture

Task 30. Determine your organization's learning culture

Task 31. Assess the relationship between knowledge and learning

Task 32. Determine if and how learning contributes to creating knowledge and business value

Task 33. Assess the relationship between knowledge cultures and learning cultures

Task 34. Determine how mistakes are recognized, rewarded, or punished

Task 35. Assess whether mistakes are hidden and if so the impact on learning

Task 36. Determine if the Double Bias is at play in your organization

Task 37. Determine if mistakes are seen as learning opportunities

	Start	Finish	Predecessors	Assigned To	% Complete	Status	Comments
Task 38. Determine what is needed to reconcile mistake acceptance and avoidance							
Task 39. Identify improvements to the learning culture							
Activity 7. Define your organizations collaboration culture							
Task 40. Determine your organization's culture of collaboration							
Task 41. Determine whether collaborative cultures are generating networked intelligence							
Task 42. Determine the relationship of collaborative cultures to trust, risk, and critical thinking							
Task 43. Determine whether collaborative cultures contribute to dynamic business capabilities							
Task 44. Determine whether collaborative cultures contribute to resilience and adaptability							
Task 45. Determine whether collaborative cultures sustain business performance							

Activity 8. Define your organization's cultural capacity

Task 46. Determine how company communications can expose and shape the company culture

Task 47. Determine how company structures affect communications at every level

Task 48. Assess the potential effect of the company's maturity and age to its ability to adapt

Task 49. Assess the potential role of transformational leaders in building cultural capacity

Task 50. Assess the potential role of knowledge workers in building the cultural capacity

Task 51. Communicate that every individual's cultural experience helps to share company culture

Task 52. Conduct a step by step assessment of your organization's cultural capacity

How to Use the Project Plan

Chapter by chapter, the book has walked the reader through the key issues and activities. Because organizations will use the book at different stages of preparing for and translating traditional human resources to future people management functions, the reader may want to consider using the project plan to assess where you stand.

A project plan is a blank form that can be expanded to suit your business needs. The project plan is a reminder that your strategy must be your own, and it must align with and be relevant to your business environment. Organizations can use the project plan to do the following:

- Assess and assign responsibility for determining the current state of the organization intelligence work.
- Identify and involve all stakeholders, both current and future, in the practicalities of intelligence work.
- Define the actions and activities that need to be completed to support your strategy. The topics covered in the individual chapters should provide practical guidance on what you need to know to develop a strategy that suits your business goals.
- Align each task in the project plan with the guiding questions presented in the supporting chapter. Walk through the questions and use the answers to help move you to the next task.
- Finally, formulate an intelligence capacity building and capital management strategy for the near and long term.

Appendix B: The Empirical Evidence of KLC Approach

The essential message of this book is that knowledge, learning, and collaboration (KLC) driven company cultures are vital company assets for generating sustainability. Organizational sustainability is a long-run perspective enabling the organization to continuously generate shared value, to survive and thrive in a knowledge economy. From this perspective, a knowledge-driven organization is a network of minds. Organizational sustainability is in effect a sustainable collaborating network of brilliant minds. In the earlier chapters, we've referenced relevant theories and case studies to support our ideas. In this appendix, though, we present empirical evidence that justifies the point that KLC-driven company cultures foster knowledge flows within an organization. As a result, the intellectual capital that is generated increases the organization's ability to change internally *(by internal innovativeness of processes; Fig. 1)*. The ability to change internally is presented in the model as a proxy of the organization's ability to change routines at greater rates *(dynamic capabilities)* and to reflect the entire organization's adaptability competency.

Below, we present the grounding theoretical model (Fig. 2). Next, we explain how we validated the model using two independent, national samples: Poland and the United States. Sample descriptions are provided for both countries to demonstrate the characteristics of respondents involved in the research (knowledge workers employed by knowledge-driven companies). Furthermore, we describe the measurement methods and data quality procedures to demonstrate scientific rigor. Finally, we concisely summarize the results and conclusions to demonstrate the core concept described throughout this text.

Samples

Given all the individual, social, and national cultural aspects of developing and sharing knowledge in organizations as presented in this book, therefore, the presented empirical research performs based on cross-country comparison: the United States and Poland. The United States is a highly developed, mature economy, while Poland is fast-growing and still developing. Mercier-Laurent (2011), in the context of innovativeness, noted that such national characteristics as institutional development, infrastructure, macroeconomic conditions, healthcare, and education levels have enhanced intellectual capital development. In addition, she characterized Poland as having high but not fully exploited innovative potential. Since this study focuses on tacit knowledge creation and sharing as a root of innovativeness, comparing Poland with not fully exploited innovativeness potential

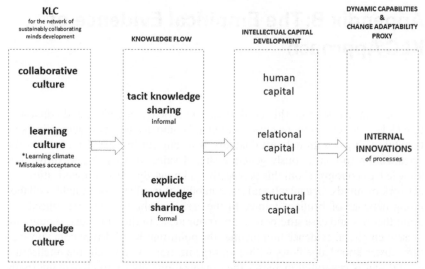

Fig. 1.   Empirical Evidence Framework – Book's Theoretical Grounding.

with the innovativeness leader is simply exciting and can bring some vital lessons. Furthermore, Vos and Boonstra (2022) noted that cultural context matters for entire enterprise systems, including tacit knowledge issues. Similarly, Andreeva et al. (2021) found that a country's environment determines its intellectual capital and innovation performance. The sample sizes and structures are given in Table 1. The sampling quota was designed according to the statistics concerning the labor market in Poland (Statistics Poland, 2017). Kucharska and Kowalczyk (2019) proved that the perception of certain organizational aspects strongly depends on the respondent's position.

With this in mind, the sampling quota was designed equally for each industry to avoid the impact of respondents' positions on particular industry findings. Moreover, all samples are characterized by gender balance for the same reasons. The sampling process focused on recruiting knowledge workers staff from the information technology (IT), construction, higher education, and healthcare industries in Poland and, from the IT, construction, and healthcare industries in the United States. Sampling administration was provided online and executed by professional partners, Qualtrics (the US) and ASM (Poland). Survey execution took two months (January to February 2020). The questionnaire started with a short introduction that provided an overview of the study, including a definition of the key terms, such as tacit knowledge. Next, a qualification question was asked to establish the respondents' minimum work experience and status as a "knowledge worker" in a knowledge-driven company. Respondents were also prompted with a short explanation of the meaning of "tacit knowledge" to ensure

Table 1. Samples Structure.

Characteristic	Total Poland/US (*n* = 1,418/1,118)	INDUSTRY			
		Construction (*n* = 350/373)	Healthcare (*n* = 350/366)	IT (*n* = 350/379)	HE (*n* = 368)
C-suite	3%	3%	3%	3%	3%
Top managers	7%	7%	7%	7%	7%
Middle managers	23%	23%	23%	23%	23%
Professionals	67%	67%	67%	67%	67%
Company size					
Micro (<10 employees)	2%/4%	3%/10%	1%/1%	3%/0%	0%
Small (10–50 employees)	57%/12%	93%/26%	57%/8%	77%/0%	0%
Medium (51–250 employees)	12%/31%	3%/30%	33%/40%	11%/24%	0%
Large (>250 employees)	29%/53%	1%/34%	9%/52%	9%/66%	100%
Sector					
Public	28%/	5%/	69%/0%	10%/	79%
Private	72%/100%	95%/100%	31%/100%	90%/100%	21%
Age					
18–24	0%/3%	0%/10%	0%/0%	1%/0%	0%
25–34	21%/37%	14%/45%	9%/38%	19%/27%	35%
35–44	32%/46%	38%/45%	26%/43%	49%/50%	23%
45–54	23%/10%	27%/0%	32%/16%	21%/16%	17%
55–64	17%/3%	15%/0%	30%/2%	9%/6%	15%
65 and over	7%/1%	6%/0%	4%/1%	2%/1%	10%

(Continued)

Table 1.   (*Continued*)

| Characteristic | Total Poland/US (*n* = 1,418/1,118) | INDUSTRY | | | | |
		Construction (*n* = 350/373)	Healthcare (*n* = 350/366)	IT (*n* = 350/379)	HE (*n* = 368)
Gender					
Female	50%	50%	50%	50%	50%
Male	50%	50%	50%	50%	50%
Other	0%/0,5%				

Note: Poland/US. The Polish sample includes one more sector than the US (Higher Education). Since the study aims to verify the assumed structure of relations using two independent samples, this sector has not been excluded. If the aim would be the cross-country comparison, then the additional sector should definitely be excluded.

they understood what they were asked. The survey's core, excluding classification items, used a seven-point Likert scale to assess the intensity of statements. Data management was straightforward, missing data were replaced with the median value. Finally, only questionnaires with SD > 0.4 were included.

Data Quality Assessment Methods

The sample quality assessment started with invariance, then the Kaiser-Meyer-Olkin (KMO) measure of sampling adequacy and Harman single-factor tests. The samples came from two countries; thus, the invariance tests of adequacy were run first to verify if the measurement instrument operated properly across different populations. Thus, it verified if the questionnaire composed of the scales presented in Table 2 measured the constructs correctly in both samples through first Cross-Loadings Matrix performing (Table 3) and next, an invariance analysis (Table 4). To measure invariance, the multi-group confirmatory factor analysis

Table 2. Scales and Their Sources.

Construct	Items
Tacit knowledge sharing Kucharska and Erickson (2023)	• I share knowledge learned from my own experience. • I have the opportunity to learn from the experiences of others. • Colleagues share new ideas with me. • Colleagues include me in discussions about the best practices.
Internal innovations Kucharska and Erickson (2023)	• We constantly improve the way we work. • We are good at managing change. • We are highly disposed to introduce new methods and procedures. • We are highly disposed to accept new rules.
IC: human capital Kianto et al. (2017)	• Our employees are highly skilled at their jobs. • Our employees are highly motivated in their jobs. • Our employees have a high level of expertise.
IC: structural capital Kianto et al. (2017)	• Our company has efficient and relevant information systems to support business operations. • Our company has tools and facilities to support cooperation between employees. • Our company has a great deal of useful knowledge in documents and databases. • Existing documents and solutions are easily accessible.

(Continued)

Table 2. (*Continued*)

Construct	Items
IC: relational capital (internal) Buenechea-Elberdin et al. (2018)	• Different units and functions within our company (e.g., research and development, marketing, production) understand each other well. • Our employees frequently collaborate to solve problems. • Internal cooperation in our company runs smoothly.
LC: climate Kucharska and Bedford (2020)	• All staff demonstrates a high learning disposition. • We are encouraged to engage in personal development. • We are encouraged to implement new ideas every day. • We are encouraged to engage in seeking new solutions.
LC: mistakes acceptance Kucharska and Bedford (2020)	• People know that mistakes are a learning consequence and tolerate it up to a certain limit. • Most people freely declare mistakes. • We discuss problems openly without blaming others. • Mistakes are tolerated and treated as learning opportunities.
Knowledge culture Kucharska and Bedford (2020)	• All employees perceive knowledge as valuable. • We have a common language to support knowledge exchange. • We are encouraged to share knowledge, ideas, and thoughts. • We care about the quality of knowledge that we share.
Knowledge processes (formalized) (Kucharska, 2021)	• Identification of knowledge sources • Knowledge capturing • Knowledge storage • Knowledge distribution • Knowledge security
Collaborative culture Kucharska and Bedford (2020)	• My company supports cooperation between workers. • Cooperation among the different duties, teams, and departments was encouraged. • Co-workers volunteer their support even without being asked. • People support each other.

Table 3a.　Cross-Loadings Matrix – Poland.

					Factor					
	1	**2**	**3**	**4**	**5**	**6**	**7**	**8**	**9**	**10**
TKS1				−0.151				0.120	**0.919**	
TKS2						−0.128	0.134		**0.556**	
TKS3									**0.911**	
TKS4									**0.891**	
KC1		**0.884**								
KC2		**0.946**								
KC3		**0.941**								
KC4		**0.842**								
CC1						**0.927**		0.132		−0.102
CC2						**0.893**		0.104		
CC3	0.106			0.444		**0.447**		−0.186		0.102
CC4				0.104		**0.671**		−0.129		
LCc1	**0.883**									
LCc2	**0.933**									
LCc3	**0.916**							−0.146		
LCc4	**0.827**		0.105							
LCm1			0.104	**0.657**				0.193		
LCm2				**0.911**						
LCm3				**0.905**						
LCm4				**0.803**						
EKS1	0.232		**0.790**	−0.101				−0.156		
EKS 2			**0.871**							
EKS 3			**0.857**					0.144		
EKS 4			**0.834**							
HC1				0.109				**0.809**		
HC2	0.148							**0.772**		
HC3	0.126							**0.666**		
SC1							0.862			
SC2							0.866			
SC3							0.842			
ReCi1	**0.668**							0.310		

(*Continued*)

Table 3a.   (*Continued*)

	Factor									
	1	**2**	**3**	**4**	**5**	**6**	**7**	**8**	**9**	**10**
ReCi2	**0.636**							0.336		
ReCi3	**0.658**							0.262		
PI1					**0.812**					
PI2					**0.800**					
PI3		0.100			**0.879**	−0.139				
PI4					**0.674**					

Notes: Loadings extraction method: maximum reliability. Rotation method: Promax with Kaiser normalization. Rotation converged in 7 iterations.

(CFA) was applied (Byrne, 2016). Since both analyzed samples size $n > 1,000$, the liberal alternative of models' global fit indices was applied – comparative fit index [CFI] and root mean square error of approximation [RMSEA] (Chen, 2007). The measured change (Δ) in model fits was about 0.01 or less for CFI, and 0.015 or less for RMSEA; thus, the measurement model was nationally invariant (Byrne, 2016; Chen, 2007; Raudenska, 2020). So, Table 2 presents measurement scales, and their sources; Table 4 presents the details of the invariance measurement, which indicate that the applied scales in the questionnaire created a nationally invariant tool.

Summarizing this stage, for all obtained KMO tests of the sample's adequacy, results were 0.929 for Poland and 0.969 for the United States, which confirmed that the samples were adequate (Hair et al., 2010). The total variance explained is for the US = 72% and for Poland = 75%. In addition, we ran one Harman single-factor test (Podsakoff et al., 2012) and both samples achieved an acceptable result, with 33% for Poland and 39% for the United States, which confirmed that the sample quality was good and enabled further analysis.

Table 3b.   Cross-Loadings Matrix, the US.

MCFA Models	**CFI**	**IFI**	**TLI**	**GFI**	**AGFI**	**RMSEA**
Unconstrained model	0.950	0.950	0.942	0.911	0.891	0.050
Loading measurement equality, measurement model (Δ)	0.946 (0.004)	0.947 (0.003)	0.940 (0.002)	0.907 (0.004)	0.889 (0.002)	0.049 (0.001)
Factor covariances equality, structural model (Δ)	0.929 (0.017)	0.932 (0.015)	0.924 (0.016)	0.888 (0.019)	0.872 (0.017)	0.051 (0.002)

Notes: Loadings extraction method: maximum reliability. Rotation method: Promax with Kaiser normalization. Rotation converged in 8 iterations.

Table 4. Invariance Measurement.

	Factor									
	1	2	3	4	5	6	7	8	9	10
TKS1					**0.823**					0.164
TKS2					**0.832**					
TKS3	0.105				**0.793**			0.109		
TKS4					**0.719**		0.117		−0.109	−0.116
KC1	0.134	−0.106					**0.654**			0.347
KC2	0.139						**0.664**			0.106
KC3				0.160			**0.732**			
KC4				0.109			**0.774**			
CC1	0.104			**0.736**			0.119			0.400
CC2		0.295		**0.824**						0.114
CC3				**0.533**			0.132	0.119		
CC4	−0.132			**0.817**						
LCc1	0.167	−0.163						**0.636**		0.545
LCc2				0.233				**0.779**		0.212
LCc3			0.135	−0.153				**0.840**		0.113
LCc4	−0.188		−0.101			0.121	0.122	**0.704**		
LCm1		**0.617**		0.205						0.403
LCm2	0.105	**0.872**								0.101
LCm3	0.121	**0.741**								
LCm4		**0.742**								
EKS1		0.121	**0.757**							0.247

(Continued)

Table 4.   (*Continued*)

	Factor									
	1	2	3	4	5	6	7	8	9	10
EKS 2			**0.846**							
EKS 3			**0.831**						0.109	
EKS 4			**0.861**				0.117			−0.112
HC1	**0.859**			−0.148						0.144
HC2	**0.759**							0.102		
HC3	**0.813**	0.224		−0.184						0.109
SC1	−0.116					−0.127	0.187		**0.977**	0.109
SC2	0.119							0.103	**0.811**	
SC3	0.168								**0.576**	−0.104
ReCi1	**0.646**			0.194		0.103	−0.128			
ReCi2	**0.640**			0.332						−0.103
ReCi3	**0.573**			0.416			−0.130			−0.106
PI1	0.178					**0.620**				0.192
PI2	0.324					**0.581**				
PI3						**0.859**				
PI4						**0.902**				

Notes: Poland, $n = 1.418$; US $n = 1.118$.

IFI, CFI, GFI, and AGFI referenced values greater than 0.90 are consider as good, greater than 0.95 as excellent; RMSEA is considered correct in the range of 0.05 to 0.08 (Hair et al., 2010; Hooper et al., 2008; Kline, 2005). GFI and AGFI depend on sample size and degrees of freedom. Therefore, given the often-detrimental effect of sample size on these indexes, they are not relied upon as a stand-alone index, so they should be always considered in a particular statistical context (Hooper et al., 2008). Furthermore, the RMSEA index is generally preferable for power analysis and model evaluation than GFI and AGFI values (MacCallum & Hong, 1997).

Table 5a.   Basic Statistics, Obtained AVE Root Square, and Correlations Between Models, Poland.

	Mn	SD	AVE	CR	KC	CC	LCc	LCm	TKS	HC	KP	RC	SC	PI
KC	6.2	0.9	**0.56**	**0.79**	**0.748**									
CC	5.8	1.2	**0.69**	**0.90**	0.523	**0.834**								
LCc	5.5	1.2	**0.68**	**0.89**	0.625	0.636	**0.824**							
LCm	5.2	1.4	**0.53**	**0.82**	0.548	0.599	0.596	**0.730**						
TKS	5.8	1.1	**0.50**	**0.74**	0.458	0.48	0.636	0.6	**0.705**					
HC	5.3	1.2	**0.75**	**0.90**	0.268	0.281	0.373	0.352	0.586	**0.868**				
KP	5.1	1.6	**0.80**	**0.94**	0.305	0.197	0.269	0.193	0.343	0.201	**0.892**			
RC	5.8	1.1	**0.82**	**0.93**	0.27	0.285	0.378	0.358	0.596	0.767	0.191	**0.904**		
SC	5.6	1.2	**0.61**	**0.83**	0.185	0.147	0.198	0.164	0.282	0.272	0.427	0.327	**0.784**	
PI	5.4	1.2	**0.58**	**0.93**	0.144	0.132	0.176	0.157	0.265	0.354	0.229	0.339	0.489	**0.761**

Notes. Poland, *n* = 1.418; US *n* = 1.118; KC = knowledge culture; TKS = tacit knowledge sharing; CC = collaborative culture; LCc = learning culture (atmosphere/climate); LCm = learning culture (mistakes acceptance); EKS = explicit knowledge sharing processes; PI = process innovation; HC = human capital; SC = structural capital; RC = relational capital (internal).

Table 5b.   Basic Statistics, Obtained AVE Root Square, and Correlations Between Models, The US.

	Mn	SD	AVE	CR	KC	CC	LCc	LCm	TKS	HC	KP	RC	SC	PI
KC	6.1	1.0	**0.67**	**0.86**	**0.817**									
CC	6.0	1.1	**0.59**	**0.85**	0.814	**0.767**								
LCc	6.0	1.0	**0.53**	**0.82**	0.818	0.802	**0.727**							
LCm	5.5	1.3	**0.62**	**0.87**	0.628	0.741	0.705	**0.786**						
TKS	6.2	0.9	**0.50**	**0.80**	0.584	0.526	0.674	0.432	**0.710**					
HC	5.8	1.2	**0.66**	**0.85**	0.309	0.278	0.357	0.228	0.529	**0.812**				
KP	5.8	1.3	**0.62**	**0.87**	0.725	0.673	0.709	0.625	0.593	0.314	**0.785**			
RC	5.8	1.2	**0.66**	**0.85**	0.422	0.386	0.448	0.339	0.527	0.808	0.508	**0.810**		
SC	5.7	1.3	**0.62**	**0.83**	0.556	0.513	0.561	0.467	0.542	0.555	0.731	0.727	**0.787**	
PI	5.8	1.2	**0.61**	**0.83**	0.4	0.365	0.429	0.318	0.52	0.811	0.473	0.809	0.708	**0.784**

Notes. Poland, *n* = 1.418; US *n* = 1.118; KC = knowledge culture; CC = collaborative culture; LCc = learning culture (atmosphere/climate); LCm = learning culture (mistakes acceptance); TKS = tacit knowledge sharing; KP = explicit knowledge sharing processes; PI = process innovation; HC = human capital; SC = structural capital; RC = relational capital (internal).

Constructs Reliability and Validity

The internal consistency of the constructs was assessed using the following reference values: Cronbach's alpha > 0.7 (Francis, 2001) and average variance extracted (AVE) > 0.5 (Byrne, 2016; Hair et al., 2010). Furthermore, composite reliability > 0.7 (Byrne, 2016; Hair et al., 2010) was used to justify the reliability of the scales.

Next, after the positively assessed statistical power of the chosen items, discriminant validity was checked (deVellis, 2017). Namely, similar theoretically related constructs were verified to ensure they did not supercharge each other (Fornell–Larcker criterion). The obtained square root of the AVE was larger than the correlation observed between the constructs for all the measured constructs. Table 5 presents the obtained basic statistics and correlations between the measured constructs.

Hypotheses

Since all the above-given book's chapters clarify our theoretical assumptions through relevant theories that enable us to formulate the hypotheses given below. So, we did not repeat the presented earlier justification supported mainly by Kucharska and Bedford (2020) and Kucharska (2017, 2021, 2022) studies, and we only listed below hypotheses that expose together the presented in this book structure of dependencies that we want it to empirically verify here.

H1. Knowledge culture and collaborative culture are correlated.

H2a. Collaborative culture positively influences learning culture climate component.

H2b. Collaborative culture positively influences learning culture mistakes acceptance component.

H2c. Learning culture climate component positively influences learning culture mistakes acceptance component.

H3a. Knowledge culture positively influences learning culture climate component.

H3b. Knowledge culture positively influences learning culture mistakes acceptance component

H4. Knowledge culture positively influences explicit knowledge sharing (formal processes).

H5. Learning culture climate component positively influences tacit knowledge sharing (informal processes).

H6. Learning culture mistakes acceptance component positively influences tacit knowledge sharing (informal processes).

H7. Learning culture mistakes acceptance component positively influences explicit knowledge sharing (formal processes).

H8. Tacit knowledge sharing (informal processes) positively influences explicit knowledge sharing (formal processes).

H9. Tacit knowledge sharing (informal processes) positively influences human capital.

H10. Tacit knowledge sharing (informal processes) positively influences relational capital.

H11. Human capital positively influences relational capital.

H12. Explicit knowledge sharing (formal processes) positively influences relational capital.

H13. Explicit knowledge sharing (formal processes) positively influences structural capital.

H14. Relational capital positively influences structural capital.

H15. Human capital positively influences internal innovativeness.

H16. Relational capital positively influences internal innovativeness.

H17. Structural capital positively influences internal innovativeness.

All the above hypotheses, formulated based on the entire book content, enable us to create the theoretical model below. This model summarizes graphically the

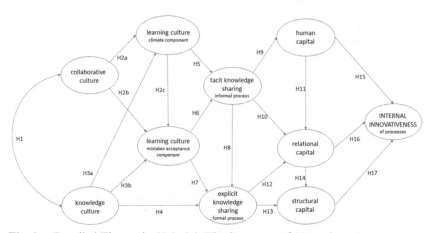

Fig. 2.   Detailed Theoretical Model (The Structure of Hypotheses).
Note: Authors' compilation based on Kucharska and Bedford (2020) and Kucharska (2017, 2021, 2022).

Table 6. Hypotheses Verification Details.

Country	USA	Poland
R^2	0.79	0.29
H1	0.81*** sustained	0.52*** sustained
H2a	0.24*** sustained	0.43*** sustained
H2b	0.62*** sustained	0.33*** sustained
H2c	0.47*** sustained	0.25*** sustained
H3a	0.62*** sustained	0.40*** sustained
H3b	−0.30*** rejected	0.22*** sustained
H4	0.43*** sustained	0.22*** sustained
H5	0.74*** sustained	0.44*** sustained
H6	−0.09** rejected	0.34*** sustained
H7	0.25*** sustained	−0.12*** rejected
H8	0.23*** sustained	0.31*** sustained
H9	0.53*** sustained	0.59*** sustained
H10	ns rejected	0.23*** sustained
H11	0.78*** sustained	0.64*** sustained
H12	0.30*** sustained	ns rejected
H13	0.49*** sustained	0.38*** sustained
H14	0.48*** sustained	0.26*** sustained
H15	0.39*** sustained	0.21*** sustained
H16	0.35*** sustained	ns rejected
H17	0.23*** sustained	0.42*** sustained
TKS→HC→RI[1]	−0.62(.19)/0.39 (**)/0.32(**) full mediation	0.23(***)/0.37(**)/0.59(**) complementary mediation
RC→SC→PI[1]	0.35(***)/0.06(***)/0.29(***) complementary mediation	−0.07(0.572)/0.07(***)/0.15(*) full mediation
χ^2	2686,26(537)	2650,085(540)
CMIN/df	5.002	5.278
RMSEA	0.062	0.062
CFI	0.914	0.907
TLI	0.905	0.897

Notes: Poland, $n = 1,418$; US $n = 1,118$; ML = standardized results.
***$p < 0.001$, **$p < 0.01$, *$p < 0.05$.
CFI referenced values greater than 0.90 are consider as good, greater than 0.95 as excellent; RMSEA is considered correct in the range of 0.05 to 0.08 (Hair et al., 2010; Hooper et al., 2008; Kline, 2005).
[1]direct/indirect/total effect (two-tailed significance effects)

book's whole manifesto that company culture is a crucial company asset enabling its survival and aims development. Precisely, we claim that the KLC cultures
approach antecedents organizational sustainability creation that consequence in
its internal innovativeness. In the presented model, the ability to change internally
is a proxy of the higher-level organizational changing routines (dynamic capabilities). Dynamic capabilities reflect organizational learning skills needed to develop
change adaptability competency (collective intelligence). Without collective intelligence – there is no chance for organizational sustainability achievement. This
above-given summary is the essence of the entire book's message.

Results

The delivered empirical evidence confirms that KLC-driven company culture fosters knowledge flow within an organization. Thanks to this flow, intellectual capital components are generated. Intellectual capital fosters the organizational ability
to change internally (by internal innovativeness of processes). These relations are
confirmed directly by the empirical model presented (Fig. 3). In the presented
model, the ability to change internally (internal processes improvement thanks to
innovativeness) is seen a proxy of the higher-level organizational changing routines (dynamic capabilities). Dynamic capabilities reflect organizational learning
skills needed to develop change adaptability competency (collective intelligence).
Without collective intelligence – there is no chance for organizational sustainability achievement. This above-given conclusion based on the applied proxy is the
essence of the entire book's message.

The correlation between knowledge culture and collaborative culture is confirmed for both nations (*H1*). Indeed, collaborative culture supports learning
culture both components (*H2a, H2b*), and it is also confirmed for both samples.
Knowledge culture also significantly influences both components of learning culture and it is positive (*H3a*), but with the exception of the US sample, where the
influence of the knowledge culture on the mistakes acceptance component of learning culture is negative (*H3b*). It reflects the attitude that "knowledge is needed to
avoid mistakes; therefore, knowledgeable people never make mistakes – they have
knowledge to avoid them" (*for more go to Chapters 4 and 5*). Therefore, knowledge
culture perfectly supports formal knowledge processes in organizations (*H4*) and,
learning culture – informal (*H5*). However, for the US sample, it is observed that
the mistakes acceptance component of learning culture does not support informal tacit knowledge sharing (*H6*), on the contrary, it positively supports formal
knowledge sharing (*H7*). Might be that in the US mistakes acceptance culture and
mistakes management are more formalized than in Poland. That suggests a set
of formal rules established to manage mistakes occurrence events. In Poland, it is
the opposite – the mistakes acceptance component supports positively informal
knowledge sharing but negatively formal. It means that formally, mistakes are not
managed. But for both countries, it is observed that informal knowledge processes
(tacit) support formal (explicit) (*H8*) and, informal knowledge processes strongly
support human capital (*H9*) in both countries and, it also supports internal, relational capital in Poland (*H10*), but it does not in the United States. But for both
countries, it is observed that human capital builds relationships (*H11*).

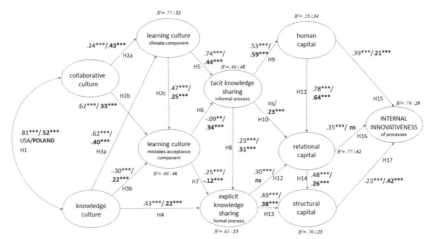

Fig. 3. Structural Model Results. *Notes:* Poland, $n = 1,418$; US, $n = 1,118$; $\chi^2 = 2686,26(537)/2850.08(540)$; CMIN/df $= 5.0/5.27$; ML $=$ standardized results; RMSEA $= 0.062/0.062$; CFI $= 0.914/0.907$; TLI $= 0.905/0.899$. ***$p < 0.001$, **$p < 0.01$, *$p < 0.05$.

So, indeed as we claim in this book, among knowledge workers, personal knowledge assets influence the ability to create an internal network of relations (*the smoothly cooperating network of brilliant minds, for more, go to Chapters 4 and 6*). Furthermore, after the TKS→HC→RI mediation analysis, we detected that human capital fully mediated for the US sample between informal knowledge sharing and relational capital, whereas for Poland complementary. So, it confirms how vital is human capital quality for the organizational ability to compose a *smoothly cooperating network of brilliant minds* and, how vital KLC-approach for this ability is. Formal knowledge sharing is not significant for internal relational capital creation in Poland (*H12*), but it is for the United States. So, in Poland, relational capital is created mostly informally. In the United States, both paths matter. Whereas structural capital in both countries comes from formal knowledge processes (*H13*) and from good relations among employees (*H14*). Finally, all intellectual capital components: human (*H15*), relational (*H16*), and structural (*H17*) support the organizational ability to improve internally thanks to internal innovations of methods of working. But for Poland, the internal relational capital influence is fully mediated by the structural capital. Altogether, the entire structure results confirm the key message of this book. Table 6 and Fig. 3 present details of the all above elaborated dependencies.

Conclusion

The presented empirical evidence confirms the entire book's message. Precisely, we claim that KLC-driven company culture is a key company asset tremendous for organizational sustainability creation. We see organizational sustainability as a long-run perspective enabling the organization to constantly generate the shared value, survive, and develop. Therefore, we see the knowledge-driven organization as a network of minds and, consequently, organizational sustainability as an effect of a sustainably collaborating network of brilliant minds. The delivered empirical evidence confirms that KLC-driven company culture fosters knowledge flow within an organization. Thanks to this flow, intellectual capital components are generated. Intellectual capital fosters the organizational ability to change internally (*by internal innovativeness of processes*). These relations are confirmed directly by the empirical model presented (Fig. 3). In the presented model, the ability to change internally (internal processes improvement, thanks to innovativeness) is seen a proxy of the higher-level organizational changing routines (*dynamic capabilities*). Dynamic capabilities reflect organizational learning skills needed to develop change adaptability competency (*collective intelligence*). Without collective intelligence – there is no chance for organizational sustainability achievement. This above-given conclusion based on the applied proxy is the essence of the entire book's message.

References

Andreeva, T., Garanina, T., Saenz, J., Aramburu, N., & Kianto, A. (2021). Does country environment matter in the relationship between intellectual capital and innovation performance? *Journal of Business Research, 136*, 263–273. https://doi.org/10.1016/j.jbusres.2021.07.038

Buenechea-Elberdin, M., Sáenz, J., & Kianto, A. (2018). Knowledge management strategies, intellectual capital, and innovation performance: A comparison between high- and low-tech firms. *Journal of Knowledge Management, 22*(8), 1757–1781. https://doi.org/10.1108/JKM-04-2017-0150

Byrne, B. M. (2016). *Structural equation modeling with Amos*. Routledge. https://doi.org/10.4324/9781315757421

Chen, F. F. (2007). Sensitivity of goodness of fit indexes to lack of measurement invariance. *Structural Equation Modeling Multidisciplinary Journal, 14*(3), 464–504. https://doi.org/10.1080/10705510701301834

deVellis, R. F. (2017). Scale development: Theory and applications. Sage.

Francis, G. (2001). *Introduction to SPSS for Windows* (3rd ed.). Pearson Education.

Hair, J. F., Anderson, R. E., Babin, B. J., & Black, W. C. (2010). *Multivariate data analysis: A global perspective*. Pearson Education.

Hooper, D., Coughlan, J., & Mullen, M. (2008). Evaluating model fit: A synthesis of the structural equation modelling literature. In *Proceedings of the 7th European Conference on Research Methods: ECRM* (pp. 195–200).

Kianto, A., Saenz, J., & Aramburu, N. (2017). Knowledge-based human resource management practices, intellectual capital and innovation. *Journal of Business Research, 81*, 11–20. https://doi.org/10.1016/j.jbusres.2017.07.018

Kline, R. B. (2005). Principles and practice of structural equation modeling. Guilford Press.

Kucharska, W. (2017). Relationships between trust and collaborative culture in the context of tacit knowledge sharing. *Journal of Entrepreneurship, Management and Innovation, 13*(4), 61–78. https://doi.org/10.7341/20171344

Kucharska, W. (2021). Leadership, culture, intellectual capital and knowledge processes for organizational innovativeness across industries: The case of Poland. *Journal of Intellectual Capital, 22*(7), 121–141. https://doi.org/10.1108/JIC-02-2021-0047

Kucharska, W. (2022). Tacit knowledge influence on intellectual capital and innovativeness in the healthcare sector: A cross-country study of Poland and the US. *Journal of Business Research, 149*, 869–883. https://doi.org/10.1016/j.jbusres.2022.05.059

Kucharska, W., & Bedford, D. A. D. (2020). Love your mistakes! – They help you adapt to change. How do knowledge, collaboration and learning cultures foster organizational intelligence? *Journal of Organizational Change Management, 33*(7), 1329–1354. https://doi.org/10.1108/JOCM-02-2020-0052

Kucharska, W., & Erickson, G. S. (2023). Tacit knowledge acquisition & sharing, and its influence on innovations: A polish/US cross-country study. *International Journal of Information Management, 71*, 102647. https://doi.org/10.1016/j.ijinfomgt.2023.102647

Kucharska, W., & Kowalczyk, R. (2019). How to achieve sustainability? – Employee's point of view on company's culture and CSR practice. *Corporate Social Responsibility and Environmental Management, 26*(2), 453–467. https://doi.org/10.1002/csr.1696

MacCallum, R. C., & Hong, S. (1997). Power analysis in covariance structure modeling using GFI and AGFI. *Multivariate Behavioral Research, 32*(2), 193–210. https://doi.org/10.1207/s15327906mbr3202_5

Mercier-Laurent, E. (2011). *Innovation ecosystems*. Wiley & Sons.

Podsakoff, P. M., MacKenzie, S. B., & Podsakoff, N. P. (2012). Sources of method bias in social science research and recommendations on how to control it. *Annual Review of Psychology, 63*(1), 539–569. https://doi.org/10.1146/annurev-psych-120710-100452

Raudenska, P. (2020). The cross-country and cross-time measurement invariance of positive and negative affect scales: Evidence from European Social Survey. *Social Science Research*, 102369. https://doi.org/10.1016/j.ssresearch.2019.102369

Statistics Poland. (2017). Polish yearbook of labour statistics. https://stat.gov.pl/en/topics/statistical-yearbooks/statistical-yearbooks/yearbook-of-labour-statistics-2017,10,6.html

Vos, J. F. J., & Boonstra, A. (2022). The influence of cultural values on enterprise system adoption, towards a culture-Enterprise system alignment theory. *International Journal of Information Management, 63*, 102453. https://doi.org/10.1016/j.ijinfomgt.2021.102453

Appendix C: Surveying Knowledge, Learning, and Collaboration Cultures

Analytical Methodology and Survey Instrument

You can provide a high-level description of your company's KLC approach by conducting a two-part assessment. The first part is a short survey. We provide a sample survey questionnaire below (Table 1). A selected set of questions is presented for the three cultures – knowledge, learning, and collaboration. Respondents will record their impressions using a 7-point Likert scale, indicating strong agreement or disagreement. In addition, respondents can mark each question. Analyzing the results will give you a starting point for understanding your KLC culture profile. This phase answers the question – "What is the nature of my KLC culture?"

The second part allows you to dig deeper through open-ended conversations with employees or follow-up surveys to learn more about why they responded the way they did. This phase answers the question – "Why are my KLC cultures what they are?" It is an important entry point to understanding what might need to be adjusted.

The survey instruments can be distributed in print form or as an automated web survey instrument. Print forms must be tallied and analyzed by hand. Automated surveys will provide you will basic statistical results.

What can you learn from the results? If you and your employee see the company culture through the same lens, there is an opportunity to build upon it. If there are different perspectives on the KLC cultures, there are opportunities for critical thinking and for discovering opportunities for improvement.

The responses to the structured survey may indicate whether any of the three cultures is dominant. Where they are perceived to be of equal value, you have a good foundation upon which to build. You may have a critical starting point if one is dominant over the others. You may have to balance or invest differently to achieve the level of synergy you desire. On the other hand, if some cultures are rated low or are not perceived as existing, you can do some critical thinking and strategizing.

KLC-approach assessment tool								
Strong knowledge culture	7	6	5	4	3	2	1	Weak knowledge culture
Based on my experience, in my place of work all of employees see knowledge as a value.								**Based on my experience, in my place of work** the all of employees **do not** see knowledge as a value
We have at work a common language to support knowledge exchange								We **have not** a common language to support knowledge exchange
We are encouraged at work to share knowledge, ideas, and thoughts								We **are not** encouraged at work to share knowledge, ideas, and thoughts. We are expected just to do our jobs.
We care about the quality of knowledge that we share								We **do not** care enough about the quality of knowledge that we share
We care about the quality of knowledge that we use								We **do not** care enough about the quality of knowledge that we use
Strong learning culture	7	6	5	4	3	2	1	Weak learning culture
Learning climate component								*Learning climate component*
Based on my experience, in my place of work: all staff demonstrate a high learning disposition								**Based on my experience, in my place of work:** nobody demonstrates a high learning disposition
We are encouraged to engage in personal development								We **are not** encouraged to engage in personal development
We are encouraged to implement new ideas every day								We **are not** encouraged to implement new ideas every day
We are encouraged to engage in new solutions seeking								We **are not** encouraged to engage in new solutions seeking
Mistakes acceptance component	7	6	5	4	3	2	1	*Mistakes acceptance component*
Based on my experience in my place of work: we know that mistakes are a learning consequence and tolerate it up to a certain limit								**Based on my experience in my place of work:** mistakes **are not** tolerated
Most people freely declare mistakes								Most people **hide** mistakes
We discuss problems openly without blaming								Problems **are not** discussed openly and blame is behind your back
Mistakes are tolerated and treated as learning opportunities								Mistakes **are not** treated as learning opportunities
Strong cooperation culture	7	6	5	4	3	2	1	Weak cooperation culture
Based on my experience in my place of work: cooperation between workers is supported								**Based on my experience in my place of work:** cooperation between workers **is not** supported.
Employees cooperate across duties								Employees **do not** cooperate across duties
Employees cooperate across teams								Employees **do not** cooperate across teams
Employees cooperate across departments								Employees **do not** cooperate across departments
My co-workers volunteer their support even without being asked								My co-workers **never** volunteer their support without being asked
We support one another								We **do not** support one another

Case Study

John, the CEO of Fixed Group Co. (FG) – which operates in consulting branch and employs 200 consultants, noticed some problems with his development strategy implementation, and his preliminary diagnosis led him to employee relations, but he needed to verify it. FG always seeks great minds – the best of the best people in the branch – and employs such "mind-profiled" people. As a result, all teams accomplish their tasks perfectly, but these teams barely cooperate. John noticed that they openly competed. The fact is that 70% of employees are men that like competition. But in John's opinion, it went too far.

However, employees have fun accomplishing tasks and competing, and the company has a substantial turnover and a perfect market position, but there is no knowledge sharing among teams. In John's opinion, it may block the company's growth in the long run. Since the company culture drives the entire company's capabilities and John appreciated the KLC approach for knowledge-driven companies, he decided to diagnose the company's KLC culture approach level. So, John fulfilled the diagnosing form (Table 1), and next asked others and compared his view with the view resulting from the average results of all employees. His view on KLC approach is marked with a solid line and employees with a dashed line. What did he find out?

John discovered that only the learning culture–climate component is developed on the highest level in his organization, and it is seen this way by him and by all employees. It means a lot to the consultancy organization. Unfortunately, the mistakes acceptance component is not developed in employees' opinion. John sees it as weaker than the component of climate, but the discrepancy between an employee's and John's view is huge. So, it suggests some leadership matters to solve – John concluded.

> It might be that my or other managers' verbal and oral communication is not consistent in this matter, or the doubled bias concerning mistakes is strongest than I expected, and my and other managers' communication and actions should be better designed and stronger.

John decided to pay more attention to this issue to be sure of what the actual point was.

In John's perception, knowledge culture is as perfect as a climate component of learning culture. In his employees, not as much. They do not see that they have a common language to support knowledge exchange. It is a severe issue probably tied to a different mindset and attitude regarding knowledge sharing. It makes sense – if employees compete, they do not share knowledge. Knowledge seen as a value is not shared to keep the advantage of one team over another or one team over others – John concluded.

The collaboration culture is the one that is seen by John and the employees in the same way and puts some light on the lack of knowledge-sharing issue. So, even though John and other managers support cooperation and the cooperation across duties is perfect, it seriously suffers across teams level. The problem lies in the attitude because employees support each other in their duties resulting from positions and the company's procedures, but not as human to human.

Finally, John decided to open an in-house project to diagnose the roots and develop an improvement plan to create a culture of collaboration. Unfortunately, this problem is deeper than it sounds because employees see that the company encourages them to cooperate, but they do not cooperate anyway. It might be that their fixed mindsets are programmed to compete instead of cooperating. If it is the case, then the entire improvement program must be very advanced in methods and tools and tailored to particular persons and teams – John summed up.

	KLC-approach assessment tool							
Strong knowledge culture	7	6	5	4	3	2	1	Weak knowledge culture
Based on my experience, in my place of work all of employees see knowledge as a value.								**Based on my experience, in my place of work** the all of employees **do not** see knowledge as a value
We have at work a common language to support knowledge exchange								We **have not** a common language to support knowledge exchange
We are encouraged at work to share knowledge, ideas, and thoughts								We **are not** encouraged at work to share knowledge, ideas, and thoughts. We are expected just to do our jobs.
We care about the quality of knowledge that we share								We **do not** care enough about the quality of knowledge that we share
We care about the quality of knowledge that we use								We **do not** care enough about the quality of knowledge that we use
Strong learning culture	7	6	5	4	3	2	1	Weak learning culture
Learning climate component								*Learning climate component*
Based on my experience, in my place of work: all staff demonstrate a high learning disposition								**Based on my experience, in my place of work:** nobody demonstrates a high learning disposition
We are encouraged to engage in personal development								We **are not** encouraged to engage in personal development
We are encouraged to implement new ideas every day								We **are not** encouraged to implement new ideas every day
We are encouraged to engage in new solutions seeking								We **are not** encouraged to engage in new solutions seeking
Mistakes acceptance component	7	6	5	4	3	2	1	*Mistakes acceptance component*
Based on my experience in my place of work: we know that mistakes are a learning consequence and tolerate it up to a certain limit								**Based on my experience in my place of work:** mistakes **are not** tolerated
Most people freely declare mistakes								Most people **hide** mistakes
We discuss problems openly without blaming								Problems **are not** discussed openly and blame is behind your back
Mistakes are tolerated and treated as learning opportunities								Mistakes **are not** treated as learning opportunities
Strong cooperation culture	7	6	5	4	3	2	1	Weak cooperation culture
Based on my experience in my place of work: cooperation between workers is supported								**Based on my experience in my place of work:** cooperation between workers **is not** supported.
Employees cooperate across duties								Employees **do not** cooperate across duties
Employees cooperate across teams								Employees **do not** cooperate across teams
Employees cooperate across departments								Employees **do not** cooperate across departments
My co-workers volunteer their support even without being asked								My co-workers **never** volunteer their support without being asked
We support one another								We **do not** support one another

Appendix D: Questions for Future Research

Many ideas arose over the three years the authors researched, discussed, and wrote this book. Some were well aligned with the structure and coverage of the book. Others, though, were out of scope for this book, or were too broad or deep and would have distracted us from completing our work. Those ideas put into a "parking lot" for future consideration. In hopes that the readers might be interested in some of these questions, we share them in this Appendix.

We caution that they are early questions which have not yet taken a solid research form. But like all good research, they begin with simple questions, generate initial ideas which raise further questions, encourage further searching, and ultimately lead to well-formed hypotheses. We hope our initial question might generate further inquiry and discussion, and continue to expand the field of knowledge cultures.

Research Question 1. Do individuals have cultural registers like they have linguistic registers? If so, what are the elements of a cultural register? If so, how do individuals manage them? Can individuals learn to "see" their cultural registers? If individuals have multiple cultural registers, when do they align and when do they conflict? How do individuals manage multiple cultural registers? Can we build a framework of a cultural register from the factors that influence individual, team, organizational, and national cultures?

Research Question 2. We have observed that organizations might not have a single company culture. It seems plausible that an organization may have multiple company cultures in place. How do these cultures interact? When do they conflict? And, when do they merge or blend? Are there some common pairings that are more or less inclined to conflict? How does the knowledge, learning, and collaboration culture function in these environments? Are there some pairings that are more common than others?

Research Question 3. As we saw in Chapter 2, national cultures are pervasive to a state. These cultures are shared by the people of the state, at least at an espoused level, if not at a lived level. National cultures have evolved in a real world, over time, in a specific place, and under known conditions. What happens when some of the people in the country are increasingly embedded in digital places where they encounter other cultures? Do these new digital places affect the national culture? If so, what is the nature of the affect?

Research Question 4. If a digitally competent younger generation is engaging with communities of other or multiple cultures, how is this affecting the individual versions of their national cultures? Is it expanding the national culture? Is it creating conflicts with traditional national non-digital cultures?

Research Question 5. We found that there is a need for a better definition and characterization of international cultures. This seems to be a much more complex idea that is currently offered. Currently, the concept is limited as it is defined by a specific context where there are multiple national cultures in play – a global company, a global project, and an international community. Is this accurate? Or, do we need more applied research to understand what "global" means? Is a global culture simply a cross-national culture?

Research Question 7. How is it that new hires learn an organizational culture? A new team culture? What are the markers and signs they look for and learn from? And, how do existing work or organizational cultures learn from new members, or adapt when members leave? Do new hires learn culture more rapidly or more slowly?

Research Question 8. National cultures have a significant effect on how people value knowledge, how they think about and approach learning, and whether they prefer collaboration or competition. When individuals are in global or multi-national cultures, do their knowledge, learning, and collaboration cultures change?

Research Question 9. Did the pandemic and its social isolation requirements shift or change our individual cultures? Did it create an international culture by propelling us all into largely digital spaces and cultures? If so, what elements were affected? Were these affects long- or short-term?

Research Question 10. How do public sector cultures vary from country to country or region to region? How do national cultures affect public sector cultures? What happens when these two cultures are in conflict or at variance? Are there common service functions across countries? Do we see similar public service cultures by sector, i.e., military, agriculture, space exploration, commerce, education, and health? Do public service cultures vary by their focus, i.e., the state, the public, and the leader?

Index